THE BIGGEST PUB JOKE BOOK Ever!

Text and design © copyright 1999 Carlton Books Limited

First published by Carlton Books Limited 1999
This edition published by Carlton Books Limited 2003

This book is sold subject to the condition that it shall not, by way of trade or otherwise, be lent, resold, hired out or otherwise circulated without the publisher's prior written consent in any form of cover or binding other than that in which it is published and without a similar condition including this condition, being imposed upon the subsequent purchaser.

All rights reserved.

ISBN 1 85868 809 4

Printed and bound in Great Britain

THE BIGGEST PUB JOKE BOOK *Ever!*

Compiled by
Ivor Baddiel, Ian Stone and Tim Dedopulos

CONTENTS

Jokes Not To Tell The Hard Bloke	9
My Wife Doesn't Understand Me	29
Don't Mix Your Drinks	77
The Lock-In	111
Medicinal Purposes	127
One For The Road	147
On The Pull	163
On The Wagon	207
Whose Round Is It?	247
Quiz Night	265
Pissed As A Fart	295
The Pub Team	329
Animal Magic	353
Down The Local	385
Pun Away! Pun Away!	421
Lads' Night Out	445
One For The Ladies	495
Professional Misconduct	539
Sporting Triumphs	589
After Dinner	611
The Day Today	633

Introduction

A drink and a laugh. The two things are bleeding synonymous. They were made for each other. I mean, when God invented the left tit, it was just right and proper that he invent the right tit to go with. The one without the other would look stupid. Batman and Robin. Morecambe and Wise. Huntley and Palmer. Mike and Berni Winters. Fish and chips. They all fit together like the finished jigsaws they are.

Of course, it's not just any drink that goes with a drink and a laugh, oh no. It's got to be a drink down the boozer with your mates. I mean, sitting at home on your own having a stiff one or cracking a few tinnies; where's the laughs in that? 'Oh ha ha, here I am alone and I'm getting pissed, ha ha ha.' What's that all about? If you do that you're just going to get more and more miserable thinking about how much of a real laugh you'd be having if you were down the pub with your mates. So, you see; a drink down the pub and a laugh – now *that's* what it's all about.

Much as the great atmosphere of the pub – with its noisy hubbub, smoky air, constant music pumping out of the jukebox, shouts at the bar and vomit – is highly conducive to a great laugh, sometimes, just sometimes, you're sitting there thinking, 'Shit, that was a great gag Barry just told and the way Barbara's looking at him now I reckon he's in there, the lucky bastard.'

Now, on the surface no one would be more pleased than your good self to see Barry get his end away with Barbara, especially as he hasn't had much luck in that department since he was discovered six months ago in a compromising position with a vacuum cleaner – come to think of it, *that* was on a night when he'd stayed in on his own with a few cans – but deep down, you know that you want to shag Barbara. In fact, Barbara knows that you want to shag her and she'd be up for it, too. It's just you can't find the right word, the right anecdote, the right line… the right gag to open the gates of heaven.

If only there was some way you could sneak off to the bogs and rub something vigorously, but lovingly. Something that would produce a genie. A genie who could turn you into the wittiest man in the boozer with a joke

Introduction

for every occasion. Then things would be different.

Oh, you'd also wish that Barry could get a shag with Barbara's mate Tracey, who's got a lovely personality, and that you could win the lottery every week – though occasionally every other week when it's a rollover – and that you could have five mansions in every continent of the world, and a new car, and be the greatest footballer in the world. But when it came down to it, what you'd really want is to be able to get those laughs. To see the adoring faces all around you, tears of happiness in their eyes, subconsciously saying, 'He's a great lad. So, so funny. They don't make many like him. He's one in a million, he is. Shame he's got such a small cock, mind.' 'Course by then it'd be too late and the genie would have gone, but there's always going to be one thing you forget to ask for.

Anyway, the point is that in some small way this book is like that genie. No, it won't give you a bigger dick, or bigger breasts if you're a woman, unless you use the correct lubricant, but it will equip you to go out there on to the social battlefield and hit 'em with a few punches. And then a few jabs. And then a few uppercuts. Maybe one or two below the belt, and then back for the big knockout finish. And it won't just be for the one night, either. There are so many laughs contained herein, that you'll be the funniest guy in the pub for years to come. Even after that you'll still be funny because the alcohol will have destroyed you and all your mate's memories, so you can just tell all the jokes again. There, you see? This is just like your own personal little genie. And you didn't even have to rub anything.

Jokes Not To Tell The Hard Bloke

1

Jokes that will get you into Trouble

You know what it's like when you've had a few. You get a bit of Dutch courage up. So you sidle over to the big, psychopathic-looking guy whose been sitting in the corner looking like it's just a matter of time before he beats someone up and, in an attempt to become his mate so that it won't be you, you tell him the one about the guy whose wife's vagina was so big there was an echo when he went down on her.

'Course the psycho's two brain cells get confused by this attempt at friendship and he thinks it's his wife you're talking about. The resulting six months you spend in hospital give you ample time to think about where you went wrong that night and what a terrible state the NHS is in.

Here are some more jokes it's best to tell only to very good friends who are not particularly strong…

****

This bloke wakes up one morning to find a gorilla in a tree in his garden. He looks in the phone book for a gorilla removal service until he finds one.

'Is it a boy gorilla or a girl gorilla?' the service bloke asks.

'Boy gorilla', replies the man.

'Righto,' says the service bloke. 'I'll be round in a jiffy.'

An hour later the service bloke shows up with a stick, a Pit Bull Terrier, a shotgun and a pair of handcuffs.

'Right,' he says to the man. 'I'm going to climb the tree and poke the gorilla with the stick until he falls. When he does, this highly trained Pit Bull will tear the gorilla's balls off. When the gorilla crosses his hands over his crotch to protect himself, you slip the handcuffs on.'

'OK,' says the man, 'but what's the shotgun for?'

'I'm glad you asked that,' says the service bloke. 'If I fall out of the tree before the gorilla does, then blow the dog's brains out.'

****

This bloke Sam's been working on the stock exchange for 15 years and the stress has finally got to him. So he quits his job and buys a cottage in the middle of nowhere, right up in the highlands of Scotland.

For six months he doesn't see a soul, until one evening, just as he's finishing his dinner, there's a knock on his front door. He opens it and there, on his door step, is a gigantic, ginger-bearded Scotsman in a kilt.

'Name's Hamish. I'm your your neighbour from the other side of the glen. I'm having a party on Saturday and I thought you might like to come along.'

'That's very kind of you,' says Sam. 'After six months of this I'm ready to meet some of the locals. Thank you very much.'

'Good,' says Hamish with a smile. 'I better warn you, though, there's gonna be some serious drinking done.'

'No problem,' replies Sam. 'After 15 years in the stock markets I can drink with the best of them.'

'More than likely be a bit of punch-up at some point as well,' says Hamish.

'Oh, I'm sure I'll be OK,' says Sam. 'I can look after myself, and besides I tend to get along with most people.'

'One last thing,' says Hamish as he turns to leave, 'I've seen some pretty wild sex at these parties, as well.'

'Well, now you're talking,' says Sam, 'what time should I come over?'

'Oh, whatever time suits you,' says Hamish. 'After all, it's only going to be the two of us.'

****

A sergeant-major in the Paras was giving a lecture to some raw recruits.

'If you want to be a part of this regiment,' he shouted at them, 'then you need to have COMMITMENT! What do you need?'

'COMMITMENT, sergeant-major!' the recruits all shouted back.

'Right, I shall now demonstrate my COMMITMENT to this regiment.' The sergeant-major then ordered one of the men to open a nearby door.

Almost as soon as the squaddie turned the handle, the door was pushed open and in slithered a 10-foot-long alligator, snarling and snapping.

The sergeant-major then undid his belt and dropped his trousers. Almost as soon as he did so, the alligator ran up and sank his teeth right into the sergeant-major's love-truncheon. The sergeant-major barely winced. 'This,' he shouted. 'is what we in the Parachute Regiment call COMMITMENT!' He waited several seconds more to make his point and then swiftly jabbed the alligator in both eyes with his fingers.

The alligator flipped over on his back, jumped up, and ran into the corner of the office, glaring angrily at the sergeant-major.

'That, you 'orrible bunch, is what we in the Paras call COMMITMENT. Now which one of you 'orrible little men is ready to demonstrate his COMMITMENT?'

There was much shuffling of feet and murmuring until finally one young lad stepped forward. 'I will, sergeant-major,' he said, 'but you've got to promise not to poke me in the eyes.'

****

Some tourists were touring an Arab bazaar when they saw a man on his knees next to a camel. The tour guide approached the man. 'Excuse me, Sir,' said the tour guide. 'You wouldn't happen to have the time, would you?'

The Arab grabbed the camel by the balls and said, 'Ten past two.'

The tour guide couldn't believe what he was seeing so he rushed off to get the rest of his party. 'You won't believe what I've just seen,' he told them. 'Follow me.'

They all trooped back to where the Arab and the camel were standing. 'Excuse me, Sir,' said the tour guide. 'Could you tell me the time again, please?'

The Arab thought this was a slightly strange request but once again, he grabbed the camel by the balls and said, 'Just gone Ten minutes past two.'

The tour party were amazed.

'Excuse me, Sir,' said the tour guide to the Arab. 'But I've worked in this part of the world for many years now, and I've never seen anything like this. If you don't mind me asking, how on earth do you tell the time by grabbing the camel's balls like that?'

'Well,' said the Arab demonstrating the manoeuvre again, 'by moving his balls over to one side I can see that clock on the wall over there.'

****

It was the stockbroker's first day in prison and on meeting his psychotic-looking cell mate he became even more nervous than ever.

'Don't worry, mate,' said the prisoner when he noticed how scared the stockbroker looked. 'I'm in for a white-collar crime, too.'

'Oh, really?' said the stockbroker with a sigh of relief.

'Yeah,' said the prisoner. 'I murdered a priest.'

****

A young man goes to a restaurant and orders a chicken dish. The waiter brings it to him and just as he's ready to tuck in, the *maître d'* comes running over and says, 'I'm terribly sorry, sir, but I'm afraid there has been a mistake. You see that police officer sitting at the next table? Well, he's a regular customer of ours and he usually orders the same dish. The problem is, this is the last chicken in the house. I'm afraid I'll have to take your meal to him and arrange for you to have something else from the menu.'

The young man, however, refuses to give up his food, so the waiter walks over to the other table and explains the situation to the policeman. A few minutes later the policeman walks over to the man's table and says, 'Now you listen to me, young man, and listen good. That is MY chicken you're about to eat and I'll warn you, whatever you do to that chicken I'll do the same to you. You pull out one of its legs, I'll pull out one of yours. You break one of its wings, I'll break one of your arms!'

The young man looks calmly at the policeman, then calmly at the chicken, sticks his finger into the bird's arse, pulls it out and licks it.

This bloke went to the Far East on business and three months later – after a successful trip – arrived home only to find he'd contracted a strange disease in the genital region. He goes to the doctor who, after a thorough examination, informs the businessman that he's got no choice but to amputate the man's penis.

'I refuse to believe that's the only option,' says the businessman. 'I shall consult another physician.'

So the businessman sees numerous doctors all over Europe and North America, but they all come to the same conclusion. His member has got to be chopped off.

Just when he's about to accept the doctors' verdict, however, the businessman has a brainwave. If it's an Oriental, Far Eastern disease, he figures, then why doesn't he consult an Oriental doctor?

An appointment is made with the finest doctor in London's Chinatown. After a full examination the Oriental doctor says to him, 'No, I don't think amputation is necessary.'

The businessman is over the moon. 'Brilliant! I saw dozens of doctors from Europe and America and they all said amputation was the only way.'

'Pah!! Western doctors!', says the Chinese doctor with disdain. 'What do they know? Any doctor worth his salt could tell you that it'll drop off by itself in four to six weeks!'

****

There was a middle-aged bloke called Steve who decided to go back to college to take a degree. Not being sure of what he wanted to take, he began to look around campus at all the different colleges. He saw the College of Physics, the College of Sociology, the College of Psychology and the College of Assuming. Having never heard of a College of Assuming, Steve was puzzled. While he stood there pondering what it was, the Dean of the college happened by and asked Steve if he needed any help.

'It's just that I've never heard of the College of Assuming,' said Steve, and I just wondered what it is.'

'Well, I'm the Dean of the college,' said the Dean, 'and here in the

College of Assuming, we raise assumption to the level of an art form.'

'I'm sorry,' said Steve, 'but I still don't understand.'

'Let's try this,' said the Dean. 'Can I assume you have a dog?'

'Why yes, I do have a dog,' replied Steve.

'And can I assume you have a garden for your dog to play in?' inquired the Dean.

'Why yes, I do have a garden for my dog,' said Steve.

'OK, and can I further assume that because you have a garden you also have a house?' said the Dean.

'Why yes, I do have a house,' said Steve beginning to be amazed.

'Now, because you have a house and a dog, and a garden, can I then assume you have a wife,' said the Dean.

'That's amazing! Yes, I do have a wife,' said Steve.

'Then because you have a wife, can I assume you are not gay?' inquired the Dean.

'Why no, I'm not gay,' replied Steve.

'There you see,' stated the Dean. 'From the simple fact of assuming you had a dog, I was able to assume you had a house with a garden, a wife, and that you are not gay.'

Clearly amazed, Steve enrolled in the class of assumptions. One day, about three weeks later while waiting for class to start, Steve saw a very puzzled man in the halls. Wanting to try his new skills and be of assistance, Steve approached the man.

'Can I help you?' asked Steve.

'Why, yes,' replied the man. 'What is the College of Assuming?'

Delighted, Steve replied, 'The College of Assuming takes assumption to the level of an art form.'

'I'm still not sure I understand,' replied the man. 'Well let me give you an example,' said Steve. 'Do you own a dog?'

'No,' replied the man.

'Aha,' said Steve, 'then you must be a poof.'

Three mice are at a bar, having drinks, talking about how tough they are. The first mouse slams down a shot of booze and says, 'Let me tell you how tough I am. I spot a trap and go for the cheese. When it snaps, I snatch the bar and bench-press it 20 or so times and before it can close I'm out of there!' and he tosses down another shot.

The second mouse slams down a shot and says, 'You think that's tough? When I find a pile of rodent poison, I crush it and snort it like it's cocaine.' With that he throws down another shot and slams his shotglass on the bar.

The first two stare at the third mouse, waiting to see what he has to say for himself. He fires down a shot of booze, throws down his glass and heads for the door. His buddies look at each other, then at him and say, 'Hey, where are you going?' The third mouse says, 'I haven't got time for this shit, I'm going home to fuck the cat.'

****

A general and his paratrooper son are sitting at home having a couple of beers.

'So, son, tell me about your first jump,' says the general.

'Well, by the time the plane got over the jump site,' says the son, 'I was really scared. When it was my turn to jump, I got to the door and I just couldn't do it.

'What happened, then?' asks the general.

'Well,' says his son, 'the sergeant came up behind me, pulled out his dick and said, "Jump or I'll stick this up your arse."'

'So you jumped? says the general.

'A little,' says the son, 'but only at first.'

****

Two old drunks were getting wankered in a pub. The first one says, 'You know, when I was 30 and got a hard-on, I couldn't bend it with both hands. By the time I was 40, I could bend it about 10 degrees if I tried really hard. By the time I was 50, I could bend it about 20 degrees, no problem. I'm 60 next week, and now I can almost bend it in half with just one hand.'

'So,' says the second drunk, 'What's your point?'

'Well,' says the first, 'I'm just wondering how much stronger I'm gonna get!'

****

An armless man walked into an empty pub. He ordered a drink and when he was served, asked the barman if he'd get the money out of his pocket for him, since he had no arms. Of course, the barman obliged.

He then asked if the barman would tip the glass to his lips. The barman did this until the man finished his drink. He then asked if the barman would get a hanky from his pocket and wipe the foam from his lips.

'It must be very difficult not to have any arms,' said the barman as he wiped the man's face.

'Yes, it can be a bit embarrassing at times,' said the armless man. 'By the way, mate; where's your bog?'

'About three miles away down the end of this road,' replied the barman.

****

Once there was a beautiful woman who loved to work in her vegetable garden, but no matter what she did, she couldn't get her tomatoes to ripen. One day when she was admiring her neighbour's garden, which had beautiful, bright red tomatoes, she asked him what his secret was.

'It's really quite simple,' her neighbour explained. 'Twice each day, in the morning and in the evening, I expose myself in front of the tomatoes and they turn red with embarrassment.'

Desperate for perfect tomatoes, she decided to take his advice and proceeded to expose herself to her plants, twice daily. Two weeks passed and her neighbour stopped by to check her progress.

'So,' he asked, 'any luck with your tomatoes?'

'No,' she replied excitedly. 'But you should see the size of my carrots!'

****

A urologist, a gynaecologist and a sex therapist met one afternoon to discuss their results from a similar study.

'I spent £100,000 on my study,' said the urologist and my results conclusively prove that the reason the head of a man's penis is wider than the shaft is so that the man will feel more pleasure during intercourse.

'Well, I spent £200,000 on my study,' said the gynaecologist, 'and my results conclusively prove that the reason the head of a man's penis is wider than the shaft is so that the woman will feel more pleasure during intercourse.'

'Oh yeah,' said the sex therapist. 'Well, I only had to spend £100 on my study and my results conclusively prove that the real reason the head of a man's penis is wider than the shaft is to prevent a man from accidentally hitting himself in the forehead while he's having a wank!'

✳✳✳✳

A husband and wife are cooing over their new born baby.

'Look at his todger,' says the man. 'It's massive!'

'Yes, dear,' says the woman. 'But at least he's got your eyes.'

✳✳✳✳

Four surgeons were taking a coffee break and discussing their work. The first said, 'I think accountants are the easiest to operate on. You open them up and everything inside is numbered.'

The second said, 'I think librarians are the easiest to operate on. You open them up and everything inside is in alphabetical order.'

The third said, 'I like to operate on electricians. You open them up and everything inside is colour-coded.'

The fourth one said, 'I prefer to operate on lawyers. They're heartless, spineless, gutless, and their heads and arses are interchangeable.'

Jokes Not To Tell The Hard Bloke

There's this woman who's a faithful churchgoer. She's been looking forward to a particular guest speaker coming to give a sermon at her local church for some months, but on the weekend he's due to speak, the woman gets ill. She's too sick to attend the service, but because she doesn't want to miss what the guest speaker has to say, she asks her husband – who never goes to church – to attend for her and give her a full report. After a big row he finally agrees and goes off to the church. On his return his wife is amazed to see he's got two black eyes.

'What in God's name happened to you?' she asks him.

'Well,' he replies, 'before the guest speaker got up to give his sermon, we were asked to stand and sing. I noticed this fat woman in front of me had her dress stuck in her crack, so I reached over the pew and pulled it out. Her husband saw me and twatted me in the eye.'

'OK,' says the wife. 'So how did you get the second black eye?'

'Well, I figured I'd upset him by taking the dress out of her crack,' said the husband, 'so I tried to make amends by slipping it back in.'

****

This little old lady calls 999. When the operator answers she yells, 'Help, send the police to my house right away. There's a damn Labour MP on my front porch and he's playing with himself.

'I beg your pardon?' said the operator.

'I said there's a damn Labour MP on my front porch playing with himself and he's weird; I don't know him and I'm afraid! Please send the police,' the little old lady repeated.

'Well, now,' said the operator. 'How do you know he's a Labour MP?'

'Because if he was a Tory,' said the old lady, 'he'd be screwing somebody!'

****

Three elderly men are talking about their aches, pains and bodily functions. The 70-year-old man says, 'I have this problem. I wake up every morning at seven and it takes me 20 minutes to tinkle.

The 80-year old man says, 'My case is worse. I get up at eight and I sit there and grunt and groan for half-an-hour before I finally have a movement.'

The 90-year old says, 'At seven I piss like a horse, at eight I shit like a cow.'

'So what's your problem?' ask the other two.

'Well, you see,' says the 90-year old, 'I don't wake up until nine.'

****

A man with a 50-inch long dick goes to his doctor to complain that he was unable to get any women to have sex with him because his knob was too long.

'Doctor,' he asks, in total frustration, 'is there any way you can shorten it?'

'Medically, I'm afraid there is nothing I can do for you,' replies the doctor, 'but, I do know this witch who may be able to help.'

So the doctor gives the man with the king-sized knob directions to the witch and the man goes off to visit her.

'Witch,' he says when he gets there. 'My dick is 50 inches long and I can't get any women to have sex with me. Can you help me shorten it?'

'Pull it out,' says the witch, 'and let me look at it.'

The man uncoils his 50-inch love wand and the witch stares in amazement, scratches her head, and then says, 'I think I may have a solution to your problem. What you have to do is go to this pond deep in the forest. In the pond you will see a frog sitting on a log who can help solve your dilemma. First you must ask the frog to marry you. Each time the frog declines your proposal, your dick will shrink by Ten inches.'

The man's face lights up and he dashes off into the forest. Sure enough he comes upon the pond in the middle of which is the frog. 'Will you marry me?' he calls out to the frog.

The frog looks at him and replies, 'No'. The man looks down and just as the witch had said, his dick is Ten inches shorter.

'WOW!' he screams out loud, 'This is great!! But it's still 40 inches too long. I'll ask the frog to marry me again 'Frog, will you marry me?'

Jokes Not To Tell The Hard Bloke

The frog rolls its eyes back in its head and screams back, 'NO!' The man feels another twitch in his dick, looks down, and finds it is another 10 inches shorter.

'This is fantastic,' says the man, 'but 30 inches is still a monster; just a little less would be ideal. So, I'll ask the frog to marry me one more time.' Grinning, he looks across the pond and yells out, 'Frog, will you marry me?'

The frog looks back across the pond shaking its head. 'How many times do I have to tell you? NO!... NO!!... and for the last time... NO!!!'

****

A girl was a prostitute, but she didn't want her grandma to know. One day, the police raided the brothel where the girl worked and the police had all the prostitutes line up outside. Just then, the girl's grandma came by and saw her granddaughter. Not wanting her granny to know the truth, the girl said the first thing that came into her head.

'I'm queueing up for some free oranges, granny, they're handing them out here today.'

'Ooh, that's nice, dear,' said the granny. 'I'll think I'll get some, too.' And with that she joined the back of the queue.

By this time, a policeman was going down the line asking for information from the prostitutes. When he got to grandma, he was bewildered and asked, 'You're so old, how do you do it?'

'Oh, it's easy,' replied Grandma. 'I just take my dentures out and suck them dry.'

****

On his first day in prison this young bloke gets put in a cell with an old con and the first thing the old con asks him is, 'Do you like church?'

'It's OK,' replies the young bloke.

'On Sundays we get to go to church,' says the old con. 'You're gonna love Sundays.'

'Yeah, right.' says the young bloke.

Next the old con asks him if he likes football.

'Yeah, I like footie,' says the young bloke.

'Well, you're gonna love Mondays then,' says the old con. 'We play football on Mondays. What about cricket?'

'Yeah, cricket's all right,' replies the young bloke. '

'Well, you're gonna love Tuesdays,' says the old con. 'We always play cricket on Tuesdays – unless, of course, it rains. Then we play cards. You like cards?'

'Yeah, I like cards,' says the young bloke.

'What about sex?' asks the old con. 'You like sex?'

'Course I do.' says the young bloke.

'Who do you like sex with best?' asks the old con. 'Men or women?'

'Women.' says the young bloke getting a little bit worried.

'You don't like sex with men?' says the old con.

'No I most certainly do not.' says the young bloke.

'Oh dear,' says the old con. 'You're gonna hate Wednesdays.'

****

Two Welshmen are out rounding up sheep when all of a sudden a ewe takes off and goes wild, runs into a fence and gets her head stuck. The two shepherds run over to the fence to get her out when one says to the other: 'Hey, boyo, this is too good an opportunity to pass up.' So he unzips his fly, yanks out his wang and fucks the this ewe for about ten minutes. When he's finally finished he looks round to his mate and says, 'That was bloody marvellous. D'you fancy a go?'

'Bloody right I do!' grins his mate, as he drops his trousers and sticks his head through the fence.

****

Two young lads are picked up by the Old Bill for smoking dope. When they appear in court, though, the magistrate says: 'You two seem like such nice young men, I'd like to give you a second chance. I want you to go out this weekend and try to show others the evils of drug use and get them to give up drugs forever. I'll see you back in court on Monday morning.'

Come Monday morning, the two lads are in court, and the magistrate says to the first one, 'So, how did you do over the weekend?'

'Well, your honour,' he replies, 'I managed to persuade 17 people altogether to give up drugs forever.'

'Seventeen people?' says the magistrate. 'That's wonderful, news. What did you tell them?'

'I used a diagram, your honour,' replied the first lad. 'I drew two circles like this:

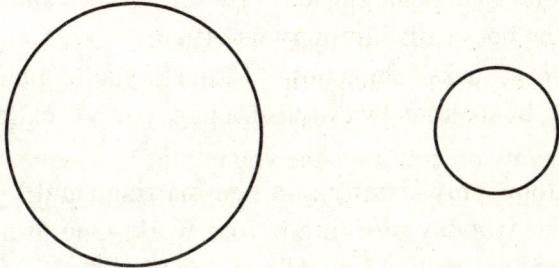

and told them this (the big circle) is your brain before drugs and this (small circle) is your brain after drugs.'

'That's admirable,' said the judge. 'And how did you do?' he asked the second lad.

'Well, your honour,' he replied. 'I persuaded 156 people to give up drugs forever.'

'One-hundred and fifty-six people!' cried the judge. 'That's amazing! How did you manage to do that?'

'Well, I used the same two circles. I pointed to the small circle and told them, 'this is your arsehole before you go to prison…'

****

This bloke John gets a new job, but on the Monday morning when he's supposed to start work he phones his new boss and tells him, 'I'm sick.' The boss excuses him and when John shows up for work on Tuesday morning the boss says he hopes he's feeling better. John works throughout the rest of the week without any problems, greatly impressing everyone with his diligence and ability. The next Monday, however, he again calls his boss to tell him, 'I'm sick'. The boss reluctantly excuses him again, but notices that this is the second Monday in a row John's claimed to be ill.

Once again, John shows up on Tuesday morning and works throughout the week, even faster and better than the previous week. The following Monday, however, he phones his boss again to tells him, 'I'm sick' and although the boss once again excuses him, he decides that this time he'll take John to task on Tuesday. Tuesday comes and as soon as John shows up, the boss calls him into his office.

'What's the story?' asks John's boss. 'I can see you're a hard worker, but you've only been here three weeks and you've called in sick every Monday.'

'Well,' says John, 'my sister's in a bad marriage and I go over to console her every Monday morning before work. One thing leads to another and we end up making love all day long.'

'With your sister!?!' says the boss. 'That's disgusting!'

'Well,' says John, 'I told you I was sick.'

****

Ten things not to say to the hard bloke in the pub:
10. Oi! Lurch! Get out of the fucking way!
9. I think of homosexuality as a perfectly acceptable extension of one's personality... my, you've got very big arms haven't you?
8. Yeah, you might be a big feller, but I reckon I'd have you.
7. Oi, you! You just spilled my pint. Tosser!
6. What'll you have, Piña Colada is it Tiny?
5. Honestly though, don't *you* think your relationship with your mum is a bit... well, unnatural?
4. Is that your bird? I heard she bangs like a barn door in a blizzard.
3. You look like Boy George. I bet you mince when you walk too.

2. What's your job then? Guard dog? Paperweight? Go on? What do you do?
1. Is this your pint… *(drinks some)* mmm, that tastes nice and that's Lager is it?

****

Q: Why did they have to draw a circle round your mouth when you were born?
A: Because you were so ugly they were afraid they might feed your arse by mistake!

****

Little Johnny thinks he's old enough to start swearing, so when he comes down for breakfast one morning and his mum wishes him a good morning and asks him what he'd like for his breakfast, Johnny replies: 'I'd like some fucking cornflakes…'

Obviously, his mum's outraged. 'Go to your room now!' she screams. Once he's gone, she turns to Johnny's brother Ivor and asks him what he'd like for breakfast.

'Well,' says Ivor. 'I'm definitely not having the fucking cornflakes…'

****

Q: What do you call a Manc lad in a filing cabinet?
A: Sorted!

****

Two friends are out taking a walk in the Australian outback when one of them goes for a piss behind a tree. In the middle of his piss a snake appears, slithers up his leg and bites him on the knob. Writhing in agony he shouts to his friend for help. Luckily his friend has a mobile phone and calls the doctor.

'Doc, doc!' shouts the friend. 'My mate just got bitten by a snake. What should I do?'

'OK, just calm down,' says the doctor. 'Firstly, take a knife and make a small incision where the bite is and then suck out all the poison; it's quite a simple operation. But if you don't do it I'm afraid your friend will die.'

By now his mate is writhing around in agony. 'What the doc say?' he asks his friend with the phone.

'Sorry, mate', he replies, 'but he says you're going to die.'

****

Q: How can you tell a Frenchman's been in your garden?
A: Your dustbin's empty and your cat is pregnant

****

Q: Why do the marines send three men out on a patrol?
A: One to read the map and two to guard the intellectual.

****

Q: What do you call a Welshman with a sheep under his arm?
A A newlywed.

****

Q: What do you call a Welshman man with two sheep under his arms?
A: A pimp.

****

During the war an officer got caught getting a blow-job by a female spy. He was later court martialed for insertion in the face of the enemy. During the war an officer got caught getting a blow-job by a female spy. He was later court martialed for insertion in the face of the enemy.

****

Q: What's the similarity between a lawyer and a sperm?
A: Only one in a million turns out to be a human.

****

Q. What did the elephant say to the naked man?
A. How do you breathe through that thing?

****

An Essex man goes to a fancy dress party, with blonde draped over his shoulder. 'I've come as a tortoise,' he says, and points to the girl on his back, 'and this is Michelle.'

****

Q: What's the violent, alcoholic, mental patient's catchphrase?
A: I'd rather have a bottle in front of me than a frontal lobotomy

****

Q: How many intelligent Arsenal fans does it take to screw in a light bulb?
A: Both of them.

****

Q: Why don't men have mid-life crises?
A: They stay stuck in adolescence.

****

Q: How do men buy lingerie for a woman?
A: They throw it on the floor to see if it looks good, 'cause that's where they want to see it anyway.

****

Q: How are men and dogs alike?
A: If they can't eat it or screw it, then they just piss on it.

****

Q: What's the difference between men and cheese?
A: Cheese matures.

****

Q: What is the difference between a puppy and a man?
A: Eventually the puppy will grow up and stop whining.

****

Q: Why is sleeping with a man like a soap opera?
A: Just when it's getting interesting, they're finished until next time.

****

Q: Why do men like love at first sight?
A: It saves them a lot of time.

****

Q: What do you call a virgin in a $300 Hat?
A: The Pope.

My Wife Doesn't Understand Me

2

Jokes about Matrimonial Bliss

Getting pissed can go three ways. Up, down or fast asleep. Up is good because you're loud, boisterous and having a laugh. Fast asleep isn't too bad until you wake up, but down is not good. When the booze starts working on you in such a way that your eyes fill with tears and you put your arm round the nearest person of the same sex (it has to be someone of the same such otherwise you're not telling them your problems, you're trying to shag them) and start telling them the most intimate details of your personal life and why it's all going wrong, you're in trouble. But don't panic; even though you're probably being more honest and open with a complete stranger than you've ever been with anyone before in your life, neither of you will remember a bleedin' word you said the next morning…

****

While on a car trip, the old couple stopped at a service station for lunch. The old woman left her glasses on the table, but didn't miss them until her and her husband were back on the motorway. By then, they had to travel quite a distance before they could find a place to turn around. The old man was fuming and moaned on at his poor wife all the way back to the service station. When they finally arrived, as the old woman got out of the car to retrieve her glasses, the old man called after her, 'And while you're in there, you might as well pick up my hat, too.'

****

You may have heard about a new bride who was a bit embarrassed to be known as a honeymooner. So when she and her husband pulled up to the hotel, she asked him if there was any way that they could make it appear as if they'd been married a long time. 'Sure,' he said. 'You carry the suitcases.'

****

A young man said to his girlfriend's dad, 'I realise this is only a formality, but could I ask you for your daughter's hand in marriage?'

'Who says it's only a formality?' replied her dad angrily.

'Her obstetrician,' replied the young man.

✳✳✳✳

This lad was getting married and two days before he was due to tie the knot, a cricket ball hit him in the bollocks.

'Sorry son,' his doctor told him. 'But your tackle will need to go in a splint.'

On his wedding night, his virginal bride strips off and points at her breasts. 'Aren't they beautiful?' she asks him. 'Never touched by human hands.'

He pulled down his Y-fronts and points at his crotch. 'That's nothing,' he says, 'mine hasn't even been unpacked.'

✳✳✳✳

A boy and his dad from a developing country were visiting the Gateshead Shopping Centre. They were amazed by almost everything they saw, but especially by two shiny, silver walls that could move apart and back together again. The boy asked his dad what it was.

'Son,' he replied, ' I have never seen anything like this in my life.'

While the boy and his dad watched wide-eyed, an old lady in a wheelchair rolled up to the moving walls and pressed a button. The walls opened and the lady rolled between them into a small room. The walls closed and the boy and his dad watched small circular numbers above the walls light up. They continued to watch as the circles lit up in the reverse direction. The walls opened up again and out stepped a voluptuous 24-year-old woman.

The dad and the son stared at each other in wide-eyed amazement until the dad said, 'Son, go and fetch your mother.'

✳✳✳✳

A Frenchman and an Italian were seated next to an Englishman on a long-haul flight. After a few cocktails, the men began discussing their home lives.

'Last night I made love to my wife four times,' the Frenchman bragged, 'and this morning she made me delicious *crêpes* and she told me how much she adored me.'

'Ah, last night I made love to my wife six times,' the Italian responded, 'and this morning she made me a wonderful omelette and told me she could never love another man.'

'And what about you?' the Frenchman smugly asked the Englishman. 'How many times did you make love to your wife last night?'

'Just the once,' he replied.

'Only once?' laughed the Italian. 'And what did she say to you this morning?'

'Don't stop,' said the Englishman.

✳✳✳✳

A bloke walks into a pub and sees a man sitting at the end of the bar with the smallest head he's ever seen. In fact, it's only about two inches high. So, he sits down next to him and says, 'Excuse me for asking, mate. But how come you've got such a small head?'

'Well, you see,' says the man with the unfeasibly small head, 'I was stranded on a deserted island and was combing the beach, when I came across an ornate bottle. When I opened it, a beautiful genie appeared and she told me I would be granted three wishes. My first wish was for a luxurious boat to take me home, and so a large yacht appeared just offshore. For my second wish, I asked to be wealthy, so I would want for nothing when I got home, and lo and behold a large pile of gold coins appeared on the deck of the yacht. For my third wish I asked the genie if I could make mad, passionate love to her, but she refused. She told me that under no circumstances could she do that for me, so I asked her, 'How about a little head?'

✳✳✳✳

This bloke walks into a pub with a monkey on a string. He sits at the bar and announces that the monkey's for sale.

'What do I want with a monkey?' replies the publican, 'they destroy everything, and they're a nuisance!'

The bloke replies, 'But this is a special monkey. It gives a really good blow-job. Look, go in the back and try it out.

After 10 minutes, the publican returns with a broad grin.

'You weren't kidding, were you mate? That monkey's really good! How much do you want for it?'

They agree on £200 and the money is duly exchanged. That evening, the publican returns home to his wife. 'Listen, love, he says to her. 'I just bought this monkey and it cost me 200 quid so I want you to teach it to cook and wash and then I want you to get the fuck out of my house.'

✳✳✳✳

Customer: (to publican) My wife and I just got into a knock-down, drag-out fight!

Publican: What happened?

Customer: When it was all over, she came crawling to me on her hands and knees!

Publican: Wow! What did she say?

Customer: She said, 'Come out from under that bed right now you coward, or I'll kick your flamin' head in!'

✳✳✳✳

A fellow decides to take off early from work and go drinking. He stays until the pub closes at 11pm by which time he's well and truly wankered. When he gets home, he doesn't want to wake anyone up, so he takes off his shoes and starts tip-toeing up the stairs. Half-way up, though, he falls arse over tit and lands flat on his backside. To make matters worse, the two bottles of lager he had in his back pockets smash, carving up his arse terribly.

Because he's so pissed, though, he doesn't realise how badly he's hurt himself until gets to his room and stars undressing. Realising that he's bleeding, he checks himself out in the mirror and, sure enough, his behind is cut up something terrible. Well, he repairs the damage as best he can under the circumstances, and goes to bed. The next morning, his head aching, and his rear's throbbing, and he's lying there under the covers trying to think up a good story, when his wife comes into the bedroom.

'Well, you really tied one on last night,' she says. 'Where'd you go?'

'I was working late,' he replies, 'and I stopped off for a couple of pints.'

'A couple of beers? That's a laugh,' she shouts. 'You got plastered last night.'

'What makes you so sure I got drunk last night?' he shouts back.

'Well,' she replies, 'my first big clue was when I got up this morning and found a load of plasters stuck on the mirror.'

✳✳✳✳

A married couple were throwing a dinner-party for all the top people in Cannes. The wife was very excited about this and wanted everything to be perfect. At the very last minute, she realised she didn't have any snails, so she asked her husband to run down to the beach and get her a bucketfull. Reluctantly, he agreed. He took the bucket, walked out the door, down the steps and out to the beach. As he was collecting the snails, he noticed a beautiful woman strolling alongside the water just a little further down the beach. 'Wouldn't it be great if she came over and just started talking to me?' he thought for a moment, before going back to gathering the snails. Moments later, he found himself staring up into the face of the beautiful woman he'd watched earlier. The two of them got talking, and she invited him back to her place. Before long they started shagging and it got so hot and heavy that when it was over he passed out from exhaustion.

At seven o'clock the next morning he woke up and, remembering his wife's dinner party, grabbed his clothes, put them on as quickly as he could, grabbed his bucket, and ran out the door. He ran down the beach all the way home. He ran up the stairs of his house, but he was in such a hurry that when he got to the top of the stairs, he dropped the bucket of snails.

Hearing the commotion his distraught wife came to the front door. On seeing her husband she became furious. 'Where the hell do you think you've been?' she screamed at him.

The man looked at the snails all down the steps, then looked at her, then back at the snails and said, 'Come on lads, we're almost there!'

****

This couple had been married for 30 years, and on their anniversary they decided to go back to the same hotel where they'd spent their wedding night. The husband was lying on the bed when his wife came out of the bathroom totally starkers, just as she had 30 years before. She stood seductively before him and said, 'Tell me, darling, what were you thinking 30 years ago when I came out of the bathroom like this?'

The husband replied, 'I took one look at you and thought I'd like to screw your brains out and suck your boobs dry.'

'And what are you thinking now, baby?' she asked huskily.

He said, 'I'm thinking I did a pretty good job of it!'

****

Eli was a just simple country boy, and though his wife longed for the sophisticated London life she read about in glossy magazines, she loved him just the same. Around the end of harvest-time she wanted to do something special for him because he'd been working so hard, so she bought a pair of crotchless knickers. The night the harvest was finally all brought in she put them on and waited for him. When he came home she lay sprawled on the couch spread-eagled. 'Hi, honey,' she purred sexily. 'You fancy some of this?'

Eli took one look at her and said, 'No thank you. Just look at what it done to your undies.'

****

A fireman came home from work one day and said to his wife, 'You know, we have a wonderful system at the fire station. Bell One rings and we all put on our jackets. Bell Two rings and we all slide down the pole and when Bell Three rings we're ready to go on the engines. From now on we're going to run this house the same way. When I say, "Bell One," I want you to strip naked. When I say, "Bell Two" I want you to jump into bed, and when I say, "Bell Three" we're going to screw all night.' So the next night he came home from work and yelled, 'Bell One,' and his wife took off her clothes. He yelled, 'Bell Two,' and his wife jumped into bed. He yelled, 'Bell Three,' and they began to screw. After a couple of minutes, though, his wife yelled, 'Bell Four!'

'What's Bell Four?' her husband asked.

'More hose,' she replied, 'you're nowhere near the fire.'

✳✳✳✳

This geezer had a very attractive wife, but she was always wanting clothes and jewellery and all sorts of expensive stuff he couldn't really afford. One day his wife came home with a diamond necklace.

'Where'd you get that?' asked the bloke.

'I won it at bingo,' she replied.

The very next night she comes home with a Gianni Versace coat.

'Where'd you get that?' asks the geezer.

'I won it at bingo,' she replied.

The following night she comes home with a brand-new Mercedes.

'Where'd you get that?' asks the bloke exasperated.

'Look,' shouts his wife. 'Don't keep asking where I get my things from. Go upstairs and run a bath for me.'

So off he went, but when his wife comes upstairs she finds only a small amount of water in the tub.

'Why's there hardly any water in the bath?' she demands.

'Well,' replied the guy, 'I didn't want to get your bingo card wet.'

Malcolm and his wife are walking down the high street one evening, window-shopping. They stop by a jewellery shop.

'Malc,' says his wife, 'I'd love those diamond earrings.'

'No problem,' says Malcolm, takes a brick out of his pocket, smashes the window and grabs the earrings. They walk hastily away and soon come upon another jewellery shop. In the window, there's this gorgeous diamond ring.

'Malc, oh please, please, please, get me that ring,' begs his wife. He looks around, sees there's nobody looking, takes another brick out of his pocket and hurls it at the window. Now she's got the earrings and this great ring, and they walk away until they come to yet another jewellery shop. This time there's this fantastic diamond necklace in the window.

'Malc, Malc, just look at it. It goes so well with the ring and the earrings. I need it!'

'For God's sake, woman,' says Malcolm. 'Do you think I'm *made* of bricks?'

****

A businessman and his secretary are overcome by passion, and the exec convinces her to nip back to his house for a lunchtime shag.

'Don't worry,' he purrs, 'my wife's on a business trip. She won't bother us.'

The pair are getting it on in the man's bedroom, when the secretary gasps, 'We've got to stop now! I'm not using any birth control.'

'No problem,' replies the man, 'I know where my wife keeps her diaphragm.'

He immediately begins rooting around in the bathroom. After half an hour, he returns to the bedroom in a fury.

'The bitch took it with her,' he said angrily. 'I knew she didn't trust me.'

****

A husband and wife were lying in bed. The husband reached over and nudged his wife. 'What do you want?' she said.

'You know,' he said.

'Can't,' she replied. 'I have to see my gynaecologist tomorrow.'
Later, the husband reached over and nudged his wife again.
'Look, I told you,' she shouted. 'I have to see my doctor tomorrow.'
'I know,' he said. 'But you don't have to see your dentist, do you?'

****

A husband comes home with a tub of ice-cream and asks his wife if she wants some.
'How hard is it?' she asks.
'About as hard as my dick,' he replies.
'OK,' she says, 'then pour me some!'

****

Man: (to friend) I'm taking my wife on an African safari.
    Friend: Wow! What would you do if a vicious lion attacked your wife?
    Man: Nothing.
    Friend: Nothing? You wouldn't do anything?
    Man: Right. Let the stupid lion fend for himself!

****

A man rushes into his house and yells to his wife, 'Debbie, pack your things, girl. I just won the lottery!'
'Shall I pack for warm weather or cold?' asks Debbie.
'I don't care,' the man responds. 'Just so long as you're out of the house by noon!'

****

Two married couples who regularly played bridge together were playing one week and took a break between hands. The wives went to the kitchen to get refreshments and the following conversation took place.

My Wife Doesn't Understand Me

'You know, Brian, you're doing much better this week as far as remembering what's trump and whose played what and everything,' said George.

'Yeah, George,' said Brian. 'I took one of them memory courses.'

'Really? which one did you take?' asked George.

'Erm, now let me think,' says Brian. 'Erm… what's it called… a red flower… got thorns…'

'A rose?' suggest George.

'That's it!' shouts Brian. 'Rose,' he shouts into the kitchen, 'what was the name of that memory course I took?'

****

A man is holding his wife's hand as she's lying on her death-bed.

'Jerry, I… I have something to tell you before I pass on,' she whispers.'

'No, no, dear,' says Jerry. 'Everything is forgiven now. All is well.'

'No, Jerry,' she mumbles. 'I've been carrying this load for years now, and I must tell you. I… I've been unfaithful to you. I slept with your best friend, Phil. I'm so terribly sorry.'

'Yes, dear, I know,' says Jerry. 'Why do you think I poisoned you?'

****

'After a few years of married life, this bloke finds he's unable to perform any more. He goes to his doctor, who tries a few things, but nothing works. Eventually the doctor says to him 'This is all in your mind', and refers him to a psychiatrist.

After a few visits to the shrink, the shrink confesses, 'I'm at a loss as to how to cure you,' and refers him to a witch-doctor.

The witch-doctor tells him, 'I can cure this, no problem,' and throws some powder on a flame. Suddenly, there's a flash followed by billowing blue smoke.

'This is powerful healing,' the witch doctor tells the bloke, 'but you can only use it once a year! All you have to do is say "One, two, three" and it shall rise for as long as you wish!'

'What happens when it's over?' asks the guy. 'All you have to say is "One, two, three, four" and it will go down again,' says the witch-doctor. 'But be warned; it will not work again for a year!'

The bloke goes home and that night he is ready to surprise his wife with the good news. As he's lying in bed with her he says "one, two, three", and suddenly he gets an erection.

His wife turns over and says, 'What did you say "One, two, three" for?'

✳✳✳✳

A woman reported the disappearance of her husband to the police. The officer in charge looked at the photo she handed them, questioned her, and then asked if she wished to give her husband any message if they found him.

'Yes,' she replied readily. 'Tell him Mother didn't come after all.'

✳✳✳✳

A married couple retire to their hotel room on their wedding night. The man, who's much larger than his petite bride, takes off his trousers and throws them over to his wife, saying, 'Put these on.'

'But they're way too big for me,' giggles his wife.

'I don't care,' says the man. 'Put them on anyway.'

So she puts his trousers on and, of course, they fall down. 'I told you I couldn't fit into these…'

'That's right,' he replied. 'Now just remember who wears the trousers in this family.'

The woman then takes off her panties and throws them over to her husband, saying, 'Put these on.'

He looks at them and says, 'I can't get into these...'

'Yes, that's right,' she replies, 'and you won't be able to in the future unless you change your attitude!'

****

Men who have pierced ears are better prepared for marriage. They've experienced pain and bought jewellery.

****

A little boy asked his father, 'Daddy, how much does it cost to get married?'
   'I don't know, son,' replied his father, 'I'm still paying for it.'

****

A tramp asked a man for £2.
   'Will you use it to buy booze?' asked the man.
   'No, sir,' replied the tramp.
   'Will you gamble it away?' asked the man.
   'No, sir,' said the tramp.
   'Then will you come home with me,' said the man, 'so my wife can see what happens to a man who doesn't drink or gamble?'

****

This couple visited a sex clinic to get treatment because their sex life had become a bore. Each night, the man would arrive home. His wife would prepare supper. After supper, they'd watch two hours of telly and immediately afterwards go to bed. From that point on, every move was routine.
   'No wonder,' the sex therapist said. 'You've made sex monotonous. Stop living on a schedule. Get into sex whenever you feel like it. Don't wait until bedtime each night to do it. Do it whenever you get into the mood.'
   The couple agreed to try the advice and said they would give him a progress report the following week.
   'How did things work out?' the sex therapist asked when they turned

up a week later. The man and his wife were beaming. 'It worked! It worked great!' they both said.

'Tell me about it,' said the therapist.

'Well, two nights after we saw you last,' said the husband, 'we were eating supper when I noticed that, although it was only seven o'clock, I had this huge erection. Sweetie-pie here was staring at it with longing eyes. So I didn't wait for any shower or any news broadcast. Instead, I reached out, ripped off her blouse and bra. Then I tore off her panties. I flung her right on to the table, spilling all the wine and soup in the process. Then I unzipped and we had sex like we've never had it before!'

'That's wonderful!' said the sex therapist. 'I told you it would work if you did it when the spirit moved you!'

'Only one thing,' said the man a little sadly. 'They're never going to let us go back in that restaurant.'

****

This old bloke who's a bit hard of hard of hearing has a bit of a funny turn, so his missus takes him to see the doctor.

The doctor runs a few tests but can't find anything wrong with him. Finally, the doctor says, 'Well, I'm baffled. I'm afraid I'm going to have to undertake some more thorough tests. Could you leave me a urine, faeces and sperm sample, please?'

'What does he want me to leave him?' says the old man.

'Your underwear, dear,' says his wife.

****

This woman goes to see a psychiatrist and says, 'I've got a big problem, doctor. Every time I'm in bed with my husband, he lets out this earsplitting scream when he climaxes.'

'My dear,' says the shrink, 'that's completely natural. I don't see what problem is.'

'The problem is,' says the woman, 'that he always wakes me up.'

My Wife Doesn't Understand Me

Since her husband became infatuated with Brigitte Bardot, Doreen's found that her love life' has gone right down the tubes. So one day she goes to the a tattoo shop, thinking that if she has the letters BB tattooed on her breasts that maybe her husband will notice and start paying attention to her again. Upon telling the tattooist her desires he explains that due to the ageing process and gravity, the tattoo on her breasts might not be so attractive in several years' time and suggests she have the initials put on her buttocks instead. She thinks it over and agrees, then leans over the table while the tattooist puts a B on each cheek. When her husband arrives home from work she greets him, turns around, bends over and lifts her dress to expose the art work.

'What do you think?' she asks.

'Who the fuck is Bob?' shouts her husband.

****

Mrs Jones goes to see her obstetrician, Dr. Smith. She says, 'Dr. Smith, I'm pregnant again. I need a hearing aid.'

'Mrs Jones,' says Dr. Smith, 'I thought we decided last time that your 12 children were more than you could handle, and that you should not get pregnant again. I'm going to give you a powerful contraceptive.'

'But doctor,' says Mrs Jones, 'I don't need a contraceptive. I need a hearing aid!'

'How come, Mrs Jones?' asks the doc.

'Well,' says Mrs Jones, 'I'm kinda hard of hearing. At night, when the old man and I turn off the lights and go to bed, he asks me, "Do you want to go to sleep, or what?" And I always say, "What?"'

****

A man came home after a night shift and went straight up to the bedroom. He found his wife with the sheet pulled over her head, fast asleep. Not to be denied, the horny husband crawled under the sheet and proceeded to make love to her. Afterwards, as he hurried downstairs for something to eat, he was startled to find breakfast on the table and his wife pouring coffee.

'How d'you get down here so fast?' he asked. 'We were just making love!'

'Oh my God,' his wife gasped, 'that's my mother up there! She came over early and had complained of having a headache. I told her to lie down for a while.'

Rushing upstairs, the wife ran to the bedroom. 'Mother, I can't believe this happened. Why didn't you say something?' The mother-in-law huffed: 'I haven't spoken to that good-for-nothing for 15 years and I wasn't about to start now!'

****

A woman was in bed with her lover when she heard her husband opening the front door. 'Hurry!' she said, 'stand in the corner.' She quickly rubbed baby oil all over him and then she dusted him with talcum powder. 'Don't move until I tell you to,' she whispered. 'Just pretend you're a statue.'

'What's this, darling?' her husband inquired as he entered the room.

'Oh, it's just a statue,' she replied nonchalantly. 'The Smiths bought one for their bedroom. I liked it so much, I got one for us too.'

No more was said about the statue, not even later that night when they went to sleep. Around two in the morning the husband got out of bed, went to the kitchen and returned a while later with a sandwich and a glass of milk.

'Here,' he said to the statue, 'eat something. I stood like an idiot at the Smiths' for three days and nobody offered me so much as a glass of water.'

****

Two deaf people get married. During the first week of marriage, they find they're unable to communicate in the bedroom when they turn off the lights because they can't see each other using sign language.

After several nights of fumbling around and various misunderstandings, the wife decides to find a solution. 'Darling,' she signs, 'why don't we agree on some simple signals? For instance, at night, if you want to have sex with me, reach over and squeeze my left breast once. If you don't want to have sex, reach over and squeeze my right breast once.'

The husband thinks this is a great idea and signs back to his wife, 'Great idea. Now if you want to have sex with me, reach over and pull on my penis once. If you don't want to have sex, reach over and pull on my penis 50 times.'

****

A couple go out to dinner to celebrate their 50th wedding anniversary. On the way home, she notices a tear in his eye and asks if he's getting sentimental because they're celebrating 50 wonderful years together.

'No,' he replies, 'I was thinking about the time before we got married. Your father threatened me with a shotgun and said he'd have me thrown in jail for 50 years if I didn't marry you. Tomorrow I would've been a free man!'

****

A little old man and a little old lady met in a nursing home and decided to get married. Both had been widowed some years before, and, naturally, it had been a long time since either had enjoyed conjugal relations. So on their wedding night, as she started to disrobe, the little old lady turned to her new husband and said, 'Now, before we get frisky, I just want you to know that I have acute angina.'

Her new husband, who was a little deaf, replied, 'WHAT WAS THAT, HONEYBUNCH?'

'I SAID, I'VE GOT ACUTE ANGINA!' she shouted.

'WHAT?' he yelled back.

'I SAID, I'VE GOT ACUTE ANGINA!' she screamed.

'Thank God for that,' the old man muttered, 'those wrinkley old tits of yours are a right turn-off.

****

Joe still enjoyed chasing girls even when he got to be 70. When his wife was asked if she minded, she answered, 'Why should I be upset? Dogs chase cars, but they can't drive.'

****

Doris and Fred had started their retirement years and decided to raise some extra cash by advertising for a lodger in their two-up, two-down terraced house. After a few days, a young, attractive woman applied for the room and explained that she was a model working in a nearby city-centre studio for a few weeks and that she'd like the room from Mondays to Thursdays, but would pay for the whole week.

Doris showed her the house and they agree to start straight away. 'There's just one problem,' explained the model. 'Because of my job, I have to have a bath every night, and I notice you don't have a bath?'

'That's not a problem,' replied Doris. 'We have a tin bath out in the yard and we bring it in to the living room, in front of the fire, and fill it with hot water.'

'What about your husband?' asked the model.

'Oh, he plays darts most weekdays, so he'll be out in the evenings,' replied Doris.

'Good,' said the model. 'That settles it. I'll go to the studio and see you tonight.'

That evening Fred dutifully went to his darts match whilst Doris prepared the bath for the model. After stripping off the model stepped into the bath and Doris was amazed to see that she had no pubic hair. The model noticed Doris staring, smiled and explained that it was part of her job to shave her pubic hair especially when modelling swimwear or underclothes. Later when Fred returned, Doris told him about this, but Fred didn't believe her.

'It's true I tell you,' says Doris. 'Look, if you don't believe me,

My Wife Doesn't Understand Me

tomorrow night I'll leave the curtains slightly open and you can peek in and see for yourself.'

The next night Fred left as usual and Doris prepared the bath for the model. As the model stepped naked into the bath Doris, standing behind her, looked towards the curtains, and points towards the model's naked snatch. Then she lifted up her skirt and, wearing no panties, points to her own hairy mass. Later Fred returned and they retired to bed.

'Well do you believe me now?' she asks Fred.

'Yes,' he replied. 'I've never seen anything like it in my life. But why did you lift up your skirt and show your hairy bits?'

'Just to show you the difference,' answered Doris. 'But why are you so bothered about it? You've seen my hairy bits millions of times?'

'I know I have,' said Fred, 'But the rest of the darts team hadn't!'

****

This couple had been married for 25 years and they decided to go to the same place as they had done for their honeymoon 25 years ago. As they were driving through the country the old man said: 'My love, I want to touch you the same way as I did 25 years ago.'

'You may, you old devil,' the old lady said and he touched her on the knee. A couple of miles later he touched her on the arm, and said, 'Let's do the same thing we did 25 years ago.' He stopped the car and the two old-timers got out the car and made love passionately up against a wire fence. When they were finished they resumed their journey.

'My love,' said the old boy, '25 years ago you didn't move like you've just moved!'

'25 years ago,' said the woman, 'the fence wasn't electrified.'

****

An older woman was doing her exercises in front of the mirror, admiring her figure.

'What are you looking at?' asked her husband.

'I'll have you know that my aerobics instructor says I have the chest of a 23-year-old woman!' she replied.

'Yeah?' said her husband. 'Well, did he say anything about your 60-year-old arse?'

'Why, no, dear,' she said, 'we never talk about you.'

✳✳✳✳

Two cannibals sat beside a large fire, after eating the best meal they'd had in ages.

'Your wife sure makes a great roast,' said the first cannibal.

'Yeah,' replied the second cannibal. 'I'm really going to miss her…'

✳✳✳✳

It was a dark, stormy night and the young soldier was on his first guard duty. A general was out walking his dog, and as he approached the sentry box, the nervous young private snapped to attention, made a perfect salute and called out 'Sir, good evening, sir!'

The general, out for some relaxation, returned the salute and said, 'Good evening, soldier; nice night, isn't it?'

Even though it was a horrible night, the private wasn't about to disagree with a general, so he saluted again and replied, 'Sir, yes, sir!'

The general continued, 'You know, there's something about a stormy night that I find soothing, it's really relaxing. Don't you agree?'

The private didn't agree, but then he was just a private, and so he said, ' Sir, yes, sir!'

The general, then pointed at his dog and said, 'This is a Golden Retriever, the best type of dog to train.'

The private glanced at the dog, saluted yet again and said, 'Sir, yes, sir!'

The General continued, 'I got this dog for my wife.'

'Yes, sir!' said the private. 'Good swap, sir!'

✳✳✳✳

My Wife Doesn't Understand Me

A keen huntsman, who just got a rise at work, decides to buy a new sight for his rifle. He goes to a rifle shop, and asks the clerk to show him a sight. The shopkeeper takes out a sight and says to the man, 'This sight is so good, you can see my house all the way up on that hill.'

The huntsman takes a look through the telescope and starts laughing. 'What's so funny?' asks the shopkeeper.

'I see a naked man and a naked woman running around in the house', the man replies.

The shopkeeper grabs the sight from the man, and looks at his house. Then he hands two bullets to the man and says, 'I'll give you this sight for nothing if you take these two bullets, shoot my wife's head off and shoot the guy's dick off.'

The man takes another look through the sight and says, 'You know what? I think I can do that with one shot!'

✳✳✳✳

While on holiday at a beautiful island getaway, a man discovers a lamp while walking on the beach. As these stories always go, he rubs the lamp and out pops a genie. The genie grants him three wishes, but adds one stipulation; 'Whatever you wish for, your wife will get double.'

This really upsets the man who's in the middle of a nasty divorce. He decides on his three wishes and tells the genie, 'First, I want to have £1 million.'

'Done,' says the genie. And, as promised, his wife receives £2 million.

'For my second wish,' says the man, 'I want a huge mansion.' Again it is done and his wife receives a house twice as large.

'So,' says the man, 'let me get this straight. I have a £1 million and my wife has £2 million. I have a huge mansion and my wife has one twice that size.'

'Correct,' says the genie. 'What do you want for your third wish?'

The man ponders momentarily and replies, 'I want you to scare me half to death.'

It was George the postman's last day on the job after 35 years of carrying the post through all kinds of weather in the same neighbourhood. When he arrived at the first house on his route he was greeted by the whole family, who roundly and soundly congratulated him and sent him on his way with a few quid. At the second house they presented him with a box of fine cigars. The folks at the third house handed him a selection of great golf clubs. At the fourth house he was met at the door by a strikingly beautiful woman in a revealing negligée. She took him by the hand, gently led him through the door, which she closed behind him, and led him up the stairs to the bedroom where she blew his mind with the most fantastic sex he'd ever had. When he'd had enough they went downstairs, where she fixed him a giant breakfast of eggs, bacon, sausages, chips, mushroom, beans and freshly-squeezed orange juice. When he was truly satisfied she poured him a cup of steaming coffee and gave him 50p.

George was baffled. 'All this was just too wonderful for words,' he said, 'but what's the 50 pence for?'

'Well,' she said, 'last night, I told my husband that today would be your last day, and that we should do something special for you. I asked him what to give you and he said, "Fuck him. Give him 50p." The breakfast was my idea.'

****

After her husband dies, a woman goes to the newspaper offices to place an obituary. Being short of money she decides on, 'Fred Dead, Funeral Monday.' Feeling sorry for her, the editor says she can have a few more words for free, so she changes it to, 'Fred Dead, Funeral Monday, Ford Escort for Sale.'

****

A husband and wife were having some problems with their marriage, so they bought a water bed to try to spice things up a bit. It did them no good, though. They started drifting apart.

After being examined by the doctor Ted's left to get dressed while the doctor takes his wife to one side to have a quiet word with her.

'To be honest,' he tells her, 'things aren't looking great for Ted. He's under a lot of pressure and if things don't ease up he could well suffer a heart attack soon. You can help by making his life at home as stress-free as possible. Bring him breakfast in bed in the morning, have his clothes ready, pressed and waiting for him, and in the evening when he comes home make him sit down, take his shoes off, run him a bath and gently massage his neck while he's in it. Anything like that will help with the stress.'

After Ted's got dressed, he's leaving the surgery with his wife when he turns to her and says, 'I noticed you were having quite a long chat with the doctor. What did he say to you?'

'He said you're going to die,' replied his wife.

****

One guy to another: 'I married Miss Right. I just didn't know that her first name was Always'.

****

Q: Did you hear about the new 'Divorced Barbie?'
A: Yeah, it comes with all of Ken's stuff!

****

An old farmer's having trouble with his prize bull. It won't breed with the cows, and he's lamenting the fact to a few of his friends down at his local.

One of them says, 'You know, I used to have the same trouble with my bull, but I got it fixed really quick.'

'How did you get it fixed?' asked the old farmer.

'Well I just dipped my finger in the cow's vagina and rubbed it all over the bull's nose and he got right after her,' explains his friend.

When the old boy goes home to the farm, he decides to try it. He grabs a cow, dips his fingers in her vagina and rubs it all around the bull's nose. The bull gets a rip-roaring boner and jumps on the cow immediately.

That night, the old farmer gets into bed with his wife and can't get the effect on the bull out of his mind. As she lies sleeping, he dips his fingers into his wife's vagina and feeling that it's nice and wet, he rubs it all around his nose and – hey presto! – he gets a rip-roaring hard on.

He quickly shakes his wife awake and cries out, 'Darling! Look at this!'

She rolls over, turns on the light and says, 'You mean you woke me up in the middle of the night just to show me that you have a nose-bleed?

****

Husband: Fancy a quickie?
Wife: As opposed to what?

****

There was once a lion-tamer who worked at the circus. His bunch of lions were well known for being the most ferocious lot around, but he never thought twice about going in with them.

After a show one night he'd been out for a few beers and, reckoning on a right bollocking from the missus, decided not to go home. He wandered around looking for somewhere to kip and eventually decided on going into the lion's cage where, resting his head on a particularly large beast, he fell asleep.

The following morning his wife woke up alone and, annoyed, came to look for him. After wandering around for some time she spied him, still dozing, in the lion's cage.

'Oi!' she shouted at him. 'Wake up, you bleedin' coward!'

****

A wife was having a go at her husband. 'Look at Mr Barnes across the road,' she moaned. 'Every morning when he goes to works, he kisses his wife goodbye. Why don't you do that?'

'Because I haven't been introduced to her yet,' replied her old man.

****

A man and a woman had been together for a few months. The woman was extremely wealthy and the man was very poor and they both knew that their relationship was a bit of fun, but one night the man took the woman out for a romantic meal with all the trimmings.

'Will you marry me?' he asked her.

'No,' replied the woman.

'I didn't think you would,' said the man.

'Well, why did you ask me then?' inquired the woman.

'Because I just wanted to know what it felt like to lose millions,' said the man.

****

A big Hollywood star fired his personal assistant one day because she hadn't been very good at keeping his personal records straight. According to her he'd had one more divorce than he'd had marriages.

****

On a particularly warm day one summer, a man decided to sunbathe naked in his back garden. Having recently built a large fence he was confident that no one would be able to see him.

'I wonder,' he mused to his wife, 'what the neighbours would say if they could see me.'

'They'd probably say that I must have married you for you money,' replied his wife.

****

Barry Davies was a very henpecked husband. In fact the only time he managed to get away from it all was at the annual school reunion where, each year, a trophy was awarded to the man who told the funniest story about making love to his wife. This particular year Barry won it and proudly took the trophy home.

'What did you get that for?' demanded his wife.

'Er, it was, er… it was for telling a story about when we played golf on holiday last summer, dear,' Barry stammered in reply.

'Hummph,' grunted his missus and wandered off. The next day Barry's wife was chatting to the wife of another man who had been at the dinner.

'Hello, Mrs Davies,' said the woman. 'I gather that your Barry won a prize for telling the best story at the do last night.'

'Yes, but I've no idea why,' replied Mrs Davies. 'We only did it once. His cap blew off, he couldn't get it in the hole and he lost a ball.'

****

A husband goes up in the loft and notices an eggbox containing no eggs but £5,000 in used notes. He says to his wife, 'What's all this money doing in this eggbox?'

She instantly breaks down and cries: 'I can't lie any more, I've been unfaithful. Every time I slept with another man, I took six eggs in payment.'

'Well that explains the eggbox,' says the husband. 'But how about the £5,000?'

'Well,' says his wife, 'every time I collected a dozen eggs I sold them.'

****

On their ruby wedding anniversary Janet turned to Jack and said, 'Do you know, Jack, we've been married for 60 years and I've been by your side all that time.'

'Yes,' said Jack. 'When I took a bayonet in the leg in the First World War you nursed me back to health. Then in the Second World War, after I was shot, you did the same. After the war when I was out of work, there you were for me. Then, when I did get a job and had to work all hours of the day just to make ends meet, you were by my side. When I was sacked and spent three years on the dole you never left me. When I developed kidney trouble and had to have an operation, there you were. And now that we're living in a B&B and I'm too old to work, you're still here. You know what Janet? You're a bloody jinx.'

****

After his beautiful wife died, John was understandably upset. 'I can feel your pain,' the local vicar told him. 'But it's good to grieve. And believe me, in time things will get better and you'll meet someone else.'

'I know,' said John, 'but what am I going to do tonight?'

****

A newly-married couple were getting ready for their wedding night but they both had a painful secret. He had terribly smelly feet and she had bad breath. To hide things he'd thrown his socks in the bath and she'd sprayed herself with breath freshener. They met in the middle of the room...

'Darling,' said the husband, 'I think there's something you should know. I've got very smelly feet.'

'That's OK,' said the wife. 'I've got something to tell you, too.'

'I know what you're going to tell me,' said the husband. 'You've eaten my socks.'

****

A woman is reading the ads in the local newspaper when she spots one that upsets her. 'Can you believe this?' she says to her husband. 'Some guy has put an advert in the paper offering to swap his wife for tickets to the Cup Final. You'd never do anything like that would you dear?'

'Course not, love,' says her husband. 'I've already got tickets for the game.'

****

On returning from the newsagent one morning a husband says to his wife, 'I've just heard a rumour that our postman's slept with every woman in this street except one. Can you believe that?'

'Hah,' says his wife, 'I bet it's that snobby, stuck-up cow at number 12.'

****

Two women are chatting. 'Dennis asked me to make him the happiest man in the world and marry him,' said the first one.

'Ooh, that's a tough one,' said the other. 'Which one did you choose?'

****

A woman was telling her friend about the tragic and sudden death of her husband.

'One minute he was with me and then he went out into the garden to pick some peas for our tea and he dropped dead,' she said.

'That's terrible,' said her friend. 'What did you do?'

'Opened a tin of beans instead,' she replied.

****

Two blokes were arguing about the merits of a particular actress.

'Look,' said the first one, 'take away her beautiful eyes, her great breasts, her fantastic figure and her lovely long hair, and what have you got?'

'My wife,' said the other sadly.

****

Two expectant fathers were waiting in the maternity ward.

'This is our first,' said one. 'Is it your first?'

'Oh no,' said the other, 'this is our fifth.'

'Really?' said the first bloke. 'Tell me something. Erm, how long before... well, you know? I mean, well... when can you have sex with your wife again after the birth?'

'Well,' said the other bloke. 'That all depends on whether she's on a ward or in a private room.'

****

A husband caught his wife in bed with another man and in a fury pulled out a gun ready to shoot him.

'No, no, don't kill him,' pleaded the wife. 'Who do you think paid for the new car? And that holiday? And who do you think paid for Kevin to go to that private school?'

'Was that you?' said the husband to the man.

'Yes,' spluttered the man, nodding. 'Well, get your clothes on then,' said the husband. 'You don't want to catch cold now, do you?'

****

A father came home one day and told his three kids that he had a surprise for them. 'Now,' he said to them, 'I've got some sweets and I'm going to give them to the person who never answers mummy back and always does what they're told. So who's going to get them?'

In unison the kids said, 'You are, Daddy!'

****

A beautiful woman was at the airport waiting for her husband to return from a long overseas trip. She spotted him at customs and waved, at which the husband waved back and shouted, 'F.F.'

'E.F,' woman shouted back the.

'F.F.' came the reply, to which the woman again shouted, 'E.F.' This went on for a while until eventually the customs officer's curiosity got the better of him and he asked, 'Is that a special code that you have with that lady?'

'Sort of,' said the man. 'She's my wife and she's just saying that she wants to eat first.'

****

An actor who'd been out of work for some time finally landed a part. Excitedly, he phoned his dad with the news. 'Dad, dad,' he said, 'Guess what? I've landed a really challenging role in the new Ken Branagh film. I'm playing a guy who's been married for 30 years.'

'That's great news son,' said his Dad. 'Soon you'll be able to move on to speaking parts.'

****

Tom and Sally had been married for 40 years. After Tom died Sally missed him terribly so she went to a medium and made contact with him on the other side. 'Tom, Tom,' she said. 'Is that really you?'

'Yes, it is,' said Tom.

'Tell me,' she asked, 'are you happy on the other side?'

'Oh yes, very,' replied Tom.

'Happier than when you were alive and with me?' asked Sally.'

'Yes Sally, I'm very much happier than when I was alive and with you,' said Tom.

'Gosh,' said Sally. 'Heaven must be such a wonderful place.'

'Who said anything about heaven?' said Tom.

****

A man rushed home excitedly one day with some great news.

'Darling, darling,' he shouted. 'I've found a fantastic job. £25,000 a year, company car, five weeks holiday a year and flexible hours.'

'That's brilliant news,' said his wife.

'Yes, I knew you'd be pleased,' he said, 'you start tomorrow.'

My Wife Doesn't Understand Me

****

The bellboy had carried the couple's luggage up to a room on the sixth floor of the hotel and was rewarded with a large tip.

'Thank you sir,' he said. 'Can I get you anything else?'

'No, thank you,' said the man.

'What about something for your wife, sir?' asked the boy.

'That's a good idea,' said the man. 'Bring me a postcard to send to her.'

****

Two businessmen were having lunch one day when two women entered the restaurant. 'Shit,' said one. 'My wife and my lover have just walked in.'

'Fuck,' said the other one. 'So have mine.'

****

Gary was down the local with his mate Ted. 'Do you know, Ted,' said Gary. 'I never slept with my wife before we were married. What about you?'

'I don't know,' replied Ted. 'What was her maiden name?'

****

'Where are you going on holiday?' John asked Trevor.

'We're off to Thailand this year,' Trevor replied.

'Oh; aren't you worried that the very hot weather might disagree with your wife?' asked John.

'It wouldn't dare,' said Trevor.

****

'Darling,' said Joan to her husband Clive. 'Every day you come in from work and I ask you how your day was and I sit patiently and listen as you tell me. You never ask me how my day was, here with the children and all the washing, ironing, cleaning and shopping to do.'

'OK, OK,' said Clive. 'How was your day, dear?'

'Terrible,' replied Joan. 'Don't ask.'

****

A husband and wife were talking about their dog. 'You know, dear,' said the wife. 'I think Fido's getting a bit old.'

'What makes you say that?' said the husband.

'Well, I think he's going a bit deaf. I often have to whistle two or three times before he comes,' said the woman.

'Nonsense,' said the man. 'Look at this. Fido! Sit!'

'I told you, dear, didn't I?' said the wife. 'Shall I get the disinfectant and the shovel?'

****

A honeymooning couple are about to get into bed when the woman bangs her foot on the bathroom door. 'Oh dear, darling,' says the man. 'Come here and I'll kiss it better.' She does so and before long they're shagging away. After a good session the woman gets up to go to the bathroom and once again she bangs her foot on the door.

'Can't you watch where you're going, you clumsy cow?' says the man.

****

Goldstein, the man with the biggest dick in Britain, dies. At the funeral an American tourist puts in a huge offer for his penis. After some discussion the relatives decide to sell the organ to the tourist. Back in the States the American rushes home and shouts to his wife, 'darling, darling. Come and see what I've got for you.'

The woman comes in, has a look and says, 'Oh my God! Goldstein's dead!'

My Wife Doesn't Understand Me

****

An Italian woman has just got married and is about to have sex for the first time. After her husband takes off his shirt she rushes downstairs and says to her mother, 'Mama, mama! He's got scars all the way up his arm.'

'Don't worry, bambina,' says her mother. 'It's OK. You go back up there and I'll carry on making the spaghetti.'

So she goes back upstairs, but after her husband has taken off his vest she runs down again. 'Mama, mama!' she shouts. 'He's got hairs all over his chest.'

'Don't worry, bambina, it's OK,' says her mother. 'Go back up there while I finish the spaghetti.'

So she goes back upstairs, but after her husband has taken off his shoes, socks and trousers she's down again. 'Mama, Mama!' she shouts. 'He's got half a foot.'

'Here, bambina,' says her mother. 'You make the spaghetti.'

****

A rich geezer rings home and when the butler picks up the phone he asks to speak to his wife.

'I'm sorry sir,' says the butler, 'but she can't speak to you at the moment.'

'Why not?' asks the rich geezer.

'Well, sir, she's busy,' says the butler.

'Doing what? asks the rich geezer.

'She's in the bedroom, sir,' the butler informs him.

'What's she doing in the bedroom?' asks the rich geezer becoming more irate by the second.

'I don't know sir, but she's with a man,' says the butler.

'Right,' says the rich geezer. 'Here's what I want you to do. Go and get the shotgun I use for hunting, go to the bedroom and shoot both of them.'

So the butler puts the phone down and goes about the task. After hearing two loud bangs down the phone the man hears the butler returning to the phone.

'Are they dead?' he asks the butler. 'Yes sir,' says the butler.

'Right,' says the rich geezer, 'I want you to take the gun into the garden and throw it into the fishpond at the bottom.'

'But sir,' exclaims the butler, 'we don't have a fishpond.'

'That is 454 7234, isn't it?' says the rich geezer.

****

A couple celebrating their 60th wedding anniversary decide to spice things up a little by sitting down to supper stark naked.

'Oh, Herbert,' says the woman, 'this is so lovely. I can feel my heart warming already.'

'I'm not surprised, Lily,' says Herbert, 'one of your tits is in the soup.'

****

A couple of American tourists are visiting London Zoo. When they get to the skunk cage the husband is so enchanted by the creatures that he sneaks in and steals one. He hides it in his bag, but as they approach the exit he becomes increasingly nervous and passes it to his wife telling her to hide it up her skirt.

'But what about the smell?' says the anxious wife.

'Don't worry,' says the man. 'If it dies I'll go back and get another one.'

****

A policeman gets home very late at night and so as not to disturb his wife creeps into their bedroom without turning on the light. Unfortunately, as he's slipping into bed his wife wakes up.

'Oh, darling,' she says, 'I've got a terrible headache. Please can you pop to the all-night garage and get me some aspirin?'

So the copper gets dressed again and goes to the shop.

'Hey,' says the assistant when he gets there. 'I thought you were a policeman.'

'I am,' says the copper.

'Then why are you wearing a fireman's uniform?' asks the shop assistant.

****

A woman who lived on a main road was having trouble with her bedroom closet. Every time a bus went past, its doors would fly open. So she called a carpenter who came round to look at it. He couldn't see any problem on the outside, so he climbed into it. Just then the woman's husband came home and sensing something was up ran straight into the bedroom and flung open the closet doors.

'What the hell are you doing in here?' he demanded.

'Would you believe I'm waiting for a bus?' said the carpenter.

****

Jane entered the kitchen one morning, reached to turn on the light, and found it didn't work. After replacing the bulb, there was still no light. When John, her husband, came home, she said, 'Darling, the light switch is broken. Could you fix it for me, please?'

To which John replied – while proudly displaying the front of his T-shirt – 'Do you see the word "Electrician" written on the front of this shirt?'

Jane said nothing.

Next day John came home and Jane said, 'Darling, the cabinet door fell off today. Could you put it back on for me, please?'

To which John replied, 'Do you see the word "Carpenter" written anywhere on the front of this shirt?'

Next day John came home and Jane said, 'Darling, the water pipe under the sink is leaking. Could you fix it for me, please?'

'Look,' John replied, 'Do you see the word "Plumber" written anywhere on the front of this shirt?'

Next day John came home and the light switch was working, the cabinet door had been replaced, and the pipe wasn't leaking. John said, 'I see you found some good repairmen'.

To which Jane replied, 'No, I just called the neighbour next door.'

'Oh, really?' said John. 'And how much did he charge?'

Jane laughed and said, 'He didn't charge anything. He said I could just bake him some "goodies" or we could trade it out in sex.'

To which, of course, John asked, 'Well, what kind of "goodies" did you bake for him?'

And Jane said proudly, while displaying the front of her shirt, 'Do you see the words "Delia Smith" written on here anywhere?'

✳✳✳✳

All men who hope to enter heaven have to queue at one of two gates: one marked, 'For Henpecked Men,' and one marked, 'For Men Who Have Not Been Henpecked.'

One morning the Angel Gabriel turns up for work and is amazed to see, along with the usual very long line at the first gate, one little geezer standing by the second. 'Hello,' said the Archangel, 'are you sure you're in the right line, mate?'

'Well, I don't really know,' said the little bloke, 'my wife told me to come and stand here.'

✳✳✳✳

Two married couples were playing bridge one night. Unfortunately, the husband of one of the couples was a bloody awful player and he and his wife were getting a drubbing. Eventually the husband decided he had to go and take a leak. After he'd left, his wife said, 'That's the only time this evening when I've known what's in his hand.'

A middle-aged woman goes to visit a fortune teller.

'I see only good for you,' says the fortune teller. 'You will meet a tall, dark, handsome stranger who will sweep you off your feet and make you incredibly happy.'

'That's fantastic,' says the woman. 'But I do have one small question.'

'And what may that be?' says the fortune teller.

'What happens to my husband?' she asks.

✳✳✳✳

A posh newly-wed woman was telling her friends all the intimate details of her recent honeymoon. 'It was truly marvellous,' she exclaimed. 'No sooner had we arrived in the hotel than Sebastian rushed me upstairs and we had a performance. Then just after lunch we had another performance, in the middle of the afternoon we had another and before dinner we had another. And then after dinner we had a dress rehearsal.'

'What is a dress rehearsal?' enquired one of her friends.

'It's the same as a performance,' said the posh woman, 'only nobody comes.'

✳✳✳✳

Not long after he'd been brought into existence, Adam couldn't help noticing that the animals would pop off into the forest in pairs and return some time later with wide, contented grins on their faces. Bemused, he asked God what it was all about.

'It's called reproduction,' said the Lord. 'Why don't you take Eve into the forest and find out about it?'

Adam did as the Lord had suggested, but returned to him the next day with another question. 'Lord,' asked Adam, 'What's a headache?'

✳✳✳✳

A husband and wife take their young son along with them when they go on holiday to a nudist camp. The boy can't help noticing that some men have, 'big ones' and some have 'little ones,' so he asks his dad about it.

His dad doesn't want to get into the whole thing, so quickly says, 'Oh, those with big ones are smart and those with small ones are stupid; now run along and find something to do.'

'Later on the family are having supper and the dad asks the little boy what he's been doing.

'Oh, I wandered around the woods and saw a lot of men getting much smarter,' said the boy.

****

There was a butler who worked for a wealthy couple. The husband was old, and the wife young and beautiful. One night the couple went out to dinner. The young wife returned home earlier than the husband, and she called the butler, Sam, into her room.

She told him: 'Sam, I want you to take my shoes off.' So Sam took her shoes off. Next she said, 'Sam, now I want you to take my stockings off.' so Sam took her stockings off. 'Now, Sam, take my dress off. Now my bra, and now my panties. And Sam, if I ever catch you wearing my clothes again…'

****

Two pairs of newly-weds went on honeymoon together. After the first week they got a bit fed up with their partners and agreed to swap to liven things up a bit. The next morning one of the husbands turned to his new partner and said, 'That was great. Shall we see how the girls are getting on?'

****

Two mates are chatting over a few beers when one of them says something that would be considered a Freudian slip. He also recalls the last slip he had when he asked a gorgeous, big-breasted travel agent for two 'Pickets to Titsburgh'. His friend says, 'Yeah, I know what you mean. Last week I was having breakfast with my wife and I meant to say, "Could you please pass the milk, dear?' but what came out of my mouth was, "You fucking bitch, you ruined my life"'.

****

A bloke is having marital problems. He and the wife aren't communicating at all and he's lonely, so he goes to a pet shop thinking a pet might help.

The shop happens to specialise in parrots and as he wanders down the rows of parrots he notices one with no feet. Surprised, he mutters to himself, 'That's strange, I wonder how he hangs on to the perch?'

To which the parrot replies: 'With my prick, you thick bastard.'

The bloke's startled and says, 'You talk really well for a parrot.'

To which the parrot replies: 'Of course I do, I'm a very well educated parrot. I can discuss politics, sports, religion – any subject you like.'

The guy says 'Blimey, you sound like just what I was looking for.'

The parrot says: 'There's not much of a market for maimed parrots. If you offer the proprietor £20 for me, I'll bet he'll sell me.'

The bloke buys the parrot and for three months things go great. When he comes home from work the parrot tells him how Tony Blair's done something new, or that Tim Henman won again, or how badly England lost the Test Match by and so and so, until one day when he comes home from work and the parrot waves a wing at him and says, 'Come in and shut the door.'

'What's up?' says the bloke.

The parrot says, 'I don't know how to tell you this but the postman came today. Your wife answered the door in her negligée and he kissed her right on the lips.'

The bloke says, 'Oh, it must have been a momentary flight of passion.'

Then the parrot says, 'Then he fondled her breasts.'

The bloke says, 'He did?'

The parrot says, 'Then he pulled her negligée down and started sucking on her tits.'

The guy says, 'My God, what happened next?'
The parrot says, 'I don't know I fell off my perch.'

****

It's a beautiful, warm spring day and a man and his wife are at the zoo. She's wearing a cute, loose-fitting, pink spring dress, sleeveless with straps. As they are walking through the monkey house and pass in front of a very large gorilla, the gorilla goes apeshit. He jumps up on the bars, holding on with one hand (and two feet), grunting, and pounding his chest with the free hand – obviously excited at the pretty lady in the pink dress.

The husband noticing the excitement, suggests that his wife tease the poor fellow. The husband suggests she pucker her lips, wiggle her bum, and play along. She does and the gorilla gets even more excited making noises that would wake the dead. Then the husband suggests that she let one of her straps fall. She does, and the gorilla is just about ready to tear the bars down. 'Now, try lifting your dress up your thighs,' says the husband. This drives the gorilla bananas. Suddenly, the husband grabs his wife by the hair, rips open the door to the cage, slings her in with the gorilla and says, 'Now, tell *him* you've got a headache!'

****

A married couple went to the hospital to have their baby delivered. Upon arrival, the doctor said he'd invented a new machine that would transfer a portion of the mother's labour pain to the father. He asked if they were willing to try it out.

They were both very much in favour of it, so the doctor set the knob to 10 per cent for starters, explaining that even 10 per cent was probably more pain than the father had ever experienced before.

As the labour progressed, however, the husband felt fine, so he asked the doctor to go ahead and bump it up a notch. The doctor then adjusted the machine to 20 per cent pain transfer. After a while, though, the husband

My Wife Doesn't Understand Me

was still feeling fine. The doctor checked his blood pressure and pulse and was amazed at how well he was doing. At this, they decided to try for 50 per cent. The husband continued to feel quite well.

Since it was obviously helping out his wife considerably, he encouraged the doctor to transfer ALL the pain to him and the wife delivered a healthy baby with virtually no pain. She and her husband were ecstatic and they were allowed to leave the hospital that evening. When they arrived home they found the milkman dead on their doorstep.

****

Bill worked in a pickle factory. He had been employed there for a number of years when he came home one day to confess to his wife that he had a terrible compulsion. He had an urge to stick his penis into the pickle slicer. His wife suggested that he should see a sex therapist to talk about it, but Bill indicated that he'd be too embarrassed. He vowed to overcome the compulsion on his own.

One day, a few weeks later, Bill came home absolutely ashen. His wife could see at once that something was seriously wrong. 'What's wrong, Bill?' she asked.

'Do you remember I told you how I had this tremendous urge to put my penis into the pickle slicer?'

'Oh, Bill, you didn't!'

'Yes, I did.'

'My God, Bill, what happened?'

'I got fired.'

'No, Bill. I mean, what happened with the pickle slicer?'

'Oh… she got fired too.'

****

Mark and Sharon decide they don't want to discuss sex in front of their four- and six-year-old children, so they decide to talk in code. One day Mark is feeling a little bit turned on and says to Katie, 'Tell your mother I would really like to type a letter.'

Katie runs off to find her mum. 'Mummy, mummy', shouts Katie, 'Daddy would like to type a letter.'

Sharon replies slightly sheepishly, 'Katie, go and tell your daddy that he can't type a letter today as there's a red ribbon in the typewriter.'

Katie tears off to her dad and says, 'Daddy, daddy, mummy says you can't type a letter today as there's a red ribbon in the typewriter.'

A few days later Sharon remembers that Mark was keen for a bit of nookie and so she called Katie, 'Katie, tell your daddy that he can type that letter today.'

So Katie runs off to look for her dad and when she finds him she says, 'Daddy, mummy says you can type that letter today.'

'That's OK, Katie,' Mark says, 'You can tell your mummy that I don't need the typewriter any more. I wrote the letter by hand.'

✳✳✳✳

Fred's boss told him that he had to work overtime. 'OK,' said Fred, 'but we've only just moved into our new home and the phone ain't connected – how can I let my old lady know I'll be late home?'

'I know where you live,' says the boss. It's not far from my house. I'll pop in and tell her on my way home.'

When the boss arrived at Fred's house, his wife comes to the door.

'I just popped round to let you know that Fred will be late home tonight,' says the boss.

'Oh, OK,' says Fred's wife. 'Can I get you a cup of tea?'

'Well, that would be nice,' said the boss, 'but how about taking me upstairs and letting me fuck you instead?'

'I've never heard such cheek,' said the wife.

'What about if I give you 50 quid?' says the boss.

'No! Fred would be furious,' said the wife.

'How about £100?' says the boss.

'No!' says the wife.'

'Alright,' says the boss. '£150.'

'OK, then,' says the wife and she takes him upstairs and screws him. Later that day, Fred arrived home.

'I'm sorry I'm late, darling. Did the boss call round and tell you about the overtime?'

'Yes he did, darling,' replied his wife.

'Oh yeah,' said Fred remembering something else. 'He said he'd drop my wages off as well. Did he give them to you?'

****

A young couple was invited to a swanky masked Hallowe'en party. The wife came down with a terrible headache and told her husband to go to the party and have a good time. Being the devoted husband, he protested, but she argued and said she was going to take some aspirin and go to bed. She told him there was no need for him to miss the fun. So he took his costume and away he went.

The wife, after sleeping soundly for an hour, woke up feeling normal and, as it was still early, decided to go to the party. Because hubby didn't know what her costume was, she thought she'd have a bit of a laugh watching her husband and seeing how he acted when she was not around.

She joined the party and soon spotted her husband cavorting around on the dance floor. He was dancing with every nice woman he could, and copping a feel here and stealing a kiss there. His wife sidled up to him and being a rather seductive babe herself, he left the partner he was with and devoted his time to the new 'action'.

She let him go as far as he wished, naturally, since he was her husband, and when he whispered a little proposition in her ear she agreed to go off with him to one of the bedrooms for a bunk-up.

Afterwards they went back to the party and, just before the unmasking at midnight, she slipped out, went home, put the costume away and got into bed. She was sitting up reading when he came in, and she asked him what he had done.

He said, 'Oh, the same old thing. You know I never have a good time when you're not there.'

Then she asked him if he danced much and he said: 'I never even danced one dance. When I got to the party, I met Pete, Bill and some other guys so we went into the kitchen and got a poker school going. But I'll tell you... the guy I loaned my costume to, he told me what he'd been up to and he had one a hell of a time…'

****

Two women were standing at a funeral. 'I blame myself for his death,' said the wife.

'Why?' said her friend.'

''Cos I shot him,' said the wife.

****

A married couple had jet-black hair, so when their daughter was born a redhead, the husband was a bit suspicious. He went to the doctor and explained the situation.

The doctor said, 'Well how often do you have sex?'

'Oh, about once every two years,' said the husband.'

'Well, that explains it,' said the doctor. 'You're a bit rusty.'

****

'You never cry out when you orgasm,' said the husband.

'How would you know?' replied his wife, 'you're never there.'

****

A very old millionaire goes for a check-up. The doctor looks him over and pronounces him in fine physical shape.

'I'm curious,' says the doctor. 'Why did you decide to have a physical now?'

''Cos I'm just about to marry an 18-year-old and we're planning on having children.'

The doctor tries not to look too astonished.

My Wife Doesn't Understand Me

'Is there anything you think I should do to help things along?' asks the old man.

The doctor thinks about this for a while and says, 'I think you should get a young lodger.'

'OK,' says the old man and leaves. A year later, the doctor sees the old man in the street and asks how things are going.

'My wife's pregnant,' says the old man.

'That's great,' says the doctor. 'And how's the lodger?'

'Oh, she's pregnant, too,' replies the old man.

****

Two bricklayers were chatting at work. 'Are you going to the match on Saturday?' said one. 'Arsenal are playing Spurs.'

'No,' said the other. 'My wife won't let me.'

'What?' said the first. 'It's easy to get out of that. About an hour before the game, what you do is pick her up, take her to the bedroom, rip off her clothes and make mad, passionate love to her. Then she'll let you do anything you want.'

'I'll try that,' said the other man.

The following Monday the two men meet on the building site. 'How come you didn't make it to the game?" asked the first man.'

'Well, I'll tell you what happened,' said the second man. 'About an hour before kick off, I did as you said. I picked her up, took her to the bedroom and ripped off her clothes. And then I thought, Spurs haven't been playing that well recently.'

****

This poor old couple were sitting in a flat. 'We've completely run out of money,' said the husband. 'You're going to have to go out and sell your body.'

'You can't be serious,' said his wife.

'Yes, I am,' said the husband.

So off she goes and comes back 12 hours later with £5 and 10 pence.

'Who gave you the 10 pence?' asked the husband.
'Everybody,' she replied.

★★★★

This man went to the doctor because he wanted to kill his wife. The doctor said to him, 'I've got the perfect solution. Take these pills every day and you'll be able to make love to your wife 15 times a day. In a month, she'll be dead.'

The man was very grateful and rushed off with the pills. Four weeks later, the doctor was walking down the street and saw his patient, in a wheelchair, moving very slowly towards him.

'What happened?' said the doctor.

'Two more days,' said the man. 'Just two more days…'

★★★★

There was this man who had just got married and was spending his wedding night with his new wife in a very posh hotel. It was to be the first time that he had ever had sex with her; indeed, he had never even seen her naked.

As they were both undressing, he looked up from taking his socks off to notice that she had huge breasts and even went so far as to compliment her on them.

Unfortunately, the poor girl had always had a bit of a complex about them and got very distraught at this. So much so that she sent him with a blanket out into the corridor to sleep. The man was pretty upset at this, but not wishing to fuel her anger further, did as he was told.

Just as he was getting off to sleep another man came into the corridor to join him. The first man asked the second why he was out there, to which he replied that he was also on his wedding night and had never had the pleasure of seeing his new wife's body before. When she was undressing, he had suddenly exclaimed out loud what an absolutely enormous bum she had. She hadn't really been very impressed with this outburst, and had ordered him to go and sleep in the corridor.

Before long jilted honeymooner number three sulkily sauntered out to join the other two.

'What's wrong with you?' asked the first, 'did you put your foot in it as well?'

'No,' replied the third, 'but I bloody well could have.'

****

An architect, an artist and a computer programmer were discussing whether it was better to have a wife or a mistress. The architect said he enjoyed time with his wife, building a solid foundation for an enduring relationship. The artist said he enjoyed time with his mistress, because of the passion and mystery he found there. The computer programmer, meanwhile, said, 'I prefer to have both.'

'Both?' said his friends incredulously.

'Yeah,' said the programmer. 'If you have a wife and a mistress, they'll each assume you're spending time with the other woman, leaving you plenty of time to mess about on the computer.'

****

A young couple hadn't been married for very long when, one morning, the man came up behind his wife as she was getting out of the shower and grabbed her by the buttocks. 'Y'know love, if you firmed these up a bit you wouldn't have to keep using your girdle.'

Her feelings were so hurt that she refused to speak to him for the rest of the day. A week or two later she was again stepping out of the shower when he grabbed both her breasts and said, 'Y'know what love? If you firmed these up a bit you wouldn't have to wear a bra.'

The young wife was infuriated, but had to wait 'til the next morning to get her revenge. Waiting until her husband stepped out of the shower she grabbed him by his dick and hissed, 'Y'know what love, if you firmed this up a little bit, I wouldn't have to use your brother.'

My Wife Doesn't Understand Me

****

Two old men are comparing their sex lives:
Man 1: I can still do it twice!
Man 2: Which time do you enjoy the most?
Man 1: I think the winter.

****

Ten things a woman will never say:
10. Could we be more physical? I'm tired of just being friends.
9. I think you should have another beer.
8. I think hairy arses are really sexy.
7. Hey, I just farted. Phew! get a whiff of that one!
6. Don't throw that smelly, old t-shirt out… it's really cute!
5. This diamond is far too big!
4. I won't even put my lips on that thing unless you let me swallow!
3. My God! It really is 14 inches.
2. Does this make my bum look too small?
1. I'm wrong. You must be right again.

Ten things a man will never say:
10. I think Peter Andre is a really cool bloke!
9. While I'm up could I get you a beer?
8. I think hairy arses are sexy.
7. Her tits are far too big.
6. Sometimes I just want to be held.
5. Why don't we invite your mother?
4. Of course! I'd love to wear a condom!
3. Hey, let's go shopping and why don't you drive!
2. Fuck the football, let's watch your 'Cagney and Lacey' videos.
1. It looks like we're lost, better pull over for some directions.

Don't Mix Your Drinks

3

Jokes for the Morning After

Don't Mix Your Drinks

It's an age-old adage and it is as true today as it ever was, mix your drinks and come a cropper: a bit of cider; a few beers; a gin and tonic; a whisky; a chocolate milkshake; another glass of wine; some Guinness; a flaming Sambuca; an Irish Coffee... stick it all in your belly, dance like a king and spend the next few days wondering what on Earth could be the matter with you. Thankfully, the same cannot be said of mixing jokes, so, here is a mighty selection of all the jokes that we couldn't crowbar into the other sections all laid out for your enjoyment and edification.

****

A woman goes into a clothes shop. 'Can I try that dress on in the window, please?' she asks.

'I'm sorry, madam,' replies the shop assistant, 'but you'll have to use the changing-rooms like everyone else.'

****

At the top-secret army HQ, two generals were testing the new computer. They asked it to answer the question: 'How long is a piece of string?'

After a few moments '5,000,' came up on the computer screen.

'5,000 what?' said one of the generals. '5,000 sir!' flashed up on the screen.

****

Van Gogh goes in to a pub and his mate asks him if he wants a drink. 'No thanks,' said Vincent, 'I've got one ear.'

****

Q: What was the first thing Dick Turpin said on completing his epic ride from London to York?
A: 'Woah!'

****

The orchestra had hired a new conductor from Russia. He started off on the first day by shouting at the orchestra, 'You bunch of lazy bastards. You don't practice enough! From now on you get here three hours before practice every day to work with your section head. Only once you are sufficiently warmed up will I grace you with my genius. You are so bad you need to practice every day!'

This really annoyed the musicians, especially the man who played the kettle drums, and he banged them – BOOM BA-DA BOOM! BOOOOOM! – in frustration.

The new conductor glared at the orchestra, 'Right, who did that?'

****

In the old Soviet Union, the secret police discovered a man who looked exactly like Stalin. This was obviously dangerous as he could impersonate the Leader so Beria, the secret police chief, reported the discovery to Stalin, and asked him for instructions.

'Why, shoot him,' said Stalin.

'Certainly, comrade Stalin – that's a great idea,' says Beria, 'but... '

'BUT?' says Stalin. 'But what?'

'Well, I just thought, if we shaved off his moustache he wouldn't be a problem... ' says Beria.

'A valuable suggestion, comrade Beria!' says Stalin. 'Give him a shave and then shoot him!'

****

One cold morning two Russian border guards, Ivan and Vladimir, are looking across the border. Ivan is smiling to himself when he notices that Vladimir is also smiling.

Ivan (suspiciously): 'What are you thinking about?'

Vladimir: 'Same thing as you, comrade.'

Ivan: 'Then it is my duty to arrest you.'

****

A nerd walks into a chemist's and says: 'I need a box of tampons.'

The sales assistant is surprised and says, 'Young man, what do you want with tampons?'

'Well,' says the nerd, 'My sister says that if you use them, you can run, go horseback riding, and take part in all kinds of dangerous sports.'

****

This traveller is driving past a psychiatric hospital in the middle of nowhere when the front wheel comes off his van. Looking into the problem he finds that all four of the wheel's nuts have come off and he hasn't got any to replace them. In despair, he sits down by the side of a road to think things out.

All this is watched by one of the mental patients from a window. After a while the mental patient calls out to the traveller and beckons him over.

The traveller looks at him and decides that the last thing he needs right now is a conversation with a nutter, and so ignores him. The mental patient, however, is insistent and keeps calling out to the traveller until, in the end, the traveller gives in and goes over to talk.

When he approaches the window the mental patient tells him to take one nut out of each of his other wheels and use it temporarily on the wheel that's come off. This way he could get to the next town and buy four more. The traveller looks at him in disbelief; this had never occurred to him. Totally blown away by this, he apologises for his previous rude behaviour and asks him why he's in a nut house when he obviously has so much common sense. To this he gets the reply, 'I may be mad but I'm not STUPID.'

****

Two old men were walking down the street when they came across a frog. The frog looked up at them and said, 'Hey, if you pick me up and kiss me I'll turn into a beautiful princess and you can have your wicked way with me.'

One old man reached down and picked the frog up and put it in his pocket. The other man said, 'Hey, aren't you gonna kiss that frog?'

The first old man says, 'No way, at my age I'll have more fun with a talking frog!'

****

Three months after having sold a fridge to an Eskimo, the world's greatest salesman decided to check up on his new customer.

'How you getting on with the fridge?' he asked the Eskimo.

'Oh, not too bad,' replied the Eskimo, 'but it's a real pain cutting the ice into squares so it will fit into the tray.'

****

A bloke walked into a posh block of flats one day and saw the following sign; PLEASE RING BELL FOR DOORMAN. So he rang the bell and the doorman appeared. 'Yes, sir?' said the doorman, 'can I help you?'

'Yes you can," came the reply. 'I just wanted to know why you can't ring the bell yourself?'

****

Two old boys are sitting on the top deck of a bus talking.

'I'm telling you my friend, it's spelt w-o-o-o-o-o-m-m-m-m-b, wooooommmmmb!" said one.'

'No, no, no. It's spelt, w-o-o-o-m-m-m-m-m-m-b-b-b-b-b, wooom-mmmmmmbbbbb!' said the other.

This went on for a while until a nurse sitting behind them leant over and said, 'I'm sorry, I couldn't help overhearing your discussion and I can tell you that it's spelt, w-o-m-b, womb.'

'I'm sorry, madam,' said the one old boy, 'but have you ever *heard* an elephant fart under water?'

****

Two sperms are swimming along and one is starting to get tired. He asks his mate, 'How far do you think is it to the uterus? I'm getting pretty tired!'

His mate says, 'I'm not sure, but I think it must be still a long way – we've only just passed the oesophagus!'

****

A horse and a chicken are playing in a meadow. The horse falls into a mud hole and is sinking. He calls to the chicken to go and get the farmer to help pull him out to safety. The chicken runs to the farm but the farmer can't be found. So he drives the farmer's Mercedes back to the mud hole and ties some rope around the bumper. He then throws the other end of the rope to his friend, the horse, and drives the car forward and saves him.

A few days later, the chicken and horse are playing in the meadow again and this time the chicken falls into the mud hole. The chicken yells to the horse to go and get some help from the farmer. The horse says, 'I think I can stand over the hole!' So he stretches over the width of the hole and said, 'Grab my love pump and pull yourself up.' The chicken does and hauls himself to safety.

The moral of the story? If you're hung like a horse, you don't need a Mercedes to pick up chicks.

****

One day, Pinocchio and his girlfriend were in bed doing what girls and wooden boys do. As they were having a cuddle afterwards, Pinocchio could tell that something was bothering his girlfriend. So, he asked her, 'What's the matter, baby?'

Pinocchio's girlfriend gave a big sigh and replied, 'You're probably the best bloke I've ever met, but every time we make love you give me splinters.'

This remark bothered Pinocchio a great deal, so the next day he went to seek some advice form his creator, Gepetto. When Pinocchio arrived, Gepetto could tell something was bothering Pinocchio, and asked him what was the matter. As Pinocchio revealed his dilemma to Gepetto, Gepetto searched up and down for a solution.

Eventually, he suggested that sandpaper might be able to 'smooth' out Pinocchio's relationship with his girlfriend. Pinocchio thanked Gepetto and went on his way.

When Gepetto didn't hear from Pinocchio for a while, he assumed that the sandpaper had solved all Pinocchio's problems. A couple of weeks later, Gepetto was in town to have some blades sharpened at the hardware store when he ran into Pinocchio. When he saw Pinocchio buying all the packs of sandpaper the store had in stock, Gepetto remarked, 'So, Pinocchio, things must be going pretty damn good with the girls.'

Pinocchio looked at him with a grin and said, 'Girls? who needs girls?'

✶✶✶✶

Ahmed Al-Mohammed was in the bazaar when he felt terrible stomach cramps. Unable to control himself, he let out a long and noisy fart. People all around stared and Ahmed felt his face redden. He ran home, packed up his few belongings and journeyed to the far side of the world vowing never to return. But over the years, he missed his home and finally, at the age of 83, he felt he could return safely, his aged face concealing his true identity.

So, Ahmed returned to his home. He walked around the bazaar feeling happier than he had for years. He was browsing in one shop and asked the trader when the paving stones had been relaid so neatly.

'By the grace of Allah,' said the trader, 'that was four years and two months after Ahmed Allah Mohammed farted.'

An elderly man stands in line for hours at a Warsaw meat store during the last days of Communism. When the butcher comes out at the end of the day and announces that there's no meat left, the man flies into a rage.

'What is this?' he shouts. 'I fought against the Nazis, I worked hard all my life, I've been a loyal citizen, and now you tell me I can't even buy a piece of meat? This rotten system stinks!'

Suddenly a thuggish man in a black leather coat sidles up and murmurs, 'Take it easy, comrade. Remember what would have happened if you had made an outburst like that only a few years ago,' and he points an imaginary gun to his head and pulls the trigger.

The old man goes home, and his wife says, 'So they're out of meat again?'

'It's worse than that,' he replies. 'They're out of bullets.'

****

A Chinese man goes for a job on a building site. 'Can you lay bricks?' asks the foreman.

'No,' says the Chinaman.'

'Can you paint?'' asks the foreman.

'No,' says the Chinaman.

'Can you plaster?' asks the foreman.

'No,' says the Chinaman. The foreman's a bit exasperated by all this, but after a bit he says, 'OK, you can work on supplies.'

Three months later, the foreman's walking around the site. 'Has anyone seen that Chinaman we took on a few months ago,' he asks. Just then, the Chinaman jumps out from behind some boxes and shouts, 'Suplise!'

****

A farmer sent his 15-year-old son to town. He gave him a duck and said, 'I want you to come back a man. Use the duck to get what is needed.'

Don't Mix Your Drinks

The son walked off into town and came across a prostitute. 'Would you sleep with me for this duck?' asked the boy.'

'Yes, I would,' said the prostitute. 'I've always liked animals.'

When they were finished, the prostitute was very impressed. 'I'll tell you what,' she said. 'If you can do it again, I'll give you the duck back.' So they did it again and the boy got his duck back.

He was walking home later that day when the duck flew out of his hands and into the path of an oncoming truck. The truck driver was very upset and came over to the boy. 'I'm very sorry about your duck,' gave him £5 and drove off.

When the boy got home, the father asked his son how the day had gone.

'Pretty good,' said the boy. 'I got a fuck for a duck, a duck for a fuck and £5 for a fucked-up duck.'

****

Jim and John, two drunks, are lying next to a hot-dog stand in the street.

'We've only get 50p and I need another drink,' said Jim.

'I know how we can drink all day for that,' said John.

John buys a hot dog and sticks it in his fly. Next, they walk into a pub, order drinks and knock them back in one. When the publican asks them to pay up, Jim gets down on the floor and started sucking the hot dog. The publican throws them out.

They do this scene 12 more times until John calls a halt.

'You must be getting tired kneeling down and standing up again and again'

'Well, I don't feel too bad,' says Jim, 'but I think you dropped the hot dog after the second pub.'

****

What's the difference between a working-class woman and a rich woman? The working-class woman has real orgasms and fake pearls.

****

What do you get when you cross LSD and the Pill? A trip without the kids.

****

Why did the Siamese twins move to France? So the other one could learn to drive.

****

What's the difference between a woman in church and a woman in a bathtub? One has hope in her soul...

****

What has six balls and fucks you twice a week?
The National Lottery!

****

What's the difference between a tyre and 365 condoms?
One's a Goodyear, and the other's a fucking excellent year!

****

Two little old ladies with very weak eyesight go shopping one day. After shopping a while, they decide to go to the toilet. Mistakenly, they walk into the Gents instead of the Ladies. Inside, two men who are equally desperate to take a leak are standing at the urinals, about to begin. When the two ladies walk in, the men not knowing what else to do, put their backs against the wall and pretend they're part of the toilet fixtures.

The first lady, mistaking one of the men for the sink, walks up to him and pulls his penis a couple of times. The man looses control and lets go.

She then turns to the other one and says, 'Oooh, you should try this one Gladys. It has lovely warm water!

To which Gladys replies, 'No dear, I think I'll stick with this one. It not only has warm water, it dispenses liquid soap as well!'

****

A frog telephones the Psychic Hotline and his Personal Psychic Advisor tells him: 'You're going to meet a beautiful young girl who will want to know everything about you.'

The frog is thrilled, 'This is great! Will I meet her at a party?'

'No,' says his Advisor, 'in her biology class.'

****

A ventriloquist cowboy walked into a little town in Texas and saw a rancher sitting on his porch with his dog.

Cowboy: Hey, cool dog. Mind if I speak to him?
Rancher: Dawgs cain't talk.
Cowboy: Hey dog, how's it going?
Dog: Doin' alright.
Rancher: (Extreme look of shock)
Cowboy: Is this your owner? (Pointing at rancher)
Dog: Yep.
Cowboy: How's he treat you?
Dog: Real good. He walks me twice a day, feeds me great food and takes me to the lake once a week to play.
Rancher: (Look of disbelief)
Cowboy: Mind if I talk to your horse?
Rancher: Horses cain't talk.
Cowboy: Hey horse, how's it goin?
Horse: Cool.
Rancher: (An even wilder look of shock)
Cowboy: Is this your owner? (Pointing at the rancher)
Horse: Yep.

Cowboy: How's he treat you?

Horse: Pretty good, thanks for asking. He rides me regularly, brushes me down often and keeps me in the barn to protect me from the elements.

Rancher: (Total look of amazement)

Cowboy: Mind if I talk to your sheep?

Rancher (Gesturing wildly and hardly able to talk): Them sheep ain't nothing but liars!

****

A man stood before the judge.

'I sentence you to three years for breaking and entering,' said the judge.

'But your honour, I didn't do anything !' said the man.

'You were caught with your burglar tools in your possession,' said the judge.

'In that case you can put me in jail for rape,' said the man.

'Did you really rape somebody?' asked the judge.

'No, your honour, but I had the equipment on me.'

****

A woman living in a rural area wanted to have an outside lav. that wouldn't stink. She advertised in the local papers for a contractor that could build such a structure. After some time, a contractor applied for the job and guaranteed that the outside lav. would not have any odour. He got the job.

Some time after completing the construction, the man got a frantic phone call from the woman.

'You better get here fast. That outside lav you built has a terrible smell.'

He rushed over, went to the lav, poked his head through the door, and exclaimed, 'No wonder it stinks – you took a shit in it!'

****

This big, rough-looking cowboy walks into the bar. He orders up bottle after bottle of rot-gut whisky and proceeds to get really wasted. In the process of doing so, he manages to anger just about everyone in the bar with offensive and obnoxious remarks.

Finally he finishes up his fifth bottle and decides he's had enough. He proceeds to get up and swagger out of the bar. He gets outside to untie his horse from the post and he notices someone's painted his horse's balls a real bright shade of yellow. This pisses him off immensely, so he rolls back into the bar, slamming the doors open and yelling out at the top of his lungs. 'JUST WHO IN THE SAM-HILL PAINTED MY HORSES BALLS YELLAH!!'

After everyone in the bar rustles around a bit, this bloke at the back of the bar stands up. He's six feet tall and built like a brick shit house. He says to the cowboy, 'I did. What you got to say about it, boy?'

The cowboy looks back at this guy and says, 'Oh, I just was going to let you know that the first coat of paint is dry.'

There were two church-going women gossiping in front of the store when a dusty old cowboy rode up. He tied up in front of the saloon, walked around behind his horse, lifted its tail and kissed the horse full on its rectum. Repulsed, one of the women asked, 'That's disgusting; why did you do that?'

To which the cowboy replied, 'I've got chapped lips.'

Confused, the other woman asked, 'Does that make them feel better?'

'No,' replied the cowboy, 'but it stops me from licking them!'

A pony walks into a pub. The publican says, 'What's the matter with you?'

'Oh it's nothing,' says the Pony. 'I'm just a little horse!'

One night, the Potato family sat down to dinner: Mother Potato and her three daughters. Midway through the meal, the eldest daughter spoke up. 'Mother Potato?' she said, 'I have an announcement to make.'

'And what might that be?' said Mother Potato, seeing the obvious excitement in her eldest daughter's eyes.

'Well,'' replied the daughter, with a proud but sheepish grin, 'I'm getting married!'

The other daughters squealed with surprise as Mother Potato exclaimed, 'Married? That's wonderful! And who are you marrying, eldest daughter?'

'I'm marrying a King Edward!'

'A King Edward!'' replied Mother Potato with pride. 'Oh, a King Edward is a fine tater, a fine tater indeed!'

As the family shared in the eldest daughter's joy, the middle daughter spoke up. 'Mother? I, too, have an announcement.'

'And what might that be?' encouraged Mother Potato.

Not knowing quite how to begin, the middle daughter paused, then said with conviction, 'I, too, am getting married!'

'You, too!' Mother Potato said with joy. 'That's wonderful! Twice the good news in one evening! And who are you marrying, middle daughter?'

'I'm marrying a Jersey!' beamed the middle daughter.

'A Jersey!' said Mother Potato with joy. 'Oh, a Jersey is a fine tater, a fine tater!'

Once again, the room came alive with laughter and excited plans for the future, when the youngest Potato daughter interrupted. 'Mother? Mother Potato? Um, I, too, have an announcement to make.'

'Yes?' said Mother Potato with great anticipation.

'Well,' began the youngest Potato daughter with the same sheepish grin as her eldest sister before her, 'I hope this doesn't come as a shock to you, but I am getting married, as well!'

'Really?'' said Mother Potato with sincere excitement. 'All of my lovely daughters married! What wonderful news! And who, pray tell, are you marrying, Youngest Daughter?'

'I'm marrying David Coleman!'

'DAVID COLEMAN?!' Mother Potato scowled suddenly. 'But he's just a common tater!'

****

An old lady is rocking away the last of her days in front of the fire, reflecting on her long life, when all of a sudden a fairy godmother appears and informs her that she will be granted three wishes.

'Well, now,' says the old lady, 'I guess I'd like to be really rich.'

POUF! her rocking chair turns to solid gold.

'And I'd like to be a young and beautiful princess.'

POUF! she turns into a beautiful young woman.

'And your third wish?' asked the fairy godmother. Just then the old woman's cat wanders across the porch in front of them.

'Ooh – can you change him into a handsome prince?' she asks.

POUF! there before her stands a young man more handsome than anyone could possibly imagine. She stares at him, smitten. With a smile that makes her knees weak, he saunters across the porch and whispers in her ear: 'Bet you wish you'd never had me neutered.'

****

There was this bloke and he suffered from terrible headaches. Finally he went to the doctor, who gave him a thorough examination.

'Well, I'm not sure exactly what's causing the problem,' said the doctor, 'but we've found a cure. You'll have to be castrated.'

The man, needless to say, was horrified. 'No, doctor, I prefer to suffer the headaches.' But as time passed, they got worse and worse and finally he was driven back to the doctor's surgery.

'OK,' he said to the doctor, 'I can't stand it any longer. I'll have the operation.' And so he was castrated.

Afterwards the man was very depressed and his doctor told him, 'I recommend you begin a new life – start afresh from this point.'

Taking the doctor's advice, the man went to a men's shop for new clothes. The salesman said, 'Let's start with the suit. Looks like you're a 38 regular.'

'That's right,' said the man. 'How did you know?'

'Well, when you've been in the business as long as I have, you get pretty good at sizing a man up,' said the salesman. 'Now for the shirt. Looks like a 15 long.'

'Exactly!' said the man.

'And for underpants, I'd say a size 36,' guessed the salesman.

'Well, there's your first mistake,' said the man. 'I've worn 34s for years.'

'No, you're a size 36 if ever I've seen one,' said the salesman.

'I ought to know,' the man replied, becoming irritable.

'Well, OK, if you insist,' said the salesman. 'But they're going to pinch your balls and give you terrible headaches.'

****

An Englishman, Frenchman, Mexican, and Texan were flying across country in a small plane when the pilot comes on the loudspeaker and says, 'We're having mechanical problems and the only way we can make it to the next airport is for three of you to open the door and jump; then at least one of you can survive. The four open the door and look at the passing countryside below. The Englishman takes a deep breath and with a shout of 'God Save The Queen!' jumps.

The Frenchman, inspired by the Englishman's bravery, shouts 'Vivé la France!' and he also jumps. This really pumps up the Texan, so he shouts out, 'Remember the Alamo!' and pushes the Mexican out of the plane.

****

A military cargo plane, flying over a populated area, suddenly loses power and starts to nose down. The pilot tries to pull up, but with all their cargo, the plane is too heavy. So he shouts to the soldiers in back to throw things out to make the plane lighter. They throw out a pistol.

'Throw out more!' shouts the pilot. So they throw out a rifle.

'More!' cries the pilot. So they heave out a missile, and the pilot regains control. He pulls out of the dive and manages to lands safely at an air base. The soldiers meanwhile get into a jeep and drive off.

Pretty soon they meet a boy on the side of the road who's crying. They ask him why he's crying and he says, 'A pistol hit me on the head!' They drive on until they meet another boy who's crying even harder. Again they ask why he's crying and the boy says, 'A rifle hit me on the head!'

Feeling severely guilty they drive on until they meet a boy who's laughing hysterically. 'Hey kid, what's so funny?' they ask him. 'What's so funny?'

The boy replies, 'You won't believe this, but I just farted and a house blew up!'

****

On reaching his plane seat a man is surprised to see a parrot strapped in next to him. He asks the stewardess for a coffee, whereupon the parrot squawks, 'And get me a whisky, you stupid cow!'

The stewardess, flustered, brings back a whisky for the parrot and forgets the coffee. When this omission is pointed out to her the parrot drains its glass and bawls, 'And get me another whisky, you slapper.'

Quite upset, the girl comes back shaking with another whisky but still no coffee. Unaccustomed to such slackness the man tries the parrot's approach. 'I've asked you twice for a coffee, go and get it now, you thick bitch,' he shouts at the stewardess.

Next moment both he and the parrot have been wrenched up and thrown out of the emergency exit by two burly stewards. As they land on the runway the parrot turns to the man and says, 'Blimey, you've got a lip for someone who can't fly!'

****

This young lady walks into a pet store to buy a parrot. The shop keeper tells her he only has one and that it's a real smart-arse, with vulgar vocabulary and rude temperament. The woman says, 'That's OK, I know how to handle arseholes like that – I want the parrot anyhow.'

So the woman gets the bird home, puts it in her room, and starts to get ready for bed. Just as she gets her skirt off the parrot says: 'AWK… NICE LEGS, BABY.' Well, the the woman isn't going take this shit, so she takes the bird out of the cage and puts it in the freezer for three minutes. While the parrot's in the freezer, he comes to the realisation that this was the wrong thing to say, and makes a mental note not to say it again.

The next night, the woman is getting ready for bed and this time the parrot knows not to say any thing about her legs, but after she removes her blouse, and then her bra, the parrot just can't resist any longer. He blurts out: 'AWK… GREAT TITS BABY! GIVE 'EM A SHAKE!'. Once again this pisses the woman right off and she decides that instead of three minutes in the freezer, she's going to keep the parrot in for five minutes.

Well, the parrot has lots of time to think this time, and remorse gives way to desperation and then anger. Finally, the woman opens the freezer door, takes out the near frozen parrot and asks, 'Well, have you learned your lesson?'

The parrot still shivering and barely able to speak says, 'AWK... YEAH, YEAH, BUT I CAN I ASK JUST ONE QUESTION?'

'Fire away,' says the woman.

'AWK... WHAT THE FUCK DID THE TURKEY DO? ASK FOR A BLOW-JOB?'

✳✳✳✳

A man walks into a pub and says, 'Landlord, give me two single whiskys.'

The landlord says, 'You want them both now or one at a time?'

'Oh, I want them both now,' the man says. 'One's for me and one's for my mate here,' and he pulls a three-inch man out of his pocket.

'Can he drink?' the landlord asks.

'Oh, sure. He can drink,' says the man. So the landlord pours the drinks and sure enough, the tiny man drinks it all up.

'That's amazing,' says the landlord. 'What else can he do – can he walk?'

The man flicks a 10p piece down to the end of the bar and says, 'Hey, Jake. Go get that.' The tiny man runs down to the end of the bar, picks up the coin, then runs back down and gives it to the man.

The landlord is in total shock. 'That's amazing,' he says. 'What else can he do? Can he talk?'

'Of course,' says the man. 'Hey, Jake, tell him about that time we were in Africa and you called that witch-doctor a wanker…'

****

A bloke walks into a pub and sits on a stool. In front of him he sees a big jar full of fivers and a little card which reads: 'Hello, if you'd like to win all of this money you have to make the horse at the end of the bar laugh. Entry fee: £5.'

'I'll have a crack at that,' thinks the bloke, sticks five quid in the jar and takes the horse into the bathroom. Two minutes later they come out and the horse is laughing so hard that he pisses on the floor. So the guy takes the money and leaves.

The very next day the same guy walks into the pub again and sees the horse and the jar, this time full of tenners, with a sign stating, 'You can win all of this if you make the horse cry. Entry fee: £10. So the bloke puts in his tenner and takes the horse into the bathroom. Two minutes later they come out and the horse is crying like a baby. So the guy takes the jar, but before he can leave the landlord asks, 'How did you do that?'

'Well, says the bloke, 'the first time I told him my dick was bigger than his and the second time I showed him!'

****

A pirate was talking to a 'land-lubber' in a pub. The land-lubber noticed that, like any self-respecting pirate, this fella had a peg leg, a hook in place of one of his hands and a patch over one eye. The land-lubber just had to find out how the pirate got in such bad shape, so he asked the pirate, 'How did you lose your leg?'

The pirate responded, 'I lost me leg in a battle off the coast of Jamaica!'

His new acquaintance was still curious so he asked, 'What about your hand. Did you lose that at the same time?'

'No,' answered the pirate. 'I lost it to the sharks off the Florida Keys.'

Finally, the land-lubber asked, 'I notice you also have an eye-patch. How did you lose your eye?'

The pirate answered, 'I was sleeping on a beach when a seagull flew over and shat right in me eye.'

'But how could a little bird-shit make you loose your eye?' the land-lubber asked.

'It was the day after I got me hook!' the pirate snapped.

****

A newly-wed couple were on their honeymoon. Before hopping into bed, the bride said to the groom, 'Darling, please be careful… you know I'm a virgin.'

The groom was shocked and replied, 'What are you talking about? I'm your third husband, for Christ's sake!'

'Well,' the bride replied, 'my first husband was a psychologist and all he wanted to do was talk about it, and my second husband was a gynaecologist and all he wanted to do was look at it. I know you'll screw me, though; that's why I married a lawyer.'

****

A guy walks into a drug store in America and asks for a pack of condoms. 'That'll be $5 with the tax,' says the shopkeeper.

'Tacks?' the guy exclaims, 'I thought you rolled them on!'

****

These three geezers went to the top of the Empire State Building to show off the length of their manhoods. The first one opened his fly and let it out. It flopped down 20 storeys.

'Top that,' he said.

So the second geezer opened his fly and let it out. It flopped down 25 storeys. 'Top that,' he said.

The last guy opened his fly and let his out. Down it went, on and on until, suddenly, he started to shift from side to side in jerky movements.'

'What's the matter? You OK?' his friends asked.

'Yeah, no problem. I'm just dodging traffic!' he replied.

****

A young man went to a chemist and asked if he could speak with the pharmacist.

'I am the pharmacist,' a little old lady informed him.

'Oh, in that case, forget it,' he replied and started to leave.

'Young man,' the old lady said to him, 'my sister and I have been pharmacists for 40 years and there's nothing we haven't seen or heard of, so come on, what's your problem?'

'Well,' the young man said reluctantly, 'I have a problem with erections. Once I get hard, it won't go down for hours and hours, no matter how much I masturbate or how many times I have intercourse! Please, can you give me something for it?'

'I'll have to go in the back and talk to my sister,' she told him.

About ten minutes later she came back out. 'Young man, I have consulted with my sister and the best we can give you is £100 a week and a third interest in the business.'

****

Mr Evans had been retired for a year when his wife of 50 years said to him one day, 'Why don't we take a cruise for a week and make wild passionate love like we did when we were young?'

He thought it over and agreed. He put on his hat and coat and went down to the corner shop. He stepped up to the counter and asked for a bottle of seasick pills and a box of condoms. Upon returning home his wife greeted him at the door saying, 'You know dear, I've been thinking it over and I see no reason why we couldn't manage a month-long cruise so we could relax and make wild passionate love like we did when we were young.'

He smiled, turned around and went back to the shop. He stepped up and ordered 12 bottles of seasick pills and a dozen boxes of condoms.

Upon returning back home his wife met him on the porch with a big smile on her face. 'Arthur, I have a marvellous idea. You know, now that our children are all grown up, there's nothing to stop us from cruising around the world for years on end.'

'I'll be right back,' he said. Back to the corner shop he went. When he approached the counter the shop keeper looked up with a puzzled grin. Mr Evans sheepishly ordered 297 bottles of seasick pills and the same number of boxes of condoms.

The startled shop keeper busied himself filling the order, then passed the wrapped package across the counter saying, 'You know, Mr Evans, you've been coming in here for over 30 years. I certainly don't mean to pry, but if it makes you that sick, why do you do it?'

****

There was an old man whose family could no longer afford to take care of him. So the family decided that a nursing home for the aged would be appropriate. Of course the old man rejected the idea, but soon he was convinced that it was the right thing to do.

On his first day at the home, he spent most of his time lying in bed reflecting on life and feeling lonely. A while later, an orderly stopped by to see how the old man's first day was going.

'How you doing today?' she asked the old man. 'First day, I see.'

The old man replied with a nod. In no time the two began talking up a storm. As the conversation began to drag on, the orderly was eyeing the room filled with fresh flowers, cards and balloons from friends and relatives. She noticed a bowl full of peanuts sitting on top of the table next to the bed, and helped herself to a handful. As the two continued to converse with each other, the orderly kept eating more helpings of the peanuts.

After two hours she looked at her watch and said, 'My goodness, the time's gone by quickly. I have to tend to other people here, too.'

'That's OK,' said the old man, 'I feel so much better being able to talk to someone.'

Looking into the bowl the orderly said, 'I feel awful! I ate almost all of your peanuts!'

'That's OK,' the old man responded. 'Ever since I got these false teeth, all I could do was suck the chocolate off of them anyhow.'

****

Elvis, Liberace, and River Phoenix were sitting around in heaven, bored of their heavenly lives. They went to see Gabriel and asked him if there was any way they could get out. He apprehensively decided to let them go back to earth for a short while, but told them if they even thought of sin, they would go straight to hell. So zap, there they are on Hollywood Boulevard.

As they are walking, Elvis sees a bar. He thinks for a moment and heads toward the door; the moment he touches it, POUF!, he's gone. The others think, 'Hmm, Gabriel was serious'.

A little while later River Pheonix sees a dollar bag of coke in the gutter. He thinks for a moment and bends over to pick up the bag and POUF!, Liberace disappears.

****

A newspaper photographer, reporter and editor are walking down the beach. They see a bottle in the sand. The reporter grabs it, rubs it and a genie pops out. So grateful is the genie he grants them each one wish.

The photographer says, 'I want to be on a mountain-top with the wisest of the wise, soaking up wisdom.' And POUF! he's gone.

The reporter says, 'I want to be on a tropical paradise being served pina coladas and bon-bons all day long.' and POUF! she's gone. And the editor says, 'I want those two hacks back here, right now!'

****

It was time for an elderly gentleman to be put into a nursing home, as his grown-up children could no longer care for him. After a week, the children went to visit their father at the nursing home. During the visit, the father leaned to the right, and a nurse quickly came over and propped him up with a pillow.

A little while later, he leaned to the left, and a nurse came and propped him up with another pillow. The man's children were amazed at how attentive the home staff seemed to be, and questioned their father on how he liked it there.

'I've been treated well,' he tells them, 'but I've got to tell you – they sure don't want you to fart round here.'

****

Two old women were sitting on a bench waiting for their bus. The buses were running late, and a lot of time passed. Finally, one woman turned to the other and said, 'You know, I've been sitting here so long, my bum has fallen asleep!'

'I know!" said the other woman. 'I heard it snoring!'

****

One morning, a teacher asked her class which part of the body went to heaven first. One little girl raised her hand and said, 'I think your mind goes to heaven first because you have to have a mind in order to believe in God.'

'Very good,' said the teacher.

Then a little boy raises his hand and said, 'I think your heart goes to heaven first because God is all about love.'

'Very good,' said the teacher. She then looked up and saw that little Johnny's hand was up. 'Johnny,' she said, 'which part of the body do you think goes to heaven first?'

Don't Mix Your Drinks

Johnny thought for a minute and then said, 'Your feet.'

'What makes you think your feet go to heaven first?' the teacher asked him.

'Well,' he replied. 'I was walking past my parent's bedroom last night and my mum had her feet up in the air and she was shouting, 'Oh God, oh God, I'm coming!'

****

Little Johnny's next door neighbours had a baby. Unfortunately, the little baby was born with no ears. When they arrived home from the hospital, the parents invited Johnny's family to come over and see their new baby. Johnny's parents were very afraid that their son would say something embarrassing about the baby, so his dad had a long talk with him before they left.

'Now, son,' he said, 'that poor baby was born without any ears. I want you to be on your best behaviour and not say a word about his ears or I promise you I'll give you a good hiding when we get back home.'

'I promise not to mention his ears at all,' said Johnny.

At the neighbours home, Johnny leaned over in the cot and touched the baby's hand. He looked at its mother and said 'Oh what a beautiful little baby'.

'Thank you very much, Johnny,' said the mother. 'This baby has perfect little hands and perfect little feet,' said Johnny. 'Just look at his pretty little eyes. Did his doctor say that he had good sight?'

'Yes,' said the mother. 'In fact, his doctor said he had perfect 20/20 vision.'

'Well, thank God for that,' said Johnny, 'because there's no way he could wear glasses.'

****

An after-dinner speaker was in such a hurry to get to his engagement that when he arrived and sat down at the table, he suddenly realised that he'd forgotten his false teeth. Turning to the man next to him he said, 'I forgot my teeth.'

'No problem,' said the man and with that he reached into his pocket and pulled out a pair of false teeth. 'Try these,' he said.

The speaker tried them. 'Too loose,' he said.

'I've got another pair,' the man said, 'try these.'

The speaker tried them but they were too tight, so the man said, 'I've got just one more pair… try these.'

The speaker said, 'Wow, these fit perfectly.' With that he ate his meal and gave his address. After the dinner was over, the speaker went over to thank the man who'd helped him. 'I want to thank you for coming to my aid and I wouldn't mind putting a bit of business your way, too.' he said. 'Where's your office? I've been looking for a good dentist.'

'I'm not a dentist,' replied the man, 'I'm the local undertaker.'

****

A man who is not qualified keeps pestering this tailor about giving him a job selling suits. Finally, the tailor tells him if he can sell this one green suit he'll give him a job. Another employee points out to the tailor that they've had that suit on the rack for four years, and that it's such an ugly, green suit that no one will ever buy it.

'Yes, I know,' the tailor tells the employee, 'that's my way of getting rid of that pest.'

Two hours later the new bloke calls his boss for his next assignment. The tailor can't believe it and heads down to the shop to find out how he managed to sell the suit.

Upon his arrival he finds the new salesman bleeding, scratched and his clothes torn in several places, but smiling.

'Congratulations, the job is yours,' he says to the man. 'Nobody has come close to selling that old, ugly, green suit. But what in the world happened to you?'

'Thank you for the job,' says the man. 'The man who bought it loved the suit, but he had a very sensitive guide-dog.'

****

This woman goes into a restaurant and orders a scoop of vanilla ice-cream, a scoop of strawberry ice-cream and a scoop of chocolate ice-cream. The waiter who takes her order, however, apologises and tells her that they don't have any chocolate.

'OK,' says the woman, I'll have a vanilla milk shake, a strawberry milk shake and a chocolate milk shake.' Once again, however, the waiter tells her there isn't any chocolate!

The woman changes her order for the third time. 'OK. I'll have vanilla cake, strawberry cake, and chocolate cake.'

This time the waiter is very annoyed and shouts, 'Madam, we have no chocolate. Let me try to explain this to you. Do you see the word 'van' in the word 'vanilla'?'

The woman replies, 'Yes.' So the waiter asks her if she sees the word 'straw' in the word 'strawberry' and once again she replies, 'Yes'. Then he asks her if she sees the word 'fuck' in the word 'chocolate' and the woman says, 'There's no fuck in chocolate.'

And the waiter screams, 'That's what I've been trying to tell you.'

****

A man returning from a overseas business trip decides to bring his son a young puppy as a present. Unfortunately, he doesn't have time to sort out the paperwork and he doesn't want the puppy to get stuck in quarantine at Heathrow for six months, so he hides the puppy down the front of his trousers and gets on the plane.

About 30 minutes into the flight a stewardess notices the man shaking and quivering. 'Are you OK, sir?' she asks him.

'Yes, I'm fine,' says the man.

Sometime later the stewardess noticed the man moaning, and shaking again. 'Are you sure you're all right sir?' she asks him again.

'Yes,' says the man, 'but I have a confession to make. I didn't have time to get the paperwork done to bring a puppy on board, so I hid him down the front of my trousers.'

'Oh dear,' says the stewardess, 'I guess he's not house-trained yet, eh?' she adds with a knowing smile.

'Oh no, that's not the problem,' says the man. 'The real problem is he's not weaned yet!'

✱✱✱✱

An army major is visiting sick soldiers. He goes up to one private and asks, 'What's your problem, soldier?'

'Chronic syphilis, sir,' says the soldier.

'What treatment are you getting?' asks the major.

'Five minutes with the wire brush each day, sir, ' replies the soldier.

'What's your ambition, soldier?' asks the major.

'To get back to the front, sir,' says the soldier.

'Good man,' says the major. He goes to the next bed and says, 'And what's your problem, soldier?'

'Chronic piles, sir,' comes the reply.

'What treatment are you getting?' asks the major.

'Five minutes with the wire brush each day, sir' replies the soldier.

'And what's your ambition, soldier?' asks the major.

'To get back to the front, sir,' replies the soldier.

'Good man,' says the major. He goes to the next bed. 'What's your problem, soldier?" he asks.

'Chronic gum disease, sir," is the reply.'

'What treatment are you getting?' asks the major.

'Five minutes with the wire brush each day, sir' says the soldier.

'And what's your ambition, soldier?" asks the major.

'To get the wire brush before the other two, sir,' replies the soldier.

✱✱✱✱

A lawyer named Strange died, and his friend asked the tombstone maker to inscribe on his tombstone, 'Here lies Strange, an honest man, and a lawyer.'

The inscriber insisted that such an inscription would be confusing, for passers-by would tend to think that three men were buried under the stone. However, he suggested an alternative: he would inscribe, 'Here lies a man who was both honest and a lawyer.' That way, whenever anyone walked by the tombstone and read it, they would be certain to remark: 'That's Strange!'

****

Did you hear about the fat bloke who tried every diet in the world in an attempt to lose weight? He tried them all but none worked. Then, one day, he was reading the paper when he noticed a small ad that read: 'Lose weight Only £1 a pound. Call 018556785-0238.'

The fat bloke decided to give it a try and called the number. A voice on the other end asked, 'How much weight do you want to lose?'

'Ten pounds,' the fat bloke replied.

'Very well,' replied the voice, 'give me your credit card number and we'll have a representative over to your house in the morning.'

About 9am the next day the fat bloke heared a knock on the door. When he opened it, there was a beautiful redhead standing on his doorstep, completely starkers except for a sign around her neck stating, 'If you catch me, you can have me.'

Well, the fat bloke chased her upstairs, downstairs, over sofas, through the kitchen, all around the house until finally, panting and wheezing like a dog, he caught her.

When he'd had his way with her she said to him, 'Quick, go into the bathroom and weigh yourself.'

He did just that and was amazed to find that he'd lost 10 pounds, right to the ounce!

That evening he called the number again. The voice on the other end asked, 'How much weight do you want to lose?' to which the not-so-fat bloke man replied, '20 pounds.'

'Very well,' the voice on the phone told him, 'Give me your credit card number and we'll have a representative over at your house in the morning.'

At about 8am the next day there was a knock on the not-so-fat bloke's door and when he opened it he saw a beautiful blonde dressed only in track shoes and a sign around her neck stating, 'If you catch me, you can have me.'

The chase took a good while longer this time and the man nearly passed out, but he finally caught her. When he was done she told him, 'Quick, run into the bathroom and weigh yourself.'

He ran to the bathroom and found he'd lost another 20 pounds! 'This is fantastic!' he thought to himself.

Later that evening he called the number again and the voice at the other end asked, 'How much weight do you want to lose?'

'Fifty pounds!' the man exclaimed.

'Fifty pounds?' the voice asked, 'That's an awful lot of weight to lose at one time.'

'Listen mate,' the man replied. 'Here's my credit card number, you just have your representative over here in the morning!'' and he hung up.

About 6am the next morning the man got out of bed, splashed on some cologne and got all ready for the next representative. At about 7am he got a knock on the door. When he opened the door, he saw this huge gorilla with a sign around his neck saying, 'IF I CATCH YOU, I'M GOING TO FUCK YOU.'

****

A rather posh lady is showing her small daughter around Rome in the back of a taxi. They pass a railway station and the daughter asks, 'Mummy, what are all those ladies doing standing around in very short dresses?'

The mother realises that she's referring to the prostitute dayshift, but hedges. 'I expect they're waiting for their friends, or looking at the Roman architecture, dear,' she tells her daughter.

The taxi driver flips back the partition and says, 'Go on, don't lie to the kid. Tell your daughter they're prostitutes!'

'Mummy, what are "prostitutes"?' asks the little girl.

With a sigh, the mother explains all. The little girl is very interested: 'But Mummy,' she says, 'don't they sometimes have babies?'

'Well, yes dear, I'm afraid they do,' replies her mother.

'But Mummy, what happens to the babies?' the little girl asks.

'Well, dear, that's the interesting thing about it,' explains her mother, 'they almost invariably turn out to be taxi-drivers.'

****

A teacher asks a class of kids if their skin could be made out of anything other than skin, what they would choose. One kid puts his hand up and says, 'Gold, Miss.'

'Why?' asks the teacher.

'Because then I'd go to a car showroom, give them a few shavings and drive off in a new car.'

Another child puts his hand up and says, 'Platinum, Miss.'

'Why?' asks the teacher. 'Because then I'd go to the car showroom, give them a few shavings and drive off in an even better car.'

A third child puts his hand up and says, 'Pubic hair miss.'

'Why pubic hair?' asks the teacher.

'Because my sister's only got a little bit, but you should see the cars outside our place.'

****

A guy goes to his local supermarket to buy some dog food. When he gets to the check-out with a couple of tins the cashier asks him where his dog is.

'He's at home,' replies the man.

'Well I'm sorry,' replies the cashier, 'but the rules state that unless you have the dog with you I can't sell you the dog food.'

The next day the same bloke is in buying cat food. When he gets to the cashier he's asked where his cat is.

'She's at home,' he replies.

'Sorry, rules are rules,' says the cashier. 'I can't sell you the cat food unless your cat is with you.'

The next day the bloke goes into the supermarket with a brown paper bag. When he gets to the check-out he asks the cashier to put his hand in.

'What is it?' asks the cashier. 'It feels soft and warm.'

'I'd like three rolls of toilet paper,' replies the man.

****

It is the wedding day of Prince Charles and Lady Di. Charles has been up late the night before boozing with his old Navy buddies. He wakes up late, throws on his clothes, rushes to the Royal Coach and sets off.

In the coach, he notices that he's forgotten his shoes, so he borrows the ones his valet's wearing. Only problem is, they're two sizes too small. Charles makes it through the ceremony, then through the reception with his feet in agony the whole time, and finally with great relief, goes upstairs with his new bride.

Their departure, however, is noticed by the Queen and Queen Mother who follows them up and listen at the the door. First they hear, 'Ohhh, ohhh, that feels so goood, that was sooo tight.'

'I told you she was,' said the Queen to the Queen Mother. Then they hear, 'Ohhh, ohhh, ohhh, ahhhh, that feels even better, that one's so much tighter.'

'Tsk tsk tsk,' said the Queen Mother. 'Once a sailor, always a sailor.'

****

A Tory MP woke up in a hospital bed after a complicated operation, and found that the curtains were drawn around him. 'Why are the curtains closed,' he asked. 'Is it night?'

A nurse replied, 'No, it's just that there's a fire across the street, and we didn't want you waking up and thinking that the operation was unsuccessful.'

****

An airplane lands at an airport with great difficulty, stopping just short of an accident. When they arrive at the gate, the captain wipes his brow and says, 'My God, that's the shortest runway I've ever seen!'

'You're not kidding,' says his co-pilot, looking out the window. 'But it sure is wide.'

****

Q: What's the difference between a small blue whale and a great white whale?
A: Size and colour.

****

Q: What's black and white, black and brown, black and black?
A: A nun on a spit

****

Q: What's black and white and walks sideways down corridors?
A: A nun with a javelin through her head

****

Q: What green and red and races at 100 mph?
A: A frog in a blender

****

Q: What goes black and white, black and white, black and white?
A: A nun falling downstairs

****

Q: What's grey and comes in half-pints?
A: An elephant.

****

Q: What's the ultimate in trust?
A: Two cannibals doing 69.

****

Mother Superior is recounting her days as she lies on her deathbed when another aged Sister asks her a question.
'Mother Superior do you remember going to the Zoo in the 1920s?'
'Yes I do.'
'And Mother Superior do you remember the gorillas?''
'Yes I do.'
'And do you remember one gorilla in particular?'
'Yes I do.'
'And do you remember this gorilla... grabbed you... a-and raped you?'
'Yes I do Sister, now what is the point of all this!' snapped the dying nun.
'Mother Superior, did it hurt?'
'Hurt? You ask did it hurt! He never wrote, he never called...'

****

Q: What's the difference between an Essex girl and a 747?
A: The 747 stops whining when it gets to Majorca

****

Q: Why do Essex girls only get half an hour for lunch?
A: So they don't need to be retrained when they get
back

The Lock-In

4

Jokes for Serious Drinkers

The Lock-In

So there you are at about quarter to eleven when the bell goes for last orders leaving you thinking, 'Shit, I've only had 17 pints and four double whisky chasers, I'm not even vaguely pissed yet.' So you're just fumbling for the car keys, resigned to the fact that a promising night has been cut off in its prime, when the landlord, God bless him, sticks a proverbial two fingers up at the ridiculous licensing laws in this country by dimming the lights, ushering in the two local coppers who've been lumbered with the night beat, and locks the door.

There's a joyous feeling of camaraderie all round, probably a bit like a black-out during the war only with a lot more booze and a lot less bombs. It's time for the serious drinking to begin, and of course the serious drinking jokes...

****

A drunken man gets on the bus late one night, staggers up the aisle, and sits next to an elderly woman. She looks the man up and down and says, 'I've got news for you; you're going straight to hell!'

The man jumps up out of his seat and shouts, 'Good heavens, I'm on the wrong bus!'

****

A man comes home very late one night, pissed out of his mind, to find his wife waiting for him at the door.

'WHERE HAVE YOU BEEN?' she screams, 'It's FOUR IN THE MORNING!'

He says, 'Aww, I just stopped at this pub, I was only going to have one pint... but this pub, it was incredible. Everything in it was gold-plated. They had a gold rail under the bar, gold ashtrays, they served the drinks in gold pint glasses, the table posts were all gold-plated, even the mirror behind the bar was gold. The cash register was gold. I was so amazed by all this gold, I just kept on ordering pints, so I could stay in the pub and look at it. Hell, even when I went to the Gents, they had gold-plated

The Lock-In

urinals… it was wonderful.'

'I don't believe that story for one minute,' his wife said. 'What was this place called?'

'Fucked if I can remember,' he replies, 'I'm far too pissed up.'

'You'll have to prove it to me tomorrow then, when you sober up, or else I'm going to divorce you!' said his wife.

The next day, the man looks through The Yellow Pages under PUBS, but none of the names ring a bell. He decides that he'll call all the boozers listed, and ask the landlords about the decor in their establishments.

He's called about 50 pubs, and still no luck. Finally he calls one pub, asks his question, and the landlord says 'Yes, this is the pub with all the gold-plated stuff.

'Here,' the man says, handing the phone to his wife. 'Ask the landlord if I'm lying!'

The wife gets on the line, and begins to ask the landlord about all the things her husband had told her about on the previous night… the rail, the pint glasses, the mirrors, the table posts and the cash register. Finally, she says, 'Now, this may seem like a strange question, but my husband says you even have gold-plated urinals, do you?'

The landlord puts the phone down on the bar, and she hears him yell, 'Hey Frankie! I think I know who pissed in your saxophone last night.'

A man stumbles out of a pub and is spied by a copper. The copper approaches and says, 'Can I help you, lad?'

'Yeah,' says the man, 'ssssomebody ssstole my car!'

'Well,' says the copper, 'where was your car last time you saw it?'

'It was at the end of this key!' says the man holding up a key. Suddenly the copper notices the man has his manhood out.

'Are you aware that you are exposing yourself?' he asks.

'Oh God,' says the man. 'They got me girl, too!'

The Lock-In

An Irishman walks into a pub in Dublin, orders three pints of Guinness and sits in the back of the room, drinking a sip out of each one in turn. When he finishes them, he comes back to the bar and orders three more. The landlord says to him, 'You know, a pint goes flat after I draw it; it would taste better if you bought one at a time.'

The Irishman replies, 'Well, you see, I have two brothers. One is in America, the other in Australia, and I'm here in Dublin. When we all left home, we promised that we'd drink this way to remember the days when we drank together.'

The landlord admits that this is a nice custom, and leaves it there. The Irishman becomes a regular in the pub, and always drinks the same way: he orders three pints and drinks them in turn. One day, he comes in and orders two pints. All the other regulars notice and fall silent.

When he comes back to the bar for the second round, the bartender says, 'I don't want to intrude on your grief, but I wanted to offer my condolences on your great loss.'

The Irishman looks confused for a moment, then a light dawns in his eye and he laughs. 'Oh, no,' he says, 'everyone's fine. I'm just off the liquor.'

****

A white horse walks into a pub, pulls up a stool, and orders a pint. The landlord pours him a tall, frothy mug and says, 'You know, we have a drink named after you.'

To which the white horse replies, 'What, Eric?'

****

A gorilla walks into a pub, pulls up a stool, and orders a pint. The landlord pours him a tall, frothy mug and says, 'That'll be five quid.'

As the gorilla's paying for his pint, the landlord adds, 'You know, we don't get many gorillas in here.'

To which the gorilla replies, 'At five quid a pint, I'm not fucking surprised.'

The Lock-In

****

A guy walks into a pub and says to the landlord, 'I want you to give me 12-year old Scotch, and don't try to fool me because I can tell the difference.'

The landlord is sceptical and decides to try to trick the man with five-year scotch. The man takes a sip, scowls and says, 'Oi, landlord, this crap is five-year old Scotch. I told you I want 12-year old Scotch.'

The landlord tries once more with eight-year old Scotch. The man takes a sip, grimaces and says, 'Oi, landlord, I don't want eight-year old Scotch like this filth. Give me 12-year old Scotch!'

Impressed, the landlord gets the 12-year old Scotch, the man takes a sip and sighs, 'Ah, now that's the real thing.'

A disgusting, grimy, stinking drunk has been watching all this with great interest. He stumbles over and sets a glass down in front of the man and says, 'Hey, I think that's really amazing what you can do. Try this one.'

The man takes a sip and immediately spits out the liquid and cries, 'Yechhh! This stuff tastes like piss!'

The drunk's eyes light up and he says, 'Yeah, now how old am I?'

****

On the top of a tall building in a large city, there was a bar. In this bar, a man was drinking heavily. He would ask the bartender for a tequila shot, then walk out to the balcony and jump off. Minutes later, he would appear in the lift and repeat the whole process. This one bloke watched this happen a number of times until curiosity got the better of him.

Finally, he went up to the man and asked, 'Hey, you keep drinking, then jumping off the balcony. And yet, minutes later, you're back again. How do you do it?'

'Well, the shot of tequila provides so much buoyancy that when I get near the ground, I slow down and land gently. It's great fun. You should try it.'

The bloke, who was also quite pissed thought to himself, 'Hey, why not?' So he went to the bar, drank a shot of tequila, then walked out to the

The Lock-In

balcony, jumped off, and whoooooooooooooshSPLAT! The bartender shakes his head, looked over at the first bloke and said, 'Superman, you're a such an arsehole when you're pissed.'

****

A drunk is standing pissing into a fountain in the middle of town, so a copper comes up to him and says, 'Stop that and put it away!' The drunk shoves his dick into his trousers and does up his zip. As the cop turns to go, the drunk starts laughing. 'OK,' asks the copper, 'what's so funny?'

'Fooled you,' says the drunk, 'I may have put it away, but I didn't stop.'

****

Steve and Ollie are good friends. Each day, they get together after work and have a pint down the local. This is a tradition that goes on for some time. One day, Ollie says, 'Steve, if I die before you, promise me that you'll have a pint for me, each day.'

Steve considers this and agrees. Well, sure enough, Ollie dies, and sure enough, Steve has an extra pint for him every day after work. This goes on for some time, and the barmaid is quite familiar with the ritual and the reason.

One day, Steve comes in and only orders one drink. Well, the barmaid is in shock, and says, 'But, Steve, aren't you going to have another drink for your friend, as usual?'

And Steve says, 'Well, you see, I joined Alcoholics Anonymous, but I don't think that Ollie should be punished for that.'

****

Two geezers were in a pub partying like mad. They were drinking doubles and triples, buying rounds and generally having a great time. When asked why they were celebrating, they boasted that they'd just finished a jigsaw

The Lock-In

puzzle and it had only taken them two months!

'TWO MONTHS?!" cried the landlord. 'That's ridiculous. It shouldn't take that long!!'

'Well,' says one guy, 'the box said two to four years!'

****

A man drinks a shot of whisky every night before bed. After years of this his wife wants him to quit, so she gets two shot glasses, fills one with water, the other with whisky. She gets him to the table with the glasses and makes him fetch his fishing bait-box. 'I want you to see this,' she says and puts a worm in the water and it swims around. She then takes the worm out and puts it in the whisky where it dies. 'So,' she says. 'What do you have to say about this experiment?' '

'Well,' he says. 'If I drink whisky I won't get worms.'

****

A drunk man was casually taking a piss into a drinking fountain in the park. A police officer comes up to him and yells frantically, 'What the hell do you think you're doing? There's a public toilet 20 metres from here!'

The man, amazed, yells back, 'What do you think I have here between my legs? A hose?'

****

A drunk walks into a pub and says loudly, 'Landlord, a round for the house, and have one yourself, too!' The crowd cheers, the landlord pours and passes out the drinks, then knocks back a shot himself.

That'll be £80 for the round,' says the landlord, to which the man replies, 'I don't have a penny on me.'

The landlord is furious and drags the man to the door and roughly throws him into the street.

The next night, the drunk again walks in and says, 'Landlord, a round for

The Lock-In

the house, and have one yourself, too!' As the crowd cheers, the landlord reasons to himself that no one would come in and do that twice, and that the man probably has the money for the previous night, so he passes out the shots and knocks one back himself.

'OK, that's £80 for last night, and £63 for tonight,' he says to which the man again replies, 'I don't have a pot to piss in or a window to throw it out of, I'm sorry to say.'

The landlord, enraged at this, smashes the man in the head over and over again as he drags him to the door and again throws him roughly into the street.

The next night, amazingly, the landlord hears over his shoulder as he's working, 'Landlord, a round for the house.' Turning around, he can't believe the drunk is back for a third time.

'What, nothing for me this time?' says the landlord.

'You gotta be joking,' says the drunk. 'You get really shitty when you drink!'

****

This bloke goes into a pub to find only two men at opposite ends of the bar and the landlord. He orders his drink and listens in on the conversation. One fellow says: 'Live here?'

'Yeah, over on Miller Road,' says the other.

'I live on Miller Road too,' says the first.

'Is that right,' replies the other, 'I live over the corner shop and have a brown and white dog.'

The first responds, 'I live over the corner shop and I have a brown and white dog. I was born there on April 23, 1947.'

From the other end of the bar comes, 'I was born on April 23, 1947, too. Ain't this a small world?'

Suddenly the telephone rings and it's the landlord's wife who wants to know if anything's going on.

'Same old thing,' replies the landlord, 'the Johnson twins are drunk again!'

The Lock-In

****

One very cold night, a young man dropped into the local brothel and the Madam said, 'You'll have to wait.'

'But there's lots of girls that aren't busy right now,' insists the man.

'Yes, but several of the rooms are closed for repairs,' the Madam informs him.

'Listen,' he says, 'I'm pretty desperate. I don't need a room.'

So she takes his money and he goes upstairs with one of the staff and, after looking for a place to consummate the transaction, they decide to do it on the roof. But it's a very, very cold night, and the two of them freeze to death and fall to the pavement below, where a passing drunk looks them over, staggers to the door and knocks.

'Go away!' says the Madam. 'We don't allow drunks in here!'

'I don't want in,' says the drunk. 'I just wanted to tell you that your sign fell down.'

****

A lad walks into a pub and orders 12 shots of the best whisky in the house. The landlord proceeds to fill 12 shot glasses and stares, puzzled, at the guy as he begins to drink them down, one by one.

As the lad's finishing the 11th shot, the landlord asks, 'What's the occasion, mate?'

'I'm celebrating my first blow-job!' says the lad as he finishes off the last shot.'

'Well,' says the bartender, 'in that case, have one on the house,' and he fills another shot glass.

'No thanks,' says the guy, 'If 12 didn't get the taste out of my mouth, one more won't!'

****

A drunk walks into a crowded pub and takes the last barstool next to an

The Lock-In

older woman. After a while, the woman starts to smell this horrible odour coming from the direction of the drunk. She turns to him and says, 'Excuse me, but did you just shit yourself?'

The drunk replied, 'Yes, I have indeed shit myself.'

'Well, why don't you go somewhere and clean yourself up?' shouts the woman.

' 'Cos I'm not finished yet,' says the drunk.

****

This bloke walks into a pub. He walks up to the landlord and asks for a rum and coke. The landlord puts an apple on the table. The bloke looks at it and says, 'I'm sorry, I said I wanted a rum and Coke.'

'Just try the apple,' says the landlord. So the guy bites into the apple.

'Wow,' he says. 'This tastes like rum. The landlord tells him to turn it around and bite it again. 'Wow, this bit tastes like Coke.'

A minute later another bloke walks into the pub and asks the landlord for a gin and tonic. The landlord puts an apple on the bar leaving this bloke just as confused as the first, but the first bloke urges him to try it, so the guy bites into it.

'Wow!' he exclaims, 'it tastes like gin.' The first bloke tells him to turn it around and bites it again.

'Wow it tastes like tonic,' says the second bloke.

Later that night a third bloke walks in and joins the two blokes at the bar. The first two are so excited about these apples that they tell this third bloke that the landlord has an apple for whichever taste you want. So the guy asks for an apple that taste like a vagina. The landlord puts the apple on the table and the guy bites into it .

'Urggh,' he shouts. 'This tastes like SHIT!!!'

'Turn it around,' says the landlord.

****

This geezer dies and is sent to Hell. Satan meets him and shows him the

The Lock-In

doors to three rooms and says he must choose one of the rooms to spend eternity in. Satan opens the first door. In the room there are people standing in shit up to their necks.

'No thanks,' says the geezer. 'Can I see the the next room?'

Satan shows him the next room and this has people with shit up to their noses. And so he says 'No' again. Finally Satan shows him the third and final room. This time there are people in there with shit up to their knees drinking cups of tea and eating cakes.

'I'll choose this room please,' says the geezer. So he goes in and is standing in there eating his cake and drinking his tea thinking, 'Well it could be worse,' when the door opens and Satan pops his head around.

'Okay,' says Satan. 'Tea-break's over. Back on your heads!'

❋❋❋❋

There was this drunk who said to the landlord at his local, 'I want a woman!' So the landlord gave him directions to a place, but the drunk was so messed up that he couldn't remember where he had been told to go and accidentally walks into a chiropodist's office.

'Can I help you?' asks the receptionist.

'Yes,' replies the drunk. 'I want some service.'

'OK, sir,' says the receptionist. 'Go in the other room and put it on the table and someone will be with you shortly.'

So the drunk goes in the other room and puts his todger on the table. When the chiropodist comes in she screams, 'That's not a foot!'

'Give it time, lady,' said the drunk, 'give it time.'

❋❋❋❋

This man who stutters badly, walks into a pub, and says, 'S-say! B-b-b-arman, g-g-g-imme a b-b-beer'. The barman, who is badly humpbacked, serves him a beer and says, 'That'll be £2.50 please!'

The guy thinks that's pretty expensive and says, 'D-d-d-damn! T-t-that's a high price!'

The Lock-In

'Yes,' says the barman, 'but that's our price and that's what we get!'. So the stutterer pays him and drinks it down.

'S-s-say! B-b-barman,' he says, 'g-g-gimme a w-whisky p-p-please!" The barman serves him a shot of whisky and says, 'That will be £5 please!'

'D-d-d-damn!' says the stutterer. 'T-t-that's a high price!'

'Yes,' says the barman, 'but that's our price and that's what we get!'

The stutterer pays him, drinks his whisky and, before leaving he says, 'B-b-barman t-thanks for n-not m-m-making f-f-fun of my st-st-st-stuttering w-w-while I w-was in h-h-here!'

'Oh, that's OK,' says the barman, 'I want to thank you for not making fun of my hump while you were in here.'

'Oh, t-t-that's OK,"' says the stutterer, 'e-everything else in t-this p-p-place w-was so h-h-high, I th-th-thought it w-was y-your ARSE!'

****

There was a bloke in a theatre, sprawled out over three seats. The usher came by and told the bloke to move. The bloke mumbled, but didn't answer, so the usher went to get the manager.

'Sir,' the manager said to the man, 'if you don't move, I'll call the police and have you removed.' Again, the bloke mumbled, but didn't answer. So the manager called the police and a copper came over.

'Excuse me, sir,' the copper said to the bloke, 'what's your name?'

'Pete,' said the bloke.

'And where are you from, Pete?' asked the policeman.

'The balcony!" replied Pete.

****

One day at the end of class, little Billy's teacher has the class go home and think of a story and then infer the moral of that story. The following day the teacher asks for the first volunteer to tell their story; little Suzy raises her hand.

'My dad owns a farm and every Sunday we load the chicken eggs on the truck and drive into town to sell them at the market. Well, one Sunday we

The Lock-In

hit a big bump and all the eggs flew out of the basket and on to the road.'

The teacher asks for the moral of the story and Suzy replies, 'Don't put all your eggs in one basket.'

Next is little Lucy ... 'Well, my dad owns a farm, too, and every weekend we take the chicken eggs and put them in the incubator. Last weekend only eight of the 12 eggs hatched.'

The teacher asks for the moral of the story and Lucy replied, 'Don't count your chickens before they're hatched.'

Last is little Billy ... 'My uncle Ted fought in the Second World War, his plane was shot down over enemy territory, but he jumped out before it crashed with only a case of beer, a machine-gun and a machete. On the way down he drank the case of beer. Unfortunately, he landed right in the middle of 100 German soldiers. He shot 70 with his machine-gun, but ran out of bullets, so he pulled out his machete and killed 20 more. The blade on his machete broke, so he killed the last 10 with his bare hands.'

The Teacher looks in shock at Billy and asks if there is possibly any moral to his story. 'Of course there is,' Billy replies, 'Don't fuck with uncle Ted when he's been drinking.'

There are these two pissed geezers in a pub. One says to the other, 'Does your watch tell the time?'

The other replies, 'No, mate. You have to look at it.'

A man goes into a pub with a newt sitting on his shoulder.

'That's a nice newt,' says the landlord, 'what's he called?'

'Tiny,' replies the man.

'Why's that?' asks the landlord.

'Because he's my newt,' says the man.

The Lock-In

A bloke goes into a pub and orders a double. The landlord says, 'You look terrible, mate. What's the problem?'

The guy says, 'I just caught my girlfriend in bed with my best friend.'

Landlord: 'That's awful. What did you do?'

Bloke: 'I threw her out on to the front lawn, threw her clothes out after her and told her that we were finished and I never wanted to see her again.'

Landlord: 'Good for you, mate – that was pretty tough. What did you do to your best friend?'

Bloke: 'I shook my finger at him and said, 'BAD DOG!'

✸✸✸✸

A group of men were having a few drinks in a pub. They were swapping stories about the dogs they used to own. One man said, 'I used to have a Labrador that killed a Bull Terrier'

Another man said, 'That's nothing, I had a Poodle that killed a German Shepherd.'

Another man said, 'Well, I had a little Yorkshire Terrier that killed an American Pit Bull'.

All the men cracked up laughing. 'Bullshit,' said one man. 'How can a Yorkshire Terrier kill a Pit Bull?'

'Quite easily,' said the man, 'if the Pit Bull chokes on him.'

✸✸✸✸

A horse walks into a bar. The barman says to him, 'Hey, why the long face?'

✸✸✸✸

I had 18 bottles of whisky in my cellar and was told by my wife to empty the contents of each and every bottle down the sink, or else... I said I would and began to pour.

I removed the lid from the first bottle and poured the contents down the sink with the exception of one glass, which I drank.

The Lock-In

I then removed the lid from the second bottle and did the same, with the exception of one glass, which I drank.

I then removed the lid from the third bottle and poured the whisky down the sink which I drank.

I pulled the lid from the fourth bottle down the sink and poured the bottle down the glass, which I drank.

I pulled the bottle from the lid of the next and drank one sink out of it, and threw the rest down the glass.

I pulled the sink out of the next glass and poured the lid down the bottle.

Then I lidded the sink with the glass, bottled the drink and drank the pour.

When I had everything emptied, I steadied the house with one hand, counted the glasses, lids, bottles, and sinks with the other, which were 29, and as the houses came by I counted them again, and finally I had all the houses in one bottle, which I drank.

I'm not under the affluence of incohol as some thinkle peep I am. I'm not half as thunk as you might drink.

I fool so feelish I don't know who is me, and the drunker I stand here, the longer I get.

****

A Russian is strolling down the street in Moscow and kicks a bottle laying in the street. Suddenly out of the bottle comes a genie.

The Russian is stunned and the genie says, 'Hello, master, I will grant you one wish – anything you want.'

The Russian begins thinking, 'Well, I really like drinking vodka.' and so finally says, 'I wish to drink vodka whenever I want, so make me piss vodka.'

The Genie grants him his wish. When the Russian gets home he gets a glass out of the cupboard and pisses in it. He looks at the glass and it's clear. Looks like vodka. Then he smells the liquid. Smells like vodka. So he takes a taste and it is the best vodka he has ever tasted.

The Russian yells to his wife, 'Natasha, Natasha, come quickly!' She comes running down the hall and the Russian takes another glass out of the cupboard and pisses into it. He tells her to drink, it is vodka. Natasha reluctant antlt takes a sip. It's the best vodka she has ever tasted.

The two drink and party all night. The next night the Russian comes home from work and tells his wife to get two glasses out of the cupboard. He proceeds to piss in the two glasses. The result is the same, the vodka is excellent and the couple drink until the sun comes up.

Finally, Friday night comes and the Russian comes home and tells his wife, 'Natasha grab one glass from the cupboard and we will drink vodka.'

His wife gets the glass from the cupboard and sets it on the table. The Russian begins to piss in the glass and when he fills it his wife asks him, 'But Boris, why do we need only one glass?'

Boris raises the glass and says, 'Because tonight, my love, you drink from the bottle.'

****

Q: Why do elephants wear small green hats?
A: So they can sneak across snooker tables unobserved.

****

Q: How is being at a singles bar different from going to the circus?
A: At the circus the clowns don't talk.

****

Q: How does a man show he's planning for the future?
A: He buys two crates of beer instead of one.

****

Q: How does a blonde give a high-5 sign?
A: Smacks herself in the forehead.

Medicinal Purposes

5

Jokes that the doctor ordered

Medicinal Purposes

If you're going to spend hours in the pub, you've got to feel it's doing you some good. 'Booze agrees with me', you'll say. The fact that it only agrees that you're a sad alcoholic who's looking for excuses to justify his excess consumption of booze has nothing to do with it.

Worse still, is the excuse that 'it's for medicinal purposes'. Not only is it not doing you any harm, but it's actually promoting a healthier lifestyle. You may end up with your head down the toilet at two in the morning but that's a small price to pay for fitness and well-being.

In short, booze is only really for medicinal purposes in the sense that if you get really pissed, you could end up in hospital. If you do end up there, you might hear some of these jokes…

****

A woman went to the doctor wanting to find out about the latest weight-loss programme.

'Well,' said the doctor, 'there's a new one that you can lose a lot of weight with. All you have to do is ingest everything anally.'

So the woman decided to follow this course of treatment. After about six weeks, she walked back into the doc's office for a follow-up. It was obvious that she'd lost an awful lot of weight, but she was walking a bit bent over, and was swaying her behind from side to side.

'Wow,'' said the doc, 'you look wonderful!'

'Thanks,' said the woman. 'I've lost four stone!

'Great!' said the doctor, 'Now let me see if I can do something about that limp of yours.'

'Limp?' said the woman. 'I'm chewing a piece of gum!'

****

Doctor: I have some bad news and some very bad news.
Patient: Well, you might as well give me the bad news first.
Doctor: The lab called with your test results. They said you have 24 hours to live.

Patient: 24 HOURS! That's terrible!! WHAT could be WORSE? What's the very bad news?

Doctor: I've been trying to reach you since yesterday.

****

Patient: I'm in a hospital! Why am I in here?

Doctor: You've had an accident involving a train.

Patient: What happened?

Doctor: Well, I've got some good news and some bad news. Which would you like to hear first?

Patient: Well... The bad news first...

Doctor: Your legs were injured so badly that we had to amputate both of them.

Patient: That's terrible! What's the good news?

Doctor: There's a guy in the next ward who made a very good offer for your slippers.

****

A doctor on his rounds in a mental hospital sees a couple of patients behaving rather strangely. The first man is sitting on the edge of his bed clutching an imaginary steering wheel and making loud noises, 'VRROOOOM, VRRROOOOMM... SCREEEECH...' he's going.

'What are you doing?' asks the doctor.

'I'm taking this juggernaut down to Barcelona,' replies the ex-trucker.

Somewhat taken aback, the doctor moves on to the next bed where he can see some very energetic activity going on underneath the covers. On pulling them back he finds a man totally naked, face down on the mattress.

'And what are you doing?' asks the doctor, a little perplexed.

'Well,' pants the man, 'While he's in Barcelona, I'm fucking his wife.'

****

Medicinal Purposes

An elderly man and his wife go to the doctor so he can get a check-up. The doctor examines him thoroughly in the presence of his wife.

'You're in perfect health!' said the doctor, 'what do you attribute this to?'

'It is the help of God,' says the old geezer. 'Even when I wake in the night and go to the bathroom, God turns the light on for me so I will not stumble, and when I leave, he turns it off again.'

'That is totally amazing!' says the doc.

'No, it isn't!' says the old geezer's wife. 'He pisses in the refrigerator!'

****

Doctor, doctor, I keep thinking I'm a set of curtains!
Pull yourself together, man!

****

Doctor, doctor, I keep thinking I'm a bell.
Well, just go home and if the feeling persists, give me a ring.

****

Doctor, doctor, I've only got 59 seconds to live.
Wait a minute, please.

****

Doctor, doctor, I keep thinking I'm invisible.
Who said that?

****

Doctor, doctor, I keep trying to get into fights.
And how long have you had this complaint?

Who wants to know?

****

Doctor, doctor, people keep ignoring me!
Next!

****

Doctor, doctor, I can't concentrate, one minute I'm OK, and the next minute, I'm blank!
And how long have you had this complaint?
What complaint?

****

Doctor, doctor, no one believes a word I say.
Tell me the truth now, what's your REAL problem?

****

A surgeon came to see his patient on the morning after her operation. The young woman asked him, somewhat hesitantly, how long it would be before she could resume her sex life.

'I really haven't thought about it,' gulped the stunned surgeon. 'You're the first patient who's asked me that question after a tonsilectomy!'

****

An artist asked the gallery owner if there had been any interest in his paintings which were on display at that time.

'I have good news and bad news,' the owner replied. 'The good news is that a gentleman enquired about your work and wondered if it would appreciate in value after your death. When I told him it would, he bought all

15 of your paintings.'

'That's wonderful,' the artist exclaimed. 'What's the bad news?'

'The guy was your doctor…'

****

A woman goes to her doctor and says, 'I'd like to have bigger breasts.'

The doctor tells her to take a piece of toilet tissue and rub it between her breasts every day.

'That will make make my breasts bigger?' she asks, amazed.'

'Well, just look what it did for your arse!' said the doc.

****

A woman rushes into the vet's surgery carrying her ailing pet.

'Please,' she begs, 'You've got to do something for my dog!'

The vet leads her to the examining room where she gently lays the animal on the table. After a brief check of the body, the vet declares, 'Madam, I'm afraid your dog is dead.'

'Oh, no,' sobs the woman, 'He can't be! Please, I beg you, there must be something you can do to help him!'

So the vet takes a closer look. He lifts one of the dog's eyes, feels its nose, feels the chest for a pulse, but there is nothing, the corpse is cold and lifeless.

'I really am sorry, madam, but your dog is gone,' the vet says.

The woman begins to sob, 'Oh, please! Isn't there something you can do to help him? ANYTHING?'

The vet sighs, then says, 'Well, there is one more thing I can try.'

He goes into the next room for a moment, and returns with a live cat. Grasping the cat firmly in one hand, he waves the hissing feline in the dog's face, all around the dog's body, then in the dog's face again. But the dog just lies there, so the vet returns the cat to the next room.

'I'm really sorry, madam," says the vet on his return, 'but your dog is really dead, and nobody can bring him back.'

Medicinal Purposes

Regaining her composure, the woman sniffs, wipes away a tear, and asks the vet, 'Well, thank you for at least trying. How much do I owe you?'

'That'll be £500,' says the vet.

Shocked, the woman exclaims, 'What?! But you didn't really do anything!'

'Standard fee,' says the vet. '£20 for the examination, and £480 for the cat scan.'

✳✳✳✳

A bloke was suffering from constipation, so his doctor prescribed suppositories. A week later he was back at the doctor's complaining his constipation was worse, not better. The doctor asked, 'Have you been taking the suppositories regularly?'

'What do you think I've been doing?' said the bloke. 'Shoving them up my arse?'

✳✳✳✳

There was once a very prim and proper older lady who had a problem with passing wind. Since she came from a generation when people didn't even talk about this kind of problem it took a long time for her to seek help.

Finally, however, she was persuaded to consult her family doctor. After she filled out all the proper forms and had waited about 20 minutes in the waiting room, the doctor called her into his office, leaned back in his chair, folded his hands into a steeple and asked her how he could help.

'Doctor,' she said, 'I have a very bad wind problem.'

'A wind problem?' replied the doctor.

'Yes. Yesterday afternoon I had lunch with the Secretary of State and his wife and had six, um, er, ahhh... silent wind emissions. Last night I had dinner with the governor and his wife and had four silent wind emissions. Then, while sitting in your waiting room I had five silent wind emissions! Doctor, you've got to help me! What can we do?'

Medicinal Purposes

'Well,' said the doctor thoughtfully, 'I think the first thing we're going to do is give you a hearing test.'

****

This lad went into a doctor's office and tells the nurse, 'I have a problem with my dick.'

The nurse, half horrified, says, 'I am amazed that you the audacity to use that language in here. I will not help you until you call it something else.'

A little embarrassed, the lad leaves. A few minutes later, he comes back in and says, 'I have something wrong with my ear.'

So the nurse says, 'That's better. Now what's wrong with your ear?'

'I can't piss out of it,' the lad replies.

****

While his wife is away, this man decides to paint the toilet seat. The wife comes home sooner than expected, sits, and gets the seat stuck to her arse. She's understandably distraught about this and asks her husband to drive her to the doctor.

She puts on a large overcoat so as to cover the frozen seat, and they go. When they get to the doctor's, the man lifts his wife's coat to show their predicament.

'Doctor,' the man asks, 'have you ever seen anything like this before?'

'Well, yes,' the doctor replies, 'but never framed.'

****

Mrs May was suffering from exhaustion and went to the doctor.

'Tell me, Mrs May,' said the doctor. 'How often do you have sex?'

'Oh, four times a week,' replied Mrs May. 'On Sunday, Tuesday, Friday and Saturday nights.'

'Well you're going to have to cut out the Sunday nights,' said the doctor.

'I can't do that,' exclaimed Mrs May. 'That's the night I'm with my husband.'

****

In the middle of the night, Karen awoke screaming in pain. 'Quick, quick,' she screamed to her husband Dave. 'Ring the doctor, I think it's my appendix.'

So Dave got on the blower. 'Doctor, it's my wife,' said Dave. 'She's screaming in pain and thinks it's her appendix.'

'Dave, Dave,' said the Doctor, 'calm down and go back to sleep. I took out your wife's appendix four years ago and in all my years as a doctor I've never heard of anyone having another one.'

'Fine,' replied Dave dryly, 'but have you ever heard of anyone having another wife?'

****

A plastic bag goes to the doctor. After a thorough examination the doctor says, 'I'm very sorry, but you've got AIDS.'

'That's impossible,' says the plastic bag. 'I've never even had sex.'

'Well,' says the doctor, 'your mother must be a carrier.'

****

A bloke working in a brewery died one day after falling into a vat of beer. The managing director and some colleagues went to tell his widow.

'Tell me, did he suffer much?' cried the widow.

'I don't think so,' replied the MD, 'he got out to go to the bog three times.'

****

This woman goes to the dentist. As he leans over to begin working on her, she grabs his balls. The dentist says, 'Madam, I believe you've got a hold of my privates.'

The woman replies, 'Yes. We're going to be very careful not to hurt each other, aren't we?'

****

An 80-year-old woman married an 85-year-old man. After about six months together the woman wasn't feeling well and she went to her doctor. The doctor examined her and said, 'Congratulations, Mrs Jones, you're going to be a mother.'

'Get serious Doctor, I'm 80!' she replied.

'I know,' said the Doctor, 'this morning I would have said it was impossible, but this afternoon you are a medical miracle.'

'Well, I'll be blowed,' said the old woman and stormed out of the office. She walked down the hall and around the corner to where the phones were. In a rage, she called her husband.

'Hello,' she heard his familiar halting voice.

'You bastard,' she screamed, 'you got me pregnant!'

There was a pause on the line. Finally her husband answered:

'Who's calling, please?'

****

One day John's tennis elbow was acting up so he decided to stop in and see a doctor. When he got to the doctor's office the nurse told him he could see the doctor in 15 minutes but first he'd have to give a urine sample.

John said that this was absurd but the nurse insisted and John complied. 15 minutes later, John was ushered in to see the doctor.

'So that tennis elbow is really acting up, huh?' the doctor said.

'The nurse must have told you,' said John, wondering how the Doctor knew.

'No. It was in your urinalysis,' and the doctor continued to say that he had just purchased this new urology machine that could diagnose every physical condition with total accuracy.

John didn't believe a word of this but he did agree to provide another urine sample on a check-up visit. Two days later, John was sitting at the kitchen table with his wife and his teenage daughter. He was telling them about this ridiculous machine, when he decided to have a little fun with the doctor. John pissed in the bottle as did his wife and teenage daughter. Then John had a brainstorm. He added a few drops of motor oil to the jar and finally had a wank and put a few drops of semen in with it too. He went to the doctors office, shook the bottle, then handed it to the nurse.

This time his urinalysis took half an hour. Finally, John was ushered in to see the doctor. The doctor looked at him and said, 'I've got some bad news. Your daughter's pregnant, your wife's got clap, your car's about to break down and if you don't stop wanking that tennis elbow's gonna get worse!'

****

This geezer was in the pub when he spotted someone he thought he knew. 'Are you Derek Maygrove?' he asked.

'No,' came the reply.

'That's weird,' said the geezer, 'you look just like him. You must have a double.'

'Thanks very much,' said the bloke, 'I'll have it on the rocks, please.'

****

A day-tripper goes up to a local and says, 'Excuse me, I'm not from round here, can you tell me where I'll find the nearest boozer?'

'You're looking at him,' says the local.

****

A very wealthy, very classy lady goes to see her doctor. 'Doctor, I have this MOST disgraceful and EMBARRASSING problem. I have VERY loud, VERY frequent flatulence. Thank HEAVENS it is COMPLETELY odourless.'

The doctor tells her, 'Well, I don't think it's likely to be anything serious but, just in case, I'll give you a thorough examination.'

So the lady takes off her clothes, lays down on the examining table and put her feet up in the stirrups. The doctor bends over to examine her when all of a sudden she lets one rip BAAAAAARRRRRR-RUUUUUUMPPPPPPPP!!!!!!

The doctor stands up immediately and says, 'This is serious. Just stay still. I'm going to call an ambulance and check you into the hospital immediately. We'll have to do exploratory surgery.'

The woman was terrified at this. She said, 'Oh my God. Is it... CANCER?'

The doctor said, 'That's a distinct possibility.'

The woman said, 'How treatable is CANCER of the BOWELS?'

The doctor said, 'Christ, woman, your bowels are fine. I'm worried about your nose.'

****

Why has Guinness got a white head on it?
So when you're drunk you know which end to drink first.

****

Two blokes are chatting in a pub one day.
  'How did you get those scars on your nose?' said one.
  'From glasses,' said the other.
  'Well why don't you try contact lenses?' asked the first.
  'Because they don't hold as much beer,' said the second.

****

A heavy drinker is warned by his doctor that if he doesn't reduce his consumption he'll be dead in five years.

'You've got to cut down to only three drinks a day,' said the doc. The drinker nods in agreement and goes off. A couple of weeks later the doctor comes across the bloke in a terrible state.

'Hey, I thought you agreed to only three drinks a day?' fumed the doctor.

'Yes I did,' said the drinker, 'but I went to five other doctors for second opinions and they all prescribed the same.'

****

A drunk bloke came upon a geezer looking under the bonnet of his car.

'What's the matter?' mumbled the drunk. 'Oh, piston broke,' replied the motorist.'

'Yeah, me too,' replied the drunk.

****

Two guys were staggering home one night after a particularly excessive bout of drinking.

'Ish thas the shum or the moon up shere?' asked one.

'Don't know,' came the reply, 'I'm not from around here.'

****

'After another night on the ale John comes home to find his wife is somewhat annoyed.

'So, what's your excuse this time?' she demands.

'Well, there I was in front of a blazing fire with a drink in me hand. It was very difficult to leave,' says John.

'Well, why didn't you just get up and walk away?' asks the wife.'

'It's not that easy when you've got to get past all those firemen and their equipment,' explains John.

****

Why did the farmer feed his chickens whisky?
Because he was hoping they would lay scotch eggs.

****

Two terrorists were driving to a bombing mission when they decided to stop for a few stiff ones along the way. On getting back into the car, the passenger put the bomb in his lap.
　'I'd better drive carefully,' said the driver, 'we don't want it going off too soon.'
　'Oh, don't worry about that,' said the passenger, 'there's another one in the boot.'

****

This bloke was tottering along the road much the worse for wear, booting old cans and litter all over the place.
　'What do you think you're up to?' asked a passing copper.
　'I'm on my works outing,' replied the bloke.
　'So where's everyone else?' asked the copper.
　'There isn't anyone else,' came the reply, 'I'm self-employed.'

****

A man goes to the doctor. 'Doctor, doctor, I keep thinking I'm a bottle of gin.'
'I think you need a little tonic,' advises the doc.

****

A woman is laying naked, except for a sheet, on a bed out in a hospital corridor waiting to go into surgery. As she lays there, a man in a white coat comes by, lifts up the sheet and then leaves. This happens a second time. The third time this happens she says, 'Doctor, am I going into surgery soon?'

The man replied, 'Don't ask me lady. I'm just a painter!'

****

Three geezers have been drinking all evening when one of them passes out on the floor. One of the others goes to the bar to buy the next round. 'What's he having?" asks the landlord pointing to the bloke on the floor.

'Oh he'd better not have any more,' comes the reply, 'he's driving.'

****

A woman was asleep at home when she was woken up by the sound of a terrible crash. Rushing downstairs, she sees her husband sitting in the car in the living room.

'How the fuck did you get into the living room?' she shouts.

'Well, I took a left at the front door, passed through the kitchen and then made a right,' came the reply.

****

A ghost went into a pub after closing time. To the terrified barmaid he asked, 'Do you serve spirits at this time of night?'

****

A man walks into a pub and asks, 'Do you serve women in this pub?'

'No,' replies the landlord, ' you've got to bring your own.'

****

A bloke walks into a pub at 11 o'clock one morning and asks the landlord, 'Was I in here last night?'

'Yes, mate,' goes the landlord.

'And did I spend a lot of money?' asks the bloke.
'Yes mate, you did,' replies the landlord, 'about £80.'
'Thank God for that,' says the bloke, 'I thought I'd wasted it.'

****

A man went to the doctor. 'Look, doc,' he said, 'I can't stop my hands from shaking.'
'Do you drink much?' asked the doctor.'
'No,' replied the man, 'I spill most of it.'

****

A stuttering man finally decides to go to the doctor to see if his speech impediment can be cured. The doctor thoroughly examines the man and finally asks him to drop his pants. Out comes this gigantic dick and the doctor pronounces the root of the problem to be strain on the vocal chords from the effects of gravity being transmitted up to the neck area.

The patient then asks, 'Wh-wh-at c-c-ca-an b-b-e d-d-done ab-b-bout- t-t i-it?'

To which the doctor replies, 'modern surgery can work miracles. We can replace your dick with one of normal size and the stuttering will disappear right after the operation.'

The patient eagerly agrees to the surgery, and as promised his stuttering disappears. About three months later the man returns to the doctor and complains, 'Doctor, I'm grateful to you for having cured me, but my wife really misses a big dick, and rather than lose her I've decided to get my old dick back and live with stuttering for the rest of my life.'

The doctor then looks straight at the man and replies, 'A d-d-de-deal's a d-d-deal.'

****

Q: What's so great about being a test tube baby?

A: You get a womb with a view.

****

Pissed and confused, this bloke is staggering home one night when he stops to ask someone the time. On getting his reply he says, 'I don't get it. That's the fourth person I've asked and I get a different answer each time.'

****

On his way home from the pub, a drunk decides to go and see a late-night film. After buying a ticket he staggers into the cinema, only to return two minutes later to buy another ticket and stagger in again. Two minutes later he's back again buying a third ticket.

'Do you realise,' says the girl in the ticket office, 'that's the third time you've bought a ticket?'

'Yes,' replies the drunk,' but every time I get to the cinema some bloke takes it from me and tears it in half.'

****

Two women are in a wine bar. They order a couple of glasses of white wine.

'And make sure my glass is clean,' says one woman. 'Last time I was here I got a dirty one.'

The waiter goes off and returns later with their wine. 'Now then,' he says, 'who was it who wanted the clean glass?'

****

The Sally Army were collecting outside a pub one day when a slightly pissed geezer wandered out of the pub and said to one of the girls collecting, 'Do you save fallen women?'

'Why yes, we do,' replied the girl.

'Well, can you save me one for Friday night, then?' asked the bloke.

****

Man goes to the doctor. 'Doctor, doctor, I keep seeing fish everywhere.'
'Have you seen an optician?' asks the doctor.
'Look I told you,' snapped the patient, 'it's fish that I see.'

****

A charity worker knocked on Mrs Smith's door and said, 'Hello, I'm collecting for a home for drunkards. Can you donate anything?'
'Yes,' replied Mrs Smith, 'if you come back after closing time you can have my husband.'

****

In desperation the alcoholic tried drinking varnish. Sadly he he came to a terrible end… but a beautiful finish.

****

A guy rang up Alcoholics Anonymous in the middle of the night.
'I need help,' he said. 'I'm currently sitting in a room with 50 bottles of wine.'
'I see,' came the reply. 'And how can we help?'
'I just wondered if you could put me in touch with one of your clients with a corkscrew they don't need any more?' said the man.

****

After sinking a good eight pints, a worse-for-wear tough guy slammed his fists down on the bar and shouted, 'Right, everyone on the left side of the pub is a bastard.'

Getting no reaction, the guy tried again with, 'Everyone on the right of the pub is a homosexual.'

On hearing this, one chap got up. 'Right,' said the tough guy,' do you want some, then?'

'No,' said the chap, 'it's just that I'm on the wrong side of the pub.'

****

An old pisshead was staggering along the road pulling a piece of string along behind him.

'Why are you pulling that piece of string along?' asked a passing policeman.

''Cos it's a damn sight easier than pushing it,' replied the pisshead.

****

The wife of a friend of mine was in an accident and is now in hospital in a coma. She's on monitors and the nurses noticed that when they bathed her, her brain waves would elevate. So the doctors called in the husband and suggested he come in everyday to wash and massage her. They even suggested having oral sex, as this would keep her mind active.

So the next day as the husband was washing her, the doctors where delighted to see the brain waves go so high. Then everything went flat-line. They rushed in to inquire as to what had happened. The husband replied, 'I did everything you told me, I guess she choked to death.'

****

Two doctors and an NHS Trust manager died and lined up at the Pearly Gates for admission to heaven. St Peter asked them to identify themselves. One doctor stepped forward and said: 'I was a pediatric spine surgeon and helped kids overcome their deformities.'

St Peter said, 'You can enter.'

The second doctor said: 'I was a psychiatrist. I helped people rehabilitate themselves.' St Peter also invited him in.

The third applicant stepped forward and said, 'I was a NHS Trust manager, I helped people get cost-effective health care.'

St Peter said, 'You can come in too.' But as the NHS Trust manager walked by, he added, 'But you can only stay three days. After that you can go to hell.'

✳✳✳✳

A mad fan of Michelle Pfeiffer wins a date with her in a competition. Naturally, he's very nervous when they meet, but she turns out to look even better than she does on the big screen, beautifully turned out in a designer dress, with her blue eyes sparkling in the light.

Clearing his throat, the fan offers Michelle a drink. 'Erm, would you like a port or a Martini, Michelle?'

'Oh, a port,' says Michelle. 'Port to me is like a deep sunset over a forest of blazing russet trees. It makes me glow and shimmer like a ray of light bouncing off an icy lake in winter. Martini, on the other hand, makes me fart.'

✳✳✳✳

Q: Why did the blonde have a sore navel?
A: Because her boyfriend was also blonde!

✳✳✳✳

Q: Why do black widow spiders kill their males after mating?
A: To stop the snoring before it starts.

✳✳✳✳

Q: How do you get a man to do situps?
A: Glue the TV remote control between his ankles.

One For The Road

Jokes about Drinking and Driving

One For The Road

OK, so we all know that drink driving is a big no no, unless of course you live in the country where in order to get your license you have to pass a special drink driving test, but that doesn't stop people going on about how they reckon they actually drive better after a few stiff ones.

It's bloody ridiculous. You don't get people claiming to play a better game of chess after 10 pints, or thinking they could scale Mount Everest that bit more smoothly after a couple of bottles of gin, do you?

Actually after a couple of bottles of gin you'd probably reckon you could scale Everest whilst playing chess, but fortunately we're not dealing with the real world here, rather the world of jokedom and gaggery in which getting into the car as pissed as a newt is almost bleedin' obligatory. And, in a strange life-imitates-art sort of way, after seven pints you'll find that even though you start thinking that your delivery of the gags is getting better, it is in fact a whole lot worse. Weird...

****

A copper sees a car weaving all over the road and pulls it over. He walks up to the car and sees a nice-looking woman is driving and smells booze on her breath.

He says, 'I'm going to have to give you the breathalyser test to determine if you are under the influence of alcohol.'

She blows into the bag and he walks over to the police car. After a couple of minutes he comes back and says, 'It looks like you've had a couple of stiff ones.'

'You mean it shows that, too?' she replies.

****

A young couple are out driving down the motorway. The lad says to the girl, 'If I go at 100 miles an hour, will you take off your clothes?'

She agrees and he begins to speed up. When the speedometer hits 100 she starts to strip. When she gets all her clothes off he's so busy staring at her that he drives off the road and flips the car. The girl is thrown clear without a scratch, but her clothes and her boyfriend are trapped in the car.

'Get help!' he pleads.

'I can't, I'm naked,' she says.

He points to his shoe that has been thrown clear and says, 'Cover yourself with that and get help.'

She takes the shoe, covers herself, and runs to the service station down the road. When she arrives she's frantic and calls to the attendant, 'HELP! HELP! My boyfriend's stuck!'

The attendant looks down at the shoe covering her crotch and replies, 'I'm sorry Miss. He's too far in.'

****

After a car crash one of the drivers was lying injured on the pavement.

'Don't worry,' said a policeman who's first on the scene, 'a Red Cross nurse is coming.'

'Oh shit,' moaned the victim, 'couldn't I have a blonde, cheerful one?'

****

A middle-aged businessman took a young woman, half his age, as his wife. The fantasy of having a young woman in his bed soon became a nightmare when he found that he could not last long enough to satisfy his young bride.

His wife, as understanding as she was exciting, told him that all was well even if he was quick to get out of the saddle.

Determined to satisfy this sweet young thing, the man visited the doctor to get some advice. 'Doctor,' he said, 'I can't seem to hold back for very long when I make love to my young wife and I can't satisfy her. What can I do?'

The doctor smiled, patted him on the shoulder, and said in a professional manner, 'Try a bit of self-stimulation before having intercourse with your wife and you'll find that you'll last longer and ultimately satisfy her.'

'OK, Doctor,' said the man. 'If you think that will help.'

Later that afternoon, his young bride called him at work to let him know that she would be attacking him at the front door when he arrived home.

'Be prepared, my darling. I'm going to ravish you,' she cooed over the phone. Undaunted, the man decided to follow the doctor's advice. But where? In the office? The toilet? What if someone walked in on him? So eventually he got in his car and began the journey home. Soon he decided he would find a spot on the road to pull over, climb underneath the car and, pretending to be inspecting the rear axle, do the deed there.

A moment later, he pulled over, crawled beneath the car, closed his eyes tightly, and fantasising about his young wife, began his 'therapy'.

A few minutes later, just as he was about to complete his therapy session, he felt someone tugging on his trouser leg. Keeping his eyes tightly shut to avoid ruining the fantasy he was enjoying, he said, 'Yes?'

'Sir, I'm a policeman. Could you tell me what you are doing, please?' said the copper.

'Yes, officer, I'm inspecting my car's rear axle,' he replied confidently.

'Well, why don't you check the brakes while you're down there. Your car rolled down the hill ten minutes ago.'

****

A policeman walked over to a parked car and asked the driver if the car was licensed. 'Of course it is,' said the driver.

'Great, I'll have a pint then,' said the policeman.

****

One day while on patrol, a policeman pulled over a car for speeding. He went up to the car and asked the driver to roll down her window. The first thing he noticed, besides the nice red sports car, was how attractive the driver was! Drop-dead gorgeous blonde, the works.

'I've pulled you over for speeding, madam... could I see your licence?' said the copper.

'What's a licence?' replied the blonde, instantly giving away the fact that she was as dumb as a stump.

'It's usually in your wallet,' replied the officer. After fumbling for a few minutes, the driver managed to find it.

'Now may I see your insurance details?' asks the copper.'

'Insurance details? What's that?' asked the blonde.

'It's usually in your glove compartment,' said the copper, impatiently. After some more fumbling, she found her insurance details.

'I'll be back in a minute,' said the copper and walked back to his car. He radioed in to run a check on the woman's details and after a few moments, the control room came back to him.

'Ummm… is this woman driving a red sports car?'

'Yes,' said the copper.

'Is she a drop-dead gorgeous blonde?'

'Uh, yes,' replied the copper.

'In that case, give her the stuff back and drop your trousers.'

'WHAT!? I can't do that,' shrieked the copper.

'Trust me, just do it...'' said the copper in the control room.

So the cop goes back to the car, gives the woman back her documents and drops his trousers. The blonde looks down and sighs, 'Oh no... not ANOTHER breathalyser.'

****

Late one night the police were following a car. The driver of the car was driving immaculately, never going over the speed limit, giving the correct signals and even being courteous to other drivers.

Eventually the police car pulled alongside and an officer said to the driver, 'Excuse me sir, you're not in trouble, we just wanted to compliment you on your exemplary driving.'

'Thank you, officer,' replied the driver, 'I always make a point of driving especially carefully when I've had a few pints.'

****

The Pope arrives at Heathrow Airport and gets straight into a chauffeur-driven car.

'I'm rather late for a very important meeting, my good man,' he tells the driver, 'so I would appreciate it if we could go as fast as possible.'

The driver agrees, but being a law-abiding fellow, doesn't do more than 70 miles per hour on the motorway. This infuriates the Pope, who badgers the driver to go faster, but with no success.

Eventually the Pope says, 'Look, I really do have to get to this meeting. It's extremely important. You sit in the back and I'll drive.'

Being a good Catholic lad the driver feels he can't refuse His Holiness, so they change places and set off. The Pope really puts his foot down and before long they're doing well over 100. Inevitably, though, a few miles down the road they get pulled over by the police.

The officer comes over to the car, looks in and then walks away to radio his boss.

'Chief, chief,' he says into his radio, 'I think I might have just pulled over someone really, really important.'

'Is it the Prime Minister?' asks the chief.

'No,' says the officer, 'more important than him.'

'Well, is it the Queen?' asks the chief.

'No sir,' replies the copper. 'More important than her.'

'Well, who on earth is it then?' asks the chief.

'I don't know, sir,' says the officer, 'but he's got the Pope driving him around.'

****

A rabbi and a priest get into a car accident and it's a bad one. Both cars are totally demolished but, amazingly, neither of the holy men is hurt. After they crawl out of their cars, the rabbi sees the priest's collar and says, 'So you're a priest. I'm a rabbi. Just look at our cars. There's nothing left, but we are unhurt. This must be a sign from God. God must have meant that we should meet and be friends and live together in peace the rest of our days.'

The priest replies, 'I agree with you completely. This must be a sign from God.'

One For The Road

'And look at this,' the rabbi says, 'here's another miracle. My car is completely demolished but this bottle of kosher wine didn't break. Surely God wants us to drink this wine and celebrate our good fortune.'

So he hands the bottle to the priest who takes a few big swigs, and hands the bottle back to the rabbi. The rabbi takes the bottle, immediately puts the cap on, and hands it back to the priest. 'Aren't you having any?' asks the priest.

'No,' replies the rabbi, 'I think I'll wait for the police.'

****

The elderly man entered the car showroom together with his young wife. The owner of the showroom spotted the couple and went over to wait upon them himself, but he could not help staring at the lady, which, of course, the elderly man noticed.

'May I propose a wager?' he said. 'If you can do everything to my wife that I can do and still end up the same way as I do, I will pay you double for the car. But if you cannot, you will give it to me for free!'

'OK, agreed!' said the owner.

The elderly man gave his wife a passionate kiss and the agency owner did the same. Then the man unbuttoned her blouse and kissed her breasts. So did the agency owner. Then the husband opened his fly, pulled out his pecker and bent it in half.

'What colour car do you want?' asked the showroom owner.

****

A policeman stops a woman and asks for her licence.

'Madam,' he says, 'it says here that you should be wearing glasses.'

'Well,' replies the woman, 'I have contacts.'

'Listen, love,' says the copper, 'I don't care who you know; You're nicked!'

****

Three cowboys were hanging out in the bunkhouse. 'I know that smart alec Tex,' said the first. 'He's going to start bragging about that new foreign car he bought as soon as he gets back.'

'Not Tex,' the second cowboy replied. 'He'll always be just a good ol' boy. When he walks in, I'm sure all he'll say is hello.'

'I know Tex better than either of you,' said the third. 'He's so smart, he'll figure out a way to do both. Here he comes now.'

Tex swung open the bunkhouse door and shouted, 'Audi, partners!'

****

A motorist parked outside the Bank of England was approached by a plain-clothes policeman.

'Will you be staying long?' inquired the officer.

'What's it got to do with you?' asked the motorist.

'I'm a policeman, sir,' replied the officer.

'Get out of it,' said the motorist, 'you're wearing an ordinary jacket.'

'That's right, sir. This is a routine check,' the officer told him.

****

A man goes out and buys a 1998 Turbo BeepBeep. It's the best and most expensive car in the world, and it costs him £750,000. He takes it out for a spin and, while doing so, stops at a red light. An old man on an even older looking moped pulls up next to him. The old man looks over the sleek, shiny surface of the car and asks, 'What kind of car's that, sonny?'

The geezer replies, 'A 1998 Turbo BeepBeep. They cost £750,000.'

'That's a lot of money!' says the old man, shocked. 'Why does it cost so much?'

' 'Cos this car can do up to 320 miles per hour!' says the geezer proudly.

'Can I take a look inside?' the old man asks.

'Sure,' replies the owner. So the old man pokes his head in the window and looks around. Leaning back on his moped, the old man says. 'That's a nice car, all right.'

Just then the lights change, so the geezer decides to show the old man what his car can do. He floors it, and within 30 seconds the speedometer reads 320 mph.

Suddenly, the geezer notices a dot in his rear-view mirror. It seems to be getting closer! Whhhoooooooooosssssshhhhhh! Something flies by him! Going maybe three times as fast! The guy wonders what on earth could be going faster than his Turbo BeepBeep. Then, ahead of him, he sees a dot coming toward him. Whooooooooooosh! Goes by again! And, it looks distinctly like the old man on the moped!

'It couldn't be,' thinks the geezer. 'How could a moped outrun a Turbo BeepBeep?' But again, he sees a dot in his rear-view mirror! WhooooooooshhhhhhhhKa-BbbbblaMMMMM! It ploughs into the back of his car, demolishing the rear end.

The geezer jumps out and is amazed to discover it is the old man. He's in a bad way so the geezer says to him, 'Is there anything I can do for you?'

'Yeah,' says the old man. 'You could unhook my braces from your near-side mirror.'

****

A yuppie opened the door of his BMW when suddenly a car came along and hit the door, ripping it off completely. When the police arrived at the scene, the yuppie was complaining bitterly about the damage to his precious BMW.

'Officer, look what they've done to my Beeeeemer!' he whined.

'You yuppies are so materialistic, you make me sick!' retorted the officer. 'You're so worried about your stupid BMW that you didn't even notice that your left arm was ripped off!'

'Oh my gaaawd...' replied the yuppie, finally noticing the bloody stump where his left arm once was. 'My Rolex!'

****

There was a young lad who was quite inventive and was always trying out new things. One day he thought he'd see just how fast a bicycle could go before it became uncontrollable. He asked his friend, who owned a Porsche, if he could tie his bike to the bumper of his car to test his theory. 'Sure,' his friend said.

So the young lad tied his bike to the back of the car and said to his friend, 'I'll ring my bike bell once if I want you to go faster, twice if I want you to maintain speed, and repeatedly if I want you to slow down.'

With that, off they went. Things were going pretty well, with the car driver slowly speeding up to well over 60 miles per hour. The young lad on the bike was handling the speed just fine until, all of sudden, a Ferrari came up beside them and before you knew it the bloke driving the Porsche forgot all about the lad on the bike and started to race the Ferrari.

A little further down the road sat Constable Pigg in his police car. As the racing cars passed him he radioed in saying, 'Hey, lads. You aren't going to believe this, but there's a Porsche and a Ferrari racing out here on the M1, and there's a bloke on a bike ringing his bell and waving his arms trying to pass them!'

****

A police officer had just pulled a car over. When he walked up to the car the man rolled down the window and said, 'What's the problem, officer?'

To which the policeman responded, 'I stopped you for going through that red light back there.'

Just then, the man's wife leaned forward from the passenger seat and said with a very loud voice, 'I told him to stop at that light. But did he listen? No. He just kept right on going.'

The man then turned to his wife and shouted, 'Shut up, bitch!'

'And just before the red light,' continued the policeman, 'I clocked you doing 50 miles per hour and the speed limit is only 30.'

His wife then leaned forward again and squawked, 'I told him to slow down. But did he listen to me? No! He never listens to me.'

And again the man shouted at his wife, 'Listen, bitch, I told you to SHUT UP!'

The policeman then looked at the woman and said, 'Does he always talk to you this way?'

'Oh no, officer,' replied the woman, 'Only when he's been drinking.'

****

Leaving the pub a bit worse for wear, this guy got into his car and decided that the best thing for him to do would be to follow the rear lights of another car that was just pulling out. Everything was fine for about five miles until the lights of the car in front went out and the drunk driver smashed into the back of it.

'Hey, what the hell do you think you're doing turing your lights off? It's pitch black,' shouted the drunk driver.

'What the hell do you expect me to do?' came the reply, 'I'm in my own garage.'

****

Two judges were booked for speeding and being friends they agreed to try each other. The next day one of them sat on the bench and the other entered the dock. He pleaded not guilty and after all the evidence was heard the case was dismissed and the judges changed places.

The second judge also pleaded not guilty, but after hearing the evidence his friend pronounced him guilty and fined him £250.

The second judge was amazed, but before he could say anything his friend said, 'This is the second case of speeding we've had this morning and I'm determined to stamp it out.'

****

A man driving down a country road was flagged down by a policeman on a motorcycle.

'Excuse me, sir, but there's a lady about a mile back who says she's your wife and she fell out of the car when you went over a bump in the road.'

'Thank God for that,' said the man, 'I thought I'd gone deaf.'

****

A flash geezer in a Porsche bombed through a quiet village at 90 miles an hour. At the other side of town he was stopped by the local bobby who asked him if he hadn't seen the, 'Dead Slow,' sign when he came in. 'Of course I did,' said the flash bloke,' but I thought it referred to the villagers.'

****

A policeman stopped a motorist in the centre of town one evening. 'Would you mind blowing into this bag, sir?' asked the policeman.
 'Why?' said the driver.
 'Because my chips are too hot,' replied the copper.

****

A distraught little boy rang his dad at work one day. 'Dad,' cried the boy, 'Mum was backing the car out of the garage this morning and she ran over my bicycle.'
 'Look,' said his dad, 'how many times have I told you not to leave your bike in the middle of the lawn?'

****

An advert in a local paper offered a brand-new Porsche for sale for only £50. On spotting this a keen motorist decided to call round to the address given. He arrived to find a very large house in a wealthy area.
 The door was opened by an attractive woman in her late forties who showed him the Porsche which was indeed brand new. Of course he snapped it up and after handing over the £50 asked, 'Why are you selling this car so cheaply? You could probably have got at least £12,000 for it.'

'Well,' explained the woman, 'my husband died recently and in his will he left strict instructions that the proceeds from the sale of his car were to go to his 21-year-old blonde secretary.'

****

A driver came to a stream to discover that the bridge over it was in need of repair. Standing nearby was an old boy, so the driver asked him if he thought the stream was shallow enough for him to drive across.

'Yes, I should think you could do that, sir,' replied the old boy.

So the driver drove into the stream and almost immediately his car sank and he only just managed to scramble out. 'What the hell's the idea of telling me I could drive across,' he shouted at the old boy. 'It must be at least 30 feet deep.'

'I don't understand it,' said the old boy, 'the water only comes halfway up the ducks.'

****

Whizzing round a sharp bend on a country road a motorist ran over a large dog. A distraught farmer's wife ran over to the dead animal.

'I'm so very sorry,' said the driver, 'I'll replace him, of course.'

'Well, I don't know,' said the farmer's wife, 'are you any good at catching rats?'

****

'Why don't you buy a car?' says a salesman to a farmer.

'Well, I'd much rather buy a cow,' replies the farmer.

'You'd look pretty silly riding around on a cow,' says the salesman.

'Not half as silly as I'd look milking a car,' says the farmer.

A woman goes to the garage and says, 'I need a longer dip-stick.'
 'Why's that?' asks the mechanic.
 'Because the one I've got won't reach the oil,' replies the woman.

****

A policeman in a lay-by is amazed when a car whizzes past at 70 miles an hour with a woman calmly knitting at the wheel. He gives chase and on catching her up shouts, 'Pull over!'
 'No, pair of socks,' she shouts back.

****

A police officer stopped a car for speeding and saw a dog in the back.
 'Does this dog have a licence?' the officer asked the driver.
 'Oh no, officer,' said the driver, 'I do all the driving myself.'

****

A copper pulls over a motorist who's been weaving erratically across all three motorway lanes. He approaches the motorist's window carefully, holds out a plastic tube and says, 'Sir, I'll need you to blow into this breathalyser.'
 'I'm sorry, officer, I can't do that,' replies the guy, 'I'm an asthmatic, and if I do that I could have a bad asthma attack.'
 'OK, sir,' says the policeman. 'Then I'm going to have to ask you to come down to the station with me to give us a blood sample.'
 'I can't do that either, officer,' says the driver. 'I suffer from a life-threatening form of haemophilia, and if my skin is punctured in any way, especially by a sharp needle, I could easily bleed to death.'
 'No problem, sir,' says the officer, 'then we'll just take a urine sample.'
 'I'm awful sorry, officer,' says the motorist, 'I also have diabetes, and if I piss this late at night, I'll get low blood sugar and possibly even go into cardiac arrest.'
 'I see sir,' replies the officer calmly, 'then I'll need you to step out of

One For The Road

your vehicle and walk a straight line for me right here and now.'

'I can't do that either, officer,' says the guy.

'And why is that, sir?' asks the policeman.

'Because I'm too pissed.'

****

A penguin was driving through the desert when his car broke down. He waddled to the nearest phone to call the AA. His car was quickly towed to the nearest garage where the mechanic told him he would need a couple of hours to check out the car.

The penguin didn't complain but wandered off to find the closest supermarket. He proceeded to the frozen foods section and hung out near the fish sticks. After an hour he got in the freezer next to the vanilla ice cream and, he couldn't help himself, ate several gallons. Then he saw the time and went back to the garage covered in ice cream.

The mechanic walked over to him wiping his hands and shaking his head, saying, 'It looks like you blew a seal.' Blushing, the penguin said, 'Oh no! It's just ice cream.'

****

An MG Midget pulled alongside a Rolls-Royce at a set of traffic light.

'Do you have a car phone?' its driver asked the guy in the Rolls.

'Of course I do,' replied the haughty deluxe-car driver.

'Well, do you have a fax machine?'

The driver in the Rolls sighed. 'I have that too.'

'Do you have a double bed in the back?' the Midget then asked.

Ashen-faced, the Rolls driver sped off. That afternoon, he had a mechanic install a double bed in his motor. A week later, the Rolls driver passes the same MG Midget, which is parked on the side of the road – back windows fogged up and steam pouring out. The arrogant driver pulls over, gets out of the Rolls and bangs on the Midget's back window until the driver sticks his head out.

'I want you to know that I had a double bed installed,' brags the

Rolls driver.

    The Midget driver is unimpressed. 'You got me out of the shower to tell me that?'

****

Q: How many mechanics does it take to screw in a light bulb?
A: Two. One to force it with a hammer and one to go out for more bulbs.

****

Q: What do you call a convertible Lada?
A: A skip

****

Q: How do you double the value of your Lada?
A: Fill it up with petrol.

****

Q: Why does a Lada have a heated rear windscreen?
A: To keep your hands warm while you're pushing it.

****

Q: What do you call a Lada at the top of a hill?
A: A miracle.

****

Q: What do you call a Lada going down a hill?
A: An accident waiting to happen.

On The Pull

7

Jokes about the Mating Game

On The Pull

Among the many and various reasons why people drink, the following juxtaposition, as it were, must surely rank highly. Without a drink inside you, you spend about two hours deciding to go over to the member of the opposite sex you've been eyeing up all night and out of you mouth comes the following: 'frmmm greeebly shtrummmp blarllll orgoonnnta.' With a few bevvies inside you, you spend about five minutes making the same decision and out of your mouth comes the following: 'frmmm greeebly shtrummmp blarllll orgoonnnta.'

However, crucially, in the latter example, if the object of your desire has had a few, you might well be on for a shag, whereas in the former example you're probably on for being sectioned.

Now being realistic, all you're really up for is a quick bunk-up without too much discussion, if any, and then you go home hoping never to have to see each other again. Then again, we've all seen *Fatal Attraction*, and if you're really unlucky you may be entering a battle of the sexes that can last an awfully long time...

✳✳✳✳

Q: Why can't dumb blondes count to 70?
A: Because 69 is a bit of a mouthful.

✳✳✳✳

Q: What do you call a dumb blonde golfer with an IQ of 125?
A: A foursome.

✳✳✳✳

Q: Why do dumb blondes get confused in the ladies toilet?
A: They have to pull their own knickers down.

✳✳✳✳

Q: What is 68 to a dumb blonde?
A: Where she goes down on you and you owe her one.

****

Q: What is an dumb blonde doing when she holds her hands tightly over her ears?
A: Trying to hold on to a thought.

****

Q: Why did the dumb blonde stare at a carton of orange juice for two hours?
A: Because it said 'concentrate'.

****

Q: Why did the dumb blonde take two acid tabs?
A: She wanted to go on a round trip.

****

Q: What's the definition of a metallurgist?
A: A man who can tell if a platinum blonde is a virgin metal or a common ore.

****

Q: How does a dumb blonde commit suicide?
A: She gathers her clothes into a pile and jumps off.

****

Q: Why did God give dumb blondes two per cent more brains than horses?
A: Because he didn't want them shitting in the streets during parades.

****

Q: Why was the dumb blonde disappointed with her trip to London?
A: She found out Big Ben is only a clock.

****

A newly-wed couple were spending their honeymoon in a remote log cabin resort way up in the Alps. They had registered on Saturday and they had not been seen for five days. An elderly couple ran the resort, and they were getting concerned about the welfare of these newly-weds. The old man decided to go and see if they were all right.

He knocked on the door of the cabin and a weak voice from inside answered. The old man asked if they were OK.

'Yes, we're fine. We're living on the fruits of love.'

The old man replied, 'I thought so… would you mind not throwing the peelings out of the window, 'they're choking my ducks!'

****

The young man had asked for a job with the circus – any job, just so he could travel with the circus. The owner of the circus, thinking he might be able to make an assistant lion-tamer out of the young man, took him out to the practice cage.

The head lion-tamer, a beautiful young woman, was just starting her rehearsal. As she entered the cage, she removed her cape with a flourish and, standing in a gorgeous costume, motioned to one of the lions.

Obediently, the lion crept toward the young woman, licked her elbow, and rolled over twice.

'Well,' said the owner to the young man, 'think you could do that?'

'I'm sure I could, sir,' said the young man, 'but you'll have to get that lion out of there.'

****

On The Pull

A guy is sitting at the pub enjoying a pint when a great-looking young woman sits down beside him and gives him a dynamite smile. Just as he's figuring out his opening line, she says in a loud indignant voice that the whole pub can hear

'Your place? Absolutely not!' and she gets up and stomps off to the other end of the bar.

He sits there in confusion and embarrassment, nursing his pint and wondering how to get out of there. After a while, she comes back, sits next to him again, and says in a low voice. 'Look, I'm sorry about that. I'm a graduate student in psychology and I'm conducting an experiment to see how people react in unexpected stressful situations. Please accept my apologies and let me pay for your beer.'

The guy stands up indignantly and says at the top of his voice, 'a £100! You must be joking!'

****

A bloke walks into a pub and orders a pint. After a couple of sips he looks up and sees a woman sitting at the end of the bar. He calls the landlord over and says he'd like to buy the lady a drink.

The landlord says, 'Listen, pal, let me save you some trouble. She's a lesbian.'

The bloke takes a second, thinks it over, shrugs his shoulders and says, 'That's OK. I'd like to buy her a drink anyway.'

So the landlord brings the woman her drink. The woman lifts her glass and gives the man a nod of thanks. The bloke gets up from his bar stool and saunters over to the woman. As he's sitting down on the stool next to her he says, 'So, what part of Lesbia are you from?'

****

As an airplane is about to crash, a female passenger jumps up frantically and announces, 'If I'm going to die, I want to die feeling like a woman.' She removes all her clothing and asks, 'Is there someone on this plane who is man enough to make me feel like a woman?'

A man stands up, removes his shirt and says, 'Here, iron this.'

****

A businessman boards a flight and is lucky enough to be seated next to an absolutely gorgeous woman. They exchange brief hellos and he notices she's reading a manual about sexual statistics. He asks her about it and she replies, 'This is a very interesting book about sexual statistics. It identifies that American Indians have the longest average penis and Polish men have the biggest average girth. By the way, my name is Jill. What's yours?'

'Tonto Kowalski,' he replies, 'nice to meet you.'

****

A guy is tending the bar at a sophisticated party when two toffee-nosed women approach.

'So, where are you two from?' he asks.

'We,' she answers, 'are from somewhere where people don't end their sentences with prepositions.'

'Oh,' says the bartender. 'So, where are you two from, bitch?'

****

This big geezer meets a woman in a pub, and after a number of drinks, they agree to go back to his place. As they're getting it on in the bedroom, ready for the act, he stands up and starts to undress.

After he takes his shirt off, he flexes his muscular arms and says, 'See there, baby? That's 1,000 pounds of dynamite!.'

She begins to drool. The man drops his pants, and strikes a bodybuilder's pose, and says, referring to his bulging legs, 'See those, baby? That's 1,000 pounds of dynamite!'. She is aching for action at this point. Finally, he drops his underpants, and she screams and legs it to the front door.

On The Pull

He catches her before she is able to run out the door, and asks, 'Why are you in such a hurry to leave?'

'With 2,000 pounds of dynamite and such a short fuse,' she replies, 'I was afraid you were about to blow!'

****

Each time this bloke visited this pub he had a little white box with him. The barmaid is finally overcome with interest, and asks, 'What's in the box?'

To which he replies, 'The most amazing frog ever. He loves to go down on women and he is really great.' He suggests she might like to find out just how good the frog is, so they go in the back room where she takes off all her clothes, and spreads her legs apart.

The man then takes the frog out of the box and places him between her legs. After several minutes nothing is happening. The man reaches down and picks the frog up, and shaking him says, 'Now listen; I am going to show you just one more time!'

****

Two men are in a disco and both are pretty drunk when one notices a beautiful woman sitting in the corner. 'Wow,' he says, 'I'd really love to dance with that bird.'

'Well, go ahead and ask her, don't be a chicken,' says his mate.

So the man approaches the lovely woman and says, 'Excuse me? Would you be so kind as to dance with me?'

Seeing the man is totally drunk the woman says, 'I'm sorry. Right now I'm concentrating on matrimony and I'd rather sit than dance.'

So the man humbly returns to his friend. 'So what did she say?' he asks.

'She said she's constipated on macaroni and would rather shit in her pants,' says his friend.

A rich lonely widow decided that she needed another man in her life so she placed an ad, which read something like this: RICH WIDOW LOOKING FOR MAN TO SHARE LIFE AND FORTUNE WITH. QUALIFICATIONS: 1) WON'T BEAT ME UP 2) WON'T RUN AWAY 3) HAS TO BE GREAT IN BED.

For several months, her phone rang off the hook, her doorbell was buzzing constantly and she received tonnes of post, but all to no avail. No one could meet her qualifications.

Then one day the doorbell rang yet again. She opened the door to find a man with no arms and no legs lying on the welcome mat.

Perplexed, she asked, 'Who are you? And what do you want?'

'Hi,' he said, 'your search is over, for I'm the man of your dreams. I've got no arms so I can't beat you up and no legs so I can't run away.'

'Well then,' she said, 'what makes you think that you're so great in bed?'

To which he replied, 'Well, I rang the doorbell, didn't I?'

****

A young woman was depressed because she was flat-chested. So when her fairy godmother appeared one day and offered to grant her most heart-felt wish, the young woman instantly requested large breasts.

'All right, my dear,' said her fairy godmother. 'From this moment on, every time a man says "Pardon" to you, your breasts will grow.'

So the next day the woman was walking down the street, lost in thought, when she bumped into a policeman. 'Pardon me,' said the copper politely. Instantly her breasts grew an inch. She was ecstatic.

A few days later the young woman was doing her shopping at the supermarket. Leaving with a large bag of groceries, she bumped into a another customer. 'Pardon me,' the man said, bending over to help her collect her groceries, and sure enough the young woman's breasts grew another inch. Very happy, she decided to treat herself to dinner at a Chinese restaurant.

Going in the door, she collided with a waiter, who bowed and said, 'Oh, miss, I beg of you a thousand pardons.'

The following morning the headline in the newspaper read, CHINESE WAITER KILLED BY TWO TORPEDOES.

****

A man walks into a chemist and asks for a pack of condoms. As soon as he's paid for them, he starts laughing and walks out. The next day, there's the same performance, with the man walking out pissing himself. Thinking this a bit odd the chemist asks his assistant to follow the man if he returns.

Sure enough, he comes in the next day, repeating his actions once more. The assistant duly follows and half an hour later, he returns.

'So did you follow him?' asked the chemist.

'I did,' replied the assistant.

'And, where did he go?' asked the chemist.

'Over to your house,' says the assistant.

****

A young man goes into a chemist to buy condoms. The chemist tells him that condoms come in packs of three, nine or 12 and asks which the young man wants.

'Well,' he says, 'I've been seeing this girl for a while and she's really hot. I want the condoms because I think tonight's the night. We're having dinner with her parents, and then we're going out. And I've got a feeling I'm gonna get lucky after that. Once she's had me, she'll want me all the time, so you'd better give me the 12-pack.'

The young man makes his purchase and leaves. Later that evening, he sits down to dinner with his girlfriend and her parents. He asks if he might say grace, and they agree. He begins the prayer, but continues praying for several minutes. The girl leans over and says, 'You never told me that you were such a religious person.'

He leans over to her and says, 'You never told me that your father was a chemist.'

On The Pull

****

A young man wanted to purchase a gift for his new sweetheart's birthday, and as they had not been dating very long, after careful consideration he decided a pair of gloves would strike just the right note – romantic, but not too personal. Accompanied by his sweetheart's younger sister, he went to Harrods and bought a pair of white gloves. The sister purchased a pair of panties for herself. During the wrapping, though, the items got mixed up.

Without checking the contents, the young man sealed the package with the panties in it and sent it to his sweetheart along with the following note: 'I chose these because I noticed that you're not in the habit of wearing any when we go out in the evening. If it had not been for your sister I would have chosen the long ones with the buttons, but she wears the short ones that are easier to remove. These are a delicate shade, but the lady I bought them from showed me the pair she had been wearing for the past three weeks and they were hardly soiled. I had her try yours on for me and she looked really smart. I wish I was there to put them on for you the first time, as no doubt other hands will come in contact with them before I have a chance to see you again. When you take them off, remember to blow in them before putting them away as they will naturally be a little damp from wearing. Just think how many times I will kiss them during the coming year. I hope you will wear them for me on Friday night. P.S. The latest style is to wear them folded down with a little fur showing.'

****

A guy on a date parks his car and gets the girl in the back seat. They make love, but the girl wants it again and the guy complies. She wants more and they do it again. She still wants more and the guy says, 'Excuse me a minute, I have to relieve myself.'

While out of the car he notices a man nearby changing a flat tyre.

'Look,' he says to the man. 'I've got this bird in my car and I've given it to her four or five times and she still wants more. I'll change your flat if you'll take over for me.'

So that's what they do. The second guy gets in the car and starts shagging the bird. Suddenly a copper knocks on the window and shines a light on them.

'What are you doing in there?' asks the copper.

'I'm making love to my wife,' replies the guy.

'Why don't you do that at home?' asks the policeman.

'To tell you the truth,' the guy answers, 'I didn't know it was my wife until you shone the light on her.'

****

A guy is shipwrecked on a celebrity cruise and he wakes up stranded on a desert island with Nicole Kidman. After a few weeks they are having passionate sex which is fine for a bit, but the guy starts getting a bit depressed. Nicole comes up to him on the beach one day and says, 'What's the matter?'

'Well, it's wonderful,' he says, 'I'm on a tropical island with a beautiful woman who I love, but… but… I miss my mates. I miss going down the pub with them.'

'Well, I'm an actress,' says Nicole. 'Maybe if I get dressed in some of those male clothes which were left behind in the trunks, I can pretend to be one of your friends, and you can talk to me as if you were down the pub.'

It sounded a bit weird, but he thought he would give it a try. So she gets into the men's clothing and they sit down next to each other.

'Hey, Joe,' says the man. 'You'll never guess who I've been shagging.'

****

A man and his wife have been stranded on a deserted island for many years. One day a new man washes up on shore. He and the wife are attracted to each other right away, but realise certain protocols must be observed.

The husband, however, is very glad to see the second man there. 'Now we will be able to have three people doing eight-hour shifts in the watchtower, rather than two people doing 12-hour shifts.'

The second man is only too happy to help and in fact volunteers to do the first shift there and then. So up the tower he goes and the husband and wife start placing stones in a circle to make a fire to cook supper.

'Hey, no fucking,' the man yells from the tower.

'We're not fucking,' they shout back. A few minutes later they start to put driftwood into the stone circle.

Again the second man yells down, 'Hey, no fucking,' and again they shout back, 'We're not fucking.'

Later they are putting palm leaves on the roof of their shack to patch leaks. Once again the second man yells down, 'Hey, I said no fucking.'

'We're not fucking!' they shout back.

Finally the shift is over and the second man climbs down from the tower and the husband starts to climb up. He's not even halfway up before the wife and second man are screwing each other's brains out. The husband looks out from the tower and says, 'Blimey, he's right. From up here it really does look like they're fucking'.

****

A man and a woman are riding next to each other in a first-class train carriage. The man sneezes, pulls out his wang and wipes the tip off. The woman can't believe what she just saw and decides she is hallucinating.

A few minutes pass. The man sneezes again. He pulls out his wang and again wipes the tip off. The woman is outraged. She can't believe that such a rude person exists. A few minutes pass. The man sneezes yet again, and he takes his wang out and wipes the tip off.

The woman has finally had enough. She turns to the man and says, 'Three times you've sneezed, and three times you've removed your penis from your pants to wipe it! What kind of degenerate are you?'

'I am sorry to have disturbed you, madam,' says the man. 'I have a very rare condition that causes me to have an orgasm every time I sneeze.'

'Oh, how strange,' says the woman. 'What are you taking for it?'

The man looks at her and says, 'Pepper.'

****

The soldier serving overseas was annoyed and upset when his girl wrote breaking off their engagement and asking for her photograph back. So he went out and collected from his friends all the unwanted photographs of women that he could find, bundled them all together and sent them back with a note saying, 'Regret cannot remember which one is you – please keep your photo and return the others.'

****

Mr Rice got himself a new secretary. Melanie was young, sweet and polite. One day while taking dictation she noticed his fly was open and, on leaving the room, she said, 'Oh, Mr Rice, did you know that your barracks door is open?'

He didn't understand her remark, but later on he happened to look down and saw that his fly was open. He decided to have some fun with his new secretary. Calling her in, he asked, 'By the way, Miss Brown, when you saw my barracks door open this morning, did you see a soldier standing at attention?'

'Why, no, Mr Rice,' she replied. 'All I saw was a disabled veteran sitting on two old duffel bags.'

****

A man mets his girl friend from 25 years ago. She was so happy to see him that she couldn't resist and asked him to come up and see her some time.

'With pleasure!' said the man. So he bought some wine and a bunch of flowers and in the evening he went to see her. When the door opens there she was, stark naked.

'What's this?' – the man was shocked.

She smiles and says, 'I wore my birthday suit for you.'

'That's great,' he says, somewhat embarrassed, 'but couldn't you have pressed it first?'

****

A guy goes to a girl's house for the first time, and she shows him into the living room. She excuses herself to go to the kitchen to make them a few drinks, and as he's standing there alone, he notices a cute little vase on the mantelpiece. He picks it up, and as he's looking at it, she walks back in.

'What's this?' he say.

'Oh,' she says, 'my father's ashes are in there.'

'Ooops... I... don't know what to say,' says the guy.

'Yeah I know, it's shocking,' says the girl. 'He's too lazy to go to the kitchen to get an ashtray.'

****

There was a girl who had one huge goal in life. Her goal was to have a baby. She got a bloke into bed with her and as soon as he was ready, she asked, 'What are we gonna name the baby?' He told her he didn't want a baby and that she was crazy. With that he got out of bed and left.

The next weekend the same thing happened. On the third weekend she finally got someone that was really horny. As he got ready to screw her she asked the question: 'What are we gonna name the baby?' The bloke ignored her and went about his business. About half-way through she asked him again only to get ignored again.

When they finally finish she asked him again. He replied, while taking off his condom and tying it in a knot, 'We'll call him Houdini if he can get out of this.'

****

Derek Rourke rented a flat in a large block, and went to the lobby to put his name on the group letterbox. While there, an attractive young woman came out of the flat next to the boxes, wearing a dressing-gown. Del smiled at the young girl and she struck up a conversation with him. As they talked, her dressing gown slipped open and it was quite obvious that she had nothing on under the robe.

Poor Del broke into a sweat trying to maintain eye contact. After a few minutes, she placed her hand on his arm and said, 'Let's go into my flat, I hear someone coming...'

They went inside and after she closed the door, she leaned against it allowing her robe to fall completely open. She purred at him, 'What would you say is my best feature?'

The flustered, embarrassed Del stammered, cleared his throat several times, and finally squeaked out, 'Oh, it's got to be your ears!'

She was astounded! 'Why my ears? Look at these boobs! They are full, don't sag, and they're all mine! My bum's firm, doesn't sag, and has no cellulite! Look at this skin; no blemishes, or scars! Why in heaven's name would you say my ears are the best part of my body?'

Clearing his throat once again, Del stammered, 'Because when we were outside and you said you heard someone coming – well, that was me'

****

One day God came to Adam to pass on some news. 'I've got some good news and some bad news,' God said.

Adam looked at God and said, 'Well, give me the good news first.'

Smiling, God explained, 'I've got two new organs for you. One is called a brain. It will allow you to be very intelligent, create new things, and have intelligent conversations with Eve. The other organ I have for you is called a penis. It will allow you to reproduce your now-intelligent life form and populate this planet. Eve will be very happy that you now have this organ to give her children.'

Adam, very excited, exclaimed, 'These are great gifts you have given to me. What could possibly be bad news after such great tidings?'

God looked upon Adam and said with great sorrow, 'The bad news is that when I created you, I only gave you enough blood to operate one of these organs at a time.'

****

Bill was approaching mid-life and physically he was a mess. Not only was he going bald, but years of office work had given him a large pot-belly. The last straw came when he asked a woman he worked with out on a date, and she all but laughed at him.

'That does it,' thought Bill. 'I'm going to start a whole new regime.' He began attending aerobics classes. He started working out with weights. He changed his diet. And he got an expensive hair transplant. After six months, he was a different man. Again, he asked his female colleague out, and this time she accepted.

So there he was, all dressed up for the date, looking better than he ever had. He stood poised to ring the woman's doorbell, when a bolt of lightning struck him and knocked him off his feet. As he lay there dying, he turned his eyes toward the heavens and said, 'Why, God, why now? After all I've been through, how could you do this to me?'

From up above there came a voice, 'Sorry, I didn't recognise you.'

****

There once was a priest who had to spend the night in a hotel and asked the girl on reception to come up to his room for dinner. After a while he made a pass at her, but she stopped him and reminded him he was a holy man.

'It's OK,' he replied, 'it's written in the Bible.' After a wild night of sex she asked to see where in the Bible it said it was OK, so the priest took the Bible out of the drawer and showed her the first page where someone had written in pencil, 'The girl on reception will shag anybody!'

****

On The Pull

There were three men who died and before God would let them into heaven, he gave them a chance to come back as anything they wanted. The first man said, 'I want to come back as myself, but 100 times brighter.' So God made him 100 times brighter.

The second guy said, 'I want to be better than that bloke, make me 1,000 times brighter.' So God made him 1,000 times brighter.

The last man decided he would be the best. So he said, 'God, make me better than both of them, make me 1,000,000 times brighter.' So God made him a woman.

****

An old man wanders away from a nursing home. He comes upon a pub that looks friendly enough, and no sooner has he sat down at the bar than a young woman comes up to him.

'Would you like a drink?' she asks him.

'I'd love one,' he replies. So she gets him drink.

'Would you like to dance?' she asks him after he's downed the drink.

'Why of course,' he replies. After a short time on the dance-floor she snuggles up close to him and whispers in his ear, 'Would you like to go home with me?'

'Wow,' says the old man, 'I'd love to!'

The next morning the old man goes to confession. 'I am 85 years old,' he says to the priest, 'and I spent last night with a 28-year-old woman.'

The priest thinks about it and decides that an 85-year-old man couldn't have done much damage.

'Go and say ten Hail Marys,' he says to the man.

'I can't do that,' exclaims the old man, 'I'm Jewish.'

'Well, then what are you doing talking to me?' asks the priest.

'Because I'm 85 years old,' replied the old man. 'I'm telling everybody I can!'

****

On The Pull

An old man decides to visit a brothel as it's been a long time since he's had any. After paying the madam, he picks out a cute little blonde girl and they go upstairs. After the preliminaries, he climbs on and starts humping away. 'How am I doing, darling? he asks halfway through.

'About three nots,' she replies.

'Three knots?' he says. 'What does that mean?'

'You're not in, you're not hard, and you're not getting your money back!' she says.

****

A guy is walking down the street and enters a clock and watch shop. While looking around, he notices a drop-dead gorgeous female sales assistant behind the counter. He walks up to the counter where she's standing, unzips his fly, and places his dick on the counter.

'What are you doing, sir?' she asks. 'This is a clock shop!'

'I know it is,' he replies. 'And I'd like two hands and a face put on THIS!!'

****

The lovers passionately embraced on her bed, their bodies fused together as they gyrated. Suddenly the woman cocked her ear.

'Quick! It's my husband coming through the front door. Hide in the bathroom!' she cried.

The lover ran into the bathroom. She hid his clothes under the bed and as she turned back, her husband came through the bedroom door.

'What are you doing lying on the bed naked?' he asked.

'Darling, I heard you coming up the drive and got ready to receive you,' she replied with a knowing smile.

'Great,' he said 'I'll just nip into the bathroom and I'll be with you in two shakes.'

Before she could stop him he was into the bathroom where he found the lover clapping his hand in mid-air.

'Who the fuck are you?' the husband demanded.

'I'm from the pest-control company. Your wife called me in to get rid of these moths,' the lover replied.

'But... but you've got no clothes on' stammered the husband.

The lover looked down, jumped backwards in surprise and said, 'Oh! The little bastards!'

✳✳✳✳

A missionary is walking through the jungle with the chief of the tribe he is teaching. As they walk, they come across a couple making love.

'What is going on here?' says the chief.

The missionary, embarrassed, says, 'Well, uhhhh, chief, he is riding a bicycle.'

So the chief, grunts, pulls out a blow-gun and shoots a poisoned dart into the man's back.

'Chief, you shouldn't have killed him,' shouts the missionary. 'It was a perfectly natural act they were performing. Why did you have to kill him?'

'He was riding my bicycle!' says the chief.

✳✳✳✳

Young Tony was courting Polly, who lived on an adjoining farm. One evening, as they were sitting on Tony's tractor watching the sun go down over the hills, Tony spied his prize bull doing the business on one of his cows. He sighed in contentment at this idyllic rural scene and figured it was a good omen about finally getting to shag Polly.

He leaned in close and whispered in her ear, 'Polly, I'd sure like to be doing what that bull is doing.'

'Well then, why don't you?' Polly whispered back. 'It's your cow.'

The elegant young lady was strolling through the zoo and walked all the way around the monkey house. There wasn't an ape or a monkey to be seen, so she sought out the keeper.

'Why are there no monkeys on view?' she asked, her displeasure evident.

'It's mating season,' replied the keeper bluntly. 'They're back in their caves.'

'But I want to see them. Will they come out if I throw them some peanuts?' she asked coolly.

'I dunno, lady,' he answered, looking her over. 'Would you?'

****

This professor had a lie-detecting chair. Whenever anybody sitting on it told a lie, the chair would open up and the person would fall flat on the ground. As a part of his experiment a young brunette came in and sat down. The professor asked her to talk about herself.

'I think,' she began, 'I'm the most beautiful girl in this region, and perhaps even in the whole world!' Immediately after she said that the chair opened up and she landed flat on her arse. She stormed out and a young blonde was invited in to sit on the chair.

She sat down and was invited to talk about herself. 'I think…' she began, and suddenly the chair opened up and she fell flat on her arse!

****

Two dwarfs decide to treat themselves to a vacation in Las Vegas. At the hotel bar, they're dazzled by two women, and wind up taking them to their separate rooms. The first dwarf is disappointed, however, as he's unable to reach a certain physical state that would enable him to shag his bird. His depression is enhanced by the fact that from the next room he hears cries of, 'ONE, TWO, THREE… HUH!' all night long.

The following morning they both meet up. 'How did it go?' his friend asked him.

'It was so embarrassing,' he replied. 'I simply couldn't get an erection.'

On The Pull

The second dwarf shook his head. 'You think that's embarrassing?' he said. 'I couldn't even jump up on the bed!'

****

A shipwreck left three men and one woman on a desert island. They wanted to be fair, and since none of them was promiscuous, they decided that each man would marry the woman for a week at a time and then divorce her. The one-week marriage arrangement went on for about nine weeks and everybody was happy until one day the woman caught a mysterious illness and died. The first week after that was bad; the week after was worse and the week after that was terrible. Then, on the fourth week they buried her.

****

A new recruit arrives in the desert with the Foreign Legion. After a couple of weeks he's feeling in need of some release, so he asks one of his colleagues what they do for sex. The other soldier makes a gesture towards a camel that's tied up nearby and leaves it at that.

The new recruit suddenly loses his sexual appetite, but as the weeks go by it builds up and up and eventually, after two months, he can't control himself any longer and gives the camel the rogering of his life.

The next day he sees the other soldier again and says to him, 'You know that camel? It was one of the best shags of my life.'

'Really?' says the soldier, 'we use it to ride to the brothel in the village.'

****

Very late one night a policeman spotted a lad and a girl sitting in a parked car. The lad was reading and the woman was knitting.

'Excuse me, sir, can you tell what you're doing?' asked the copper.

'Well, I'm reading, officer,' replied the man.

'I see, and what about you, miss, what are you doing?'

'I'm knitting,' said the girl.

'I see,' replied the policeman, 'and can I ask exactly how old you are, madam?'

'Well,' she said glancing at her watch, 'in 15 minutes I shall be 16.'

****

A brunette, a redhead and a blonde all went to see their obstetrician. Trying to make conversation, the brunette said, 'I'm going to have a boy. I'm sure of it because I was on top.'

The redhead said, 'I know I'm going to have a girl. I'm sure because I was on the bottom.'

The blonde suddenly burst into tears. The other women tried to comfort her and asked what was wrong. 'I think I'm going to have puppies,' she sobbed.

****

A computer programmer was on holiday on a cruise ship in the Caribbean for the first time. It was wonderful; the experience of a lifetime. He was being waited on hand and foot. Unfortunately it did not last. A hurricane blew in unexpectedly, and the ship went down almost instantly.

The programmer found himself swept up on the shore of an uncharted island. There was nothing to be seen anywhere: no people, no supplies, nothing. The man foraged around. There were some bananas and coconuts, but that was it. He was desperate and forlorn, but decided to make the best of it. So for the next four months he ate bananas, drank coconut juice and mostly looked out to sea hopefully for a ship to come to his rescue.

One day, as he was lying on the beach stroking his beard and looking for a ship, he spotted movement out of the corner of his eye. Could it be true, was it a ship? No, from around the corner of the island came this rowboat. In it was the most gorgeous woman he had ever seen, or at least seen in four months. She was tall, tanned, and her blonde hair flowing in the sea breeze gave her an almost ethereal quality.

When she saw him waving and yelling and screaming to get her attention, she rowed her boat toward him. Overjoyed, he asked, 'Where did you come from? How did you get here?'

'I rowed from the other side of the island,' she said. 'I landed on this island when my cruise ship sank.'

'Amazing,' he said, 'I didn't know anyone else had survived. How many of you are there? Where did you get the rowboat? You must have been really lucky to have a rowboat wash up with you!'

'It's only me,' she said, 'and the rowboat didn't wash up. Nothing did.'

'Well, then,' said the man, 'how did you get the rowboat?'

'I made it out of raw material I found on the island,' replied the woman. The oars were whittled from gum tree branches, I wove the bottom from Palm branches, and the sides and stern came from a eucalyptus tree.'

'But,' asked the man, 'what about tools and hardware? How did you manage that?'

'Oh, no problem,' replied the woman. 'On the south side of the island there is a very unusual stratum of alluvial rock exposed. I found that if I fired it to a certain temperature in my kiln, it melted into forgeable ductile iron. I used that for tools, and used the tools to make the hardware. But enough of that,' she said. 'Where do you live?' At last the man was forced to confess that he'd been sleeping on the beach.

'Well, let's row over to my place,' she said. So they both got into the rowboat and left for her side of the island. The woman easily rowed them around to a wharf that led to the approach to her place. She tied up the rowboat with a beautifully-woven hemp rope. They walked up a stone walk and around a palm tree, and there stood an exquisite bungalow painted in blue and white.

'It's not much,' she said, 'but I call it home. Sit down, please. Would you like to have a drink?'

'No,' said the man, 'one more coconut juice and I'll puke.'

'It won't be coconut juice,' the woman replied. 'I have a still. How about a Piña Colada?' Trying to hide his continued amazement, the man accepted, and they sat down on her couch to talk.

After a while, having exchanged their stories, the woman asked, 'Tell me, have you always had a beard?'

'No,' the man replied, 'I was clean-shaven all of my life, even on the cruise ship.'

'Well, if you would like to shave, there is a man's razor upstairs in the cabinet in the bathroom.'

So the man, no longer questioning anything, went upstairs to the bathroom. There in the cabinet was a razor made from a bone handle, two shells honed to a hollow-ground edge were fastened on to its end inside of a swivel mechanism. The man shaved, showered and went back downstairs.

'You look great,' said the woman. 'I think I'll go up and slip into something more comfortable.'

While she was gone, the man continued to sip his pina colada. After a short time, the woman returned wearing fig-leaves strategically positioned and smelling faintly of gardenia.

'Tell me,' she said, 'we've both been out here for a very long time with no companionship. You know what I mean. Have you been lonely? Is there anything that you really miss? Something that all men and women need. Something that it would be really nice to have right now?'

'Yes, there is,' the man replied, as he moved closer to the woman while fixing a winsome gaze upon her. 'Tell me... do you happen to have a set of golf clubs?'

****

There was a small bakery shop in a town that had a very attractive female assistant and it became known throughout the town that the pretty woman didn't like to wear panties under her skirt while she was at work.

Men would come in to the store, all day long, to buy a loaf of raisin bread because when they requested raisin bread, the assistant would have to climb a ladder to reach the bread on a high shelf behind the counter which revealed quite a show for the male customers.

As the day went on, the woman became quite exhausted from climbing the ladder to fetch raisin bread and just as she was on the ladder retrieving another loaf of raisin bread for a customer, an elderly gentleman walked into the bakery to purchase a pie for his wife.

The assistant shouted down to the old man, who was pretending not to be looking up and asked, 'Sir, I'll bet yours is raisin, too?'

The old gentleman replied, 'No, it isn't, but it is starting to twitch.'

****

A shy young student had been asked out for a date by a particularly good-looking and intelligent bloke from the college. She was determined not to look stupid and spent much of the time before the evening reading the quality newspapers and brushing up on her political and philosophical viewpoints. The pair met in the Student Union bar.

'Two pints,' ordered the bloke.

Not to be outdone the girl said, 'Two pints for me, too, please.'

****

A bloke's giving head to a woman. 'My word! You've got a large vagina. My word! You've got a large vagina,' he says.

'There's no need to say it twice,' says the woman.

'I didn't,' says the man.

****

A sheep farmer was very concerned because none of his sheep were producing offspring. He was chatting with a neighbouring farmer who told him that he had the horniest ram in the world and would give him a lend of the beast.

'But how will I know if it's worked?' asked the first farmer.

'Well,' said the second, 'if, in the morning, your sheep are at the top of the hill, they're pregnant. If they're at the bottom, they're not.'

So the very next morning the farmer loaded his sheep into his truck and took them round to his neighbour's farm. After leaving them for a good while he took them back home and the next morning looked out of the window. He was dismayed to find his flock at the bottom of the hill, so he loaded them into the truck again and took them back round to his neighbour's. This time he left them even longer, but the following morning when he looked out of the window they were still at the bottom of the hill. Hoping it would be third time lucky, he set off for his neighbour's farm again and this time left the sheep with the ram for what seemed like an age. The following morning he couldn't bring himself to look out of the window so he asked his wife to do so.

'Are the sheep at the bottom of the hill?' he asked her.

'No,' she replied.

'So are they at the top of the hill?' he asked excitedly.

'No,' she replied.

'Well, where are they then?' he said.

'They're in the truck,' said his wife, 'and one of them is honking the horn.'

****

Two fleas are chatting in an airport lounge. 'That's a nasty cold you've got there,' says one.

'Yeah,' says the other. 'I nestled down in a biker's moustache and must have caught it as he was driving along here.'

'Listen,' said the first. 'You should do what I do and find a stewardess. Hole up in her pubic hair and you'll be nice and warm.'

The following week the two fleas meet up again and the one with the cold is no better. 'Why didn't you do what I suggested and find a stewardess?' said the first.

'I did,' said the other, 'but before I knew it I was back in the biker's moustache.'

****

An ant and an elephant get it together and have a fantastic night of non-stop sex. Unfortunately, when the ant wakes up in the morning, the elephant is dead.

'Oh shit,' moaned the ant. 'I get one night of heaven and a life-time digging a grave.'

****

Two guys are driving out in the country when their car breaks down. After a look in the engine one of them decided that if they can get some Vaseline they might just make it to the next garage. So they head off to the farmhouse in the distance.

It just so happens that in the farmhouse the farmer, his wife and two daughters are having an argument about who should hang out the washing. Eventually the father decides that the next person who speaks shall do the chore.

At that moment the two guys arrive and knock on the door. There's no reply, so they go in. They try to introduce themselves to the family but get no response and so, reckoning the family are deaf and dumb, start fooling around with one of the daughters. Before long they've both shagged her and move on to the other daughter and then the mother.

Suddenly one of them remembers why they came to the house in the first place.

'Do you have any Vaseline?' he asks.

'Right, that's it,' says the father. 'I'll hang the washing out.'

****

A Doberman and a poodle are at the vet's. 'What are you here for?' asks the poodle.

'Well,' says the Doberman. 'The other day I got really horny. So I fucked the pillow, I fucked the mattress, I fucked the settee, I fucked the letter box, and then I ran outside and fucked every bitch in the area. Now I'm being neutered. What about you?'

'Well,' says the poodle. 'I also got really horny the other day. I fucked the pillow, I fucked the mattress, I fucked a piece of meat in the kitchen and then I fucked my master's wife who was doing the dishes.'

'So you're going to be neutered, too?' says the Doberman.

'No,' replies the poodle. 'I'm here for a manicure.'

****

A guy goes to a brothel with only a fiver in his pocket.

'I'm sorry, sir,' says the madam. ' The only thing we've got for a fiver is a goat.'

Reluctantly, the guy agrees and goes off to give the kid a damn fine rogering. A week later he's back, but this time he's only got a pound on him.

'I'm sorry, sir,' says the madam, 'but for a pound the only thing we've got is a peep show.'

So he goes in and discovers lots of blokes watching a man toss off a donkey.

'Christ,' says the guy, 'I've never seen anything like this before.'

'You should have been here last week,' says the bloke next to him. There was a guy in there shagging a goat.'

****

Dave the lad has struck it lucky with a bit of well posh tottie. They've been going out together for three months when he gets invited round to her parents' house for dinner. He puts on his best clobber and sitting nervously at the table, is trying his hardest to be polite and courteous.

The first course is a particularly heavy soup, after which Dave has a terrible desire to fart. Much as he tries to hold it in, out comes the slightest of bottom burps.

'Rover!' shouts his girlfriend's dad, and to Dave's immense relief he spots a large dog lying under the table.

'Fucking brilliant,' thinks Dave. 'The old boy thinks it was the dog. I'm in the clear.'

The second course is also very heavy with all the trimmings and once again Dave has to fart afterwards. This time though he lets one rip with rather more bravado.

'Rover!' shouts the Dad again. By now Dave is well relaxed and after the pudding throws caution to the wind and lets rip with a real earbuster.

'Rover!' shouts the Dad. 'Get out of there before he shits on you!'

****

They set up the greatest whorehouse in the world. On the ground floor are the French beauties. On the first floor are the Swedish nymphettes. On the second floor are the African Amazons and on the third floor is the whore of whores. The first customer is this big stud. He pays his money and goes in. After half an hour they go to find him. The French beauties are all exhausted and the guy is crawling up the stairs to the Swedish nymphettes.

The next customer is an even bigger stud who pays his money and goes in. After half an hour, they find him halfway up the stairs heading towards the African Amazons, gasping for air.

The third customer is the biggest man-mountain in the world. He slaps his money on the table and struts in. Half an hour later they find him scratching at the door of the whore of whores, on his last legs.

The next bloke to come in is a little geezer with glasses. After they've stopped laughing they take his money and give him five minutes before going to find him. On the ground floor the French beauties are packing their bags and leaving. The Swedish nymphettes on the first floor are aching all over, the African Amazons are hanging out of the windows for air and they find the whore of whores cowering in the corner of her room.

'My God,' they say. 'Where's the little geezer?'

'He's out on the balcony,' whispers the whore of whores, 'having a wank.'

****

Pierre the French fighter pilot was holding his gilrfriend Marie in an amorous embrace. Suddenly, he pulls away from her and pours red wine over her lips.

'Pierre, Pierre, what are you doing?' she demands.

'I am Pierre the French fighter pilot and before I taste red meat, I must taste red wine,' he replies.

As things get saucier, Pierre ripped off Marie's blouse and pours white wine over her breasts.

'Pierre, Pierre, what are you doing?' demands Marie again.

'I am Pierre the French fighter pilot and before I taste white meat, I must taste white wine,' he replies.

As things get even steamier Marie was begging Pierre to go down on her when he ripped off her panties, poured brandy between her legs and lit it.

'Pierre, Pierre, what are you doing?' screamed Marie.

'I am Pierre the French fighter pilot,' said Pierre. 'And when I go down, I go down in flames.'

****

A dumb blonde goes in to the doctor's office for a pregnancy test. A short time later, the doctor returns with the results.

'Yes, madam, you're pregnant!' he announces, beaming.

The dumb blonde is stunned. 'Oh my God,' she says, 'is it mine?'

****

A fantastic-looking woman was walking down the road in the tightest of tight body-hugging jeans one day. It was amazing that she could actually walk in them. Eventually a plucky geezer went up to her and asked, 'Your trousers are incredible. How could anyone get into them?'

'Well,' replied the woman, 'you could start by buying me a drink.'

****

Two mates were chatting down the pub one day. 'You know, no matter what type of girl I bring home, my mother always disapproves and hates her,' complained the one guy.

'I'll tell you what,' said his mate. 'Find a bird who is just like your mum in looks and personality. She can't hate her then.'

A couple of weeks later they meet up again. 'Did you find a bird just like your mum?' asked the one lad.

'Yeah, I did. It was uncanny. She even spoke and dressed like her,' said the other.

'So, what happened?' said the first lad.

'Oh,' replied the second lad, 'when I got her home, my dad hated her.'

****

An irate woman rang up her local vet in the middle of the night and asked him if he could do anything about a dog and a bitch who were making a lot of noise hard at it in her garden.

'Why don't you try telling them they're wanted on the phone?' suggested the vet through slightly clenched teeth.

'Do you think that'll stop them?' asked the woman.

'Well, it worked on me,' replied the vet.

****

An attractive secretary walks into her boss's office and announces that she has some good news and some bad news. Harassed, the boss angrily snaps, 'Look, I haven't got much time today, just tell me the good news.'

'OK then,' says the secretary, 'the good news is that you're not shooting blanks.'

****

Billy goes to the doctor and says, 'Doc, I'm having trouble getting my penis erect. Can you help me?'

After a complete examination the doctor tells Billy that the problem with him is that the muscles around the base of his penis are damaged.

There is nothing he can do for him unless he's willing to try an experimental treatment. Billy asks sadly, 'What is the treatment?'

'Well,' the doctors explains, 'what we would do is take the muscles from the trunk of a baby elephant and implant them in your penis.'

Billy thinks about it for a while then decides that the thought of going through life without ever having sex again is too much, and tells the doctor to go for it.

A few weeks after the operation Billy is given the green light to use his improved equipment. So he plans a romantic evening with this girl that he's been meaning to ask out for a while but didn't dare to until now.

They go to this very nice restaurant in the city. In the middle of dinner Billy feels a stirring between his legs that continues to the point of being uncomfortable. To release the pressure, he unzips his fly under the table thinking nobody is going to see it anyway, but his penis immediately springs from his trousers, grabs a roll from the table and returns to his gaping fly.

His date was completely stunned at first but then says with a sly smile, 'That was incredible! Can you do that again?'

To which Billy replied, 'Well, I guess so, but I don't think I can fit another roll up my arse.'

****

Running Bear finally woke up one morning to discover that he was a man. As such, he deduced, he would require a woman. So he trekked on over to the Medicine Man's teepee to requisition a woman.

'What you want, Running Bear?' queried the Medicine Man.

'Running Bear want woman!'

'Hmmm,' said the Medicine Man, 'do you know what to do with a woman once you've got her?'

'Uh,' said Running Bear, 'no…'

'Then go into the woods for two months. Find a tree with a hole in it, and practice on the tree. Once you have perfected your technique with the tree, come back to me and I will give you a woman.'

Running Bear agreed, and set off into the woods. Sure enough, he found a tree with the appropriately sized hole, and began his two months of practice.

Two months later, he returned to the Medicine Man with pride in his eyes. 'OK,' he said to the Medicine Man, 'me know what to do. Give me woman.'

The Medicine Man nodded and brought a pretty young squaw from the back of the teepee. 'Little Flower,' he said to her, 'you now belong to Running Bear. Do as he asks.'

Running Bear and Little Flower then retire to a vacant teepee where Running Bear instructs her to bend over. She shrugs and complies. Running Bear then gives her a swift kick in the arse.

'Hey!' cried Little Flower. 'What did you do that for?'

'Me no stupid,' explained Running Bear. 'Me check for bees first.'

✱✱✱✱

A young woman in a REALLY skimpy skirt was at the bus stop. When the bus arrived and the doors opened she tried to climb the steps. However, her skirt was too tight and her legs couldn't move. So, she reached behind her and undid her zip. She tried to step up again, and still couldn't, so she reached behind again and played with the zip. She tried to climb the steps again, but still no luck. So, she reached behind again, but a pair of strong hands picked her up and placed her on the top step.

'What do you think you're doing?' she asked the guy behind her.

'Well, I figured the second time you undid my fly we were at least good friends!'

✱✱✱✱

One evening after attending the theatre, two men were walking down the street when they saw a well-dressed, attractive young woman walking just ahead of them. One turned to the other and said, 'I'd give 50 quid to spend the night with that woman.'

To their surprise, the woman turned and said, 'I'll take you up on that.'

After bidding his friend goodnight the man accompanied the woman to her apartment, where they immediately went to bed. The following morning the man presented her with 25 quid as he prepared to leave.

'If you don't give me the other 25 quid I'll sue you for it,' said the woman.

The man just laughed and said, 'I'd like to see you get it on these grounds.'

The next day he was surprised when he was served with a summons ordering his presence in court as defendant. He hurried to his lawyer and explained the details of the case.

His lawyer said, 'She can't possibly get a judgement against you on such grounds, but it will be interesting to see how her case will be presented.'

After the usual preliminaries, the woman's lawyer addressed the court as follows: 'Your Honour, my client is the owner of a piece of property, a garden spot surrounded by a profuse growth of shrubbery, which property she agreed to rent to the defendant for a specified length of time for the sum of £50. The defendant took possession of the property, used it extensively for the purpose for which it was rented, but upon evacuating the premises tendered only £25. The rent is not excessive since it was restricted property, and we ask judgment to be granted against the defendant to assure payment of the balance.'

The defendant's lawyer was impressed and amused at the way the case had been presented. His defence was therefore somewhat altered from what he had planned.

'Your Honour,' he responded, 'my client agrees the young lady has a fine piece of property, for a degree of pleasure was derived from the transaction. However, my client found a well on the property, around which he placed his own stones, sank a shaft and erected a pump, all labour being personally performed by him. We claim these improvements to the property are sufficient to offset the unpaid balance, and that the plaintiff was adequately compensated for the rental of the said property. We therefore ask that the judgment not be granted.'

The young woman's lawyer's comeback was this: 'Your Honour, my client agrees that the defendant did find a well on the property, and he did make improvements such as described by my opponent; however, had the defendant not known the well existed, he would never have rented the property; also, on evacuating the premises, the defendant moved the stones, pulled out the shaft and took the pump with him. In so doing he not only dragged his equipment through the shrubbery, but left the hole much larger than it was prior to his occupancy, making it easily accessible to little children. We therefore ask that judgment be granted.'

****

There once was a man who had three girlfriends, and he couldn't decide which one to marry. He decided to give £5,000 to each woman to see what she would do with it. The first woman bought new clothes for herself. She got an expensive new hairdo, a massage, a facial, a manicure, and a pedicure. She said, 'I spent the money so that I would look pretty for you because I love you so much.'

The second woman bought a VCR, a CD player, a set of golf clubs and a tennis racket and gave them to the man. 'I used the money to buy you these gifts because I love you,' she told him.

The third woman invested the money in the stock market and within a short time had doubled her investment. She returned the initial £5,000 to the man and reinvested the profit. 'I'm investing in our future because I love you so much,' she said.

The man carefully considered how each woman had spent the money, and then married the woman with the biggest tits.

****

We all know how Cinderella wanted to go to the ball but her wicked stepmother wouldn't let her and then the fairy godmother pops up and gives Cinderella some good news. The fairy godmother tells Cinderella that she'll provide everything she needs to go to the ball, but only on two conditions.

Cinderella asks what she needs to do and the fairy godmother replies, 'First, you must wear a diaphragm.'

Cinderella's mouth drops open and says, 'You must be crazy! I'm on the pill, and I don't need to wear a diaphragm.'

The fairy godmother reminds Cinderella about all the handsome princes that will be attending the ball that night, and Cinderella agrees to wear a diaphragm.

'Well, what's the second condition?' Cinderella asks.

The fairy godmother replies, 'You must be back home by 2am.'

Well, Cinderella explains that if she's gonna party with the princes, she wants to be out all night long. The fairy godmother tells Cinderella that if she's not home by 2am, then her diaphragm will turn into a pumpkin and reminds her that at least she'll be with the princes most of the evening, so Cinderella agrees to be home at 2am.

At 2am, Cinderella doesn't show up. By 3am, there's still no Cinderella. By 4am, still no Cinderella... finally, at 5am, Cinderella shows up at the door with a huge grin on her face.

The fairy godmother stands up and looks at Cinderella and says, 'Where the hell have you been? Your diaphragm was supposed to turn into a pumpkin three hours ago!!!'

Cinderella tells the fairy godmother that she met a prince and he took care of it for her. The fairy godmother wonders about a prince with this type of power and asks Cinderella his name – to which she sheepishly replies, 'Peter, Peter the pumpkin-eater.'

****

Jill was sitting around with her mum, waiting for a bus, on a particularly cold day. When Jill started to complain her mother told her the way to get warm and to be very lady-like is to put your hands between your legs so that they can warm up. Jill tried this, and was amazed at how well it did warm her hands.

A month later Jill and her boyfriend, Paul, were parked up at Lover's Leap when Jill started to feel the cold. Again, very lady-like, she placed her hands together and put them between her legs. Quite bewildered, her boyfriend asked what she was doing, So Jill explained how it warms your hands. Fifteen minutes later Paul starts rubbing his hands together and complaining about the cold... Jill gently takes his hands and very lady-like places them between her legs. Ten minutes later Paul starts rubbing his nose saying how cold it feels. After a short time Paul complains how his penis is so cold it has gone stiff...

The next morning Jill's mother asks how she coped with the cold night. 'Fine, mum,' she replied, 'but penises make a right mess when they thaw out, don't they?'

****

King Arthur was getting ready to go on a quest, but was worried about leaving Queen Guinevere alone with all the horny knights of the Round Table. So he went to Merlin the Magician for advice.

After explaining his problem to Merlin, the wizard thought about the problem for a while and then told the king to come back in a week and he would have a solution to the problem.

The next week the king returned to Merlin to see the new invention. It was a chastity belt, except that it had a rather large hole in the most obvious place.

'This is no good,' said the king . 'Look at this opening. How is this supposed to protect the queen?'

'Ah sire, just observe,' said Merlin as he pulled out an old wand that he was going to throw away. Merlin then inserted the wand into the hole in the chastity belt whereupon a guillotine blade came down and cut the wand neatly in two halves.

'Merlin, you are a genius. Now I can leave knowing that my Queen is fully protected,' said the king.

After putting Guinevere in the device, King Arthur then set out on his quest. Several years later the King returned to Camelot. Immediately, the king assembled all the Knights of the Round Table into the courtyard and had them drop their trousers for inspection. Sure enough every knight was either amputated or damaged in some way, all except for Sir Galahad.

'Sir Galahad, you are the one and only true knight. What is in my power to grant you? Name it and it is yours,' said the King.

Sir Galahad was speechless.

****

A doctor was giving a talk on safe sex and was asking the class who had sex once a week. Most of the hands went up. He then asked who had it once a month. A few hands went up. This went on for a while until the doctor noticed that only one man had not put his hand up.

'And how often do you have sex?' asked the doctor.

'Once every two years,' replied the man happily.

'Once every two years!!' said the doctor. 'You don't seem too unhappy.'

'Well, tonight's the night!' replied the man.

****

A new recruit arrived in a remote fort in the desert for his first day in the French Foreign Legion. He asked the sergeant what the men did for recreation. 'You'll see soon enough,' said the sergeant.

A week later, 300 camels were herded in to a corral and the men went wild trying to fuck the camels.

The new recruit was a bit stunned. 'Why do the men rush?' he asked. 'There are hundreds of camels and only 50 men.'

'That is true,' said the sergeant. 'But do you want to be stuck with the ugly one?'

****

An agent discovered that his leading actress had been selling her body. Having long lusted after her, he asked if he could have a go as well. She said to him, 'OK, but you'll have to pay the same as everyone else.'

He thought this was a bit unfair but agreed and met at her flat later that night. He turned the lights out and they fucked. She fell asleep. Ten minutes later he woke her up and fucked her again. This went on for two hours.

She was amazed at her agent's vitality.

'I never knew agents were so virile,' she said to him.

'I'm not your agent,' came the reply. 'He's at the door selling tickets.'

****

An 84-year-old man went to a famous brothel. 'I want a girl please,' he said.

'I'm sorry?' said the receptionist.

'I want a girl, please,' said the old man.

'How old are you?' said the receptionist.

'Eighty-four,' he replied.

'Eighty-four? You've had it,' she said.

'Oh, have I?' said the old man. 'How much do I owe you?'

****

A blonde gets on an airplane and sits down in the first-class section. The stewardess tells her she must move to economy because she doesn't have a first-class ticket. The blonde replies, 'I'm blonde, I'm smart, I have a good job and I'm staying in first class until we reach Jamaica.'

The stewardess gets the head stewardess who asks the woman to leave and she says, 'I'm blonde, I'm smart, I have a good job and I'm staying in first class until we reach Jamaica.'

The stewardesses don't know what to do because they have to get the rest of the passengers seated to take off, so they get the co-pilot. The co-pilot goes up to the blonde and whispers in her ear. She immediately gets up and goes to her seat in the economy section.

The head stewardess asks the co-pilot what he said to get her to move. The co-pilot replies, 'I told her the front half of the airplane wasn't going to Jamaica.'

****

One day this fellow noticed that a new couple had moved into the house next door. He was also quick to notice that the woman liked to sunbathe in the back garden, usually in a skimpy bikini that showed off her magnificent breasts. He made it a point to water and trim his lawn as much as possible, hoping for yet another look. Finally, he could stand it no more. Walking to the front door of the new neighbour's house, he knocked and waited. The husband, a large, burly man, opened the door.

'Excuse me,' our man stammered, 'but I couldn't help noticing how beautiful your wife is.'

'Yeah? So?' his hulking neighbour replied.

'Well, in particular, I'm really struck by how beautiful her breasts are. I would gladly pay you £10,000 if I could kiss them.'

The burly gorilla is about to deck our poor guy when his wife appears and stops him. She pulls him inside and they discuss the offer for a few moments. Finally, they return and ask our friend to step inside.

'OK,' the husband says gruffly, 'for ten thousand quid you can kiss my wife's tits.'

At this the wife unbuttons her blouse, and the twin objects of desire hang free at last. Our man takes one in each hand, and proceeds to rub his face against them in total ecstasy. This goes on for several minutes, until the husband gets annoyed.

'Well, come on, kiss them!' he growls.

'I can't,' replies our awe-struck hero, still nuzzling away.

'Why not?' demands the husband, getting really angry now.

'I don't have ten thousand quid.'

****

It was a cold, dark winter night (aren't they all?), and this is woman driving home through the countryside, when suddenly she her tire blows out and she has to stop the car. Since it's late and she doesn't relish the thought of changing the wheel, she walks to a nearby farmhouse to ask if she can stay the night and phone a garage in the morning to fix the car. The farmer agrees to let her stay in his house as long as she doesn't touch the farmers' two sons.

On The Pull

The farmer explains that his wife has died when the boys were young and due to the farm's isolation, the two, who are now young men, have never seen a woman at close quarters before. So the woman goes to bed and halfway through the night, she starts to feel quite randy, and decides to pay one of the lads a visit.

Now, being a careful and sensible woman, she gives him a condom to wear, telling him it will prevent her from getting pregnant. After they make love she goes back to bed. Unfortunately, soon afterwards, she gets the urge again, and goes to see the other son. Once again giving him a condom to wear, they make love.

The next morning she thanks the farmer for his hospitality and phones the garage and goes on her way. Three months later the two sons are working in the fields together, and they discuss their experience with the woman.

The youngest son asks the eldest son, 'Do you really care if that woman gets pregnant?'

'No, not at all,' replies the eldest.

'Well, why don't we take off these damn rubber things, then?'

****

This bloke took a blind date to a fair. They went for a ride on the Ferris wheel. The ride completed, she seemed rather bored. 'What would you like to do next?' he asked.

'I wanna get weighed,' she said.

So the bloke took her over to the guess-your-weight.

'Eight stone,' said the man at the scale, and he was absolutely right.

Next they rode the roller-coaster. After that, he bought her some popcorn and some candyfloss, then he asked what else she would like to do.

'I wanna get weighed,' she sighed. I really latched on to a saddo tonight, thought the young man, and using the excuse that he had developed a headache, he took the girl home.

The girl's mother was surprised to see her home so early, and asked, 'What's wrong, dear? Didn't you have a nice time tonight?'

'Wousy,' said the girl.

****

Two engineering students meet on campus one day. The first engineer calls out to the other, 'Hey, nice bike! Where did you get it?'

'Well,' replies the other, 'I was walking to a lecture the other day when this pretty young student rides up on this bike. She jumps off, takes off all of her clothes, and says 'You can have ANYTHING you want!!'

'Clever,' says the first, 'her clothes wouldn't have fitted you anyway.'

****

Q: What's the difference between a vitamin and a hormone?
A: You can't hear a vitamin.

****

Q: How do blonde braincells die?
A: Alone.

****

Q: Why is a blonde like a turtle?
A: They both get fucked up when they're on their back.

****

Q: Why are blondes bad with cattle?
A: Because they can't keep two calves together!

****

Q: Why do blondes have orgasms?
A: So they know when to stop having sex!

****

Man: You should learn to iron, then we could do without the ironing lady.
Blonde wife: Well, if you would learn to fuck me properly we could do without the gardener.

****

Q: How can you tell that a blonde's having a bad day.
A: She has a Tampax tucked behind her ear, and she can't find her pencil.

****

Q: Why do men like blonde jokes?
A: Because they can understand them.

****

Q: What kind of clothes are there?
Woman replies: Clean and dirty
Man replies: Clean, almost clean, sort of clean, not bad, dirty, really dirty, pretty shitty, nasty and smelly, really, really shitty. Men will voluntarily wear all but the last of these clothes listed.

****

Q: How was Colonel Sanders a typical male?
A: All he cared about were legs, breasts, and thighs.

****

Q: What would men do if they had breasts?
A: They'd stay at home and play with them all day.

****

Q: Why do men find it difficult to make eye contact?
A: Breasts don't have eyes.

****

Q: Why do men get paid twice as much to complete the same job?
A: The woman can do it right the first time.

****

Q: How can you tell if a man is sexually excited?
A: He's breathing.

****

Q. What did the Leper say to the Hooker?
A. Keep the tip

****

Q: How do you get a blonde pregnant?
A: Come on her shoes and let the flies do the rest.

****

Q: Why did the pervert cross the road?
A: To get to the chicken!

****

Q: What's an Essex girl's favourite wine?
A: 'I wanna go to Spaiiiiiiiiiin.'

On The Wagon

8

Jokes for Drying Out

Now, strange as it may seem, there are non-alcoholic drinks available in a pub. And, incredibly, some people do choose to drink them. Now, for most folk the only time they consider getting within a hundred miles of an orange juice is if they're having a bad acid trip or if it's mixed with some other highly alcoholic beverage, but there are those who, because they've overdone it a bit in the past or are only aged nine and are in one of those pubs that allow children in, undergo a more sedate pub experience altogether.

Not for them the deep belly laughs and bits of dribble down the shirt-front of the full, raucous, pissed night out. Their evening is one of gentle banter and amusing jokes, that neither offend nor insult. Incredibly, such jokes do actually exist…

****

'Jimmy, did your mother help you with your homework last night?' the teacher asked.

'No, she did it all,' he replied.

****

Two guys are walking in the jungle. One is carrying a lamp-post, the other one has a telephone box. 'Why are you carrying a telephone box?' the first one asked.

'When the lions come,' says the second, 'I'll put it down, get inside it and I'll be saved'

'Oh,' says the first.

'And why are you carrying a lamp-post?' asks the one carrying the telephone box. 'When the lions come,' he replies, 'I'll throw it away, so I can run faster.'

****

A teacher was working with a group of underprivileged children, trying to broaden their horizons through sensory exploration. With their eyes closed, they would feel objects from pumice stones to pine cones and smell aromatic herbs and exotic fruits. Then one day, the teacher brought in a great variety of boiled sweets, more flavours than you could ever imagine.

'Children, I'd like you to close your eyes and taste these,' announced the teacher. Without difficulty, they managed to identify the taste of cherries, lemons and mint, but when the teacher had them put honey-flavoured sweets in their mouths, every one of the children was stumped.

'I'll give you a hint,' said the teacher. 'It's something your daddy and mummy probably call each other all the time.'

Instantly, one of the children spat the sweet out of his mouth and shouted, 'Ugh... they're arseholes.'

****

While crossing the US-Mexican border on his bicycle, this man was stopped by a guard who pointed to two sacks the man had on his shoulders. 'What's in the bags?' asked the guard.

'Sand,' said the cyclist.

'Get them off – we'll take a look,' said the guard.

The cyclist did as he was told, emptied the bags, and proving they contained nothing but sand, reloaded the bags, put them on his shoulders and continued across the border.

Two weeks later, the same thing happened. Again the guard demanded to see the two bags, which again contained nothing but sand. This went on every week for six months, until one day the cyclist with the sand bags failed to appear.

A few days later, the guard happened to meet the cyclist downtown. 'Say friend, you sure have us beat,' said the guard. 'We know you're smuggling something across the border. I promise I won't say a word, please tell me what it is?'

'Bicycles!' replied the man.

On The Wagon

****

Three bulls heard via the grapevine that the farmer was going to bring yet another bull on to the farm, and the prospect raised a discussion amongst them.

'Boys,' said the first bull, 'we all know I've been here five years. Once we settled our differences, we agreed on which 100 of the cows would be mine. Now, I don't know where this newcomer is going to get HIS cows, but I'm not giving him any of mine.'

'That pretty much says it for me, too,' says the second bull. 'I've been here three years and have earned my right to the 50 cows we've agreed are mine. I'll fight him till I run him off or kill him, but I'M KEEPING ALL MY COWS.'

'I've only been here a year,' says the third bull, 'and so far you guys have only let me have 10 cows. I may not be as big as you fellows yet, but I am young and virile, so I simply MUST keep all MY cows.'

They'd just finished their big talk when an 18-wheel lorry pulls up in the middle of the pasture with only ONE ANIMAL IN IT. The biggest bull these guys had ever seen!

'You know,' says the first bull, 'it's actually been some time since I really felt I was doing all my cows justice, anyway. I think I can spare a few for our new friend.'

'I'll have plenty of cows to take care of if I just stay on the opposite end of the pasture from HIM,' says the second bull. 'I'm certainly not looking for an argument.'

They look over at their young friend, the third bull, and find him pawing the dirt, shaking his horns, and snorting the bull's equivalent of 'Stay away from my bird.'

'Son,' says the first bull, 'let me give you some advice. Let him have some of your cows and live to tell about it.'

'Hold on, mate,' says the third bull, 'he can have ALL MY COWS. I'm just making sure he knows I'M a bull!'

****

Waiter, there's a dead fly in my soup!
Yes sir, I expect it's the hot water that kills them.

****

Waiter, there's a fly in my soup!
Keep it down, sir, or they'll all be wanting one.

****

Waiter, what's this fly doing in my soup?
It's fly soup sir!

****

Waiter, what's this fly doing in my soup?
Um, looks to me to be backstroke, sir...

****

Waiter, there's a fly in my soup!
Don't worry sir, the spider on the bread roll will get him.

****

Waiter, there's a fly in my soup!
No sir, that's a cockroach, the fly is on your steak.

****

Waiter, this coffee tastes like dirt!
Yes, sir, that's because it was ground this morning.

****

On The Wagon

Waiter, what is this stuff?
That's bean salad sir.
I know what it's been, but what is it now?

****

Waiter: And how did you find your steak sir?
Well, I just rolled a pea over, and there it was!

****

Two hunters got a helicopter pilot to fly them into the highlands for deer hunting. They were quite successful in their venture and bagged six big bucks. The pilot came back, as arranged, to pick them up. They started loading their gear into the chopper, including the deer. But the pilot objected, 'The chopper can only take four of your deer,' he said. 'You'll have to leave two behind.'

They argued with him; the year before they'd shot six and the pilot had allowed them to put all aboard. The helicopter was the same model and capacity. Reluctantly, the pilot finally allowed them to put all six aboard. But when they attempted to take off and leave the valley, the little chopper couldn't make it and they crashed into the wilderness.

Climbing out of the wreckage, one hunter said to the other, 'Do you know where we are?'

I think so,' replied the other hunter. 'Isn't this the same place we crashed last year?'

****

A customer was bothering the waiter in a restaurant. First he asked that the air conditioning be turned up because he was too hot, then he asked it be turned down because he was too cold, and so on for about half an hour.

Surprisingly, the waiter was very patient, he walked back and forth and never once got angry. Finally a second customer asked him why he didn't throw the git out.

'Oh, I don't care,' said the waiter with a smile, 'we don't even have an air conditioner.'

****

When Beethoven passed away, he was buried in a churchyard. A couple of days later, the town drunk was walking through the cemetery and heard some strange noises coming from the area where Beethoven was buried.

Terrified, the drunk ran and got the priest to come and listen to it. The priest bent close to the grave and heard some faint, unrecognisable music coming from the grave.

Frightened, the priest ran and got the town magistrate. When the magistrate arrived, he bent his ear to the grave, listened for a moment, and said, 'Ah, yes, that's Beethoven's Ninth Symphony, being played backwards.' He listened a while longer, and said, 'There's the Eighth Symphony, and it's backwards, too. Most puzzling.' So, the magistrate kept listening; 'There's the Seventh... the Sixth... the Fifth...'

Suddenly, the realisation of what was happening dawned on the magistrate; he stood up and announced to the crowd that had gathered in the cemetery, 'My fellow citizens, there's nothing to worry about. It's just Beethoven decomposing.'

****

Three convicts were going to be executed. As they went out, the first was given one last request. He pointed behind the firing range and shouted, 'Tornado,' and when the firing squad looked round he ran away.

When the second took up his position he was also given one last request. He pointed behind the firing squad and shouted, 'Hurricane,' and he too ran away.

Sadly, the third one didn't get away. When he was given a last request, he pointed behind the squad and shouted, 'Fire!'

On The Wagon

A waiter brings the customer the steak he ordered with his thumb over the meat. 'What the hell are you doing holding on to my dinner like that?' screamed the customer.

'What?' answers the waiter, 'You want it to fall on the floor again?'

✳✳✳✳

Long ago, when sailing ships ruled the waves, a captain and his crew were in danger of being boarded by a pirate ship. As the crew became frantic, the captain bellowed to his First Mate, 'Bring me my red shirt!'

The First Mate quickly retrieved the captain's red shirt, which the captain put on and led the crew to battle the pirate boarding party.

Although some casualties occurred among the crew, the pirates were repelled.

Later that day, the lookout screamed that there were two pirate vessels sending boarding parties. The crew cowered in fear, but the captain, calm as ever, bellowed, 'Bring me my red shirt!' And once again the Captain and his crew repelled the boarding parties, although this time more casualties occurred.

Weary from the battles, the men sat around on deck that night recounting the day's occurrences when an ensign looked to the captain and asked, 'Sir, why did you call for your red shirt before the battle?'

The Captain, giving the ensign a look that only a captain can give, exhorted, 'If I am wounded in battle, the red shirt does not show the wound, and thus, you men will continue to fight unafraid.'

The men sat in silence marvelling at the courage of such a man. As dawn came the next morning, the lookout screamed that there were pirate ships, ten of them, all with boarding parties on their way. The men became silent and looked to the captain, their leader, for his usual command. The captain, calm as ever, bellowed, 'Bring me my brown trousers!'

Two atoms were walking down the street when they bumped into each other. 'Are you OK?' asked the first one.

'No,' replied the second. 'I lost an electron!'

'Are you sure?' asked the first one.

'I'm positive!' replied the second.

****

So there's this magician working on a small cruise ship. He's been doing his routines every night for a year or two now. The audiences appreciate him, and they change over often enough for him not to worry too much about new tricks. However, there's this parrot who sits in the back row and watches him night after night, year after year.

Finally, the parrot figures out how the tricks work and starts giving it away for the audience. For example, when the magician makes a bouquet of flowers disappear, the parrot squawks, 'Behind his back! Behind his back!'

Well, the magician gets really annoyed at this, but he doesn't know what to do. The parrot belongs to the captain, so he can't just kill it. One day, the ship springs a leak and sinks. The magician manages to swim to a plank of wood floating by and grabs on. The parrot is sitting on the other end of the plank. They just stare at each other and drift. They drift for three days and still don't speak. On the morning of the fourth day, the parrot looks over at the magician and says, 'OK, I give up. Where did you hide the ship?'

****

During camouflage training, a private disguised as a tree trunk had made a sudden move that was spotted by a visiting general.

'You simpleton!' the officer barked. 'Don't you know that by jumping and shouting the way you did, you could have endangered the lives of the entire company?'

'Yes sir,' the solder answered apologetically. 'But, if I may say so, I did stand still when a flock of pigeons used me for target practice. And I never moved a muscle when a large dog pissed on my lower branches. But when two squirrels ran up my trouser leg and I heard the bigger say, "Let's eat one now and save the other until winter," that did it.'

Two rhinos have been in a cage at the zoo for 10 years when one turns to the other and says, 'Do you know, we've been in this cage for all this time and I don't even know your name.'

'It's Neil,' replies the other.

'Not Rhino Neil?' says the first.

Two elephants fell off a cliff. Boom, boom.

A guy goes into a pet shop and asks for a wasp. The owner tells him they don't sell wasps, to which the man says, 'Well, you've got one in the window.'

Luke Skywalker and Darth Vader are fighting with the light sabres. To put Luke off Darth says, 'Luke, I am your Father.'

'I don't believe you,' says Luke.

'I can prove it,' says Darth.

'OK, prove it then,' says Luke.

'I know what you're getting for Christmas,' says Darth.

'How do you know?' says Luke.

'Because, Luke, I've felt your presents.' says Darth.

A sausage walks into pub and asks for a pint. The landlord says, 'Sorry, we don't serve food.'

****

One ghost says to the other, 'How long have you been dead?'
'Six foot two, the same as when I was alive,' says the other.

****

In a restaurant. 'Waiter, why is there a small coffin floating in my wine?'
'Well you did order something with a little body, sir.'

****

Have you heard about the rude ghost?
She goes bum in the night.

****

Man at the restaurant. 'Waiter, there's a dead vampire bat in my meal.'
'Yes, sir, it's the steak that kills them.'

****

Guy goes into a fish shop and says, 'I'd like a piece of cod, please.'
Fishmonger says, 'It won't be long sir.'
'Well, it had better be fat then,' replies the guy.

****

Two peanuts walking down the road. One's assaulted.

****

Two flies were on a lavatory seat. One got pissed off.

****

This guy goes to a camel salesman and says, 'I want to buy a camel, please.'

The salesman hands him two bricks and says, 'This one here is very fast but you'll need these.'

The man asks why. The salesman says, ' 'Cos when you want the camel to go, you have to take the bricks, place them either side of the camel's balls and smash them together.'

The man asks, 'Doesn't it hurt?'

The salesman says, 'Only if you get your thumbs caught.'

****

There once was a young person named Red Riding Hood who lived with her mother on the edge of a large wood. One day her mother asked her to take a basket of fresh fruit and mineral water to her grandmother's house. Not because this was woman's work, mind you, but because the deed was generous and helped engender a feeling of community. Furthermore, her grandmother was not sick, but rather was in full physical and mental health and was fully capable of taking care of herself as a mature adult.

So, Red Riding Hood set off with her basket through the woods. Many people believed that the forest was a foreboding and dangerous place and never set foot in it. Red Riding Hood, however, was confident enough in her own budding sexuality that such obvious Freudian imagery did not intimidate her. On the way to Grandma's house, Red Riding Hood was accosted by a wolf who asked her what was in her basket. She replied, 'Some healthful snacks for my grandmother, who is certainly capable of taking care of herself as a mature adult.'

The wolf said, 'You know, my dear, it isn't safe for a little girl to walk through these woods alone.'

'I find your sexist remark offensive in the extreme,' said Red Riding Hood, 'but I will ignore it because of your traditional status as an

On The Wagon

outcast from society, the stress of which has caused you to develop your own, entirely valid, world view. Now, if you'll excuse me, I must be on my way.'

Red Riding Hood walked on along the main path. But, because his status outside society had freed him from slavish adherence to linear, Western-style thought, the wolf knew a quicker route to Grandma's house. He burst into the house and ate Grandma, an entirely valid course of action for a carnivore such as himself. Then, unhampered by rigid, traditionalist notions of what was masculine or feminine, he put on Grandma's night-clothes and crawled into bed.

Red Riding Hood entered the cottage and said, 'Grandma, I have brought you some fat-free, sodium-free snacks to salute you in your role of a wise and nurturing matriarch.'

From the bed, the wolf said softly, 'Come closer, child, so that I might see you.'

'Oh,' said Red Riding Hood, 'I forgot you are so optically challenged. Grandma, what big eyes you have!'

'They have seen much, and forgiven much, my dear,' said the wolf.

'Grandma,' said Red Riding Hood, 'what a big nose you have, only relatively, of course, and certainly attractive in its own way.'

'It has smelled much, and forgiven much, my dear,' said the wolf.

'Grandma, what big teeth you have!' said Red Riding Hood.

'I am happy with who I am and what I am,' said the wolf and leaped out of bed. He grabbed Red Riding Hood in his claws, intent on devouring her.

Red Riding Hood screamed, not out of alarm at the wolf's apparent tendency toward cross-dressing, but because of his wilful invasion of her personal space. Her screams were heard by a passing woodchopperperson (or solid-fuel technician, as he preferred to be called). When he burst into the cottage, he saw the mêlée and tried to intervene. But as he raised his axe, Red Riding Hood and the wolf both stopped.

'And just what do you think you're doing?' asked Red Riding Hood. The woodchopperperson blinked and tried to answer, but no words came to him. 'Bursting in here like a Neanderthal,' continued Red Riding Hood, 'trusting your weapon to do your thinking for you! Sexist! Speciesist! How dare you assume that women and wolves can't solve their own problems without a man's help!'

When she heard Red Riding Hood's impassioned speech, Grandma jumped out of the wolf's mouth, seized the woodchopperperson's axe, and cut his head off. After this ordeal, Red Riding Hood, Grandma, and the wolf felt a certain commonality of purpose. They decided to set up an alternative household based on mutual respect and co-operation, and they lived together in the woods happily ever after.

****

Man: Doctor, I've just swallowed a pillow.
Doctor: How do you feel?
Man: A little down in the mouth.

****

Did you hear about the paranoid with low self-esteem?
He thought that nobody important was out to get him.

****

Man: Doctor, I can't stop singing, 'The Green, Green Grass Of Home.' Can you help me?'

Doctor: Ah yes, you appear to be suffering from Tom Jones Syndrome.

Man: Is it rare?

Doctor: Well… it's not unusual.

****

A Mother and Father are talking about their son's school progress. 'So how did Peter do in his history exam?' asked the father.

'Not very well,' said his Mother, 'but then he can't really be blamed. A lot of the questions were about things that happened before he was born.'

On The Wagon

****

Two women are talking. 'My youngest has trouble with eczema and asthma,' said one.

'Oh, that's nasty,' said the other. 'How did he get them?'

'He hasn't got them,' said the first woman. 'He just can't spell them.'

****

The teacher is handing back the class's homework. 'Johnny,' she says. 'Your homework is very poor. I really don't see how one person can make so many mistakes.'

'It wasn't one person, Miss,' says Johnny. 'My Dad helped me.'

****

A mother is shouting at her cheeky son. 'Stephen, just for once I'd like to go through a whole day without having to tell you off or punish you,' she shouts.

'OK, Mum,' says Stephen. 'You have my consent.'

****

Teacher to pupil: Tell me two pronouns.
Pupil: Who? Me?

****

The young kid went to the sweet shop. 'I want one of those all-day gobstoppers please,' he said. The shop assistant gave him one. 'Here,' said the kid. 'This looks smaller than the one I had before.'

'Well,' said the shop assistant. 'The days are getting shorter.'

****

A Hollywood actor was testifying in a court case. When asked to identify himself he said, 'I am the world's greatest actor.'

The next day his agent was talking to him. 'Don't you think that was a bit much yesterday?' he said.

'Not at all,' replied the actor. 'Don't forget I was under oath.'

****

A doctor is on the phone to a farmer, 'I'm sorry,' says the doc, 'but I can't come out to see you any more.'

'Why not?' asks the farmer.

'Because every time I come to your place your ducks insult me,' says the doctor.

****

Two goldfish are in a tank. One turns to the other and says, 'Do you know how to drive this thing?'

****

A tortoise goes to the police station to report being mugged by three snails. 'What happened?' says the policeman.

'I don't know,' says the tortoise. 'It was all so quick.'

****

A duck goes to a chemist and says, 'Can I have some lipsalve please?'

The chemist goes and gets it and says, 'Will you be paying cash?'

'No thanks,' says the duck, 'put it on my bill.'

****

A tortoise knocks on the door of this big house in winter. A gruff old geezer answers the door. 'What do you want?' he says.

'Please, sir,' says the tortoise, 'I'm so very cold. Can I come in and warm myself by your fire?'

'Certainly not,' says the man, and kicks the tortoise to the end of the garden.

Next Spring there's another knock at the door and the same man answers it. 'Yes?' he says.

'What did you do that for?' says the tortoise.

****

Two Moroccans are introduced to each other at a party. One says to the other, 'I'm sure we've met before. Your fez is very familiar.'

****

This kid walks into a general store one day and asks for a job. The owner tells him that he doesn't need any help. The kid is persistent so the bloke tells him to watch him when the next customer comes in. If he can do what he does, he'll give him a job.

A few minutes later a customer comes in. 'Good afternoon, sir. What can I do for you?'

The bloke says, 'I need some grass seed.' So the owner goes and gets it. When he gets back he says, 'How about a lawnmower to go with this?'

'What do I need a lawnmower for?'

'Well, when the grass grows you're going to need something to cut it with.'

'Yeah, OK, I'll take a lawnmower, too.'

After the customer's gone, the owner turns to the kid and said, 'That's how it's done. Can you do that?'

The kid says, 'Sure.'

So the next customer comes in and says, 'I need some Tampax.'

The kid says, 'Yes sir,' and goes to get them. When he gets back he says, 'Would you like a lawnmower to go with that?'

On The Wagon

The bloke says, 'What the hell do I need a lawnmower for?'

The kid replies, 'You might as well cut the grass. Your weekend is shot, that's for sure…'

****

A mother was working in the kitchen and listening to her son playing with his new electric train in the living room. She heard the train stop and her son say, 'All of you fuckers who want to get off, get the fuck off now 'cos this is the last stop. And all of you fuckers who are getting on get your arses in the train 'cos we're leaving.'

The mother went into the living room and told her son, 'We don't use that kind of language in this house. Now I want you to go to your room for two hours. When you come out you may play with your train. But I want you to use nice language.'

Two hours later the son comes out of the bedroom and resumes playing with his train. Soon the train stops and the mother hears her son say, 'All passengers who are disembarking the train please remember to take all of your belongings with you. We thank you for riding with us today and hope your trip was a pleasant one. We hope you will ride with us again soon. For those of you just boarding we ask you to store all your luggage under your seat. Remember there is no smoking on this service. We hope you have a pleasant and relaxing journey with us… And for those of you who are pissed off about the two-hour delay, please see the bitch in the kitchen.'

****

A young lad was playing with his food one dinner time. 'Come on,' said his mum, 'eat up your greens. They'll make you big and strong.'

'Well, why don't you give them to Grandpa, then?' replied the boy.

On The Wagon

Young Johnny turned up late for Sunday school one morning and the teacher wanted to know why. 'Well, I was going to go fishing, but my dad wouldn't let me,' said Johnny.

'I should think not,' replied the teacher. 'And did your father explain why you should not go fishing on this day?'

'Oh yeah,' said Johnny. 'He said he didn't have enough bait for both of us.'

****

One day, the teacher walks into her classroom and announces to the class that on each Friday, she will ask a question of the class and anyone who answers correctly doesn't have to go to school the following Monday.

On the first Friday, the teacher asks, 'How many grains of sand are on the beach?' Needless to say, no one could answer. The following Friday, the teacher asks the class, 'How many stars are in the sky?' and again no one could answer.

Frustrated, little Johnny decides that the next Friday, he would somehow answer the question and get a three-day weekend. So Thursday night, Johnny takes two ping-pong balls and paints them black. The next day, he brings them to school in a paper bag. At the end of the day, just when the teacher says, 'Here's this week's question,' Johnny empties the bag to the floor sending the ping-pong balls rolling to the front of the room.

Because they are young kids who find any disruption of class amusing, the entire class starts laughing. The teacher says, 'OK, who's the comedian with the black balls?' Immediately, little Johnny stands up and says, 'Lenny Henry, see you on Tuesday!'

****

What do you call a cross between a rooster and an owl?
A cock that stays up all night.

A whole family was caught in a small boat during a sudden storm off the coast of Cornwall, but were towed to safety by the coastguard.

'I always knew God would take care of us,' said the composed five-year old daughter of the boat owner after the family got home.

'I like to hear you say that,' beamed the mother. 'Always remember that God is in His heaven watching over us.'

Oh, I wasn't talking about THAT God,' the five-year-old interrupted. 'I was talking about the COAST God.'

****

A little girl says, 'Grandpa, can I sit on your lap?'

'Why sure you can,' her grandfather replied.

As she's sitting on granddad's lap she says, 'Grandpa, can you make a sound like a frog?'

Perplexed, her granddad says, 'Sweetheart, why do you want me to make a sound like a frog?'

And the little girl says, ''Cause Grandma said that when you croak, we're going to EuroDisney.'

****

A very confused little boy goes to his mother and asks, 'Mummy? Is God male or female?'

'Well, honey,' says his mother. 'He's both.'

'Oh,' says the little boy. 'Mummy? Is God black or white?'

'Well, he's both,' replies his mother.

'Oh…' says the little boy. 'Mummy?'

'Yes, sweetie?'

'Is Michael Jackson God?'

****

A little boy is in school working on his arithmetic. The teacher says,

'Imagine there are five blackbirds sitting on a fence. You pick up your gun and shoot one. How many blackbirds are left?'

The little boy thinks for a moment and says, 'NONE!'

The teacher replies, 'None, how do you figure that?' The little boy says, 'If I shoot one, all the other birds will fly away scared, leaving none on the fence.'

The teacher replies, 'Hmmmm, not exactly, but I do like the way you think!'

The little boy then says, 'Teacher, can I ask you a question? There are three women sitting on a park bench eating ice cream cones. One is licking her cone, another is biting it, and the third one is sucking it. How can you tell which one of the women is married?'

The teacher ponders the question uncomfortably and then finally replies, 'Well, I guess the one sucking her cone.'

To which the little boy replies, 'Actually, it's the one with the wedding ring, but I do like the way YOU think!'

****

A 999 operator gets a call one evening but nobody says anything. Fearing the worst, the operator calls back, and a little boy answers the phone in a whispering voice.

Boy (barely audible): Hello!

Operator: Hello little boy. Did you just call 999?

Boy (barely audible): No!

Operator: O.K., is your mum home?

Boy (barely audible): Yes.

Operator: Can I speak to her, please?

Boy (barely audible): No.

Operator: Why not?

Boy (barely audible): Because she's busy!

Operator: Oh, OK. Is your daddy home then?

Boy (barely audible): Yes.

Operator: Well, can I speak to him?

Boy (barely audible): No!
Operator: Well, my goodness, why not?
Boy (barely audible): Because he's busy too!
Operator: Oh, goodness! What's he busy doing?
Boy (barely audible): Talking to the police.
Operator: Oh, so the police are there?
Boy (barely audible): Yes.
Operator: Can I speak to one of them?
Boy (barely audible): No!
Operator: Why not?
Boy (barely audible): Because they are really busy.
Operator: Well, what's your mum busy doing?
Boy (barely audible): Talking to the firemen.
Operator: Can I speak to one of the firemen then, please?
Boy (barely audible): No.
Operator: Well, goodness, why not?
Boy (barely audible): Because they are really busy, too!
Operator: Well, what are all of these people busy doing?
Boy (barely audible): Looking for me.

✱✱✱✱

A little boy is in a queue with his dad at the supermarket check out. In front of them is a really fat woman. The little boy looks her over and turns to his day and says: 'She is really big and fat, isn't she, daddy?'

The father is embarrassed and tries to get his son to quieten down. In a few minutes the little boy yells out: 'She is the biggest woman I have ever seen!'

The father is embarrassed to tears and bends over and tell his son: 'We do not talk about people looking different from us, especially if they are fat. Don't do it again.'

The little boy got the message and stood for a long time, until the woman's beeper went off. He then shouted: 'Look out, daddy, she's backing up!'

On The Wagon

****

A secondary school student asked his teacher if a person should be punished for something he hadn't done. 'No,' said the teacher. 'Of course not,'
   'Good,' said the boy. 'I haven't done my homework.'

****

A father and his small son were standing in front of the tiger cage at the zoo. The father was explaining how ferocious and strong tigers are, and the son was taking it all in with a serious expression.
   'Dad,' the boy said finally, 'if the tiger got out of his cage and ate you…'
   'Yes, son?' the father said expectantly.
   'What bus should I take home?' the boy finished.

****

'Are caterpillars good to eat?' asked little Tommy at the dinner table.
   'No,' said his father, 'what makes you ask a question like that while we are eating?'
   'You had one on your lettuce salad, but it's gone now,' replied Tommy.

****

Mr Baldwin, the biology teacher, asked Mary, 'Tell me the part of the body that, under the right conditions, expands to six times its normal size, and state the conditions.'
   Mary gasped and said in a huff, 'Why, Mr Baldwin! That is an inappropriate question and my parents are going to hear of it when I get home!' She sat down, red-faced.
   'Susan, can you tell me the answer?' asked Mr Baldwin, 'The pupil of the eye, under dark conditions,' said Susan.
   'Correct. Now Mary, I have three things to say to you. First, you have not studied your lesson. Second, you have a dirty mind. And third, boy, are

you going to be disappointed some day!'

****

A stern father was taking his little son Johnny for a walk in the park when a bee landed on a rock in front of them. The little boy stepped forward and crushed the bee with his shoe. The father said, 'That was cruel, you'll get no honey for a whole year.'

Later, Johnny deliberately stepped on a butterfly. 'Just for that,' his father said, 'you'll have no butter for a year.'

When they returned home, Johnny's mother was making dinner. As they walked into the kitchen, she spied a cockroach and immediately crushed it. Johnny looked at his father and asked, 'Shall I tell her, Dad, or will you?'

****

A small boy walked into a gents. He saw a sailor in full dress uniform. The little boy got really excited, and asked the sailor, 'Are you a REAL Sailor?'

The sailor replied, 'Why, yes, son, I am. Would you like to wear my hat?'

The little boy said, 'Yes!' and put on the hat.

A Royal Marine entered the bathroom. The little boy, very excitedly asked, 'Mister, are you a REAL Marine?' The Marine answered, 'Yes, son, I am! Why, do you want to suck my dick?'

The little boy exclaimed, 'I'm not a REAL sailor! I'm just wearing the hat!'

****

Little Johnny's teacher asked him, 'Johnny, give me a sentence using the phrase, "bitter end" in it.'

Little Johnny thought for a moment and replied, 'Our dog chased our cat and he bitter end.'

****

One blistering hot day when guests were present for dinner, a mother asked her four-year-old son to say grace.

'But, Mother, I don't know what to say,' he protested.

'Just say what you've heard me say,' she told him. Obediently, he bowed his head and said, 'Oh, Lord, why did I invite those people here on a hot day like this?'

****

This young girl about five years old had a dog which she took for a walk every day after school. Well, one day her dog was on heat, so her father told her that she couldn't walk the dog for a week or so because it wasn't feeling well. His daughter became very upset and cried for most of the night.

The next day the father came up with a plan. He put some petrol on the dog's rear end to conceal the smell from the male dogs. Well, when the girl got home she was happy to find that she could now walk her dog again. About an hour later the girl returned without the dog. The father asked her what on earth had happened to the dog?

The girl replied: 'She ran out of petrol a few streets back and she's being pushed home by another dog.'

****

A couple of young lads were fishing at their special pond off the beaten track when out of the bushes jumped the gamekeeper. Immediately, one of the boys threw his rod down and started running through the woods like a bat out of hell, and hot on his heels came the game keeper. After about half a mile the young lad stopped and stooped over with his hands on his thighs to catch his breath and the gamekeeper finally caught up with him.

'Let's see your fishing licence, lad!' the game keeper gasped.

With that, the young lad pulled out his wallet and gave the gamekeeper a valid fishing licence.

'Well, son,' said the gamekeeper, 'you must be really stupid! You don't have to run from me if you have a valid license.'

'Yes, sir,' replied the young lad, 'but my friend back there, well, he doesn't have one.'

****

Little Johnny sat playing in the garden. When his mother came out to collect him, she saw that he was slowly eating a worm. She turned pale. 'No, Johnny! Stop! That's horrible! You can't eat worms!' Trying to convince him further she said, 'Now the mother worm is looking all over for her nice baby worm.'

'No, she isn't,' said Johnny.

'Why not?' said his mum.

'Because I ate her first!'

****

Eight-year-old Johnny comes into the house for dinner after playing outside all afternoon. His parents ask him what he did today. He says that he played football and then he proposed to seven-year-old Jane, the nextdoor neighbour. They are going to get married. His parents think this is cute, and they don't want to make fun of Johnny so they ask him, 'How are you and Jane going to pay for the expenses of being married?'

Johnny replies, 'Well, with the £1 I get each week from you and the £1 she gets from her mum and dad, we should do OK.'

His father says, 'That's fine, but how will you pay the extra expenses if you and Jane have a baby?'

Johnny answers, 'Well, so far, we've been lucky...'

****

Every day an eight-year-old boy walks home from school past an eight-year-old girl's house. One day he is carrying a football, and he stops to taunt the little girl. He holds up the football and says, 'See this football?

Football is a boy's game and girls can't have one!'

The little girl runs in the house crying and tells her mother about the encounter. She runs out and buys the girl a football. The next day the boy is riding home on his bike, and the girl shows him the football, screaming, 'Nah na nah na nah.'

The little boy gets mad and points to his bike. 'See this bike? This is a boy's bike, and girls can't have them!'

Next day, the boy comes by and the little girl is riding a new boy's bike. Now he's really mad. So he drops his pants, points at his most private of parts, and says, 'You see THIS? Only BOYS have these and your mother can't buy you one!'

The next day as he passes the house he asks the little girl, 'Well, what do you have to say NOW?'

So she pulls up her dress and says, 'My mother told me that as long as I have one of these, I can have as many of THOSE as I want!'

****

'Is your mother home?' the salesman asked a small boy sitting on the frontstep of a house.

'Yeah, she's home,' the boy said, moving over to let him past. The salesman rang the doorbell, got no response, knocked once, then again. Still no one came to the door. Turning to the boy, the salesman said, 'I thought you said your mother was home.'

The kid replied, 'She is, but I don't live here.'

****

One day, a father and his son were walking in the woods on their way home when suddenly they came upon two dogs mating in the bushes.

'What are they doing, Dad?' asked the small child, staring intently at the scene before them.

'They, um, they're making a puppy,' said the boy's father, as he grabbed his coat and moved him along quickly.

A few nights later, the little boy woke up and got up from his bed to go to the bathroom. As he walked by his parents' room, he heard strange noises coming from within. He opened the door and was surprised to see his father on top of his mother, moving in a strange way. His father looked up and saw his son – instantly, both mother and father froze. As the boy's mother grabbed for the sheets to cover herself up, the father got up and hustled his son out of the bedroom.

'What were you doing to Mum, Dad?' asked the little boy, who still wasn't sure what he saw.

'Your mother and I were, well, we were, ah, trying to make a baby – you know, maybe a brother or sister for you,' said the boy's father, now confident that this would satisfy his son's curiosity.

'Oh,' said the little boy, thinking hard for a minute. 'Y'know Dad, when you go back to bed with mum, turn her over, please – I'd rather have a puppy.'

****

This little boy wakes up three nights in a row when he hears a thumping sound coming from his parents' room. Finally, one morning he goes to his mum and says, 'Mummy, every night I hear you and daddy making noises and when I look in your bedroom you're bouncing up and down on him.'

His mum is taken by surprise and says, 'Oh... well... ah... I'm, er bouncing on his stomach because he's fat and that makes him thin again.'

And the boy says, 'Well, that won't work'

His mum says, 'Why?'

And the boy replies, 'Because the lady next door comes by after you leave each day and blows him back up!'

****

Mother: Why are you home from school so early?
Son: I was the only one who could answer a question.
Mother: Oh, really? What was the question?

Son: Who threw the rubber at the headmaster?

****

Little Johnny has a problem. He swears like a trooper. Johnny's teacher is aware of this, so she has got to be extra careful not to let Johnny swear.

'OK, class. We're going to play a game today. I'm going to name a letter of the alphabet and I want you to come up with a word that starts with that letter and put it in a sentence.'

The kids are excited, especially Johnny, who's thinking of every swear word he can.

'OK, class, let's start with the letter A.'

Johnny raises his hand.

'Susie,' the teacher calls.

'A is for apple. Apples grow on trees,' she replies.

'Very good,' the teacher says. 'OK, class, let's do the letter B.'

Johnny raises his hand excitedly.

'Mikey,' the teacher calls.

'B is for brown. Brown is my favourite colour.'

'Very good,' the teacher says. 'OK, class, let's do the letter C.'

Johnny raises both hands! He's going mad! He's got a great word for C!

'Bobby,' the teacher calls.

'C is for cat. A cat lives in my back garden.'

'Very good,' The teacher says. This goes on and on, and the teacher is not going to call on Johnny if there's a swear word that starts with the letter she calls out.

Finally, she gets to the letter R. The teacher can't think of a single swear word that starts with R, and even Johnny looks a little puzzled. So she calls out R and asks Johnny to respond.

Johnny nervously stands up. He looks around the room. Then he says, 'R is for a Rat…' he suddenly gets excited and stretches both arms wide, '…a rat with a dick this big!'

****

A vampire bat came flapping in from the night covered in fresh blood and parked himself on the roof of the cave to get some sleep. Pretty soon all the other bats smelt the blood and began hassling him about where he got it. He told them to piss off and let him get some sleep but they persisted until finally he gave in.

'OK, follow me,' he said and flew out of the cave with hundreds of bats behind him. Down through a valley they went, across a river and into a forest full of trees. Finally he slowed down and all the other bats excitedly milled around him. 'Now, do you see that tree over there?' he asked.

'Yes, yes, yes!' the bats all screamed in a frenzy.

'Good,' said the first bat, 'Because I didn't!'

****

There was once a Scotsman and an Englishman who lived next door to each other. The Scotsman owned a hen and each morning would look in his garden and pick up one of his hen's eggs for breakfast.

One day he looked into his garden and saw that the hen had laid an egg in the Englishman's garden. He was about to go next door when he saw the Englishman pick up the egg. The Scotsman ran up to the Englishman and told him that the egg belonged to him because he owned the hen. The Englishman disagreed because the egg was laid on his property. They argued for a while until finally the Scotsman said, 'In my family we normally solve disputes by the following actions: I kick you in the balls and time how long it takes you to get back up, then you kick me in the balls and time how long it takes for me to get up; whoever gets up quicker wins the egg.'

The Englishman agreed to this and so the Scotsman found his heaviest pair of boots and put them on. He took a few steps back, then ran toward the Englishman and kicked him as hard as he could in the balls. The Englishman fell to the floor clutching his nuts, howling in agony for 30 minutes.

Eventually the Englishman stood up and said, 'Now it's my turn to kick you.'

The Scotsman said, 'Keep the fucking egg.'

****

A Daughter's Letter Home

Dear Mum and Dad,

It has been three months since I left for college. I have been remiss in writing and I am very sorry for my thoughtlessness. I will bring you up to date now, but before you read on, please sit down. You are not to read any further unless you are sitting down, OK?

Well, I'm getting along pretty well now. The skull fracture and the concussion I got when I jumped out of the window of my halls of residence when it caught fire shortly after my arrival are pretty well healed now. I only spent two weeks in the hospital and I now can see almost as well as before and I only get those nauseating headaches once a week. Fortunately, the fire in the halls of residence and my jump was witnessed by an attendant at the petrol station near the halls and he was the one who called the fire brigade and the ambulance. He also visited me at the hospital and since I had nowhere to live because of the burnt-out halls, he was kind enough to invite me to share his flat with him.

It's really a basement, but it's really quite nice. He is a very good man and we have fallen deeply in love and are planning to get married. We haven't exactly set the date yet, but it will be before my pregnancy begins to show. Yes, Mum and Dad, I am pregnant! I know how you are looking forward to being grandparents and I know you will welcome the baby and give it the same love and devotion and tender care you gave me as a child.

The reason for the delay in our marriage is that my boyfriend has some minor infection which he is waiting to clear up. I carelessly caught it from him. This will soon clear up with the penicillin injections I am taking daily. I know you will welcome him into the family with open arms. He is kind, and, although not well-educated, has ambitions.

Although he is of a different race and religion than ours, I know your oft-expressed tolerance will not permit you to be bothered by the fact that his skin colour is somewhat darker than ours. I am sure you will love him as I do. His family background is good, too, for I hear that his father is an important gun-bearer in the village in Africa from which he comes.

Now that I have brought you up to date, I want to tell you that there was no fire. I do not have a concussion or a skull fracture, I was not in the hospital, I am not pregnant, I am not engaged, I do not have syphilis and there is no African in my life. However, I did fail my exams and I wanted you to see these results in their proper perspective.

Your loving daughter, Gail xxx

****

John Wayne rides in to town, ties up his horse and walks into the saloon.

'Give me a shot of red eye,' says John.

He downs it in one and then walks outside. He notices that his horse is gone so he comes back inside the saloon. 'If my horse isn't returned after I've had another drink,' says John, 'the same thing will happen here that happened in Dodge City. Now, give me another red eye.'

He downs the red eye in one and walks outside to find his horse tied up against the rail. he mounts up and is just about to ride off when this cowboy walks up to him.

'Say, John,' says the cowboy. 'What happened in Dodge City?'

'I had to walk home,' John replies.

****

A three-legged dog walks into a saloon in the Wild West. The piano stops playing, everyone stops talking and a nervous hush descends upon the room.

'What do you want here?' says one brave soul.

'I've come for my paw,' replies the dog.

****

This man went to a casino. Very soon, he'd lost almost all his money. He decided to put the rest on number five on the roulette. The wheel spun and it came up number five. He'd made all his money back and a bit to spare. He was just about to leave the table when the devil appeared on his shoulder.

'Let it ride on number five,' said the devil. The man decided to go for it, the wheel spun and number five came up again. The man was very happy and went to grab his chips when the devil spoke again. 'Let it ride on number five again,' said the devil.

The man wasn't very sure but he decided to have one more go. The wheel spun and number five came up again. The man was now quite rich and was just about to leave the table when the devil piped up once more.

'Let it ride on number five again,' said the devil. The man didn't want to. He'd already planned to start a new life in the Caribbean. But the devil insisted. 'Let it ride on number five again,' said the devil.

The man was extremely doubtful but he left the money where it was. The wheel spun and came up on number five again.

'You jammy git,' said the devil.

****

A posh woman owned a very talented parrot called Charles. Not only could Charles talk but he played the piano as well. Unfortunately, he had one failing. He loved to fuck chickens. Any chance he could get to fuck a chicken, he'd be in there.

This really upset the farmer next door and he complained to the posh lady. She went and told Charles. 'If you mess with those chickens again, you're really going to get it,' she said.

Charles said nothing. He tried to resist, but the next day, he was caught messing around with the chickens. His mistress was very annoyed and punished Charles by shaving his head and nailing him to the piano. That evening, the posh lady had a gala party and all Charles could do was announce the guests.

'Mr and Mrs David Lloyd… Mr and Mrs John Silverman… ' he was saying. Just then two bald-headed men appeared at the door. 'And you two chicken fuckers can come up on the piano with me.' said Charles.

****

'Give me two hot dogs. One with mustard and one without.'
'Which one without?'

****

A man was seen walking through town with a desk strapped to his back, a typewriter under one arm, and a wastebasket under the other. A policeman stopped him and asked him what he was doing. He was arrested when he replied, 'Impersonating an office, sir!'

****

What do Saddam Hussein and Little Miss Muffet have in common?
They both have Kurds in their way.

****

This man was walking along a street and met a young boy. The man asked the boy, 'What's your name?'
   The boy replied, 'Six and Seven-Eighths.'
   The man asked, 'Where did your parents get a name like that?'
   The boy said, 'They picked it out of a hat.'

****

A group of chess enthusiasts had checked into a hotel, and were standing in the lobby discussing their recent tournament victories. After about an hour, the manager came out of the office and asked them to disperse. 'But why?'

they asked.

'Because,' he said, 'I can't stand chess nuts boasting in an open foyer.'

✯✯✯✯

The first Jewish woman Prime Minister is elected. She calls her Mother: 'Mama, I've won the elections, you've got to come to the swearing-in ceremony.'

'I don't know, what would I wear?'

'Don't worry, I'll send you a dressmaker.'

'But I only eat kosher food!'

'Mama, I am going to be the Prime Minister, I can get you kosher food.'

'But how will I get there?'

'I'll send a limo, just come Mama.'

'OK, OK, if it makes you happy.'

The great day comes and Mama is seated between the Lord Chancellor and the future Cabinet ministers, she nudges the gentleman on her right. 'You see that girl, the one with her hand on the Bible? Her brother's a doctor!'

✯✯✯✯

There were three guys on top of this big construction platform. One was a German, the other Italian, and the third one was an Irishman. The German opened his lunchbox and saw sauerkraut for his lunch and said, 'If I haff this stuff vun more time, I'll jump off zis beam.'

The Italian also looked in his lunchbox and saw pasta and said, 'If I 'ave disa pasta one more time I jump offa dis beam.'

Then the Irishman looked in his lunchbox and saw a cheese and tomato sandwich and said, 'If I have this sandwich one more time, I'll jump off this beam.'

So, the next day came and the German opened his lunchbox and saw sauerkraut, and jumped off the beam. Then the Italian looked in his lunchbox and saw pasta, and jumped off the beam. So, the Irishman looks in

On The Wagon

his lunchbox and sees a cheese and tomato sandwich and jumps.

The three workers' wives showed up at the scene and the workers' boss came over and told them why. He told them he had overheard the conversation saying that the workers would jump if their lunch was the same the next day.

Suddenly the German wife spoke up, 'Dat's veird, he neffer said anyzing to me. If he would haff I wouldn't haff packed it!'

The Italian wife said the same thing. But the Irishman's wife was crying worse now, and was barely able to say, 'That is strange, because he packs his own lunch!'

****

One day a man was walking in the woods when he got lost. For two days he roamed around trying to find a way out. He had not eaten anything during this period and was famished. Over on a rock ledge he spotted a bald eagle, killed it, and started to eat it. Surprisingly a couple of park rangers happen to find him at that moment, and arrested him for killing an endangered species.

At court, he pleaded innocent to the charges against him claiming that if he didn't eat the bald eagle he would have died from starvation. The judge ruled in his favour. In the judge's closing statement he asked the man, 'I would like you to tell me something before I let you go. I have never eaten a bald eagle, nor ever plan on it. What did it taste like?'

The man answered, 'Well, it tasted like a cross between a whooping crane and a lesser spotted owl.'

****

A father decided his son was showing signs of taking him and his mother for granted so he sat him down one day for a chat.

'Right,' said the dad, 'I think it's time you started treating your mother and I with a little more respect, young man. I mean, where would you be if we both died suddenly?'

'Here,' replied the boy. 'The question is, where would you two be?'

****

Q: Why can't women play hockey?
A: They have to change their pads after every period.

****

Q: Do you know how men and floor tiles are alike?
A: If you lay them right the first time you can walk on them the rest of your life.

****

Q: What did the banana say to the vibrator?
A: 'What are you shaking for? She's gonna eat me.'

****

Q: Why do they call seagulls seagulls?
A: Cause if they flew over the bay, they'd be bagels!

****

So these two cannibals were eating this clown and the one cannibal says to the other cannibal, 'Does this taste funny to you?'

****

Q: What is the result of a bomb blast in the middle of a herd of cows?
A: Udder destruction.

****

On The Wagon

Q: What did one fly say to another?
A: Time is fun when you're having flies.

****

Q: How do you get down from an elephant?
A: You don't, you get down from a goose.

****

Q: How many mice does it take to screw in a light bulb?
A: Two, the trick is getting them in there.

****

Q: What does a women have two of that a cow has four of?
A: Feet.

****

Q:What's the difference between a porcupine and a Porsche owner?
A:With a porcupine, the prick is on the outside!

****

Q: What happened to the Pope when he went to Mount Olive?
A: Popeye almost killed him!

****

Q: Did you hear about the man who ate his son?
A: He didn't know his wife was pregnant!

****

Q: What's the difference between a pervert and a kinky person?
A: A pervert uses a feather, a kinky person uses the whole chicken!

****

Q: What goes, 'Marc, Marc?'
A: A dog with a hare lip!

****

Q: What's the hardest part about eating a vegetable?
A: Manipulating the wheelchair!

****

Q: What's red and has seven dents?
A: Snow White's cherry!

****

Q: How can you tell a head nurse?
A: She's the one with the dirty knees!

****

Q: What do you have if you have a moth ball in one hand and a moth ball in the other hand?
A: One HELL of a moth!

****

Q: How many Zen masters does it take to screw in a light bulb?

On The Wagon

A: None. The Universe spins the bulb, and the Zen master merely stays out of the way.

****

Q: Why did the polygamist cross the aisle?
A: To get to the other bride.

****

Q: Why did the teacher draw a dot on the floor for his students?
A: He wanted to illustrate a point.

****

Q. What do you call a dog with no hind legs and steel balls?
A. Sparky!

****

Q: How do you confuse an idiot?
A: 26

****

Q: How many dope smokers does it take to screw in a light bulb?
A: Two. One to roll it and one to light it up.

****

Q: How many mystery writers does it take to screw in a light bulb?
A: Two. One to screw it almost all the way in and the other to give it a surprising twist at the end.

Whose Round Is It?

9

Jokes about Money

Whose Round Is It?

It's a difficult moment, but ultimately unavoidable. At the start of the evening everyone's clear-headed and when John bought the first round, followed by Pete getting the next lot in and then Sandra sharing a round with Ted all was well. Then things became a bit blurred. Firstly, Karl and Janine turned up and got involved in a mini-round of their own with Dave, Ian and Louise. Then Barry, who had been in at the beginning, went to the bog and missed out on Steve's round, and of course with three beers in him John's begun to think that Sandra and Ted sharing a round wasn't really fair and that when it comes round to him again he's only going to buy one of them a drink.

It's complicated, and with money being the root of all evil and alcohol being, well, alcohol, it's surprising that more friendships don't end this way. However, more often than not, the desperation to get more bevvied becomes the overriding drive and that tenner you were saving for the cab home soon becomes two large ones for Sandra and Ted, who have strangely gone to the toilet next time it's their round…

****

A travelling salesman stopped alongside a field on a country road to rest for a few minutes. The man had just closed his eyes when a horse came to the fence and began to boast about his past. 'Yes sir, I'm a fine horse. I've run in 25 races and won over £5 million. I keep my trophies in the barn.'

The salesman computed the value of having a talking horse, found the horse's owner and offered a handsome sum for the animal.

'Aw, you don't want that horse,' said the farmer.

'Yes I do,' said the salesman, 'and I'll give you £10,000 for him.'

Recognising a good deal, the farmer said without hesitation, 'He's yours.'

While he wrote out his check, the salesman asked, 'By the way, why wouldn't I want your horse?'

'Because', said the farmer, 'he's a liar – he hasn't won a race in his life.'

****

The local pub was so sure that its landlord was the strongest man around that they offered a standing £1,000 bet. The landlord would squeeze a lemon until all the juice ran into a glass, and hand the lemon to a customer. Anyone who could squeeze one more drop of juice out would win the money.

Many people had tried over time, but nobody could do it. One day this scrawny little man came into the pub, wearing thick glasses and a polyester suit, and said in a tiny, squeaky voice, 'I'd like to try the bet.'

After the laughter had died down, the landlord said OK, grabbed a lemon, and squeezed away. Then he handed the wrinkled remains of the rind to the little man. But the crowd's laughter turned to total silence as the man clenched his fist around the lemon and six drops fell into the glass.

As the crowd cheered, the landlord paid the £1,000, and asked the little man, 'What do you do for a living? Are you a lumberjack, a weight-lifter, or what?'

The man replied, 'I work for the Inland Revenue.'

****

There's a guy in a pub, it's late, and the guy and the landlord are the only ones left in the pub. The guy pushes his empty pint glass over to the edge of the counter, walks to the other end of the room and says to the landlord, 'If I could spit from here, and get it in the glass without getting any anywhere else, would you give me £50?'

The landlord, not seeing how this bet could be cheated, says, 'OK, you're on. Show me.'

So the guy spits and gets it in the glass without getting any on the counter or the floor. The landlord says, 'That's amazing! You deserve the £50!'

The next day the guy's in the pub again, and asks the landlord, if he could do it again, but with two glasses side by side, would he give him £100.

The landlord agrees and the guys spits from across the pub and makes it in both glasses, without getting any anywhere else.

So the evening rolls on, and the landlord sticks glasses all over the pub and says to the guy, 'If you can spit in all of these glasses at the same time, without getting any anywhere else, I'll give you £200.'

'Sure,' says the guy, 'but I need a little time to get ready.' So after a minute, the guy comes up, and proceeds to spit everywhere at lightning speed. The landlord, seeing that the guy has missed every single glass, jumps up and down for joy, screaming. The guy then pays the landlord and says, 'I don't see what you're so happy about, I just bet the guy in the corner £500 that I could spit all over your pub, and you'd be happy about it.'

****

A man goes into a pub and sees a pile of cash on a table beneath a big sign that reads, '£2,000 Cash Prize! See landlord for details.' Keeping one eye on the stack of money, the man goes over and asks the landlord what he has to do to win the prize. 'You have to do three things and it's all yours,' the landlord says.

'Just three things?' the bloke asks, rubbing his hands now and imagining about walking out of the pub £2,000 richer. 'What are the three things?'

'Well,' the landlord says, 'first you have to go over to that 16-stone bouncer and knock him out. After that, I've got a mean-tempered Pit Bull in the back room who needs a tooth pulled. Then you have to go upstairs and give the 80-year-old lady an orgasm.'

'No problem,' the guy says. He struts over to the bouncer and says, 'Hey pal your shoelace is untied.' When the bouncer looks down at his shoes, the man flattens him with a single, solid uppercut. Next he heads to the back room where the Pit Bull is housed. The landlord can hear a tremendous commotion from the back room and, after a few minutes the man emerges from the back room, quite bloody and cut up and breathing heavily.

'OK,' he says, 'where's the old lady that needs her tooth pulled?'

****

There was a couple who were big over-spenders. They always dreamed of holidaying in Hawaii, but were never able to save any money to do so. One day they had an idea. Each time they had sex, they would put £10 into a piggy bank. So they bought the piggy bank, and followed that procedure for about a year. After that time, they decided that there was enough money for their dream vacation and broke the piggy bank. The husband looked at their savings and said, 'Isn't it strange? Each time we had sex, I put £10 into the piggy bank. But I see here that there are quite a few £20 notes and a few £50 notes.'

'Well,' said his wife. 'Do you think that everybody is as stingy as you are?'

****

After the wedding, the bride's dad took a taxi to the bankruptcy court. As he got out he said to the driver, 'You might as well come, too.'

****

A couple were having a discussion about family finances. Finally the husband exploded, 'If it weren't for my money, the house wouldn't be here!'

'My dear,' the wife replied. 'If it weren't for your money I wouldn't be here.'

****

A man's credit card was stolen but he decided not to report it because the thief was spending less than his wife did.

A man walks into a restaurant has a few drinks and then asks what his bill is.

'20 quid,' the waiter says.

'I'll tell you what,' says the man, 'I'll bet you my bill, double or nothing that I can bite my eye.'

The waiter accepts and the man pulls out his glass eye and bites it. He has a few more drinks and asks for his bill again. This time it's £30.

'OK,' says the man. 'I'll bet you my bill, double or quits, that I can bite my other eye.' Knowing that the man can't have two glass eyes the waiter accepts the bet, at which point the guy takes out his false teeth and bites his other eye.

✳✳✳✳

A rabbi and a priest were discussing their respective collection boxes and how the money was split.

'We give three-quarters of it to Christian charities,' said the priest, 'and the last quarter we keep for ourselves and for the upkeep of the vicarage.'

'I see,' said the rabbi. 'Well, what we do is this. Each week, my wife and my two children take one corner of a table cloth and put all the money into the middle. We toss the money very high into the air up to God. Whatever he wants, he takes, and the money that falls back to earth we keep!'

✳✳✳✳

A priest and a rabbi were talking when the rabbi asked the priest about confession. 'I have an idea,' said the priest. 'Why don't you sit with me on my side of the confession booth and hear it for yourself? No one will ever know.'

A woman came into the booth and said, 'Bless me, Father, for I have sinned.'

'What did you do?' asked the priest.

'I cheated on my husband,' replied the woman.

'How many times?' asked the priest.

'Three times,' says the woman.

'Well,' said the priest, 'say five Hail Marys and put five pounds in the offertory box.'

Another woman came in and said, 'Bless me, Father, for I have sinned.'

'What did you do?' asked the priest. 'I cheated on my husband,' said the woman.

'How many times?' asked the priest.

'Three times,' said the woman.

Again the priest said, 'Say five Hail Marys and put five pounds in the offertory box.'

Then the priest turned to the rabbi and said, 'Would you like to do the next confession?' The rabbi started to object, but the priest said, 'Go ahead. It's easy.'

So another woman came in and said, 'Bless me, Father, for I have sinned.'

'What did you do?' asked the rabbi.

'I cheated on my husband,' said the woman.

'How many times?' asked the rabbi.

'Twice,' said the woman.

'Well, go and do it again,' said the rabbi. 'They're three for five pounds today.'

****

A young boy goes off to college, but about a third of the way through the term, he has foolishly squandered what money he had. 'Hmmmm,' he wonders, 'how am I gonna get more dosh?' Then he gets an idea. He calls his father. 'Dad,' he says, 'you won't believe the wonders of modern education. Why, they actually have a course here that will teach Fido how to talk!'

'Why that's absolutely amazing!' his father says. 'How do I get him on to this course?'

'Just send him down here with £1,000,' the boy says, 'I'll get him on to the course.'

So his father sends the dog and the money, but very shortly the boy has spent all the money again, so he calls his father.

'So how's Fido doing, son?' his father asks.

'Great dad, he's talking up a storm,' he says, 'but you just won't believe this – now they have a course here that will teach Fido to READ!'

'READ!' says his father, 'That's amazing! What do I have to do to get him on that course?'

'Just send £2,500, I'll get him in the class,' says the boy.

So his father sends the money. At the end of the term, the boy has a problem. When he gets home, his father will find out that the dog can neither talk nor read. So he strangled the dog.

When he gets home, his father is all excited. 'Where's Fido?' he shouts, 'I just can't wait to hear him talk and listen to him read something!'

'Dad,' the boy says, 'I have some grim news. This morning when I got out of the shower, Fido was in the living room sitting on the sofa reading the paper, like he usually does. Then he turned to me and asked, 'So, is your old man still shagging that little redhead that lives down on Oak Street?'

'I hope you wrung the lying bastard's fucking neck!' says his Dad.

****

This geezer just started at his new job, working at a porn shop. His boss comes out and tells him that he has to leave for a while. 'Can you handle it?' he asks the new employee. The new employee is somewhat reluctant, but with the boss' positive comments he finally agrees.

So, the geezer is there by himself for a little while and a white woman comes in. 'How much for the white dildo?' she asks.

'£35,' he answers.

'And how much for the black one?' she asks.

'It's the same price,' he says.

'£35 for the black one, £35 for the white one. I think I'll take the black one,' she says. 'I've never had a black one before.'

She pays him, and off she goes. A little bit later a black woman comes in and asks, 'How much for the black dildo?'

'£35,' says the new employee.

'And how much for the white one?' she asks.

'It's the same price,' he says. '£35 for the black one, £35 for the white one.'

'Hmmm,' says the woman, 'I think I'll take the white one. I've never had a white one before.'

She pays him, and off she goes. About an hour later a young blonde woman comes in and asks, 'How much are your dildos?'

'£35 for the white, £35 for the black,' says the man.

'Hmmmmm....' she muses, 'and how much is that tartan one on the shelf?'

'Well,' he says, 'that's a very special dildo... it'll cost you £165.'

She thinks for a moment and answers, 'I'll take the tartan one, I've never had a tartan one before.'

She pays him, and off she goes. Finally, the guy's boss returns and asks, 'How did you do while I was gone?'

'Really good,' said the new employee. 'I sold one white dildo, one black dildo, and I sold your Thermos flask for £165!'

✱✱✱✱

A rather scruffy-looking man went into a bank. Reaching the head of the queue, he said to the bank clerk, 'I wanna open a fucking bank account.'

'Certainly, sir,' answered the bank clerk, 'but there's no need to use that kind of language.'

'Look, lady. I just wanna open a fucking bank account,' growled the would-be customer.

'I'll be glad to be of service, sir,' said the bank clerk, blushing slightly, 'but I would appreciate not being spoken to in that way.'

'Just lemme open a fucking account, OK?' he said.

'I'm afraid I'm going to have to speak to the branch manager,' said the pissed-off bank clerk, slipping off her stool and returning shortly with a dapper middle-aged man who asked how he could be of service.

'I just won 10 million pounds on the lottery,' snarled the man, 'and all I wanna do is open a fucking account.'

'I see,' said the manager sympathetically. 'And this fucking BITCH is giving you trouble?'

****

A man was caught for speeding and went before the judge. 'What will you take, 30 days or £30?' said the judge.

'I think I'll take the money,' the man replied.

****

A biker appeared in court one day to testify on behalf of a friend, when the prosecuting lawyer asked him, 'Isn't it true that you were offered £5,000 to throw this case?' The biker calmly gazed out the window, ignoring the lawyer. Most annoyed, the lawyer again thundered, 'I said, isn't it true that you were offered £5,000 to throw this case?'

The judge, seeing that the biker continued to ignore the question, leaned over and said, 'You will answer the question,' to which the biker replied,

'Oh, sorry, your honour. I thought he was talking to you.'

****

After the student delivered the pizza to old Ken's house Ken asked: 'What is the usual tip?'

'Well,' replied the youth, 'this is my first trip here, but the other blokes say if I get 5p out of you, I'll be doing great.'

'Is that so?' snorted Ken. 'Well, just to show them how wrong they are, here's five quid.'

'Thanks,' replied the youth, 'I'll put this towards my studies.'

'What are you studying?' asked Ken. The lad smiled and said:

'Applied psychology.'

****

A shoplifter was caught red-handed trying to steal a watch from an exclusive jewellery store. 'Listen,' said the shoplifter, 'I know you don't want any trouble either. What say I just buy the watch and we forget about this?'

The manager agreed and wrote up the sales slip. The crook looked at the slip and said, 'This is a little more than I intended to spend. Can you show me something less expensive?'

****

A man walks into a bank and says he wants to borrow £200 for six months. The manager asks him what kind of collateral he has. The man says, 'I've got a Rolls-Royce. Keep it until the loan is paid off. Here are the keys.'

Six months later the man comes into the bank, pays back the £200 loan, plus £10 interest, and regains possession of the Rolls-Royce. 'Sir,' says the manager, 'if I may ask, why would a man who drives a Rolls-Royce need to borrow £200?'

'I had to go to abroad for six months, and where else could I store a Rolls-Royce for that long for only £10?'

****

There were two evil brothers. They were rich, and used their money to keep their ways from the public eye. They even attended church, and looked to be perfect Christians. Then their vicar retired, and a new one took over. Not only could he see right through the brothers' deception, but he also spoke well and true and the church started to swell in numbers.

A fund-raising campaign was started to repair the roof. All of a sudden, one of the brothers died. The remaining brother sought out the new vicar the day before the funeral and handed him a cheque for the amount needed to finish paying for the roof.

'I have only one condition,' he said. 'At his funeral, you must say my brother was a saint.' The vicar gave his word, and deposited the cheque. The next day, at the funeral, the vicar did not hold back.

'He was an evil man,' he said. 'He cheated on his wife and abused his family.' After going on in this vein for some time, he concluded with, 'But compared to his brother, he was a saint.'

****

A man tried to sell his neighbour a new dog. 'This is a talking dog,' he said. 'And you can have him for £5.'

'Who do you think you're kidding with this talking-dog stuff?' said the neighbour. ' There's no such animal.'

Suddenly the dog looked up with tears in his eyes. 'Please buy me, sir,' he pleaded. 'This man is cruel. He never buys me a meal, never bathes me, never takes me for a walk. I used to be the richest trick dog in Asia. I performed before kings. I was in the army and was decorated 10 times.'

'Hey!' said the neighbour. 'He can talk. Why sell him for just £5?'

'Because,' said the seller, 'I'm getting tired of all his damn lies.'

****

A new man is brought into prison cell 102. Already there is a long-time resident who looks 100 years old. The new man looks at the old-timer inquiringly. 'Look at me,' says the old timer. 'I'm old and worn out. You'd never believe that I used to live the life of Riley. I wintered on the Riviera, had a boat, four fine cars, the most beautiful women, and I ate in all the best restaurants in France.'

'What happened?' asked the new man.

'One day Riley reported his credit cards missing!' said the old-timer.

****

A group from Chicago spent a weekend gambling in Las Vegas. One of the men on that trip won $100,000. He didn't want anyone to know about it, so he decided not to return with the others, but took a later plane home, arriving back at 3am.

He immediately went out to the back garden of his house, dug a hole and planted the money in it.

The following morning he walked outside and found only an empty hole. He noticed footsteps leading from the hole to the house next door, which was owned by a deaf mute. On the same street lived a professor who understood sign language and was a friend of the deaf man. Grabbing his pistol, the enraged man went to awaken the professor and dragged him to the deaf man's house.

'You tell this guy that if he doesn't give me back my $100,000 I'm going to kill him!' he screamed at the professor. The professor conveyed the message to his friend, and his friend replied in sign language, 'I hid it in my backyard, underneath the cherry tree.'

The professor turned to the man with the gun and said, 'He's not going to tell you. He says he'd rather die first.'

****

The neatly-dressed salesman stopped a man in the street and asked, 'Sir, would you like to buy a toothbrush for 10 quid?'

Aghast, the man said, 'I should say not, that's robbery!'

The salesman seemed hurt. 'Well, then, how about a piece of homemade chocolate cake for 5p?'

This seemed fair, and the man handed a five-pence piece to the salesman. Unwrapping the cake, he took a bite.

'Urgh,' he snarled, 'this chocolate cake tastes like shit!'

'It is,' replied the salesman. 'Want to buy a toothbrush?'

****

A little old lady walked into the main branch the Bank of England holding a large paper bag in her hand. She told the young man at the window that she wished to take the £3 million that she had in the bag and open an account with the bank. But first, she said that she wished to meet the manager of the bank due to the large amount involved.

Whose Round Is It?

After looking into the bag and seeing an awful lot of money the bank clerk called the manager's office and told him the old lady wanted to see him.

The lady was escorted upstairs and ushered into the manager's office. Introductions were made and she explained that she liked to know the people that she did business with on a more personal level.

The manager then wondered her how she came into such a large amount of money. 'Was it an inheritance?' he asked.

'No,' she replied.

'Was it the lottery?' he asked.

'No,' she replied.

He was quiet for a minute trying to think where she could have come into £3 million.

'I bet,' she stated.

'You bet!' repeated the manager. 'As in horses?'

'No,' she replied. 'I bet on people.' Seeing his confusion, she explained that she just bet different things with people. All of a sudden she said, 'I'll bet you £25,000 that by 10am tomorrow morning your balls will be square.'

The bank manager figured that she must be off her rocker and decided to take her up on the bet. He didn't see how he could lose. For the rest of the day he was very careful. He decided to stay home that evening and take no chances – after all there was £25,000 at stake.

When he got up the next morning and took his shower, he checked to make sure that everything was OK. There was no difference, he looked the same as he always had. He went to work and waited for the little old lady to come in at 10am, humming as he went about his business. He knew that this would be a good day. How often do you get handed £25,000 for doing nothing?

At 10 sharp, the little old lady was escorted into his office. With her was a younger man. When the manager inquired as to the purpose of his being there, she informed him that he was her lawyer, and that she always took him along when there was a large amount of money involved.

'Well,' she asked. 'What about our bet?'

'I don't know how to tell you this,' he replied, 'but I'm the same as I have always been, only £25,000 richer!'

The lady seemed to accept this, but requested that she be able to see for herself. The manager thought that this was reasonable and dropped his trousers. She instructed him to bend over, then she grabbed hold of him. Sure enough, everything was fine. The manager then looked up and saw her lawyer banging his head against the wall.

'What's wrong with him?' the manager asked.

'Oh, him,' she replied. 'I bet him £100,000 that by 10am this morning, I would have the manager of the Bank of England by the balls.'

****

A man calls his lawyer and asks: 'How much would you charge me to answer three questions?'

'£400,' the lawyer replies.'

' Jesus,' says the man, 'that's a lot of money, isn't it?'

'I guess so,' replies the lawyer. 'What's your third question?'

****

One day little Johnny went to his father, and asked him if he could buy him a £200 bicycle for his birthday. Johnny's father said, 'Johnny, we have an £80,000 mortgage on the house, and you want me to buy you a bicycle? Wait until Christmas.'

Christmas came around, and Johnny asked again. The father said, 'Well, the mortgage is still extremely high, sorry about that. Ask me again some other time.'

Well, about two days later, the boy was seen walking out of the house with all his belongings in a suitcase. The father asked him why he was leaving. The boy said, 'Yesterday I was walking past your room, and I heard you say that you were pulling out, and mummy said that you should wait because she was coming too, and I'll be damned if I'm going to get stuck with an £80,000 mortgage!'

****

Whose Round Is It?

A newly-wed couple had recently opened a joint bank account. 'Darling,' said the man. 'The bank has returned that cheque you wrote last week.'

'Great,' said the woman. ' What shall I spend it on next?'

****

John's wife was not so good with money and, determined to economise, he'd decided to have a chat with her about it. The following day he met up with his mate.

'So,' asked his mate, 'do you think your little chat worked?'

'Yes, I think so,' said John. 'I'm going to give up beer and fags.'

****

Three engineers and three accountants are travelling by train to a conference. At the station, the three accountants each buy tickets and watch as the three engineers buy only a single ticket.

'How are three people going to travel on only one ticket?' asks an accountant.

'Watch and you'll see,' answers an engineer.

They all board the train. The accountants take their respective seats but all three engineers cram into a toilet and close the door behind them. Shortly after the train has departed, the conductor comes around collecting tickets. He knocks on the toilet door and says, 'Ticket, please.' The door opens just a crack and a single arm emerges with a ticket in hand. The conductor takes it, clips it and moves on.

The accountants see this and agree it's quite a clever idea. So after the conference, the accountants decide to copy the engineers on the return trip and save some money (being clever with money and all that). When they get to the station, they buy a single ticket for the return trip. To their astonishment, the engineers don't buy a ticket at all.

'How are you going to travel without a ticket?' says one perplexed accountant.

'Watch and you'll see,' answers an engineer.

When they board the train the three accountants cram into a toilet and the three engineers cram into another one nearby. The train departs. Shortly afterward, one of the engineers leaves his toilet and walks over to the toilet where the accountants are hiding. He knocks on the door and says, 'Ticket, please.'

✸✸✸✸

A butcher is in his shop and he's busy working when he notices a dog in the shop. He shoos him away, but later, he notices the dog is back again. So he goes over to the dog, and notices he has a note in his mouth. He takes the note and it reads, 'Can I have 12 sausages and a leg of lamb, please? The dog has money in his mouth.' The butcher looks inside the dog's mouth and, lo and behold, there is a £10 note in there. So he takes the money, and puts the sausages and lamb in a bag and places it in the dog's mouth. The butcher is well impressed, and since it's close to closing time, he decides to shut up shop and follow the dog.

So off he goes. The dog is walking down the street, when he comes to a level crossing. The dog puts down the bag, jumps up and presses the button and waits for the lights to change. They do, and he walks across the road, with the butcher following him all the way. The dog then comes to a bus stop, and starts looking at the timetable. The butcher is in awe by this stage. The dog checks out the times, and then sits on one of the seats provided. Along comes a bus. The dog walks around the front, looks at the number, and goes back to his seat. Another bus comes. Again the dog goes and looks at the number, sees it's the right bus, and climbs on.

The butcher, by now open-mouthed, follows him onto the bus. The bus travels through the town and out into the suburbs with the dog looking at the scenery. Eventually he gets up, and moves to the front of the bus. He stands on his hind legs and pushes the bell to stop the bus. Then he gets off, his groceries still in his mouth.

Well, dog and butcher are walking along the road, and then the dog turns into a house. He walks up the path, and drops the bag on the step.

Then he walks back down the path, takes a big run, and throws himself – whap!– against the door. He goes back down the path, runs up to the door and – whap!– throws himself against it again.

There's no answer at the house, so the dog goes back down the path, jumps up on a narrow wall, and walks along the perimeter of the garden. He gets to the window, and beats his head against it several times, walks back, jumps off, and waits at the door. The butcher watches as a big guy opens the door, and starts laying into the dog, kicking him and punching him and swearing at him. The butcher runs up, and stops the guy.

'What the hell are you doing ? The dog is a genius. He could be on TV, for God's sake !'

The big guy responds, 'Clever, my arse. This is the second time this week that he's forgotten his key.'

✶✶✶✶

Two weevils grew up in London. One went to Hollywood and became a world-famous actor. The other stayed behind in the cotton fields and never amounted to much. The second is now known as the lesser of two weevils.

✶✶✶✶

An engineer, a manager and a computer programmer driving down a steep mountain road. The brakes failed and the car careered down the road out of control. Halfway down the driver managed to stop the car by running it against the embankment, narrowly avoiding going over a cliff. They all got out, shaken by their narrow escape from death, but otherwise unharmed.

The manager says, 'To fix this problem we need to organise a committee, have meetings, and develop a solution.'

The engineer says, 'No, that would take too long, and besides that method never worked before. I have my trusty pen-knife here and will take apart the brake system, isolate the problem and correct it.'

The computer programmer says, 'I think you're both wrong! We should all push the car back up the hill and see if it happens again.'

Quiz Night

10

Those Tricky Questions

It is now a legal requirement for each and every pub in the land to have a night where some local loudmouth is given a microphone so that they can become even louder, as they blast out an astonishing array of questions supposed to be general knowledge, but in fact requiring a PhD or 10 hours a day surfing the Internet to answer.

They do this to various groups of people huddled round tables masquerading under some highly comical team name such as 'The Studs,' or 'The Cranial Crusaders,' who then scribble answers down whilst simultaneously operating a NATO-style defence manoeuvre so that other comically-named teams can't see their answers. At the end of it all the winners get a bottle of whisky, containing about the amount they would have drunk if they hadn't been spending so much time trying to answer the questions. Now that's entertainment…

****

Q: What's the last thing to go through a bug's mind as it hits the windscreen?
A: His arse!

****

Q: How do most men define marriage?
A: A very expensive way to get your laundry done free.

****

Q: Why do policemen have bigger balls than firemen?
A: They sell more tickets.

****

Q: How do you make a bunch of little old ladies say 'fuck'?.
A: Shout 'Bingo!'

****

Q: What do you call a man with a shovel in his head?
A: Doug.

****

Q: What do you call a man without a shovel in his head?
A: Douglas.

****

Q: What do you call a lady with a toothpick in her head?
A: Olive.

****

Q: What do you call a lady with one leg longer than the other?
A: Eileen.

****

Q: What do you call a Chinese lady with one leg longer than the other?
A: Irene.

****

Q: What do you call a lady with both legs the same length?
A: Nolene.

****

Q: What do you call an epileptic in a pile of leaves?
A: Russell.

Quiz Night

****

Q: What do you call a man with a wooden head?
A: Edward.

****

Q: What do you call a man with three wooden heads?
A: Edward Woodward.

****

Q: What do you call a man with four wooden heads?
A: I don't know, but Edward Woodward would.

****

Q: What do you call a man with a rabbit up his bum?
A: Warren.

****

Q: What do you call a man with his legs chopped off at the knees?
A: Neil.

****

Q: What do you call a man who is being electrocuted?
A: Buzz.

****

Q: What do you call a man who sits at your front door?
A: Matt.

****

Q: What do you call a man who has his head stuck under your car?
A: Jack.

****

Q: What do you call a man who has no arms and legs who is nailed to the wall?
A: Art.

****

Q: What do you call the arms and legs of the above-mentioned man?
A: Pieces of Art.

****

Q: What do you call a man with no arms and legs floating in the ocean?
A: Bob.

****

Q: What do you call a lady who is the stand-in for Polly in *Fawlty Towers*?
A: Polly-filler.

****

Q: What do you call a whole bunch of dead, bald, smokers floating in the ocean at Christmas?
A: Yul-tide.

****

Quiz Night

Q: What do you call a man with toilet paper in his mouth?
A: John.

****

Q: What do you call a man who has been buried for 2,000 years?
A: Pete.

****

Q: What do you call a dog with no legs?
A: It doesn't matter what you call him – he still won't come.

****

Q: What do you call a deer with no eyes?
A: No idea.

****

Q: What do you call a deer with no eyes and no legs?
A: Still no idea.

****

Q: What do you call a deer with no eyes and no legs who is chewing a razor?
A: Still no bloody idea.

****

Q: What do you call a man who hangs off the back of a car?
A: Reg.

****

Q: What do you call the man who hangs off the back of a car's brother?
A: Our Reg.

****

Q: What do you get when you cross a penis and a potato?
A: A dictator!

****

Q: What's the difference between a terrorist and a women with PMS?
A: You can negotiate with a terrorist!

****

Q: Why was the mushroom invited to all the parties?
A: Because he was a fungi.

****

Q: Why does a prostitute earn more money than a drug dealer?
A: 'Cos she can wash her crack and use it again.

****

Q: How do you turn a duck into a soul singer?
A: Put it in a microwave till its bill withers.

****

Q: What do you call a man with no arms and no legs swimming the Channel?

Quiz Night

A: Clever Dick.

****

Q: What do you call a man with no arms, no legs and no dick, swimming the Channel?
A: Smart Arse.

****

Q: What's red and invisible?
A: No tomatoes.

****

Q: What do you call a sheep with no legs?
A: A cloud.

****

Q: What do you call a greenfly without legs?
A: A bogey.

****

Q: What's green and spongey?
A: A green sponge.

****

Q: How do you reunite The Beatles?
A: Three more bullets.

****

Quiz Night

Q: What's 10 foot long and stinks of piss?
A: Old people doing the conga.

****

Q: What do ghosts do if they want to have a party?
A: See if they can dig up a few old friends.

****

Q: What do you call two ghosts in an aeroplane?
A: High spirits.

****

Q: Why did King Kong buy 15 pairs of shoes?
A: Because he was a 30-foot monster.

****

Q: Why did the ghost spend so long in the bathroom?
A: Because the spirit was willing but the flush was weak.

****

Q: What's got a big stomach and lives in the Himalayas?
A: The Abdominal Snowman.

****

Q: How could the vampire's mum tell he'd been smoking?
A: Because of his coffin.

****

Quiz Night

Q: What lies in a garden and trembles?
A: A nervous rake.

****

Q: What sits on the beach and cackles?
A: A sand witch.

****

Q: What sits in the desert and cackles?
A: A toasted sand witch.

****

Q: Where does Quasimodo keep his pet rabbit?
A: In a hutch, back of Notre Dame.

****

Q: What's brown and sticky?
A: A stick.

****

Q: What do you call a boomerang that doesn't come back?
A: A stick.

****

Q: What does a ghost take for constipation?
A: Spirit of figs.

Quiz Night

****

Q: What's hot, meaty and chases Ebeneezer Scrooge?
A: The ghost of Christmas Pasties.

****

Q: Why do hippos make love in water?
A: Do you have any idea how difficult it is to keep a seven-pound clitoris moist.

****

Q: What's the difference between cheese and men?
A: Cheese matures.

****

Q: Why is a cucumber and a beer better than a man?
A: Because the beer comes in a can, not your mouth, and the cucumber stays hard for a week.

****

Q: Why did God create men?
A: Because vibrators can't mow the lawn.

****

Q: How many men does it take to open a beer?
A: None: it should be open by the time she brings it to the couch.

****

Quiz Night

Q: What's the smelliest thing in the world?
A: An anchovy's bottom.

****

Q: What's the difference between ignorance and apathy?
A: I don't know and I don't care!

****

Q: How are a haemophiliac and a virgin alike?
A: One prick… and it's all over!

****

Q: What's green and red and faster than an airplane?
A: A frog in a blender!

****

Q: Why is a man like a Rubik cube?
A: The longer you play with one, the harder it gets.

****

Q: How many Zen Masters does it take to change a lightbulb?
A: Two, one to change it and one not to change it.

****

Q: What's blue and screws old ladies?
A: Hypothermia.

****

Quiz Night

Q: Why do farts smell?
A: So that deaf people can enjoy them, too!

****

Q: What do you call a truck full of vibrators?
A: Toys for twats.

****

Q: How many Vietnam vets does it take to change a light bulb?
A: I don't know. That's right, you don't know because you weren't there.

****

Q: Why do blondes wear panties?
A: To keep their ankles warm.

****

Q: What do you call two lesbians in a boat?
A: Fur traders!

****

Q: What should you do with your arsehole before you have sex?
A: Drop him off at the golf club.

****

Q: How do you make six pounds of fat look attractive?
A: Put a nipple on it.

****

Quiz Night

Q: What do you get when you mix a Jehovah's Witness with a Hell's Angel?
A: Someone who knocks on your front door at 7.30 on a Sunday morning, and tells you to fuck off.

****

Q: What do men and parking spaces have in common?
A: The good ones are always gone first and the ones that are left are disabled.

****

Q: How do you kill a circus?
A: Go for the juggler.

****

Q: What do you call the useless bit of skin at the end of a penis?
A: A man.

****

Q: What do elephants use as a vibrator?
A: A python with Parkinson's disease.

****

Q: What's the difference between a pub and a clitoris?
A: Most men can find a pub.

****

Q: What does tofu have in common with a vibrator?
A: They're both meat substitutes.

****

Q: What's the best way to get in touch with your long-lost relatives?
A: Win the lottery.

****

Q: Did you hear about the devil-worshipping dyslexic?
A: He sold his soul to Santa.

****

Q: How do you stop a dog from barking in the back garden?
A: Put it in the front garden.

****

Q: Why do cows have bells?
A: Because their horns don't work.

****

Q: How do you get two whales in a Mini?
A: One in the back, one in the front.

****

Q: How do you get two ants in the same Mini?
A: You can't, it's full of whales.

****

Q: Why was Cinderella chucked out of Disneyland?

Quiz Night

A: Because she was caught sitting on Pinnochio's face saying, 'Lie, lie, lie.'

****

A man goes into a fish and chip shop and orders fish and chips twice. The shop owner says, 'I heard you the first time.'

****

Two crisps were walking down the road when a passing motorist offers them a lift. 'No thanks,' say the crisps, 'we're Walkers.'

****

Two lepers were walking down the street. 'How are you?' says one. 'Mustn't crumble,' replies the other.

****

Q: What do you call a Spice Girl with two brain cells?
A: Pregnant.

****

Q: What do you call a Spice Girl sitting behind a steering-wheel?
A: An airbag.

****

Q: What do you call a polar bear in the jungle?
A: Lost.

****

Q: What do you get if you cross a hyena with an Oxo cube?
A: An animal that makes itself a laughing stock.

****

Q: What do you get if you cross a grass field with a cow?
A: A lawn-mooer.

****

Q: What do you get if you cross a herd of cows with an emergency?
A: Udder chaos.

****

Q: What do you get if you cross a cow with a major American city?
A: Moo York.

****

Q: What do you get if you cross a whale with a nun?
A: Blubber and sister.

****

Q: What do you get if you cross a cow with a sheep and a baby goat?
A: The milky baa kid.

****

Q: What do you get if you cross a thief with an orchestra?
A: Robbery with violins.

****

Quiz Night

Q: What do you get if you cross a successful book with perfume?
A: A best smeller.

****

Q: What do you get if you cross a pool of water with a spy?
A: James Pond.

****

Q: What do you get if you cross a lost property office with two vicars?
A: The missing parsons bureau

****

Q: What do you get if you cross a famous composer with an Indian?
A: Haydn Sikh.

****

Q: What did Snow White say when the chemist lost her film?
A: Some day my prints will come.

****

Q: Why couldn't the viper viper nose?
A: Because the adder adder handkerchief.

****

Q: What do you get if you cross an ancient English king with a chiropodist?
A: William the Corn-curer.

****

Q: How do you know when elephants have been making love in your garden?
A: The grass is rolled flat and all the bin-liners are missing.

****

Q: Why do elephants paint the soles of the feet yellow?
A: So they can hide upside-down in the custard.

****

Q: How do you know when an elephant has been in your fridge?
A: There are footprints in the butter.

****

Q: Why are elephants large, grey and wrinkled?
A: If they were small, round and white they'd be aspirins.

****

Q: Have you ever seen an elephant swimming in the custard?
A: No, but that just proves the efficiency of their camouflage.

****

Q: What's grey, has four legs, and a trunk?
A: A mouse going on holiday.

****

Q: What's brown, has four legs, and a trunk?
A: The same mouse coming back from holiday.

Quiz Night

****

Q: How can you tell when there's an elephant in bed with you?
A: Because they have a big 'E' on their pyjamas.

****

Q: How can you tell when there's an elephant under the bed?
A: Your nose is touching the ceiling.

****

Q: What should you do if you come across an elephant in the jungle?
A: Wipe it off and say you're sorry.

****

Q: How do elephants get up trees?
A: They sit on an acorn and fall asleep.

****

Q: How do elephants get down from trees?
A: They sit on a leaf and wait for Autumn.

****

Q: Why are crocodiles long, thin and flat?
A: They walk under trees in Autumn.

****

Q: How do you get four elephants into a Mini?

A: Two in the front, two in the back.

****

Q: How do you know when an elephant is visiting your house?
A: There's a Mini outside with three elephants in it.

****

Q: What do elephants use as tampons?
A: Sheep.

****

Q: Why do elephants have long trunks?
A: Sheep don't have strings.

****

Q: How do you get an elephant into a matchbox?
A: Take out all the matches first.

****

Q: Why are elephants large, grey and wrinkled?
A: Have you ever tried ironing one?

****

Q: What's the similarity between an elephant and a blue plum?
A: They are both grey. Well, except the plum.

****

Quiz Night

Q: What did Tarzan say, when he saw the elephants coming down the hill?
A: 'Look, the elephants are coming down the hill.'

****

Q: What did Julius Caesar say, when he saw the elephants coming down the hill?
A: 'Look, the plums are coming down the hill' – he was colour-blind.

****

Q: How many hippies does it take to screw in a light bulb?
A: Oh wow, is it like dark, man?

****

Q: How many Paras does it take to screw in a light bulb?
A: 50. One to screw in the light bulb and the remaining 49 to guard him.

****

Q: How many members of the U.S.S. Enterprise does it take to change a light bulb?
A: Seven. Scotty will report to Captain Kirk that the light bulb in the Engineering Section is burnt out, to which Kirk will send Bones to pronounce the bulb dead. Scotty, after checking around, notices that they have no more new light bulbs, and complains that he can't see in the dark to tend to his engines. Kirk must make an emergency stop at the next uncharted planet, Alpha Regula IV, to procure a light bulb from the natives. Kirk, Spock, Bones, Sulu, and three red shirt security officers beam down. The three security officers are promptly killed by the natives and the rest of the landing party is captured.

Meanwhile, back in orbit, Scotty notices a Klingon ship approaching and must warp out of orbit to escape detection. Bones cures the native king

Quiz Night

who is suffering from the flu, and as a reward the landing party is set free and given all of the light bulbs they can carry. Scotty cripples the Klingon ship and warps back to the planet just in time to beam up Kirk et al. The new bulb is inserted, and the Enterprise continues with its five-year mission.

****

Q: How many pygmies does it take to screw in a light bulb?
A: At least three.

****

Q: How many actors does it take to change a light bulb?
A: Only one. They don't like to share the spotlight.

****

Q: How many Dadaists does it take to screw in a light bulb?
A: To get to the other side.

****

Q: How many consultants does it take to change a light bulb?
A: We don't know. They never get past the feasibility study.

****

Q: How many Ukrainians does it take to screw in a light bulb?
A: They don't need to, they glow in the dark.

****

Q: How many stockbrokers does it take to change a light bulb?
A: Two. One to take out the bulb and drop it, and the other to try to sell it

before it crashes (knowing that it's already burned out).

****

Q: How many magicians does it take to change a light bulb?
A: Depends on what you want to change it into.

****

Q: How many missionaries does it take to change a light bulb?
A: 101. One to change it and 100 to convince everyone else to change light bulbs, too.

****

Q: How many Californians does it take to change a light bulb?
A: Six. One to turn the bulb, one for support, and four to relate to the experience.

****

Q: How many psychiatrists does it take to change a light bulb?
A: Only one, but the bulb has got to really WANT to change.

****

Q: How many graduate students does it take to screw in a light bulb?
A: Only one, but it may take upwards of five years for him to get it done.

****

Q: How many 'Real Men' does it take to change a light bulb?
A: None: 'Real Men' aren't afraid of the dark.

****

Q: How many folk singers does it take to screw in a light bulb?
A: Two. One to change the bulb, and one to write a song about how good the old light bulb was.

****

Q: How many surrealists does it take to change a light bulb?
A: Two. One to hold the giraffe, and the other to fill the bathtub with brightly coloured machine tools.

****

Q: How many Hassidic Jews does it take to change a light bulb?
A: None. They will never change anything.

****

Q: How many accountants does it take to screw in a light bulb?
A: What kind of answer did you have in mind?

****

Q: How many civil servants does it take to change a light bulb?
A: 45. One to change the bulb, and 44 to do the paperwork.

****

Q: How many nuclear engineers does it take to change a light bulb?
A: Seven. One to install the new bulb and six to figure out what to do with the old one for the next 10,000 years.

****

Quiz Night

Q: What do you get if you cross a Cuban with an Icelandic person?
A: An ice cube.

****

Q: What do you get if you cross a piece of paper with two composers?
A: A Chopin Listz.

****

Q: What do you get if you cross a joker with a pile of knickers?
A: A jester drawers.

****

Q: What do you get if you cross a fruit with a Welshman?
A: A taffy apple.

****

Q: What do you get if you cross a Greek singer with a yellow fruit?
A: Banana Mouskouri.

****

Q: What do you get if you cross a highwayman with a pickle?
A: Dick Gherkin.

****

Q: What do you get if you cross a chicken with a parrot?
A: Fowl language.

****

Quiz Night

Q: What do you get if you cross a mass murderer with a fish?
A: Jack the Kipper.

****

A down and out approached a well-dressed bloke. 'Ten pence for a cup of tea, Guv?' he asked.
The bloke gave him the money and after waiting for five minutes said, 'So where's my cup of tea, then?'

****

Q: How many ears did Davy Crockett have?
A: Three. A left ear, a right ear and a wild frontier.

****

Q: What's a Hindu?
A: Lay eggs.

****

Q: Who rides around on a camel carrying a lamp?
A: Florence of Arabia.

****

Q: What do zebras have that no other animals have?
A: Baby zebras.

****

Q: What's the difference between a dead skunk on the road and a

Quiz Night

dead lawyer?
A: There are skid marks in front of the skunk.

****

Q: Why did the chicken cross the road
A: Because is was stuck to the chicken-fucker's knob.

****

Q: Why was the skeleton afraid to cross the road?
A: He had no guts!

****

Q: Why have elephants got big ears?
A: Because Noddy won't pay the ransom

****

Q: What do vampires become after they reach the age of 200?
A: 201

****

Q. Why is 6 afraid of 7?
A. Because 7 ate 9

****

Q: Why was the legless dog called Woodbine
A: Because it's owner took it out for a drag in the garden twice a day

****

Quiz Night

Q: What do you call two elephants on a bicycle ?
A: Optimistic!

****

Q: What do you get if you take an elephant into the city?
A: Free Parking.

****

Q: What do you get if you take an elephant into work ?
A: Sole use of the lift.

****

Q: How do you know if there is an elephant in the pub?
A: It's bike is outside.

****

Q: How do you know if there are two elephants in the pub?
A: There is a dent in the cross-bar of the bike outside.

****

Q: How do you know if there are three elephants in the pub?
A: Stand on the bike and have a look in the window.

****

Q: What do you call a small box with a sattelite dish on the side?
A: A council house.

Quiz Night

****

Q: Why did the chicken cross the road?
A: To get to the other side.

****

Q: How can keep an Irishman busy?
A: Give him two shovels and tell hims to take his pick.

****

Q: Did you hear about the Irish woodworm?
A: It was found dead in a brick.

****

Q: How can you spot an Irish aeroplane?
A: It's got an outside lav.

****

Q: What happened at the Irish Water Polo championships?
A: All the horses drowned.

****

Q: What do you call a scouser in a suit?
A: The accused.

****

Q: What do you call a cockney in a detatched house?
A: A burglar.

Pissed As A Fart

11

Jokes for the End of the Night

Pissed As A Fart

Reality, eh? Maybe as the philosophers would have us believe we're all living in some ludicrous dream where nothing is real, yet everything is real, and we could all fly if we really wanted to in craft made out of eggshells and those bits of black stuff you get between your toes. Then again maybe philosophers are the biggest bunch of pissheads around, who spend their lives in that state somewhere just past 'lively' and just before, 'pass out' where the most ludicrous of suggestions seems like a very sensible idea, and the worst puns and crappiest jokes get massive laughs. At least we hope they do…

****

Two bits of vomit were walking down the street when one of them began to cry.

'What's the matter?' asked the first.

'I'm sorry,' said the other, 'but I always get a bit sentimental when I pass the place I was brought up.'

****

'Hello, and welcome to the Psychiatric Hotline. If you are obsessive-compulsive, please press 1 repeatedly. If you are co-dependent, please ask someone to press 2. If you have multiple personalities, please press 3, 4, 5 and 6. If you are paranoid-delusional 36.

****

Three cons escape from prison. They make it to a nearby town, but are confronted by a policeman. 'Hey, aren't you those three escaped cons?' asked the policeman.

Thinking on his feet the first con looked around him and said 'no, I'm Mark… Mark Spencer.'

The second followed his lead and said, 'My name is William, W H Smith.'

The third said, 'My name is Ken… Tucky Fried Chicken.'

****

A man sits down at a restaurant and looks at the menu. He tells the waiter, 'I think I will have the turtle soup.' The waiter leaves, but the man changes his mind to pea soup. He yells to the waiter, 'Hold the turtle, make it pea!'

****

A drunk decides to go ice fishing, so he gathers his gear and goes walking around until he finds a big patch of ice. He heads into the centre of the ice and begins to saw a hole. All of a sudden, a loud booming voice comes out of the sky and says, 'You will find no fish under that ice.'

The drunk looks around, but sees no one so he starts sawing again. Once more, the voice speaks. 'As I said before, there are no fish under the ice.'

The drunk looks all around, high and low, but can't see a single soul, so he picks up the saw and tries one more time to finish. Before he can even start cutting, the huge voice interrupts. 'I have warned you three times, now. There are no fish!'

'The drunk is now flustered and somewhat scared, so he asks the voice, 'How do you know there are no fish? Are you God trying to warn me?"

'No,' the voice replies. 'I am the manager of this ice rink.'

****

A man walks into a pub with his monkey. He orders a pint and sits down to drink it. While he's sitting at the bar, his monkey is out of control. It jumps up on the pool table and eats the cue ball. The landlord runs up to the man and says, 'Did you see what your stupid monkey just did?'

'No, what did that stupid fucker do this time?' says the man.

'He just ate the cue ball!' shouts the landlord.

'I hope it kills the stupid bastard,' says the man.

About two weeks later, the man comes back to the pub with his monkey.

Pissed As A Fart

While he's drinking at the bar, his monkey is again out of control. The monkey finds a grape at the bar, picks it up, sticks it up his arse, and eats it. The landlord, having seen this, asks the man: 'Did you see what your sick monkey just did?'

'No,' says the man.

'He just stuck a grape up his arse and ate it,' the landlord tells him.

'Well, what do you expect?' asks the man. 'Since that pool ball he measures everything first.'

✳✳✳✳

A thirsty-looking big, bad, brown bear comes walking into a pub and shouts, 'Oi, landlord, give me a pint!'

The landlord walks over to the bear and confidently says, 'Sorry but we don't serve beers to big, bad, brown bears in this pub.'

This pisses the bear off as he's growing thirstier by the second. So, the bear leans on the bar and says, 'Just give me a beer.'

The landlord replies again, 'Sorry, but we don't serve beers to big, bad, brown bears in this pub.' The bear, who is really pissed off now, leans over the bar, looks the landlord square in the eyes and says, 'If you don't give me a beer, I'm going to go bite that girls head off!' pointing to the women at the end of the bar.

The landlord repeats himself, 'Sorry but we don't serve beers to big, bad, brown bears in this pub.'

So the bear walks down to the girl… GGGRRRRRRRR… CHOMP… GULP. He bites her head off and swallows it whole. The bear walks back over to the bartender, slams his bloody paws on the table and says, 'Give me a fucking beer!'

The landlord looks the bear straight in the eyes and says, 'Sorry but we don't serve beers to big, bad, brown bears WHO DO DRUGS in this pub.'

The bear, who's a bit confused, shouts, 'WHAT?'

The landlord points to the half-eaten girl and says, 'that was a Bar-Bitch-U-ate.'

A panda sauntered into the pub, sat down at the bar and said to the landlord, 'Give me a sandwich and a pint.'

The landlord had seen many strange characters in his time, and knew it was important to keep his cool, so he replied, 'Sure, mate,' and slapped a ham sandwich and a lager in front of the panda. The panda chomped on the sandwich and gulped down the beer. He then deftly pulled out a pistol, aimed at a whisky bottle behind the counter, and pulled the trigger. The bottle exploded into pieces and shattered onto the floor. The landlord was dumbfounded as he watched the panda return his gun to his holster and walk out the front door.

'Hey, what the hell is going on?' shouted the landlord as he ran after the beast.

The panda stopped and said, 'What do you want?'

'Well, I didn't expect you to come into my pub and start shooting the place up. Besides, you still owe me for lunch.'

'I'm a PANDA. Look it up,' replied the panda and went on his way.

The landlord was too upset and nervous to rile such an unpredictable sort, so he picked up his unabridged dictionary from the shelf, and found the entry for 'panda'. 'Shit!' he muttered. He realised that there was nothing he could do about it. There it was, in black and white, written by an authority no less than Oxford University itself: 'panda n. A large bear-like member of the raccoon family native to the mountains of China and Tibet, with distinctive white and black markings. Eats shoots and leaves.'

An Indian tribe had a chief named Shortcake. He was highly regarded by all the members of the tribe and when he died, all the braves took him out and prepared to bury him. Just then his wife came running up and shouted, 'Wait! Wait! Squaw bury Shortcake.'

****

Pissed As A Fart

Charles was working for many years as the elephant trainer in a local circus. Then, after a few rough years, the circus went bust and he was let go with a 'thank you', one of the elephants and a few bales of hay.

Feeling rather depressed, Charles got to wondering how he was going to survive with only an elephant and no career. Then he remembered his days in the circus and realised he was on to a good thing. In all his years in the circus, he had trained elephants to lift one leg off the ground, lift two legs off the ground and even lift three legs off the ground, but NEVER had he seen four legs off the ground at once. Near and far he advertised, '£1 a go, win £1,000 if you can make the elephant lift four legs off the ground at once.'

People came from near and far to try and Charles was raking in the money. He had made about £700 when one day a fellow arrived in a red convertible. He asked about the rules of the contest and paid his money. He walked back to the car, took out a baseball bat, walked to the front of the elephant, looked him in the eye long and hard. Then he walked around the back of the elephant, took a mighty swing and struck the animal in the testicles. At once the elephant leapt into the air and Charles was down £1,000 and feeling very sorry for himself. Then he remembered his days at the circus and in all his days he had never seen an elephant move his head from side to side. Up and down he had seen, round and round he had seen but NEVER from side to side.

Near and far he advertised, '£1 a go, win £1,000 if you can make the elephant move his head from side to side. People came from near and far to try and Charles was raking the money in when one day the same fellow arrived in his red convertible. Again he asked the rules and walked to his car. He returned with a baseball bat, walked to the front of the elephant, looked the animal in the eye long and hard and said, 'You remember me, don't you?'

The elephant nodded.

'You remember what I did to you?'

The elephant nodded.

'You remember the PAIN?'

The elephant nodded.

'Do you want me to do it again?'

****

So, this guy, Bill is sitting at the bar and pulls out this tiny little piano and a little guy about a foot tall. The little guy sits down and starts playing the piano quite beautifully. The fellow on the next bar stool, Joe, says, 'That's amazing. Where did you get him?'

Bill says, 'Well, I got this magic lamp with a genie.'

'That's great,' says Joe. 'Could I use it?'

Bill says, 'Sure,' and hands him the lamp.

Joe rubs the lamp and out comes the genie. He says,' I want a million quid.' Suddenly the room is entirely filled with octopuses! Joe exclaims, 'Hey! I asked for a million QUID! not SQUID!'

'Yeah, sorry about that, the genie is a bit deaf,' says Bill. 'You don't think I really asked for a 12-inch-pianist, do you?'

****

Then there's the drunk who went out on a long bender. Somewhere in the course of his wanderings the right pocket was ripped out of his trousers. The drunk, sobering up somewhat after several days, begins to take stock of himself and his condition. He reaches into his coat pocket, pulls out the contents and checks them. All is well. He reaches into his left trouser pocket, pulls out the contents – again all is well. Then he reaches into his right trouser pocket. He feels around a bit then, with a quizzical look on his face says to himself, 'Prunes, prunes… now why in the hell did I buy prunes?'

****

A neutron walks into a pub. 'I'd like a beer,' he says. The landlord promptly serves him a beer. 'How much will that be?' asks the neutron.

'For you?' replies the landlord, 'no charge.'

****

Three bits of string walked by a pub and noticed a sign outside it that said, 'NO STRING ALLOWED'. Indignant at the discrimination the first piece of string decided to go in and order a drink.

'Can't you read?' said the landlord, and when the string refused to leave he picked it up and tossed it out the door. The second piece of string tried the same thing and when it also refused to leave, the landlord punched it and threw it out the door as well. The third piece of string thought for a few seconds, then scraped itself along the pavement harshly until it was ragged all over. Then it twisted itself inside out and around and around until its middle was all in a bunch, then it entered the pub, got upon a stool and ordered a pint.

'Hey,' asked the landlord suspiciously, 'aren't you the string I just threw out of here?'

'No,' replied the string, 'I'm a frayed knot.'

A duck goes into a pub and asks the landlord, 'You got any fish?'

The landlord says, 'No. This is a pub, we don't sell fish.' So the duck leaves. The next day, the duck goes back to the pub and asks, 'You got any fish?'

The landlord says, 'I told you yesterday. This is a pub and we don't sell fish.'

The following day, the duck returns and asks, 'You got any fish?'

The landlord loses it, grabs the duck by the neck, and screams, 'I TOLD YOU TWICE. THIS IS A PUB! WE DON'T SELL FISH! IF YOU ASK AGAIN, I'M GONNA NAIL YOUR FUCKING WEBBED FEET TO THE FLOOR!'

The next day, the duck goes in the pub and asks, 'Got any nails?'

The landlord sighs and says, 'No, we don't have any nails.'

'Good,' says the duck. 'Got any fish?'

The landlord got tired of hearing these five drunks arguing about who had the biggest dick. So he shouts out, 'I'm tired of this shit. Pull them out and put them up on the bar and I'll tell you who has the biggest.'

They were drunk enough that all five of them responded and placed their dicks up on the bar. Just then a gay guy walks in, and the landlord asks, 'May I help you?'

To which he responds: 'Well, I came in for a pint and a sandwich but I think I'll have the smorgasbord.'

****

The first little pig walked into the pub and said, 'Can I have a rum and Coke?'

'OK,' said the landlord. Then the little pig said, 'Can I use your toilet?' and similarly the landlord agreed.

Then a second little pig walked into the pub and said, 'Can I have a rum and Coke?' and once again the landlord poured him one.

Then the little pig said, 'Can I use your toilet?' to which the landlord similarly agreed. Then a third little pig walked into the pub and said, 'Can I have a rum and Coke?'

'OK,' said the landlord, 'and I suppose you want to use the toilet, too'.

But the third little pig said, 'No, I'm the lttle pig that goes wee, wee, wee all the way home'

****

One night, after closing time, a landlord is sitting at his bar minding his own business, when a spectral hound floats in through the door. The landlord, being an exceptionally cool kind of geezer, asks, 'Yeah, what do you want?'

The phantom hound explains, in a haunting voice, 'I've lost my tail and cannot rest until a kindly landlord stitches it back on.' At this request the landlord stands back astonished and says to the phantom dog.

'Sorry, but we don't re-tail spirits at this time of night.'

****

A doctor made it his regular habit to stop off at a bar for a hazelnut daiquiri on his way home. The bartender knew of his habit, and would always have the drink waiting at precisely 5:03pm. One afternoon, as the end of the working day approached, the bartender was dismayed to find that he was out of hazelnut extract. Thinking quickly, he threw together a daiquiri made with hickory nuts and set it on the bar.

The doctor came in at his regular time, took one sip of the drink and exclaimed, 'This isn't a hazelnut daiquiri!'

'No, I'm sorry,' replied the bartender, 'it's a hickory daiquiri, doc.'

****

A bloke goes to the doctor with a heavily-infected arm, all yellow and pussy. After examining it the doc asks, 'What is it that you do?'

'I work in the circus,' replies the man.

'I see,' says the doc. 'And what do you do in the circus?'

'I work with the elephants,' replies the man.

'I see,' says the doc. 'And what do you do with the elephants?'

'Well,' says the man. 'It's my job to give them enemas. I put my arm right up their backsides and get on with it.'

'I think,' says the doc, 'that therein lies your problem. You're going to have to stop doing that and find another job.'

'What and give up showbiz?' replies the man.

****

There was a woman who was pregnant with twins, and shortly before they were due, she had an accident and went into a coma. Her husband was away on business, and couldn't to be reached. While in the coma, she gave birth to her twins, and the only person around to name her children was her brother.

When the mother came out of her coma to find she had given birth and that her brother had named the twins, she became very worried, because he wasn't a very bright guy. She was sure he'd named them something absurd or stupid. When she saw her brother she asked him about the twins.

He said, 'The first one was a girl.'

'What did you name her?' asked the woman.

'Denise!' said her brother.

'Oh, that's not bad,' she said. 'What about the second one?'

'The second one was a boy,' said her brother.

'Oh, and what did you name him?' she asked.

'Denephew,' said the brother.

****

One afternoon this young woman called on her neighbour for a chat. She walked in and said, 'You look depressed.'

'You bet I am,' replied the neighbour. 'Look what my bloody husband sent me – six dozen roses. Now I'm going to have to spend the entire weekend flat on my back with my legs open.'

'Don't be silly,' said the first woman, 'why don't you just use a vase?'

****

It seems a man got turned in by his neighbour who saw him having sex with a goat. He was arrested and told to get a lawyer. He had a choice of two. It was a small town. One lawyer was very expensive. He usually won his case by having costly out-of-town experts testify. The other was cheap. His forte was jury selection, he could usually get a juror or two that would be sympathetic to his client. The defendant chose the less expensive lawyer.

The first day of the trial the witness was told to tell the jury exactly what he saw on the morning of March 15th. He stated that he happened to look out his kitchen window about 8am and he saw farmer Brown drop his pants and have sex with a tan-coloured goat. And when he finished the goat turned around and licked his penis. At this time a front-row juror was heard to say to another juror, 'You know, a good goat will do that.'

****

Woman goes to the doctor and says, 'Doctor, my husband limps because his left leg is an inch shorter than his right leg. What would you do in his case?'

'Probably limp, too,' says the doc.

****

A 60-year-old woman came home one day and heard strange noises in her bedroom. She opened the door and discovered her 40-year-old daughter playing with her vibrator. 'What are you doing?' asked the Mum.

'Mum, I am 40 years old and look at me,' said the daughter. 'I am ugly. I will never get married, so this is pretty much my husband.' The mother walked out of the room, shaking her head.

The next day the father came home and heard noises in the bedroom and upon entering the room found his daughter using the vibrator. 'What the hell are you doing?' he asked.

His daughter replied, 'I already told Mum. I am 40 years old now and ugly. I will never get married so this is as close as I'll ever get to a husband.' The father walked out of the room shaking his head too.

The next day the mother came home to find her husband with a beer in one hand and the vibrator sitting next to him, watching the football.

'For Christ's sake, what are you doing?' she cried.

'What does it look like I'm doing?' replied her husband. 'I'm having a beer and watching the game with my new son-in-law!'

****

Two guys wandered into a pub. One of the men shouted to the landlord, 'Hiya, Mike. Set 'em up for me and my mate here.' Then he turned to his slightly dim partner and boasted, 'This is a great pub. For every two drinks you buy, the house gives you one and the fruit machines are free!'

'"That's not so great,' responded the friend. 'There's a pub across town that'll match you drink for drink, and you can get laid for free.'

'Where is this place?' the first guy exclaimed.

'Oh, I don't know,' the dim fellow replied, 'but my wife goes there all the time.'

****

A man walked in to a pub after work. As he began to drink his beer, he heard a voice say seductively, 'You've got great hair!' The man looked around but couldn't see where the voice was coming from, so he went back to his beer.

A minute later, he heard the same voice say, 'You're a handsome man!' The man looked around, but still couldn't see where the voice was coming from. When he went back to his beer, the voice said again, 'What a stud you are!' The man was so baffled by this that he asked the landlord what was going on. The landlord said, 'Oh, it's the nuts – they're complimentary.'

****

An 80-year-old couple decide they want kids again. They visit the doctor who suggests, since they are a little older than usual, some tests might be in order. He hands the couple a small jar and asks them to go next door and for the gentleman to fill it so they can test his sperm count.

A few minutes later the couple returns and hands back the jar. 'But it's still empty!' exclaims the doctor.

'I know,' replies the man. 'I tried with my right hand, I tried with my left hand, then I tried with both hands, and I still couldn't do it. Then my wife tried with her right hand, then her left hand, and with both hands. She tried with her teeth in and her teeth out, and we still couldn't get the lid off that jar!'

Two old ladies were waiting for a bus and one of them was smoking a cigarette. It started to rain, so the old lady reached into her handbag, took out a condom, cut off the tip and slipped it over her cigarette and continued to smoke. Her friend saw this and said, 'Hey that's a good idea! What is it that you put over your cigarette?'

The other old lady said, 'It's a condom.'

'A condom?' said her friend. 'Where do you get those?'

The lady with the cigarette told her friend that you could purchase condoms at the chemist.

When the two old ladies arrived in town, the second old lady went into a chemist shop and asked the pharmacist if he sold condoms. The pharmacist said yes, but looked a little surprised that this old lady was interested in condoms. 'What size do you want?' he asked her.

The old lady thought for a minute and said, 'I'd like one that will fit a Camel.'

****

Two missionaries in Africa were apprehended by a tribe of very hostile cannibals who put them in a large pot of water, built a huge fire under it, and left them there. A few minutes later, one of the missionaries started to laugh uncontrollably. The other missionary couldn't believe it!

'What's wrong with you?' he shouted. 'We're being boiled alive! They're gonna eat us! What could possibly be funny at a time like this?'

' Well,' said the other missionary. 'I just pissed in the soup!'

****

It's been a hard year in the jungle, so when these two cannibals finally catch this one missionary they have a discussion about how they are each going to get a fair share. They finally reach the conclusion that they will start at opposite ends and meet in the middle.

After starting the meal one cannibal asks the other, 'How you doing down there?'

'Oh I'm having a ball!' replies the other cannibal.

'No, no!' screamed the first cannibal, 'you're eating too fast!'

****

The devil told the Pope, 'No one in the world has a better memory than I do.'

'Oh!' replied the Pope. 'Well, I know this American Indian who has the best memory in the world and I'll even prove it.'

'OK,' said the devil, 'I'll take up your offer and if I have a better memory I get your soul.'

'It's a deal,' said the Pope.

So off they went to a remote village. There they met Roaming Bull, who was the Indian the Pope had been talking about. The devil asked Roaming Bull what meal he had eaten 20 years ago to the day.

'Eggs,' replied Roaming Bull.

'Thank you,' said the devil and left. Although a short while after leaving town he realised that this could quite easily have been a trick answer and vowed to clear this up the next time he was free.

The devil can be a busy chap, what with all the idle hands in the world and 50 years passed before he returned to the village. This time he greeted the now wizened Roaming Bull in the traditional Indian way. 'How,' said the devil.

'Scrambled,' replied the Indian.

****

A vicar stepping up into the pulpit spots a woman he thinks he knows wearing a mini-skirt seated on the front pew. He leans over to his organist and asks, 'Isn't that Fanny Blue?'

'No,' says the organist, 'I think it's just the way the light's coming through the stain-glass window.'

****

Pissed As A Fart

A woman telephoned a vet and asked him to come and examine her cat.

'I don't know what's wrong with her,' the woman told him. 'She looks as if she's going to have kittens, but that's impossible. She's never been out of the house except for when I had her on a leash.'

The vet examined the cat and said there was no question about her pregnancy.

'But she can't be,' protested the woman. 'It's impossible.'

At that point a large tom-cat emerged from under the sofa.

'How about him?' asked the vet.

'Don't be silly,' answered the woman. 'That's her brother.'

✳✳✳✳

Three monks are meditating far from the madding crowd, in the Himalayas. One year passes in silence, and one of them says to the others, 'Pretty cold here.'

Another year passes and the second monk says, 'You know, you are quite right.'

Another year passes and the third monk says, 'Hey, I'm going to leave unless you two stop jabbering!'

✳✳✳✳

One day two nuns were sitting in their convent talking and drinking tea when a priest arrived. The nuns invited him to sit and have tea with them. He accepted and sat down to discuss upcoming events at their parish.

Suddenly the priest stopped talking in mid-sentence because his eyes had wandered to the piano in the room. Sitting on top of it was an opened unrolled latex condom. He was appalled. 'Sisters,' he said pointing to the piano, 'what do you call that?'

The nuns were oblivious to his shock and simply explained to the priest why the condom was sitting on the piano, 'Well,' said the first nun, 'we saw them advertised on the TV…'

'…And,' finished the second nun, 'the people in the ad said they were really good for you and that everybody should use them every time.'

'So,' said the first nun, 'we went to the shop and bought some. When we got back to the convent, we read the instructions on the back of the box. It said, "Carefully place it on your organ." So we did.'

****

A man saw a priest walking down the street. Noticing his collar, he stopped him and said, 'Excuse me, but why are you wearing your shirt backwards?'

The priest laughed, 'Because, my son,' he said, 'I am a Father!'

The man scratched his head. 'But I am a father too,' he said, 'and don't wear my shirt backwards!'

Again the priest laughed. 'But I am a Father of thousands!'

To which the man replied, 'Well then you should wear your underwear backwards!'

****

Ian is sitting on a bench in front of the Pearly Gates waiting for St Peter to show up when his best friend Tim comes and sits down next to him. They talk for a while until St Peter shows up at the gate.

'I'm sorry, lads,' says the winged one, 'but we only have room for one more person right now.' So the two friends started arguing about who should go in.

'You go Tim,' says Ian.

'No, no,' says Tim. 'You go Ian.'

'No, Tim, I couldn't,' says Ian. 'You go.'

This continues for some time until St Peter stops them and says, 'Right, each one of you will write me a poem about my favourite place, Timbuctoo, and whoever's is best will go to heaven.'

So they both wrote a poem and Ian, wanting his friend Tim to go to

Pissed As A Fart

heaven rather than him, decides to write a really bad one. When they're both done they go back to St Peter who asks Tim to read his poem first. He does so and it's pretty good. Next St Peter asks the Ian to read his poem. He clears his throat and reads, 'Me and Tim a-hunting went, spied three maidens in a tent, since they were three and we were two, I bucked one and Tim bucked two.'

****

Three old ladies are sitting in a cafe chatting about various things. 'You know,' says one lady, 'I'm getting really forgetful. This morning, I was standing at the top of the stairs, and I couldn't remember whether I had just come up or was about to go down.'

'You think that's bad?' says the second lady. 'The other day, I was sitting on the edge of my bed, and I couldn't remember whether I was going to bed or had just woken up!'

The third lady smiles smugly. 'Well, my memory's just as good as it's always been,' she says, 'touch wood,' and she knocks the table. Then with a startled look on her face, she says, 'Who's there?'

****

An elderly husband and wife noticed that they were beginning to forget many little things around the house. They were afraid that this could be dangerous, as one of them might accidentally forget to turn off the stove and thus cause a fire.

So, they decided to go to see their doctor to get some help. Their doctor told them that many people their age found it useful to write themselves little notes as reminders. The elderly couple thought this sounded wonderful, and left the doctor's office very pleased with the advice. When they got home, the wife said, 'Dear, will you please go to the kitchen and get me a dish of ice cream? And why don't you write that down so you won't forget?'

'Nonsense,' said the husband, 'I can remember a dish of ice cream!'

'Well,' said the wife, 'I'd also like some strawberries on it. You'd better write that down, because I know you'll forget.'

'Don't be silly,' replied the husband. 'A dish of ice cream and some strawberries. I can remember that!'

'OK, dear, but I'd like you to put some whipped cream on top. Now you'd really better write it down now. You'll forget,' said the wife.

'Come now, my memory's not all that bad,' said the husband. 'No problem, a dish of ice cream with strawberries and whipped cream.' With that, the husband shut the kitchen door behind him. The wife could hear him getting out pots and pans, and making some noise inconsistent with his preparing a dish of ice cream, strawberries, and whipped cream.

He emerged from the kitchen about 15 minutes later. Walking over to his wife, he presented her with a plate of bacon and eggs. The wife took one look at the plate, glanced up at her husband and said, 'Hey, where's the toast?'

****

There is this guy who really takes care of his body. He lifts weights and jogs five miles every day. One morning he is looking into the mirror and admiring his body when he notices that he is really sun-tanned all over, except for his penis. So he decides to do something about it.

The next day he goes to the beach, strips completely and buries himself in the sand, except for his penis which he leaves sticking out. Two little old ladies are strolling along the beach and one looks down and says 'There is no justice in this world.'

'What do you mean?' says her friend.

'Look at that,' she says. 'When I was 10 years old I was afraid of it. When I was 20, I was curious about it. When I was 30, I enjoyed it. When I was 40, I asked for it. When I was 50, I paid for it. When I was 60, I prayed for it. When I was 70, I forgot about it. And now that I'm 80, the damn things are growing wild!'

****

Two teenage boys are talking, and the first boy asks the second boy, 'How many wings does a bird have?'
　'Two wings,' the second boy replies.
　'How many stingers does a bee have?' the first boy asks next.
　'One stinger,' responds the second boy.
　'And how many ribs does a cat have?' asks the first boy.
　'I don't know,' replies the second boy.
　'Well,' says the first boy. 'You may know about the birds and the bees, but you don't know much about pussy.'

****

A murderer, sitting in the electric chair, was about to be executed. 'Have you any last requests?' asked the chaplain.'
　'Yes,' replied the murderer. 'Will you hold my hand?'

****

Once upon a time there were two deaf mutes standing on a street corner talking to each other with sign language.
　Mute One: 'What would you like to do?'
　Mute Two: 'I don't know, what about you?'
　Mute One: 'Let's get my car, find some girls, drive to a dark space and have some fun.'
　Mute Two: 'Good idea.'
　So they get his car, find some girls, drive to a dark spot and are having a ball when the guy in the back seat taps the guy in the front seat on the shoulder.
　Front Seat Mute: 'What?'
　Back Seat Mute: 'Have you got any protection?'
　Front Seat Mute: 'No. Have you?'
　Back Seat Mute: 'No. We'd better go to a chemist and get some.'

They drive to a chemist and the man in the back seat gets out and goes inside. In two minutes he is back outside and taps on the car window.
Inside Mute: 'What?'
Outside Mute: 'I can't make the chemist understand what I want.'
Inside Mute: 'I know what to do.'
Outside Mute: 'What?'
Inside Mute: 'Go back inside. Put £5 on the counter and put your pecker on the counter. He'll know what you want.'
Outside Mute: 'Good idea.'
The man goes back into the chemist and two minutes later he's back at the car window.
Inside Mute: 'Well?'
Outside Mute: 'It didn't work.'
Inside Mute: 'What do you mean?'
Outside Mute: 'I did what you told me to do. I went inside. I put £5 on the counter and I put my pecker on the counter. Then he put his on the counter. It was bigger than mine so he took my £5.'

****

A blind man was standing on the corner with his dog when the dog raised his leg and pissed on the man's trouser leg. The man reached in his pocket and took out a doggie biscuit. A busybody who had been watching ran up to him and said, 'You shouldn't do that. He'll never learn anything if you reward him when he does something like that!'

'I'm not rewarding him,' the blind man retorted, 'I'm just trying to find his mouth so that I can kick him up the arse.'

****

There were these two guys out hiking when they came upon an old abandoned mine-shaft. Curious about its depth they threw in a pebble and waited for the sound of it striking the bottom, but they heard nothing. They went and got a bigger rock, threw it in and waited. Still nothing. They searched the area for something larger and came upon a large metal fence.

With great difficulty, the two men carried it to the opening and threw it in. While waiting for it to hit bottom, a goat suddenly darted between them and leapt into the hole! The guys were still standing there with astonished looks upon their faces from the actions of the goat when a man walked up to them. He asked them if they had seen a goat anywhere in the area and they said that one had just jumped into the mine shaft in front of them.

'Oh no,' replied the man, 'that couldn't be my goat, mine was tied to a fence.'

****

There were these two statues and they were both a couple of hundred years old. One day, a fairy flew over them and tapped their heads with her wand.

'You have 24 hours to do WHATEVER YOU WANT,' she said to the statues.

Twenty-three hours and 57 minutes later the male statue says to the female statue, 'Why don't we do it again?'

'We don't have enough time!' says the female statue.

'Sure we do!' says the male statue.

'Just ONE MORE TIME, please?'

'Oh, all right!' says the female statue, 'but this time YOU hold the pigeon and I'LL crap on it!'

****

One sunny afternoon Superman was out flying around. Crime was slow that day, so he decided to go over to Spiderman's house. 'Hey, Spidey,' said Superman, 'let's go get a burger and a beer'

'No can do, Supe,' said Spiderman, 'I've got a problem with my Web-shooter. Can't fight crime tomorrow without it.'

So Superman went over to the Bat Cave to see what was up there.

'Hey, Batman!' said Superman, 'Let's go get a burger and a beer!'

'Not today, my friend,' said Batman, 'my Batmobile is down and it must be fixed today. Can't fight crime tomorrow without it.'

Disgruntled, Superman takes to the air, cruising around the skies when he flies over a penthouse apartment. Thanks to his supervision he is able to see Wonderwoman, lying on the balcony, spread eagle and stark naked! So he zooms down and thanks to his superspeed shags her in a flash and is gone before anyone can notice. All of a sudden Wonderwoman sits up and says, 'What was that!?'

'I don't know,' says the Invisible Man, 'but it hurt like hell!'

✶✶✶✶

The curator of an art gallery asked an artist for a painting depicting General Custer's last thoughts. Two weeks later, the artist unveiled a painting of an enormous canvas with a lovely blue lake painted in the centre, with a fish leaping from the water with a shining halo around its head.

On the shores of the lake were the most detailed pictures of American Indians fornicating. After gaping at the painting for some time, the enraged curator demanded to know what the theme was supposed to be.

'You asked for a painting of Custer's last thoughts,' he explained. 'That's it... Custer was thinking: 'Holy Mackerel, look at all those fucking Indians?'

✶✶✶✶

Two men are approaching each other on a pavement in America. Both are dragging their right foot as they walk. As they meet, one man looks at the other knowingly, points at his foot and says, 'Vietnam, 1969.' The other hooks his thumb behind him and says, 'Dog shit, 20 feet back.'

Two British Gas servicemen, a senior training supervisor and a young trainee, were out checking meters in a suburban neighbourhood. They parked their van at the end of the street and worked their way to the other end.

At the last house a woman looking out her kitchen window watched as the senior supervisor challenged his young colleague to a race down the street back to the van to prove that an older guy could outrun a younger one. As they came tearing up to the van, they realised the lady from that end house was huffing and puffing right behind them.

They stopped immediately and asked her what was wrong. 'When I saw two gasmen running as fast as you were,' gasped the woman, 'I figured I'd better run too!'

****

Unable to attend the funeral after his father died, a son who lived far away called his brother and told him, 'Do something nice for Dad and send me the bill.'

Later, he got a bill for £200, which he paid. The next month, he got another bill for £200, which he also paid, figuring it was some incidental expense. Bills for £200 kept arriving every month, and finally the man called his brother again to find out what was going on.

'Well,' said the other brother, 'you said to do something nice for Dad. So I rented him a dinner jacket.'

****

A tourist is travelling through the thickest jungles in South Africa when he comes across an temple. The tourist is entranced by the temple, and asks a local guide for details. The guide says that archaeologists are excavating, and still finding great treasures. The tourist then asks how old the temple is.

'This temple is 1,503 years old,' replies the guide. Impressed at this accurate dating, he inquires as to how he gave this precise figure. 'Easy,' replies the guide, 'the archaeologists said the temple was 1,500 years old, and that was three years ago.'

****

Three men are abducted by cannibals and thrown into a hut to await their fate. The chief tells them that they will be dealt with on a one per day basis. The first day, one man is dragged out and presented with a choice.

'Death or JoJo,' says the chief. The man has no idea what JoJo is, but at least it can't be worse than death, so he accepts JoJo. Immediately, he is strapped naked to a tree face first and one by one the cannibals all fuck him. Torn and bleeding, he is thrown into the hut after that, where he pleads to his companions, 'Don't accept JoJo, accept death.'

The second man is dragged out the second day and presented with the same choice. With his partner's condition still fresh in his mind, he is very afraid, but thinks that at least the guy survived. Hence he also opts for JoJo. He gets fucked again and again and is thrown back into the hut looking twice as bad as his first partner.

The third person is scared out of his wits. When asked the third day, he immediately selects death. The chief nods and passes the sentence, 'Death by JoJo.'

****

Upon entering a fashionable restaurant a couple saw a sign proclaiming it to be 'The World's Most Sanitary Restaurant.' Their waiter came to their table and used a pair of tongs to hand them the menus. All of the silverware and place settings were also placed on their table using tongs. When they questioned the waiter about this, he indicated tongs were used to perform all service functions and was the primary reason the restaurant claimed to be so sanitary.

During the meal, they noticed their waiter had a string hanging out of his fly. The husband called the waiter over and asked about it. The waiter explained the string was tied to his penis and when he had to urinate, he used it to pull it out of his pants without having to touch it which made things even more sanitary. The couple was impressed with all these sanitary procedures.

However, after a few minutes the husband got a puzzled look on his face, again called the waiter over and asked, 'I'm curious about something. How do you manage to get your penis BACK in your trousers?'

'With the tongs, sir,' the waiter replied.

****

A local policeman had just finished his shift one cold November evening and was at home with his wife.

'You just won't believe what happened this evening,' he said to his wife. 'In all my years on the force I've never seen anything like it.'

'Oh yes dear,' she said, 'what happened ?'

'I came across two guys down by the canal,' he told her. 'One of them was drinking battery acid and the other was eating fireworks.'

'Drinking battery acid and eating fireworks?' exclaimed his wife. 'What did you do with them?'

'Oh, that was easy,' said the copper. 'I charged one and let the other off.'

****

An Avon lady was alone in an elevator when suddenly she had to fart. She promptly reached into her bag and sprayed the air with her deodoriser. Two floors later, a gentleman got on the elevator. He began to sniff, and the Avon lady asked, 'Do you smell something?'

'Well, yes I do,' he replied.

'What does it smell like?'

The bemused gentleman answered, 'I'm not sure, but it kind of smells like someone crapped in a pine tree.'

****

Mickey Mouse is in the divorce court and the judge is explaining to him that he can't grant him a divorce on the grounds that Minnie has buck teeth.

'You don't understand,' cries Mickey, 'that's not what I meant when I said she was fucking Goofy.'

✳✳✳✳

A fellow was going on a tour of a factory that produces various latex products. At the first stop, he's shown the machine that manufactures baby-bottle teat. The machine made a loud 'hiss pop!' noise.

'The hiss is the rubber being injected into the mould,' explained the guide. 'The popping sound is a needle poking a hole in the end of the teat.'

Later, the tour reached the part of the factory where condoms were manufactured. The machine made a 'hiss, hiss, pop' noise

'Wait a minute!' said the man. 'I understand what the "hiss, hiss" is, but what's that "pop" every so often?'

'Oh, it's rather like the baby-bottle teat machine,' said the guide, 'but here the needle pokes a hole in every fourth condom.'

'Well, that can't be good for the condoms!' said the man.

'No,' the guide said, 'but it's great for the baby-bottle teat business!'

✳✳✳✳

A guy goes to work in a zoo. The first job he's given is to clean out the finches' cage, but he's told to be careful because finches are expensive and it'll cost him a tenner for each one he kills. So he's cleaning away when he reaches for a bucket and treads on two finches. 'Shit,' he thinks, 'I know, I'll throw them into the lions' cage and they'll get eaten.'

The next job he's given is to clean the chimps' cage and this time he's told it will cost him £400 if he accidentally kills one. Unfortunately he's a clumsy fellow and in reaching for the polish treads on two chimps. As with the finches, though, he bungs them in the lions' cage and no one is any the wiser.

His final job that day is to clean out the apiary where the bees are kept. Each dead bee will cost him a pound, he's told, and this time he slips over and squashes a large number which of course find their way into the lions' cage, too.

The following day a new lion comes along. Eager to find out about his new home he asks one of the other lions what the food's like.

'It's terrible,' says the other lion, 'all we get are finch, chimps and mushy bees.'

****

A bell ringer is happily ringing the bells one day when he tugs a bit too hard and the rope comes down. Undeterred, he goes up into the bell tower and pushes the bell with his hands. Unfortunately, after a while he loses concentration and the bell smashes into his face. He goes flying out of the window and is killed instantly as he lands on the ground outside.

Two passers by are the first to the scene of the accident. One turns to the other and says, 'Do you know him?'

And the other say, 'No, but his face rings a bell.'

****

During a particularly harsh winter a farmer discovers that all his cows are frozen solid in the meadows. Whilst he's contemplating what to do a little old lady drives up to him in her car and asks for directions. She can see he's a bit down so asks him what's wrong. After finding out the lady goes round every meadow and miraculously, as she goes past each cow, it defrosts and comes back to life.

Amazed and very grateful the farmer says, 'That's incredible Miss, Miss… I'm sorry, I don't even know your name.'

'Oh, it's Thora Hird,' says the little old lady.

****

A man goes into a pub and order a pint of bitter. Halfway through drinking it he has to go for a piss and while he's gone a large black woman, who'd been sitting in the pub, positions herself over his pint and farts into it. She then goes and sits back down again.

When the man comes back from the toilet he's just about to finish his drink when the barman stops him and tells him what happened. Somewhat annoyed the man storms over to the woman and says, 'Oi, you fart in my Whitbread?'

'No,' says the woman, 'I'm Tessa Sanderson.'

****

A missionary goes to Africa. As soon as he gets off the plane he is amazed at how authentic everything looks. It's all exactly as he expected. Even the sounds are what he had come to associate with Africa, an incessant beating of drums. As he leaving the airport he turns to the baggage handler and asks him, 'Do the drums continue all the time?'

'Oh yes,' he replies, 'if the drums stop, it's very bad news'

'So he gets into a taxi and, still hearing the beating drums, asks again, 'Do the drums ever stop?'

'Oh no,' replies the taxi driver, 'if the drums stop, it's very bad news.'

Eventually he arrives at his hotel and still the drums are beating. 'Tell me,' he says to the hotel receptionist, 'do the drums continue all the time?'

'Oh yes,' he replies, 'if the drums stop, it's very bad news.'

That evening he comes down from his room and still the drums are beating. He goes for a drink in the hotel bar and, of course, has to have a word about the drums to the barman. 'Tell me,' he says to the barman, 'do the drums ever stop?'

'Oh no,' replies the barman, 'if the drums stop, it's very bad news.'

'But why,' asks the missionary, 'is it such bad news when the drums stop?'

'Because,' explains the barman, 'when the drums stop it's the bass solo.'

****

It's a son's birthday and he asks his father for a ride in a helicopter for a present. The father phones up a mate of his who works as a helicopter stuntman and asks him if that will be OK. The pilot says, 'OK, I'll do it but I can only fly in complete silence. If you make a noise, I'll have to charge you double.' The father thinks about this for a while and says OK.

The next week, father and son strap themselves in and the father says, 'Now listen to me son. The pilot can only fly in complete silence so you mustn't make a sound.'

'OK, dad,' says the son as they take off. Pretty soon, they're soaring through the sky and the pilot thinks to himself, 'I don't want to pay for this flight. I'll do some really scary stunts and the boy will make a noise.' So he starts doing loop-the-loops and flying upside-down. Not a sound comes from behind him. He lands 40 minutes later and shakes the father's hand. 'That was amazing. I tried everything to make you to make a noise but you were completely quiet.' The father says 'Yes, it was hard. I really had to keep my lip buttoned when the lad fell out.'

****

A director is talking to an actor. 'Now, in the next scene,' he says. 'Make love to her like an animal. Imagine you're a gorilla or a lion or a bear or something.'

'OK,' says the actor. 'I'll do the beast I can.'

****

An MP was in bed with his wife when there was a massive thunderstorm. A huge bolt of lightning landed nearby and lit up the whole area at which point the MP sat up and shouted, 'I'll buy the negatives, I'll buy the negatives.'

****

Two office workers were chatting during the lunch break one day. 'It really pisses me off,' said one. 'The boss keeps taking an hour-and-a-half for his lunch break, whilst you and I only get half an hour. That's not fair. I mean if I had an extra fifteen minutes I could pop home for lunch.'

' Well, why don't you?' said the other one. 'The boss is away so long he'd never know.'

So the very next day the first guy decides to do just that. On arriving at home he can't find his wife anywhere downstairs so he goes up to the bedroom. As he's opening the bedroom door he catches a glimpse of his missus in bed with the boss. Before they see him, he shuts the door and rushes back to work.

When he gets back his mate says, 'So, are you going to do that again tomorrow?'

'No way,' he says. 'I nearly got caught today.'

****

A highly excited man rang up for an ambulance. 'Quickly, come quickly,' he shouted, 'my wife's about to have a baby.'

'Is this her first baby?' asked the operator.'

'No, you fool,' came the reply, 'it's her husband.'

****

After having been woken up in the middle of the night by his wife pouring petrol over him, the husband was recounting the incident to the police. 'What do you think she was going to do to you?' asked the officer.

'I'm not sure,' said the man, 'but I think she was trying to make a fuel of me.'

****

'I don't think we should have any more kids,' said the wife to her husband.

'But why not, dear?' said the husband. 'I thought you always wanted four.'

'Not any more,' said the woman. 'I've just heard on the radio that every fourth child born in the world today is Chinese.'

****

Did you here about the dyslexic pimp?
He bought a warehouse.

****

A bear and a rabbit are chatting in the woods.
'Tell me, rabbit,' says the bear, 'when you shit, does it stick to your fur?'
'Why, no,' says the rabbit, 'it doesn't.'
'That's great,' says the bear, picking up the rabbit and wiping his arse with it.

****

Brian is walking by the canal when he sees a guy drowning. He dives in and saves him. When they get back on to dry land the guy says to him, 'I am the grand wizard of Pittiland. For saving me I grant you three wishes.'
'Right,' says Brian. 'First up I want a million quid.'
'OK,' says the wizard. 'It's in your bank account.'
'Now I want a massive mansion in the country with a swimming pool and tennis courts,' says Brian.
'Consider it done,' says the wizard.
'And I want 500 women at my beck and call,' says Brian for his third wish.
'They will be waiting for you at the mansion,' says the wizard, 'as long as I can fuck you first.'
Still reeling from all this, Brian agrees to the wizard's request. After they've had sex, the wizard turns to Brian and says, 'Tell me Brian, how old are you?'
'Thirty,' replies Brian.
'And you still believe in wizards, eh?' says the wizard.

A carpet layer had just finished installing a carpet for a lady. He stepped out for a smoke, only to realise he'd lost his cigarettes. In the middle of the room, under the carpet, was a bump.

'No sense pulling up the entire floor for one pack of smokes,' he said to himself and proceeded to get out his hammer and flatten the hump. As he was cleaning up, the lady came in. 'Here,' she said, handing him his pack of cigarettes. 'I found them in the hallway. Now if only I could find my parakeet.'

****

Late one night, a burglar broke into a house he thought was empty. He tiptoed through the living room, but suddenly froze in his tracks when he heard a loud voice say, 'Jesus is watching you!' Silence returned to the house, so the burglar crept forward again. 'Jesus is watching you,' the voice boomed again. The burglar stopped dead again. He was frightened. Frantically, he looked all around. In a dark corner, he spotted a bird cage and in the cage was a parrot. He asked the parrot, 'Was that you who said Jesus is watching me?'

'Yes,' said the parrot. The burglar breathed a sigh of relief, and asked the parrot: 'What's your name?'

'Clarence,' said the bird. 'That's a stupid name for a parrot,' sneered the burglar. 'What idiot named you Clarence?'

'The same idiot who named the Rottweiler Jesus,' said the parrot.

****

In a busy hotel lobby, a receptionist shouts out, 'Telephone call for Mr Grobenstatermeisterhimbergmansturnumbagrat!'

At which an old geezer comes to the desk and asks, 'What's the initial?'

****

Pissed As A Fart

Everybody who has a dog calls him, 'Rover' or 'Fido'. I call my dog 'Sex'. Now, Sex has been very embarrassing to me. When I went to get his licence, I told the official I would like to have a licence for Sex. He said, 'I'd like to have one, too.'

Then I said, 'But this is a dog.' He said I didn't care what she looked like. Then I said, 'You don't understand, I've had Sex since I was nine years old.' He said I must have been quite a kid.

When I got married and went on my honeymoon, I took the dog with me. I told the hotel receptionist that I wanted a room for my wife and me and a special room for Sex. She said that every room in the place was for sex. I said, 'You don't understand, Sex keeps me awake at night.'

She said, 'Me too.'

One day I entered Sex in a contest but before the competition began, the dog ran away. Another contestant asked me why I was just standing there looking around. I told him I had planned to have Sex entered in the contest. He told me that I should have sold tickets. 'But you don't understand,' I said, 'I had hoped to have Sex on television.' He called me a show-off.

When my wife and I separated, we went to court to file for custody of the dog. I said, 'Your Honour, I had Sex before I got married.'

The judge said, 'Me too.' Then I told him that after I was married, Sex had left me. He said, 'Me too.'

Last night Sex ran off again. I spent hours looking around town for him. A copper came over to me and asked, 'What are you doing in this alley at four in the morning?'

I said, 'I'm looking for Sex…' My case comes up on Friday.

Q: Why don't blind people go skydiving?
A: It scares the shit out of their dogs.

//

The Pub Team

12

Jokes for the Active

The Pub Team

It's a mystery how they came about, but at some point in time someone must have spoiled a perfectly good drink by suggesting to the gathered throng that they do something active. Presumably this person was drummed out of town time and time again, but at some point someone must have agreed to play a game with them.

This was a defining moment because from then on the human competitive element kicked in and spread like wildfire. Before you knew where you were people were spending valuable drinking time at the dart board and pool table, and then actually organising teams to play football or cricket, games which don't even take place in the pub.

Today, of course, there isn't a pub in the land that doesn't boast a crack team of super-fit athletes ready to represent their gaff at whatever contest they've been challenged to. People who put in hours of speech training every day so that they can come back to the pub after the match and talk the best game of their lives…

✸✸✸✸

A golfer, encountering a genie, was granted one wish. The man thought a while and said, 'Well, I've always been embarrassed by being rather small, if you know what I mean; could you make me larger?'

'Done,' said the genie and disappeared. Continuing his game, the man noticed an immediate change in his 'size'. Within several holes, it was down to his knee, and by the 18th, it had crept into his sock. After holing his final putt, the man hurriedly returned to where he'd met the genie.

'Problem?' inquired the genie.

'Yes,' the man responded, 'Do you think I could trouble you for one more wish?'

'And what might that be?' asked the genie.

'Could you make my legs longer?'

✸✸✸✸

While playing golf, the man finds a corked bottle on the green. Upon opening it, a genie appears and grants the fellow one wish. After thinking about it for a while, the man says, 'I'd like to shoot par golf regularly.'

'No problem,' says the genie, 'But understand that your sex life will be greatly reduced as a side effect.'

'I can handle that,' the man says, and POUF! the deed is done. Several months later, the genie reappears on the same golf hole and asks the man how his golf is going.

'Fantastic!' says the man, 'I'm now carrying a scratch handicap.'

'And what effect has it had on your sex life?' the genie inquires.

'I still manage to have relations a couple of times a month,' the fellow answers calmly.

'A couple of times a month,' the genie says, 'That's not much of a sex life.'

'Well,' the fellow responds, 'It's not bad for a middle-aged priest with a very small parish.'

✳✳✳✳

Fay Lewis was a busy housewife with a demanding husband, six children and a large house. The only relief she got from her chores was the weekly bridge game she shared with a dozen other women. The only flaw in the bridge club relationship was that Fay loved to tell off-colour stories and the girls didn't want to hear them.

To teach Fay a lesson, the other women decided that the next time she told such a story, they'd just get up, walk out and meet at another home, but without Fay. Sure enough, at the next meeting, Fay started, 'You know, girls, there's a rumour going around that a plane-load of prostitutes will be leaving Heathrow in the morning for that big gold find in Alaska, and they say…'

Just then, the women all stood up and started for the door. Fay was disconcerted, but only for a moment. 'Hey! Girls!' she shouted. 'Hold on, hold on! There's plenty of time. The plane doesn't leave till morning!'

****

A man phones home from his office and tells his wife, 'Something has just come up. I have a chance to go fishing for a week. It's the opportunity of a lifetime. We leave right away. So pack my clothes, my fishing equipment, and especially my blue silk pyjamas. I'll be home in an hour to pick them up.'

He goes home in a hurry and grabs everything and rushes off. A week later he returns.

'Did you have a good trip, dear?' asks the wife.

'Oh yes, great,' he says, 'but you forgot to pack my blue silk pyjamas.'

'Oh no I didn't,' replies the wife. 'I put them in your tackle box!'

****

A vicar wanted to raise money for his church, and being told that there was a fortune in horse racing, decided to buy a horse and enter him in the races. However, at the local auction, the going price for a horse was so high that he bought a donkey instead. He figured that since he had it he might as well go ahead and enter it in the races, and to his surprise the donkey came in third.

The next day, the racing papers carried this headline:" 'VICAR'S ASS SHOWS'. The vicar was so pleased with the donkey that he entered it in the races again, and this time it won! The paper read: 'VICAR'S ASS OUT IN FRONT.'

The bishop was so upset with this publicity that he ordered the vicar not to enter his donkey in another race. The headlines read: 'BISHOP SCRATCHES VICAR'S ASS.'

This was too much for the bishop and he ordered the vicar to get rid of the animal. The vicar decided to give it to a nun in the nearby convent. The headlines read: 'NUN HAS BEST ASS IN TOWN.'

The bishop fainted! He informed the nun that she would have to dispose of the donkey. She finally found a farmer willing to buy him for £10. The paper read:'NUN PEDDLES ASS FOR TEN POUNDS.' They buried the bishop the next day. The headline?: 'NUN'S ASS KILLS BISHOP.'

****

One day a nun was fishing and caught a huge, strange-looking fish. A man was walking by and said, 'WOW!! What a nice Gauddam Fish!'

'Sir,' said the sister, 'you shouldn't take God's name in vain.'

'But that's the SPECIES of the fish,' said the man. 'It's a Gauddam Fish.'

So the Sister took the fish back home and said, 'Mother Superior, look at the Gauddam Fish I caught.'

Shocked, the Mother Superior said, 'Sister, you should know better than that.'

'No, Mother Superior,' said the sister, 'you don't understand. That's the name of the species of fish. It's a Gauddam Fish.'

'Well, give me the Gauddam Fish and I'll clean it,' said the Mother Superior. While she was cleaning the fish, the Monsignor walked in.

'Monsignor,' said the Mother Superior, 'look at the Gauddam Fish that the sister caught.'

'Mother Superior!' said the Monsignor rather taken aback, 'you shouldn't talk like that!'

'But that's the species of fish Monsignor,' explained the Mother Superior. 'It's a Gauddam Fish.'

'Well,' said the Monsignor, 'give me the Gauddam Fish and I'll cook it.'

That evening at supper there was a new priest at the table, and he said, 'Wow, what a nice fish.'

'Thank you,' said the sister. 'I caught the Gauddam Fish.'

'And I cleaned the Gauddam Fish,' said the Mother Superior.

'And I cooked the Gauddam Fish,' said the Monsignor.

The priest looked around in disbelief, quite shocked, and said, 'Well let's eat the fucking thing.'

****

A man went to confession and said to the priest, 'Forgive me, Father. I used the F-word this week.'

'Ah, my son,' said the priest. 'Tell me the circumstances which caused you to use the F-word. After all, I can understand a person being provoked into using it.'

'Well, I was golfing,' said the man, 'and I had just hit a beautiful tee-shot that sailed straight as an arrow for 280 yards, but then suddenly sliced into the woods.'

'That is when you used the F-word?' said the priest. 'I can appreciate your frustration my son, as I am a golfer myself.'

'No, I stayed cool at that point, Father,' said the man. 'I then hit a perfect shot out of the woods, but suddenly it landed in the sand trap.'

'Now, I can understand you saying the F-word at that point,' said the priest.

'No, Father, I was calm even then,' said the man. 'I got out my sand wedge and hit a perfect shot out of the trap right at the pin, but suddenly the ball stopped an inch from the cup.'

'Ah, that is when you used the F-word. How frustrating,' said the priest.

'No, Father, I was still cool at this point,' said the man.

'Don't tell me you missed the fucking putt?' said the priest.

****

It was a cold winter day when an old man walked out on to a frozen lake, cut a hole in the ice, dropped in his fishing line and began waiting for a fish to bite.

He was there for almost an hour without even a nibble when a young boy walked out onto the ice, cut a hole not to far from the old man and dropped in his fishing line. It only took about a minute and WHAM!, a Largemouth Bass hit his hook and the boy pulled in the fish.

The old man couldn't believe it, but figured it was just luck. But the next time the boy dropped in his line, within just a few minutes he had pulled in another one. This went on and on until finally the old man couldn't take it any more, since he hadn't caught a thing all this time.

He went to the boy and said, 'Son, I've been here for over an hour without even a nibble. You have been here only a few minutes and have caught about half-a-dozen fish! How do you do it?'

To which the boy responded, 'Roo raf roo reep ra rums rrarm.'

'What was that?' the old man asked.

Again the boy responded, 'Roo raf roo reep ra rums rrarm.'

'Look,' said the old man, 'I can't understand a word you're saying.'

So the boy spat into his hand and said, 'You have to keep the worms warm!'

One night, at the lodge of a hunting club, two new members were being introduced to other members and shown around. The man leading them around said, 'See that old man asleep in the chair by the fireplace? He is our oldest member and can tell you some hunting stories you'll never forget.'

They awakened the old man and asked him to tell them a hunting story. 'Well,' he began, 'I remember back in 1944, we went on a lion-hunting expedition in Africa. We were on foot and hunted for three days without seeing a thing. On the fourth day, I was so tired I had to rest my feet. I found a fallen tree, so I laid my gun down, propped my head on the tree, and fell asleep. I don't know how long I was asleep when I was awakened by a noise in the bushes. I was reaching for my gun when the biggest lion I've ever seen jumped out of the bushes at me like this, ROOOAAAARRRRRRRRRR! I tell you, I just shit myself.'

The young men looked astonished and one of them said, 'I don't blame you, mate. I would have shit myself too if a lion jumped out at me.'

The old man shook his head and said, 'No, no, not then, just now when I said ROOOAAAARRRRRRRRRR!'

The Pub Team

A blackjack dealer and a player with a 13 count in his hand were arguing about whether or not it was appropriate to tip the dealer. The player said, 'When I get bad cards, it's not the dealer's fault. By the same token, when I get good cards, the dealer obviously had nothing to do with it so why should I tip him?'

The dealer said, 'When you eat out do you tip the waiter?'

'Yes,' said the player. 'Well then,' said the dealer, 'he serves you food, I'm serving you cards, so you should tip me.'

'OK,' said the player, 'but the waiter gives me what I ask for... I'll take an eight.'

✳✳✳✳

While sport-fishing off the Florida coast, a tourist capsized his boat. He could swim, but his fear of alligators kept him clinging to the overturned craft. Spotting an old beachcomber standing on the shore, the tourist shouted, 'Are there any 'gators around here?'

'Naw,' the man hollered back, 'they ain't been around for years!'

Feeling safe, the tourist started swimming leisurely toward the shore. About halfway there he asked the guy, 'How'd you get rid of the 'gators?'

'We didn't do nothin',' the beachcomber said. 'The sharks got 'em.'

✳✳✳✳

There was a Liverpool fan with a really crappy seat at Anfield. Looking with some binoculars, he spotted an empty seat on the halfway line. Thinking to himself, 'What a waste' he made his way down to the empty seat. When he arrived at the seat, he asked the man sitting next to it, 'Is this seat taken?'

'This was my wife's seat,' said the man. 'She passed away recently... She was a big Liverpool fan.'

'I'm so sorry to hear of your loss,' said the first man.

'May I ask why you didn't give her ticket to a friend or a relative?'

'Because they're all at her funeral,' replied the man.

****

A group of blind people are playing a round of golf. Naturally enough they are going round quite slowly. Behind them are a priest, an imam and a rabbi. The priest says, 'What a marvellous achievement to see them overcoming their disability.'

The imam says, 'Much as I'm humbled to see these people doing what they're doing I do wish they could go a bit faster,' and the rabbi says 'What, they can't play at night?'

****

After a particularly poor game of golf, a popular club member skipped the clubhouse and started to go home. As he was walking to the car park to get his car, a policeman stopped him and asked, 'Did you tee off on the 16th hole about 20 minutes ago'

'Yes,' replied the golfer.

'Did you happen to hook your ball so that it went over the trees and off the course?' asked the policeman.

'Yes, I did. How did you know?' he asked.

'Well,' said the policeman very seriously, 'your ball flew out on to the highway and crashed through a driver's windscreen. The car went out of control, crashing into five other cars and a fire engine. The fire engine couldn't make it to the fire and the building burned down. So, what are you going to do about it?'

The golfer thought it over carefully and responded, 'I think I'll close my stance a little bit, tighten my grip and lower my right thumb.'

****

Matt and his secretary are having an affair. They decide to leave the office early one day and go to the secretary's flat for an afternoon of lovemaking. They fall asleep after and don't wake up until 8pm. They quickly get dressed and the man asks his secretary to take his shoes and go and rub them in the grass.

The secretary thinks this is pretty weird, but she does it anyway. The man finally gets home and his wife meets him at the door. The wife is very upset and asks him where he has been.

The husband replies, 'I can not tell a lie. My secretary and I are having an affair. We left work early today, went to her place, made love all afternoon, and then we fell asleep. That's why I'm late!'

The wife looks at him, notices the grass stains on his shoes and says, 'You lying bastard. You've been playing golf again, haven't you?'

✳✳✳✳

A bishop was an active golfoholic. But he always put his clubs away on saturday night and would not pick them up again till Monday morning. One Sunday, after a particularly ugly week of rain, the bishop got up very early and sneaked on to a public golf course to play one quick round before mass.

At that moment, St Peter looked down from heaven and saw what the Bishop was up to. 'God,' St Peter cried, 'God... Get over here and take a look at this. He is BLASPHEMOUS.'

'Don't worry, Pete,' said the Lord. 'I saw this coming. I'll take care of it.'

At that very moment, the Bishop teed off at the first hole, a 515-yard, dog-leg right, par five. The ball leapt from the pin, soared through the air, executed a text book right curve, struck the ground 298 yards from the tee with incredible velocity, jumped forward and, miracle of miracles, after three bounces dropped into the hole without even striking the flag stick.

The bishop is astonished, as is St Peter. 'Did You see that? He dropped it straight into the hole. That was a miracle. I thought You were punishing him.'

'With time, you will understand,' said God as he walked away. St Peter watched with astonishment as the bishop, hole after hole, dropped the tee shot into the cup. As the bishop puts his ball down on the tee at 18, St Peter summoned God once again. 'He's about to set a record, sir, and You are doing nothing about it.'

The Pub Team

God said nothing and they watched as the bishop's shot flew threw the air and dropped effortlessly into the hole.

'I am most confused,' said St Peter to his boss.

'Pete,' explained the Lord, 'think about it. He is a man of God, a vicar of the holy word. He has just shot the perfect game... on a Sunday.... without paying the green fees. Who can he tell?'

****

Harry sliced his tee shot way off into a field beside the golf course. Finally, he found the ball nestled in some buttercups. On his back swing he heard a voice say, 'Please don't hurt my buttercups.' He stopped his swing, looked around, sees no one, and prepares to hit again. 'Please don't hurt my buttercups,' comes the voice again. He stopped again, looked up and sees a beautiful woman approaching. 'I am mother nature,' she said. 'If you promise not to harm my buttercups, I can guarantee you an abundant supply of butter for the rest of your life.'

Harry thought about this and said, 'Where were you last week when I hit my ball into the pussywillows?'

****

At the Olympic wrestling event it is narrowed down to the Russian or the American for the gold medal. Before the final match, the American wrestler's trainer comes to him and says, 'Now don't forget all the research we've done on this Russian. He's never lost a match because of this "pretzel" hold he has. Whatever you do, don't let him get you in this hold! If he does, you're finished!' The wrestler nods in agreement.

As the match begins the American and the Russian circle each other several times looking for an opening. All of a sudden the Russian lunges forward, grabbing the American and wrapping him up in the dreaded "pretzel" hold. A sigh of disappointment goes up from the crowd, and the trainer buries his face in his hands for he knows all is lost. He can't watch the ending.

The Pub Team

Suddenly, though, there's a scream, a cheer from the crowd, and the trainer raises his eye just in time to see the Russian flying up in the air. The Russian's back hits the mat with a thud, and the American weakly collapses on top of him, getting the pin and winning the match.

The trainer is astounded! When he finally gets the American wrestler alone, he asks, 'How did you ever get out of that hold? No one has ever done it before!'

The wrestler answers, 'Well, I was ready to give up when he got me in that hold, but at the last moment, I opened my eyes and saw this pair of balls right in front of my face. I thought I had nothing to lose, so with my last ounce of strength I stretched out my neck and bit those babies just as hard as I could. You'd be amazed how strong you get when you bite your own balls!'

****

Two old boys were playing golf. After one particularly long and arduous hole one turned to the other and said, 'So how many did you take?'

'Nine,' came the reply.

'Well, I took eight,' said the first. 'So I guess that's my hole then.'

The next hole was equally long, after which the same old boy turned to his pal and asked the question again.

'No, no,' said his pal. 'It's my turn to ask first.'

****

A passer-by spots a fisherman by a river. 'Is this a good river for fish?' he asks.

'Yes,' replies the fisherman, 'it must be. I can't get any of them to come out.'

****

Two women were talking. 'Listen, I don't want to bring you down,' said one, 'but surely you don't believe that story about your husband being out all night fishing? I mean, he hasn't even brought any fish back.'

'That's why I believe him,' said the other.

****

One day at the golf club Jim spots the most beautiful woman he's ever seen in the clubhouse. Even more incredibly, she comes over and suggests that they play a round together.

She turns out to be a very fine player and gives Jim a good game, after which they go back to his place for some oral sex.

The following day they meet up for another game, followed by another bout of oral sex. This goes on for a week, at the end of which Jim says, 'I'm sorry, but I don't think I can keep this up much longer.'

'That's OK,' says the woman. 'There's something I have to tell you as well. I'm a transvestite.'

'Shit,' says Jim. 'All week you've been playing off the ladies' tees.'

****

A cricket player's wife rang the club during a game to be told that her husband had just gone in to bat. 'That's fine,' she said. 'I'll hold.'

****

A husband and wife were celebrating their anniversary with a romantic dinner. 'Do you remember proposing to me?' said the wife.

'Yes of course,' said the husband. 'It was just next to the pavilion when we were playing Little Sedgewick.'

'Oh, you were bold,' recalled the wife.

'No, as far as I remember it was LBW,' said the husband.

****

The Pub Team

A fielder who had dropped eight easy balls in one particularly awful match was blaming his poor display on ill health.

'I'm not well,' he said. ' I think I must have caught a cold.'

'Thank God you're able to catch something,' came the retort.

****

The top scorer of a Premier League team was tragically killed in a car accident one season. Seeing an opportunity for glory, the reserve striker went in to see the boss. 'How about the possibility of me taking his place?' he asked.

'I'm not sure about that,' said the guv'nor, 'I'll have to speak to the undertaker first.'

****

At a football match one day a man tried to get into the game with a gorilla. 'Look,' said a copper, 'I saw you with him yesterday and told you to take him to the zoo.'

'Yes I did that, and then we went to the cinema and had a meal. So today I thought he might like to see a football match.'

****

On Cup Final day a massive crowd is approaching Wembley when a funeral procession goes past. Seeing this, one bloke takes his hat off and stands motionless for a moment before walking on. 'That was a nice thing to do,' said his mate.

'Well,' said the bloke, 'she was a good wife to me.'

****

At a Celtic/Rangers match one season, things got a bit hairy in the crowd and bottles began flying from one set of supporters to the others. A young spectator stuck in the middle of this was naturally somewhat concerned, so an old boy went to reassure him. 'Don't worry son,' he said. 'It's like bombs in the war. One of those won't hit you unless it's got your name on it.'

'That's what I'm worried about,' said the young fellow. 'My name's Johnny Walker.'

****

After a string of ten defeats on the trot the manager of a local football team was at the end of his tether. 'Look,' suggested a friend. 'Why don't you take the whole squad out for a ten mile run every day?'

'What good will that do?' moaned the manager. 'Well, today's Sunday,' said his pal. 'By next Saturday they'll be 60 miles away and you won't have to worry about them.'

****

A fan arrives at a football match midway through the second half. 'What's the score?' he asks his mate as he arrives.

'Nil-nil,' is the reply.

'And what was the half-time score?' he asks.

****

Stuck in the centre of a defensive wall at a free kick, the centre forward took a ball full in the cods and was knocked out cold. When he woke up he found himself in hospital. Still in some pain he asked the doctor, 'Doc, is it bad? Will I be able to play again?'

'Yes, you should be able to,' confirmed the doc.

'Oh, great. So I can play for my club again?' said the relieved forward.

'Well, just as long as they've got a women's team,' said the doctor.

****

After a considerable win on the footie pools, Mr Smith was asked if it would change him. 'No, not at all. My life won't change a bit,' he insisted.

'But what about the begging letters?' asked a reporter.

'Oh, I'll still send them,' he replied.

✳✳✳✳

A group of Catholic priests were due to play a group of rabbis in a big inter-faith game. A couple of days before the match, disaster struck the Catholic team when their star player broke his ankle.

'What are we going to do?' moaned Father Bradley.

'Well,' said Father Turner. 'I just happen to be a good friend of Teddy Sheringham's. We could ask him to play for us.'

'But that wouldn't be ethical, now would it?' said Father Bradley.

'No, but if we called him Father Sheringham, no one need know,' replied the other priest.

Having agreed to this devious plan, Father Bradley was then called away and was unable to watch the match. However, as soon as he could he phoned Father Turner for the result.

'I'm afraid they beat us,' said Father Turner, 'Six-two.'

'But how come?' exclaimed Father Bradley, 'we had Father Sheringham on our side.'

'Yes,' said Father Turner, 'but they had Rabbi Seaman and Rabbi Shearer playing for them.'

✳✳✳✳

A great footballer was tragically killed and arriving at heaven met the angel on duty at the gates. 'Is there any reason,' asked the angel, 'why you should not be allowed to enter the kingdom of heaven?'

'Well,' said the footballer, 'there was this one time when I cheated in a big international football match.'

'I see,' said the angel, 'tell me about it.'

'Well,' said the player, 'I was playing for Wales against England and I used my hand to push the ball past an English defender. The ref never saw it and I went on to score.'

'And what was the final score?' asked the angel.

'That was the only goal,' said the player, 'we won one-nil.'

'Well, that's not too bad. I think we can let you in,' said the angel.

'Oh great!' exclaimed the footballer, 'that's been on my mind for years. Thanks a lot, St Peter.'

'That's OK,' said the angel as he ushered the player in, 'and by the way, it's St Peter's day off today, I'm St David.'

****

A wee lad was crying his eyes out at a football match one day. 'What's the matter?' asked a policeman.

'I've lost my Dad,' cried the boy.

'What's he like?' asked the copper.

'Beer, women and fags,' said the boy.

****

Two boys were playing with a new football in the street outside their house. 'Hey,' shouted their mother, 'where did you get that football?'

'We found it,' replied one of the boys.

'Are you sure it was lost?' asked the mum.

'Yes,' replied the other boy, 'we saw people looking for it.'

****

Midway through what was turning into a disastrous season, the coach of a third-division side decided to get the team together and really go back to basics. Picking up a football he went, 'Right now, lads, what I have in my hands is called a football, and the object of the game is…'

'Hang on a minute,' came a shout, 'you're going too fast.'

The Pub Team

****

A so-called football widow was having a go at her husband. 'Your whole life is football,' she moaned. 'You never take me out, you never buy me presents. You're either at a match or watching one on the telly. I bet you can't even remember when our wedding anniversary is'

'Yes, I can,' retorted the husband, 'it's the same date that Slovan Bratislava beat Barcelona in the Cup-Winners' Cup.'

****

In a nasty challenge a football player dislocated his shoulder. He was still screaming in agony when they got him to hospital.

'For God's sake,' shouted the doctor, 'you're supposed to be a big, tough defender. There's a woman having a baby next door and she's not making anything like the noise that you are.'

'That's as may be,' wailed the player, 'but in her case, nobody's trying to push anything back in.'

****

A team of mammals were playing a team of insects. The first half very much belonged to the mammals, and at half-time they were leading 46-nil. However, at half-time the insects made a substitution and brought on a centipede, which turned out to be a top move.

The centipede scored 300 goals as the insects went on to win 401-290. After the game the captain of the mammals was chatting to the insect captain. 'That centipede of yours isn't half bad, is he? Why don't you play him from the start?' he asked.

'We'd like to,' replied the insect captain, 'but it takes him 45 minutes to get, his boots on.'

****

The Pub Team

A Sunday League team were in the dressing-room, one player short. 'Where's Jeff?' said the full back to the captain. 'Oh, apparently he was getting married at 2.30,' said the captain.

'Shit,' said the full back, 'that means he won't get here till the second half'.

****

Another Sunday League team were in the pub having a constitutional before a match. 'Why are you looking so glum, Pete?' asked the landlord.

'My wife ran off with my best mate last night,' replied Pete.

'Oh no,' said the landlord, 'that's bad news.'

'You're not wrong,' said Pete, 'he was meant to be playing in goal today.'

****

A defender with a reputation for being well hard was sent off during a football match. Returning to the changing room, he had a terrible leg on him. It was covered in cuts and bruises and had a massive gash from the top of the thigh to the knee. He had no idea whose it was.

****

Two guys were watching a live Premiership footie game between Manchester United and Arsenal in their local. 'You see the Arsenal,' said one of them, 'their manager's been after me for months.'

'Really?' said his mate.

'Yeah,' he said, 'I'm shagging his wife.'

****

Amazingly, Torquay found themselves at the top of the third division one season mainly due to the goal-scoring talents of their striker. Eager to keep him at the club the manager called him into his office one day about halfway through the season.

'Well done, son,' said the boss. 'Here's a token of our appreciation.' And with that he handed the player a cheque for £5,000.

'Cheers boss,' said the player. 'This really means a lot to me.'

'Pleased to hear it, lad,' said the manager, 'and if you keep this up all season the chairman might even sign it for you.'

****

An old boy turned up at the offices of a large company one afternoon. 'Hello, I'm Tommy Wheeler's Uncle. I've come to ask if he can have the afternoon off so I can take him to the match.'

'I'm afraid he's not here,' came the reply, 'we already gave him the afternoon off so he could attend your funeral.'

****

A young autograph hunter was chuffed to bits when he got Julian Dicks' autograph after a game. The following week he accosted Mr Dicks again and got his autograph, and after the very next game he tried to get it again.

'Look,' said Julian, 'this is the third time you've asked me for my autograph. What's going on?'

'Well,' said the youngster, 'if I can get eight more of yours I can swap them for one of Gazza's.'

****

After going to the doctor a man popped into his local for a stiff one. 'What's up pal?' asked his mate, 'you look perturbed.'

'Yeah, I am,' he said. 'I've just been to the doctor's and he told me I can't play football.'

'Oh, really?' said his mate. 'He's seen you play, then.'

The Pub Team

****

A woman goes to the doctor. 'Doctor, doctor. I'm really worried about my son. All he does is play football all day, then come in covered in mud and walk all over my clean carpet,' she said.

'I think you're over-reacting,' said the doctor. 'Sons do those kind of things.'

'Yes,' said the woman, 'but it's not just me that's worried. His wife is also very concerned.'

****

Two men are discussing a golf game. 'Well, I was playing golf with my wife. I'd been having a great game but unfortunately she wasn't. On the 15th tee I hit a beautiful shot, 270 yards straight down the fairway. My wife steps up and hits a tremendous slice that leaves the course and lands in the pasture out of bounds. We both went looking for the ball and just as we were about to give up I spotted a glint of white coming from a cow's behind, just under its tail. I lifted the tail to make sure and then called to my wife saying, "Here, honey, this looks like yours." That's the last thing I remember.'

****

Fred got home from his Sunday round of golf later than normal and very tired. 'Bad day at the course?' his wife asked.

'Everything was going fine,' he said. 'Then Harry had a heart attack and died on the 10th tee.'

'Oh, that's awful!'

'You're not kidding. For the whole back nine it was hit the ball, drag Harry, hit the ball, drag Harry…'

****

The Pub Team

A couple of women, Janice and Sherrill, were playing golf one sunny Saturday morning. Sherrill, the first of the twosome teed off and watched in horror as the ball headed directly toward a foursome of men playing the next hole. Indeed, the ball hit one of the men, and he immediately clasped his hands together at his crotch, fell to the ground and proceeded to roll around in agony.

Sherrill rushed down to the man and immediately began to apologise. She then explained that she was a physical therapist and offered to help ease his pain. 'Please allow me to help. I'm a physical therapist and I know I could relieve your pain if you'd just allow me!' she told him earnestly.

'Ummph, oooh, nnooo, I'll be alright… I'll be fine in a few minutes,' he replied as he remained in the fetal position still clasping his hands together at his crotch. But she persisted; and he finally allowed her to help him.

She gently took his hands away and laid them to the side, loosened his trousers and put her hands inside, beginning to massage him. 'Does that feel better?' she asked.

'It feels great,' he replied. 'But my thumb still hurts like hell.'

****

Barely 20 minutes after teeing off, a woman came into the clubhouse, grimacing in pain. 'What happened?' the club pro asked.

'I got stung by a bee,' she replied.

'Where?'

'Between the first and second holes.'

'Hmmm,' the pro murmured. 'Sounds like your stance was a little too wide.'

****

There was an engineer, a manager and a computer programmer driving down a steep mountain road. The brakes failed and the car careered down the road out of control. Halfway down the driver managed to stop the car by running it against the embankment, narrowly avoiding going over a cliff.

They all got out, shaken by their narrow escape from death, but otherwise unharmed.

The manager said, 'To fix this problem we need to organise a committee, have meetings, and, through a process of continuous improvement, develop a solution.'

The engineer said, 'No, that would take too long, and besides that method never worked before. I have my trusty pen-knife here and will take apart the brake system, isolate the problem and correct it.'

The computer programmer said, 'I think you're both wrong! I think we should all push the car back up the hill and see if it happens again.'

****

Once the club duffer challenged the local golf pro to a match, with a £100 bet on the side. 'But,' said the duffer, 'since you're obviously much better than me, to even it a bit you have to let me have two "gotchas".'

The golf pro didn't know what a 'gotcha' was, but he went along with it. And off they went. Coming back to the 19th hole, the rest of the club members were amazed to see the golf pro paying the duffer £100.

'What happened?' asked one of the members.

'Well,' said the pro, 'I was teeing up for the first hole, and as I brought the club down, the lunatic stuck his hand between my legs, and grabbed my balls and yelled "Gotcha!" Have you ever tried to play 18 holes of golf, waiting for the second "Gotcha"?'

****

An international sports star is on a long-haul flight and he desperately needs to go to the bog, but there's a long queue of people in front of him. He isn't averse to taking advantage of his status as an instantly recognisable brat and so he starts having a temper tantrum.

The stewardess, having little option, and wanting to spare the other passengers' patience tells him to go into the Ladies, but warns him not to play with any of the buttons.

The man agrees. While he's sitting on the toilet in the Ladies, however, he sees four buttons in front of him – one marked WW, one marked WA, another marked PP, and one marked ATR. Despite his promises his curiosity gets the better of him, and, he decides what the fuck does it matter if he presses them or not – so he presses the button marked WW. Suddenly, a jet of warm water sprays gently on his arse. Then he presses the button marked WA and warm air dries his arse.

'Wow,' says the man, 'the girls really have it easy!'

Next he presses the button marked PP and a power puff pats his arse with a scented powder.

'This is great!' he thinks. 'I wonder what the last button does?'

On pressing it he's suddenly knocked unconscious. When he wakes up he finds he's in the hospital. Totally confused he calls out for a nurse to find out what the fuck happened.

'The flight attendant told you not to touch any of the buttons,' explains the nurse. 'And you pressed the one marked ATR.'

'What does ATR stand for?' asks the man, completely bewildered.

'Automatic tampon remover,' replies the nurse. 'You'll find your penis under your pillow.'

Animal Magic

13

Jokes about the Natural World

A vicar wanted to buy a parrot. "Are you sure it doesn't swear?" he asked the storekeeper. "Oh, absolutely. It's a religious parrot," the storekeeper assured him. "Do you see those strings on his legs? When you pull the right one he recites the Lord's Prayer, and when you pull on the left one he chants the 23rd Psalm." "That's wonderful!" said the vicar, reaching for his chequebook, "and what happens if you pull both strings?" "I fall off my fucking perch, you piece of shit!" screeched the parrot.

Two soldiers stationed in the Falklands were handed spades and told to bury a large, dead animal. While they were digging, they got into an argument about exactly what it was they were burying. "This is a bloody big mule!" "It isn't a mule, you idiot, it's a donkey." "Mule!" "Donkey!" "Mule!" "Donkey!" They went on like this for a while until the camp chef came out to see what the noise was. "What are you lads up to?" he asked. "We're diggin' a grave for this mule," said the first. "Donkey, dammit!" replied the other. The chef cut in, "Lads, this isn't either. It's an ass." An hour later, the commander of the garrison came up and said, "What are you men digging, a foxhole?" They nodded respectfully, then the first one said "No, sir! We're digging an asshole, sir!"

Why do birds fly south? Because it's just too far to walk.

****

A farmer, upset at the small number of eggs that his hens were laying, decided to go to town to buy a fresh cockerel who could liven things up a bit. Down at the supply shop, the bloke behind the counter apologised; all he had was one incredible randy cockerel. "But that's just what I need!" the farmer said. "Not this cockerel," said the bloke, "he's trouble. I've never seen anything so sex-obsessed." But the farmer insisted, and eventually agreed to buy the cockerel on the condition that he wouldn't ever bring him back into the town, let alone return him to the shop. Once back at the farm, the cockerel immediately jumped into the hen-house and shagged every hen repeatedly until they were all exhausted and near death. Undaunted, the cockerel then hopped the fence, got in with the ducks and fucked all of them unconscious. He then leaped another fence and proceeded to decimate the geese. This continued for three days until the farm had been devastated. That afternoon the farmer found the cockerel flat out in the middle of the yard, with buzzards circling overhead. "Serves you right, you filthy little bastard," said the farmer, at which point the cockerel pointed up at the sky, winked and said, "Shhhhhhhhh."

****

Why do hens lay eggs? It's obvious. If they dropped them, they'd break.

A pair of chickens walk up to the withdrawals desk at a public library and say, 'Buk Buk BUK.' Deciding that the chickens want three books, the librarian hands some over and the chickens cluck in thanks and leave. Around midday, the chickens come back to the desk and say, 'Buk Buk BuKKOOK!' The librarian passes over another three books and the chickens leave as before. The chickens then return to the library in the early afternoon, approach the librarian and, looking very annoyed, cluck, 'Buk Buk Buk Buk Bukkooook!' The librarian is by now a bit suspicious of these chickens, so she gives them a further five books, and decides to follow them. Trailing at a safe distance, she follows them out of the library, out through the town centre and to a park. Hiding behind a tree, she peeks out at the birds, who head down to the pond. When they get to the water's edge, she's horrified to see them throw all the books into the water. Suddenly, they come flying back out again and this frog sticks its head up and, in a smug tone of voice, says "Rrredit Rrredit Rrredit Rrredit Rrredit..."

Is it polite to eat fried chicken with your fingers? No. You should always eat your fingers separately.

****

What do you get when you cross a chick with an alley cat? A peeping tom.

****

This bloke with a parrot is getting married. On the day of the wedding, he says, "Listen, I know you're always in that bloody window. My wife and I are coming back here to pack after the wedding, and no matter what you hear, do not turn around or I'll break your damned neck! We want some privacy!" The parrot reluctantly agrees. The happy couple then come back from the wedding and start packing, but they can't get the suitcase closed. "Get on top," says the bloke, "that'll do it." She gives it a shot, but despite much effort and grunting it doesn't close. His wife then says, "Look, you get on top, that'll be better." They heave away again, with no luck. Finally, the bloke says, "I tell you what, let's both get on top; that should fix it!" The parrot immediately turns around and says, "Neck or no neck, I have got to see this!"

****

Diner: Do you serve chicken here? Waiter: Sit down, sir. We serve anyone.

****

What do you get when you cross a parrot with a centipede? A walkie-talkie.

****

An elderly lady buys a pair of parrots, but she cannot identify their sexes. She calls the pet shop, and the man there advises her to watch them carefully and all will become clear in time. She spends weeks staring at the cage, and eventually catches them shagging. To make sure she doesn't get them mixed up again, she cuts a ring out from a piece of cardboard and puts it round the male parrot's neck. The following week, the local vicar calls in for a cup of tea. He's just making himself comfortable when the male parrot notices his dog-collar. "Eh up," leered the parrot, "Who did she catch you screwing?"

****

Kath was expecting the plumber. He was supposed to arrive at ten o'clock. Ten o'clock came and went - no plumber. Eleven o'clock, twelve o'clock, and one o'clock sailed past, still with no plumber. She decided he wasn't coming, and went out to do some chores. Naturally, no sooner had she left than the plumber arrived. He knocked on the door and, from the lounge, Kath's parrot called, "Who is it?" Presuming the parrot to be the lady of the house he called back, "It's the plumber," and waited for her to come and let him in. When no-one opened the door, he knocked again. Again the parrot called, "Who is it?" Frustrated, he yelled, "It's the plumber!" He waited some more, and again no-one came to the door. He knocked again, long and hard. Again the parrot called, "Who is it?" and he shouted, "IT'S THE PLUMBER!" Once again he waited, and again she didn't come. Furious at the way she was taking the piss, he hammered on the door again and again. The parrot, who was having a great time, called, "Who is it?" innocently. It was too much for the plumber, who went berserk. With a loud scream he took a wrench to the lock, hammered it to bits and broke the door down. The excitement proved too much for the poor bloke, though, and he had a massive heart attack, dropping dead in the hall. When Kath got back an hour later she found the door ripped open and a corpse lying in the doorway. "Fuck!" she shrieked, "WHO IS IT?" Gleefully, the parrot howled "IT'S THE PLUMBER!"

****

Diner: I can't eat this chicken. Call the manager. Waiter: It's no use, sir. He can't eat it either.

****

Which side of a chicken has the most feathers? The outside.

Animal Magic

****

When her dishwasher packed up, Mrs Williams phoned the repair man. He couldn't accommodate her request for an after-hours appointment, and because she had to go to work she told him, "I'll leave the key under the mat. Fix the dishwasher, leave your invoice on the counter and I'll post you a cheque. By the way, I have a large Rottweiler called Fang, but don't worry, he's very well-trained and he won't bother you. I also have a large parrot. Whatever you do, no matter what he says to you, do not say anything to the bird!" Well, sure enough, the dog totally ignored the repair man, but the whole time he was there the parrot swore, yelled, screamed and just about drove the bloke mad. As he was getting ready to leave, he just couldn't resist saying to the parrot, "You stupid fucking mangy ball of feathers, shut the fuck up!" The bird went quiet for a moment, fixed him with a malicious glare, then shouted at the top of its voice: "Kill, Fang. Kill, boy!"

****

Two morons are standing on a cliff with their arms outstretched. One has some budgies lined up on his arms, and the other has parrots tied to his. After a couple of minutes they leap off the cliff and splat! Lying next to each other in intensive care at the hospital, the first moron says to the second one, "I don't think much of this budgie jumping." The other moron replies, "Yeah, I'm not too keen on this parrotgliding either."

****

Two tall trees are growing in the woods. A small tree begins to grow up between them. One turns to the other and says, "Is that a son of a beech, or a son of a birch?" The other says he cannot tell. When a woodpecker lands on the small tree, the first big tree says, "Woodpecker, you're a tree expert. Can you tell if that is a son of a beech or a son of a birch?" The woodpecker takes a taste of the small tree, and replies, "It is neither a son of a beech nor a son of a birch. That, gentlemen, is the best piece of ash I have ever had my pecker in!"

****

A farmer was sitting in his farmyard eating a sandwich when a hen zoomed by, with a cockerel in hot pursuit and closing fast. Suddenly the cockerel slammed on the anchors, screeched to a halt and began pecking at the crumbs from the sandwich. "Damn," muttered the farmer, "I hope I never get that hungry!"

****

A bloke walks into a pet shop and asks if he can buy a canary. The proprietor replies, "I'm sorry, we've sold out. You won't find a canary in town. I do have a parakeet, though." The bloke insists he wants a canary, so the shop owner tells him that a parakeet can be made to sound just like a canary if you file the beak down. "But you have to be careful not to file too much off, or the parakeet will drown when he goes to take a drink of water." The bloke reckons that this is complete bullshit, but thanks the shop owner politely and leaves. He goes into another pet shop and asks for a canary, but again he has no luck. "But", says the girl behind the counter, "I do have a parakeet, and if you file the beak down carefully it can be made to sound just like a canary." She, too, then goes on to explain that filing off too much beak will jeopardise the bird's life, due to the potential for drowning. The bloke decides that there might be something to it, and buys the parakeet. "Besides", he tells himself, "parakeets are much cheaper." His next stop is a hardware shop, where he wanders into the tools section, holding his recently-purchased bird. The owner wanders by and asks if he needs some help. The bloke sheepishly explains how he intends to make his parakeet sing like a canary. The hardware store owner knowingly picks up a file and hands it to him. "Here, this is what you want - a Simonson No.5 rough-edged file. But be careful not to file too much off, or the poor thing will drown." The bloke thanks the hardware store owner, pays up and leaves for home. A few weeks later, the bloke wanders into the hardware store again. The owner, recognising him, asks how it went with the parakeet. The bloke looks down and sadly reports, "Actually, the bird's dead." The hardware store owner looks sympathetic and asks, "Did you file off too much beak?" The bloke shakes his head and says, "Nope. He was dead when I took him out of the vice."

****

Have you heard about that disease that you get from shagging birds? Chirpes? It's one of those canarial diseases. I hear it's untweetable.

****

Some feline definitions - Human being: An automatic door opener for cats. Purranoia: The fear that your cat is up to something. Purring: The sound of a cat making cuteness. Purrpetual motion: A kitten at play. Purrverse: Poem about a kinky cat. Pussy Whip: The dessert topping for cats.

****

How do you make a cat go woof? Douse it in petrol and throw a match at it. How do you make a dog go meow? Freeze it solid in the freezer, then take a chainsaw to it.

****

Radioactive cats have 18 half-lives.

****

Cats know how we feel. They don't give a damn, but they know.

****

Cats took many thousands of years to domesticate humans.

****

Dogs come when called. Cats take a message and get back to you.

****

It's really the cat's house. I just pay the mortgage.

****

Do not meddle in the affairs of cats, for they are subtle and will piss on your computer.

****

According to an animal protection group in Jerusalem, there have been many recent cases of people throwing cats out of cars, apparently in an attempt to abandon them to the streets...

****

A bloke is in his back garden one lazy Sunday afternoon when he hears some crunching next door. Being nosy, he looks over the fence and sees his neighbour digging a hole in his garden. Naturally, he asks what the hole is for. "My canary died and I'm burying it," said the neighbour. "Oh, I'm sorry about that," says the bloke insincerely. "That's a pretty big hole for a canary, isn't it?" he added. "Well, yes," replies the neighbour, "but it's inside your fucking cat!"

****

Janet went to a bridge club every Thursday night, and after a peaceful game or two with the ladies she would return home to fix her husband dinner when he got home from the pub. One Thursday she was playing a great game, and had an incredible hand, when she noticed the time. "Oh, no! I have to go fix my husband his dinner! He's going to be so angry if it's not ready on time." She dashed out of her friend's house, her great hand forgotten on the table. When she got home, she realised she had very little food in the cupboard and not enough time to go to the grocery store. All she had was a wilted lettuce leaf, an egg and a can of cat food. In a panic, she opened the can of cat food, stirred in the egg and garnished it with the lettuce leaf just as her husband was pulling up. While she watched in horror he sat down to his dinner - and then she realised he was really enjoying it! "Mmmm, darling, this is the best dinner you've made for me in 40 years of marriage. You can cook this for me whenever you want!" That night they had sex for the first time in months, and it was incredible! Needless to say, every Thursday from then on she made the cat food dinner for her husband. She told her bridge friends about it and they were horrified. "You're going to kill him," one said. "He's just winding you up," accused another. Janet continued to make him his cat food dinner on a Thursday, and then afterwards they would shag like fiends. Two months later, Janet's husband died. On the Thursday after the funeral, the bridge ladies attacked her for being so callous. "You killed him!" one said. "We told you that feeding him that cat food every week would do him in! How can you just sit there so calmly and play bridge knowing you murdered your husband?" Janet calmly replied, "Ahh, come off it. I didn't kill him. He smashed his skull falling off the mantelpiece while licking his arse."

****

What do you call a cow that has had an abortion? Decalfinated.

****

A New York family bought a ranch out in the West, where they intended to raise cattle. When some stockbroker friends came out for a visit, they asked if the ranch had a name. "Well," said the new cattleman, "I wanted to name it the Bar-J, my wife favoured Suzy-Q, one son liked the Flying-W and the other wanted the Lazy-Y. We argued about it for a bit and then we decided to compromise, so we're calling it the Bar-J-Suzy-Q-Flying-W-Lazy-Y." "But where are all your cattle?" a friend asked. The rancher sighed. "Actually, none survived being branded."

****

Two cows were chatting to each other over the fence between their fields. The first cow said, "I'm telling you, this mad cow disease really scares me. They say it's spreading fast - I heard it hit some cows down on old Patterson's farm." The other cow replied, "Oh, I'm not worried. It doesn't affect us ducks."

****

A tourist went into a restaurant in Spain and ordered the speciality of the house. When his dinner arrived, he asked the waiter what it was. "These, señor," replied the waiter in broken English, "are the cojones - how you say, the testicles - of the bull that was killed in the ring today." The tourist swallowed hard but tasted the dish and, lo and behold, it was delicious. So he went back the next evening and ordered the same item. When it arrived, he had a look and said to the waiter, "These cojones, or whatever you call them...they're much smaller than the ones I had last night." "Si, señor," replied the waiter, "You see, the bull...he does not always lose."

A dog is a dog, except when he is facing you. Then, he is Mr. Dog.

The more people I meet, the more I like my dog.

Old Farmer Giles got a hefty loan from the bank to buy an expensive bull. A few days later the banker dropped by and asked, "So, how's the new bull doing?" Giles looked downcast and said, "The bull ain't doing none too good, see. I got him out there in the pasture with a lovely bunch of young heifers and he don't want nothing to do with 'em." The banker frowned and said, "You'd better call the vet, and I'll come back in a few days." A week later the banker came back and asked, "Well, Giles, how's that bull doing now?" Smiling, Giles said, "A whole bushel better, he be. He's had his way with all of my cows, jumped over the fence, and he's working his way through Silas's cows next door." The banker was much relieved and said, "Great! What did the vet give him?" Giles said, "He gave him some pills." The banker said, "What kind of pills were those?" Giles said, "I don't rightly know, but they had a strange lemony taste."

****

Outside of a dog, books are a man's best friend. Inside of a dog, it's too dark and cramped to read.

****

What is the difference between a poodle humping your leg and a pit-bull humping your leg? The pit-bull gets to finish...

****

What is meaner than a pit-bull with AIDS? Whatever gave it AIDS in the first place.

****

Did you hear about the new breed of dog? They crossed a pit bull with a collie, and came up with a long-haired mutt that bites your leg off and then goes for help.

****

What is the difference between a Rottweiler and a social worker? You can get your children back from a Rottweiler.

****

What do you do with a dog with no legs? You take it out for a drag.

****

A man went to visit a friend and was amazed to find him playing chess with his dog. He watched the game in astonishment for a while. "I can hardly believe my eyes!" he exclaimed. "That's the smartest dog I've ever seen." His friend shook his head, "Nah, he's not that bright. I beat him three games in five."

A blind man with a guide dog walks into a big department store. The man goes to the middle of the department, picks up the dog by the tail and starts swinging it around over his head in circles. The manager, who couldn't fail to see this, is rather upset by the apparent cruelty, so he decides to find out what's going on. He goes up to the blind man and says, "Good afternoon. May I help you?" The blind man shakes his head and says, "No thanks. I'm just looking around."

A father gave his teenage daughter a pedigree puppy for her birthday. An hour later when he went to make himself a drink he found her looking at a puddle in the centre of the kitchen. "My pup," she murmured sadly, "runneth over."

It was a boring Sunday afternoon in the jungle, so the Elephants decided to challenge the Ants to a game of soccer. The game was going well for the big pachyderms - the Elephants were leading the Ants ten goals to nil

- when the Ants gained possession. The Ants' star player was dribbling the ball towards the Elephants' goal when the Elephants' left back came lumbering towards him. The elephant trod on the little ant, killing him instantly. The referee, a monkey, stopped the game. "What the hell do you think you're doing? Do you call that sportsmanship, killing another player?" The elephant replied, "Well, I didn't mean to kill him. I was only trying to trip him up..."

****

Dad, Mum and little Jimmy decide to go to the zoo one day. Eventually they end up at the elephant house. Jimmy looks at the elephant, sees its penis, points to it and says, "Mum, what is that long thing?" His mother replies, "That's the elephant's trunk, Jimmy." "No, at the other end." "That's the elephant's tail." "No, mummy," said Jimmy, "the thing under the elephant." A short embarrassed silence followed, after which she said, "Oh, that's nothing." Mum then went to buy some ice-cream and Jimmy, not being satisfied with her answer, asks Dad the same question. "Dad, what is that long thing?" "That's the elephant's trunk, Jimmy," replied his father. "No, at the other end." "Oh, that's the elephant's tail." "No, dad, the thing below," asked Jimmy in frustration. "Ah. That's the elephant's penis, Jimmy. Why do you ask?" "Well, mum said it was nothing," said Jimmy. Dad shook his head wryly and said, "I tell you, I spoil that woman..."

****

Hickory Dickory Dock, an elephant ran up the clock. The clock is now being repaired.

****

Why are elephants wrinkled? Well, have you ever tried to iron one?

****

What is grey and white on the inside and red on the outside? An elephant turned inside out.

****

An elephant was down by a watering hole having a drink when he saw a turtle out of the corner of his eye. Reacting with immediate swiftness he ran down to the water's edge, jumped up into the air and landed on the turtle, turning it into a revolting pulp. A giraffe standing nearby noticed this and, faintly sickened, asked the elephant why he'd squished the turtle. The elephant calmly replied by saying that particular turtle had bitten him nastily on the trunk some 50 years earlier, with no provocation, and he had now got his revenge. "Wow," said the giraffe, "you must have an incredible memory." The elephant nodded proudly, "Yes, it's turtle recall!"

What's the biggest drawback of the jungle? An elephant's foreskin.

A guide at the zoo: "Now, ladies and gentlemen, this is the elephant, the largest living animal to roam the earth today. Every day, the elephant eats three dozen bunches of bananas, six tons of hay, and 2,000 pounds of assorted fruits. Madam, please don't stand there...Excuse me, madam, please don't stand near the elephant's backside...Madam, yes, you in the...Madam...Oh, fuck, too late. George, get digging."

Have you heard about Hannibal crossing the Alps with elephants? None of the offspring survived.

****

The United Nations held a competition to discover which nation could produce the best book on elephants. The British submitted a dry historical account, "The Elephant and the British Empire." The French entered a text "The Sensuality of the Elephant - A Personal Account." The Germans submitted an extensive 47-volume work entitled, "An Elementary Introduction to the Foundation of the Science of the Elephant's Trunk." The Americans submitted an article from Money magazine entitled, "Elephants - the Perfect Tax Shelter for the '80s." Sweden commissioned Greenpeace to write a counter-entry "Elephants: They're Better Than People." The Russians put in a terse, melancholy manuscript entitled "The Superiority of the Soviet Elephant," and the Polish submitted a poem, "The Joy and Freedom Brought Forth by the Soviet Elephant." The Greeks sent in a short recipe for clay-baked elephant in a garlic yoghurt sauce, scribbled on the back of a beer-mat. The prize, however, went to the Japanese, for their promotional flyer: "We Have No Elephants, but Wouldn't You Just Love to Buy a Honda Instead?"

****

This tiger woke up one morning and felt just great. He felt so powerful that he went out, cornered a small monkey and roared at him, "Who is the mightiest of all the jungle animals?" The poor quaking little monkey replied, "You are, of course; no one is mightier than you." A little while later, the tiger confronted a deer and bellowed out, "Who is the greatest and strongest of all the jungle animals?" The deer was shaking so hard it could barely speak, but it managed to stammer, "Oh great tiger, you are by far the mightiest animal in the jungle." The tiger, on a roll, then swaggered up to an elephant that was quietly munching on some weeds and roared at the top of his voice, "Who is the mightiest of all the animals in the jungle?" At this, the elephant grabbed the tiger with his trunk, picked him up, slammed him down, picked him up again, shook him until he was just a blur of orange and black and finally threw him violently against a nearby tree. The tiger staggered to his feet, looked up at the elephant and says, "Hey, guy, there's no need to get so wound up just because you don't know the answer."

****

Why was the bluefish blue? Because the blowfish wouldn't.

Animal Magic

****

A door-to-door salesman had suffered a really rough day and decided to try one more house before heading home. He knocked on the door, determined that this time he was going to make a sale. He could almost taste it. A boy opened the door and the salesman starts in with his sales pitch. The boy just stood there, speechless, staring at him and the salesman, seeing that he wasn't getting anywhere, asked the boy where his mother was. The boy didn't say a word, he just pointed upstairs. The salesman went up the stairs, opened the bedroom door, and found the boy's mother in bed, fucking a goat! Completely flabbergasted, the salesman slammed the door shut and charged down the stairs. He grabbed the little boy by the shoulders and yelled, "Don't you know what's in bed with your mother? Don't you know what they're doing? Doesn't it bother you?" The boy looked at him, then shook his head and answered, "Na-a-a-a-a-a-a."

****

What do you get when you cross an onion with a donkey? A piece of ass that'll bring tears to your eyes.

****

Some racehorses are chatting together in a stable. One of them starts to boast about his track record. "Out of my last 15 races, I've won eight!" he says, proudly. Another horse breaks in, "That's good. In my last 27 races, I've won 19!" "Not bad, but out of my last 36 races, I've won 28!" says another, flicking his tail. At this point, they notice a greyhound that has been sitting there listening. "I don't mean to butt in," says the greyhound, "but I've won 88 of my last 90 races." The horses are clearly amazed. "Fuck me!" says one, after a hushed silence. "A talking dog!"

****

Two cockroaches were munching on garbage in an alley. "I was in that new restaurant across the street," said one. "It's so clean! The kitchen is spotless, the floors are gleaming white. It's so sanitary the whole place shines." "Please," said the other cockroach, frowning, "not while I'm eating!"

****

How do you spot a gay termite? He'll only eat woodpeckers.

****

This termite walks into a pub and says "Is the bar tender here?"

****

Two goldfish in a tank. One turns to the other and says, "So, do you know how to drive this thing?"

****

A chicken and an egg were lying in a post-coital glow. The egg turned to the chicken and said, "Well I think we just answered that old question..."

****

Two cockney owls were in a bar playing pool, one missed a shot and said to his mate, "That's two 'its mate." His mate replied, "Two 'its to who?"

****

On the most recent flight of the space shuttle, astronauts conducted an important scientific experiment with fruit flies and gleaned a valuable insight. Zero gravity makes the little buggers far easier to swat.

****

A city bloke went out to spend a holiday on a small farm, out in the country. While he was there, he saw the farmer feeding his pigs in a most extraordinary manner. The farmer would lift a pig up to a nearby apple tree and let the pig eat the apples off the tree directly. He moved the pig from one apple to another until the pig was satisfied, then he would start again with another pig. The city man watched this activity for some time with great astonishment. Finally, he could not resist sharing his time management expertise with the farmer, and said, "Forgive me, but that is the most inefficient method of feeding pigs that I can imagine. Just think of the time that would be saved if you simply shook the apples off the tree and let the pigs eat them from the ground!" The farmer looked puzzled, and replied, "What's time to a pig?"

****

How do monkeys pick up rumours? Through the apevine.

****

There was a terrible bus accident. Unfortunately, no one survived except a monkey who was on board, and there were no witnesses. The police tried to investigate further, but got no results. At last, desperate, they tried to interrogate the monkey. The monkey seemed to respond to their questions with gestures. Seeing that it was trying to communicate, they started asking questions. The police inspector asked, "What were the people doing on the bus?" The monkey shook his head in a condemning manner and starts dancing around; he obviously meant that the people were dancing and having fun. The inspector asked, "Hmm, OK, but what else were they doing?" The monkey moved his hand to his mouth as if holding a bottle. The chief says, "Oh! They were drinking, eh?" The inspector continued, "Were they doing anything else?" The monkey nodded his head and moved his arms back and forth, indicating that they were having sex. "If they were having such a great time," asked the inspector, "who was driving the damn bus?" The monkey cheerfully swung his arms by his sides, as if grabbing a wheel...

****

Why does the Easter bunny hide his eggs? He doesn't want anyone to know he's screwing a chicken!

****

Two rabbits escape from the laboratory and see grass for the first time. They're bouncing through the grass when they meet an older rabbit. "Hello," says the older rabbit. "Would you like to come and stay at my warren?" "What's a warren?" ask the two rabbits. "Don't worry," replies the older rabbit. "Come and see." So off they go. They like the tunnels and chambers of the older rabbit's warren, and decide to stay. In the morning, the two rabbits are awaken by the thumping of the older rabbit. "Come on out for the cabbages," calls the older rabbit. "What's a cabbage?" ask the two rabbits. "Don't worry," replies the older rabbit. "Come and see." So off they go, and they enjoy a day in the fields, eating cabbages. They return very satisfied, with their tummies full of cabbage, and agree a good day was had by all. The following day it's, "Come on out for the cabbages" again, and the same for the day after that. At the end of the third day Rabbit 23 says to Rabbit 17, "These cabbages are good but there must be more to life. Let's go and find it." Rabbit 17 agrees, so off they go, across the grass. They meet a younger rabbit. "Hello," says the younger rabbit. "Come and live in my warren. I've got lots of young girly rabbits staying, and I could use some help." "Girly rabbits?" they ask. "Don't worry," replies the younger rabbit. "Come and see." So they agree, and for three days it's thump-thump-thump. At the end of the third day Rabbit 23 says to Rabbit 17, "It's no good: I've got to get out of here." "Why?" asks Rabbit 17. "This is the best time of our lives!" he exclaims. "Yes," agrees Rabbit 23, "but it's been a week and I'm dying for a fag."

Why do Scotsmen wear kilts? So the sheep won't hear the zip.

Two shepherds are flying their flock to a new farm. Suddenly the engine fails and the plane begins to plunge quickly to the ground. "Quick!" shouts one, "Grab a parachute and jump!" The other one blinks. "What about the sheep?" The first shepherd stares at him. "Eh? Fuck the sheep!" The second one pauses for a moment, then asks him "Do you think we have time?"

A cowboy goes out to seek his fortune on the frontier of the Old West. He finally settles on a ranching town near the edge of civilisation. It's so near the edge, in fact, that there aren't any women to be found, not for love nor money. Well, he's young and full of hormones, and after a month or so he starts getting randy, so he goes to the saloon to ask around. After a couple of nervous, whispered conversations, it comes out that everybody uses the sheep. He isn't particularly happy about this, but he's really desperate. He buys a bottle to provide some Dutch courage, goes and finds the nearest flock and decides that if he's going to do it at all, he's going to do it right. He spends most of the afternoon picking out the prettiest sheep in the flock. He shampoos her, ties ribbons around her neck and even puts a little bell on her collar. He's also getting pretty drunk. By evening he's finished cleaning up the sheep, and he's not thinking particularly clearly. He's so proud of the way the sheep looks, he decides to take her in to town to show her off at the saloon. When he walks in with the sheep, the room goes quiet. Everybody stares at him. They're not just staring either, but recoiling in shock and horror. He's mortally ashamed, but he's very drunk, so he slurs out, "Whassamada? I thought ever'body went out to the sheep?" Finally, one old timer pipes up. "Yeah, boy, but you got the sheriff's girl."

****

Why do Welsh sheep farmers like to screw sheep on the edge of cliffs? Because they scrabble backwards so charmingly.

****

A young man is on holiday in Wales and starts talking to an old man from the village outside the pub. Trying to be friendly, he asks the old man what his name is, but the old boy gets very irate at this point and says, "Do you see that line of houses over there? I built them all, with my own hands, but do they call me Jones the Builder? Do they buggery! And you see those railway lines over there, now? I laid them all myself, but do they call me Jones the Train? Never! And you see those bridges over that river? I built all of them, too, look you, but do they call me Jones the Bridge? No, boyo, they do not! But, a long, long time ago, when I was young, foolish and drunk, I fucked one sheep..."

****

Down the Local

14

Jokes about Boozers

Down the Local

So this baby seal walks into a club... Fucking tragedy.

****

A duck walks into a bar and says, "Got any bread?" And the barman says, "No." And the duck says, "Got any bread?" And the barman says, "No." "Got any bread?" "I said N-O, NO." "Got any bread?" "For cryin' out loud – N-O spells NO and I mean NO!" "Got any bread?" "NO, NO, NO, NO, NO, NO, NO, NO, NO, NO!!!" "Got any bread?" "Look, if you ask me one more time if I've got any bread, I'm going to nail your fucking beak to the fucking bar!!" "Got any nails?" "No!" "Got any bread?"

****

An Indian walks into a saloon dressed like a cowboy. He goes up to the bar, looks at the landlord and says, " Me wantum beer." So the landlord gives him a beer. He drinks it. He then goes into the bathroom, pulls out his rifle, shoots the toilet, walks back out, grabs his bag, opens it, pulls out a mangy-looking cat and takes a big bite out of it. The landlord looks at him and says, "Son, what the Sam Hill are you doing?" The Indian replies, "Me being like the white man. Me drink beer, shoot shit and eat pussy."

****

A bloke walked into the pub and said, "Give me three shots, one each for my best friends and one for me." All through the following month, the bloke drank there in the same way - each time he had three shots, one each for his best friends and one for him. One day he went in and only ordered two shots. The landlord looked sympathetic and said, "What's up, did one of your friends pass away?" "Oh, no," the man replied, "the doctor made me give up drinking."

****

Two fat blokes in a pub, one says to the other "Your round." The other one says, "So are you, you fat bastard."

Down the Local

Two cannibals walked into a pub and sat down beside a clown. Suddenly the first cannibal whipped out his hunting knife, stabbed the clown through the heart and proceeded to butcher him on the spot. He then cut off a couple of big chunks, handed one to his mate and they both started eating. Suddenly the second cannibal looks up at his friend and says, "Wait a moment. Do you taste something funny?"

****

Two blokes go into a pub to check out the local talent. The first one looks around, and says "Wow, look at the blonde over there in the crop-top. I bet she's really wild in the sack." He goes over to her and starts to make small-talk. Before long, the two of them are heading off out back to her place for a quick shag. The two blokes meet up again the next night in the same bar, and sure enough the blonde is there again. "She's really up for it," says the first one, "Why don't you go give it a shot?" Well, the second bloke goes over and pinches her ass; they start chatting, and five minutes later they're out the back of the pub. When he gets back after 20 minutes or so, he goes over to compare notes with his mate. "So, what do you think? I reckon my wife is better," says the first bloke. "Yeah," says the second bloke, "your wife is better."

****

A baby seal walks into a bar and sits down. "What can I get you?" asks the landlord. "Anything but a Canadian Club," replies the seal.

****

This rural bloke goes into his local one afternoon and to his amazement spots a pair of absolutely stunning babes sitting in one corner of the pub. He goes up to the bar, calls the landlord over and nodding at the girls says, "Keith boy, you'd best tell me what it is they're drinking, 'cos I'm going to get them another one." The landlord gives him a funny look, and says, "Well, I don't know if that's such a good idea, Tom. They're lesbians, see." Tom looks blank. "Lesbians? What's that, then?" The landlord shakes his head and says, "Tell you what, why don't you go ask them?" So Tom shrugs, strolls over to the girls and says, "Well now, forgive my ignorance, but old Keith over at the bar tells me you two are lesbians. What does that mean?" They both smile, and one says, in a slow, sexy drawl, "Well, it means that we like to fuck girls. We like to kiss and stroke each other, suck each other's nipples, finger each other and lick each other's pussies." Tom nods, smiling broadly, and calls to the landlord, "Keith lad, three drinks over here for us lesbians!"

****

A skeleton walks into a pub one night and plops down on a stool. The landlord asks "What can I get you?" The skeleton says, "I'll have a beer, thanks." The landlord passes him a beer and asks "Anything else?" The skeleton nods. "Yeah...a mop..."

✳✳✳✳

A man was trying to get into a town centre pub, but the doorman stopped him saying, "Sorry mate, you can't get in here unless you're wearing a tie." The man said, "Okay, I'll be right back," and popped back to his car to find something to use. All he could find, sadly, was a set of jump leads, so he tied them around his neck, went back, and asked, "How's this?" "Well," replied the doorman doubtfully, "Okay, I guess that'll do, but I'm warning you now, don't start anything."

✳✳✳✳

A snake slithers into a pub and up to the bar. The landlord says, "I'm sorry, but I can't serve you." "What? Why not?" asks the snake. "Because," says the landlord, "you can't hold your booze."

A man went into a small Yorkshire pub and ordered a beer. The landlord served him, and then turned to the news on the TV. Tony Blair was busy giving yet another speech. "God, not that horse's arse again!" said the man. The landlord immediately leaped over the bar and punched the man so hard he knocked him clean off the bar stool. "Look, sorry," said the man, "I didn't know I was in Blair country." The landlord said, "Watch it, lad. You're not in Blair country...You're in horse country."

A circus-owner walks into a pub to see everyone crowded around a table watching a little show. On the table is an upside-down pot, and a duck tap-dancing on it. The circus-owner is so impressed that he immediately offers to buy the duck from its owner. After some haggling, they settle on £5,000 for the duck and the pot. Three days later the circus-owner comes back to the pub, furious. He goes up to the bloke he bought the duck from and says: "Your duck is a bloody rip-off! I stuck him on the pot before a whole audience, and he didn't dance a single step!" The bloke looks unimpressed. "Well," he asks, "did you remember to light the candle under the pot?"

What's the difference between an Irish wedding and an Irish funeral? There's one fewer drunk at the funeral.

****

A white Texan, a black Texan and a Mexican are walking along a beach. The Mexican spots an old oil lamp, picks it up and rubs it. A genie immediately appears and says that since there are three of them, they can each have one wish. The black Texan thinks for a bit and says, "I wish that my brothers and sisters world-wide were all free of American oppression and back in our ancestral homelands, living happy, successful, wealthy, contented lives." The genie grants his wish, and the black guy vanishes. The Mexican says, "Yeah, that would be nice," so he makes the same wish, but for all Latin Americans, and he too vanishes. The genie then turns to the white Texan, and asks if he too wants freedom and contentment for himself and his fellow-Caucasians. He looks around slowly, grins, and says "Nope. Reckon I'll just have me a beer, boy. It don't get much better than this..."

****

Two tubs of yoghurt walk into a pub. The landlord - himself a tub of cottage cheese - says, "Get out. We don't serve your kind in here." One of the yoghurt cartons looks at him and says, "Why not? We're cultured individuals!"

One day, after striking a rich seam of gold in Alaska, a miner came down from the mountains and walked into the nearest saloon in the nearest town. "Ah'm a-lookin' for the meanest, roughest, toughest whore in the Yukon!" he said to the barman. "Well, we got her!" replied the barkeep. "She's upstairs, second room on the right." The miner handed the landlord a gold nugget to pay for two beers and the whore. He grabbed the bottles, stomped up the stairs, kicked open the second door on the right and yelled, "Ah'm a lookin' for the meanest, roughest, toughest whore in the Yukon!" The woman inside the room looked at the miner and said, "Honey, you just found her!" Then she stripped naked, turned her back on the guy, bent over and grabbed her ankles. "Hey, hold on a minute!" said the miner, "I should get to say how we screw." "Relax, sugar, you will," replied the whore, "but I thought you might like to open those beers first."

An English bloke, an Irish bloke and a Scots bloke went into a pub for a beer. When the pints rolled up, each one had a fly floating in the top. "Bloody hell!" said the English bloke, disgusted, "That's a bit much. Pour me another one, landlord." The Irish bloke shrugged, said, "Ah, stop making such a fuss, you big lemon," to the English bloke, "Sure now and it's only a little fly," and took a hearty swing. The Scots bloke was horrified. He snatched the fly out of his pint, shook it really hard and yelled, "Spit that oot, ye wee bastard! G'wan, spit it oot or ye'll be sorry!"

****

Yesterday scientists in Canada announced that beer contains small traces of female hormones. To prove the theory, they fed 100 men 12 pints of beer and observed that 100% of them started talking nonsense and lost the ability to drive.

****

A man's disembodied head floats into a pub and orders a pint of beer. When it is served he uses his long tongue to lap up all the beer. No sooner has he finished than his torso appears. He orders another drink, laps it up, and suddenly he has legs, too. "This is great," he says to the landlord, "Give me another drink and we'll see if I can get my arms back, so that I can reach into my trousers, fetch my wallet and pay you." The landlord pours him another one and he laps that one up too. Next thing the landlord knows he's completely vanished. A bloke at the end of the bar turns to the landlord and says, "He should have quit while he was a head."

****

A fly goes into a pub and orders a drink. The customer on the next stool glances at him and says to the landlord, "What's with him?" The landlord says, "Oh, he works in the restaurant down the street." The man says to the fly, "That's fascinating. What kind of work do you do?" The fly sighs, "They put me in bowls of soup. It's tough on my health."

****

What's the difference between an Irish woman and an Irish goddess? About five pints.

****

A man walks into a bar – he sits down and orders a drink. The bar man gives him his drink, accompanied by a bowl of peanuts. To his surprise a voice comes from the peanut bowl. "You look great tonight!" it said, "You really look fantastic... and that aftershave is just wonderful!" The man is obviously a little confused, but tries to ignore it. Realising he has no cigarettes he wanders over to the cigarette machine. After inserting his money, another voice comes from the machine. "You WANKER... Oh my god you STINK... Do you know, you're almost as ugly as your mother." By now, the man is extremely perplexed. He turns to the barman for an explanation. "Ah yes sir," the barman responds, "The peanuts are complimentary, but the cigarette machine is out of order."

Down the Local

****

Descartes walks into a pub. "Would you like a beer, sir?" asks the landlord politely. Descartes replies, "I think not" and ping! he vanishes.

****

This bloke walks into a pub and there's a horse behind the bar serving the drinks. The bloke stares at the horse in amazement, so the horse says, "Look, what are you staring at, mate? Haven't you ever seen a horse serving drinks before?" The bloke says, "No, it's not that...it's just that I never dreamed that the parrot would sell the place."

****

John met Lisa down the pub one night and began buying her drinks. They got on pretty well together, and John suggested they go to his flat for a little light entertainment. Well it wasn't long before they found themselves in bed screwing passionately. As they were making love, John noticed that Lisa's toes curled up whenever he thrust into her particularly firmly. When they were done John laid back on the bed and said, "I must have been pretty good tonight. I noticed your toes curling up when I was going deep." Lisa looked over at him and smiled. "That usually happens when someone forgets to remove my tights."

****

Have you heard the new pickup line currently in fashion at gay bars? "Excuse me, can I push your stool up for you?"

****

A drunk bloke staggers into a pub, bumping into customers and spilling drinks as he makes his way to the bar. "Get the fuck out of here!" shouts the landlord when the drunk bloke finally makes it over. "I've gotta use the bog," slurs the drunk. "Fuck off right this instant or I'll throw you out myself," yells the landlord. "I gotta use the bog," says the drunk bloke again and starts to unbutton his trousers. "For fuck's sake! Hold on, hold on," says the landlord. "Alright, you can go to the toilet, but afterwards you piss off!" The drunk agrees and stumbles off to the toilet. After about five minutes a loud scream rips through the crowded bar, and everyone goes absolutely silent. Suddenly there's another loud scream. The landlord and a couple of regulars sprint to the bathroom to find out what's going on. When they get there, they find the drunk sitting down in the corner. "What the fuck is going on?" asks the landlord. "Look, 's your bog. I've had a pony, and every time I try to flush it crushes my balls!" says the drunk. "You stupid wanker!" screams the landlord, "You've crapped in my mop bucket!"

****

A bloke opens a bar, but he's having difficulty thinking of a name for it. "Name it after something you remember happily," a friend tells him; so remembering an old girlfriend of his he calls it "Lucy's Legs". A couple of weeks later, three blokes are waiting outside the bar for opening time. A policemen walks up to them, and curiously asks "Everything alright, gentlemen?" One of the blokes turns round to him and says, "Yes, thanks, officer. We're just waiting for Lucy's Legs to open so we can pop in and get a bite to eat."

****

A cowboy walked into a bar, dressed entirely in paper. It wasn't long before he was arrested for rustling.

****

A bloke was watching the football, drinking a few tinnies and popping peanuts into his mouth, when his wife called him from the kitchen. He turned his head towards her and accidentally popped a peanut into his ear. Well, they both tried and tried but neither could get it out. "Alright then," she said, "We'd better get you to hospital." As they walked out, their teenage daughter and her boyfriend came up and the daughter asked, "Where are you and dad going, mum?" The mother replied, "Oh, we're just off to the hospital. Your father has a peanut stuck in his ear." The boyfriend then said, "I tell you what; before you go, let me try to dislodge it." They agreed, so the lad stuck two fingers up the father's nose and told him to blow. The father blew, and out popped the peanut. As they headed back inside, the mother turned to her husband and said, "That lad's pretty clever. What do you think he'll be when he grows up?" The father replied, "By the smell of his fingers, he'll be our son-in-law."

****

Down the Local

Three blokes are driving around, necking beers and having a laugh when the driver looks in the mirror and sees the flashing lights of a police car telling him to pull over. The other two are really worried. "What are we going to do with our beers? We're in trouble!" "No," the driver says, "it's OK, just pull the label off of your bottle like this and stick it on your forehead. Let me do the talking." So they all pull the labels off their bottles and stick them to their foreheads, and the bloke pulls over. The policeman then walks up and says, "You lads were swerving all around the road back there. Have you been drinking?" "Oh, no, officer," says the driver, pointing to his forehead, "We're trying to give up, so we're on the patch."

A bloke walks into a pub with a pet crocodile at his side. He puts the crocodile up on the bar, turns to the astonished customers and says, "I'll do you a deal. I'll open this crocodile's mouth and place my dick inside it. The croc will close his mouth for one minute. He'll then open his mouth, and I'll remove my dick unscathed. In return for witnessing this feat, each of you will buy me a beer." The crowd nodded their agreement. The man got up on the bar, dropped his trousers, and placed his dick in the crocodile's open mouth. The croc closed his mouth, and the crowd winced in sympathy for the guy. After a minute, the bloke grabbed a beer bottle and rapped the crocodile hard on the top of its head. The croc opened his mouth, and the man removed his dick unscathed, as promised. The crowd cheered, and the first of his free beers was delivered. A couple of minutes later, the bloke stood up again and made another offer. "There's fifty quid here waiting for anyone else who's willing to give it a try." A hush fell over the crowd, and everyone shuffled their feet. After a while, a hand went up at the back of the crowd and a woman timidly called out. "Well, I'll try, but you have to promise not to hit me on the head with that beer bottle."

A bloke walks into a pub and orders a double whisky. He pays up, gulps it down and looks into his shirt pocket. He then orders another double, pays, gulps it down and look into his shirt pocket again. He orders a third drink and does the same thing. After the sixth double, he gets up and starts to stagger out. Curiosity gets the better of the landlord, and he says to the bloke, "Excuse me, but I noticed that every time you had a drink, you looked inside your pocket. I was wondering what's in there." The blokes looks at him for a moment, then slurs, "Well, I keep a picture of my wife in that pocket. Every time I have a drink, I take a look. When she starts looking good, I go home."

****

An obviously drunk bloke staggers into a pub and seats himself at the bar. After being served, he notices a woman sitting a few stools down. He motions the landlord over and says "Landlord, I'd like to buy that old douchebag down there a drink." Somewhat offended, the landlord replies, "Sir, I run a respectable establishment, and I don't appreciate you calling my female customers douchebags." The man looks ashamed for a moment and says "Yes, you're right, that was uncalled-for...please allow me to buy the woman a cocktail." "That's better," says the landlord, and he goes over to the woman. "Madam, the gentleman at the bar there would like to buy you a drink. What would you like?" "How nice!" replied the woman, "I'll have a vinegar and water, thanks."

Down the Local

One night a policeman was staking out a particularly notorious pub for drunk drivers. Towards closing time he saw a bloke stumble out of the pub, trip on the kerb and try his keys in five different cars before his own. Then he sat in the front seat of his car fumbling with his keys for several minutes. The policeman sat and waited for him to start up, then almost as soon as the man had left the car park he pulled the guy over and gave him a breathalyser test. After asking a few pointless questions and fumbling with the device for a minute or two, he blew into the box. The results showed no alcohol at all. Puzzled, the policeman made the driver repeat the test, and got the same result again - the bloke was sober. Worried, the policeman offered to fetch medical assistance if the driver was ill. The chap just smiled at him and said "Everything is fine, officer. I'm tonight's designated decoy!"

****

A dishevelled man, stinking like a distillery, flopped onto a bar stool next to the local Catholic vicar. His tie was tattered, his face was covered with lipstick prints and a half-empty bottle of gin was sticking out of his coat pocket. He pulled a newspaper out of his coat and began reading. After a few minutes, the dishevelled bloke turned to the vicar and asked, "Tell me Father, what causes arthritis?" The priest looked at the chap for a moment or two, and then disapprovingly said: "Actually, it's caused by loose morals, cavorting with cheap, wicked women, drinking excessive quantities of alcohol and having contempt for your fellows." "Well, I'll be damned," the drunk muttered, returning to his paper. The vicar thought about what he had said for a few moments, then nudged the man and apologised. "I'm sorry, I didn't mean to be so heavy with you. How long have you had arthritis?" The dishevelled bloke shook his head, and said, "I don't have arthritis, Father. I was just reading here that the Pope does."

****

After a major beer festival, the biggest brewery presidents decided to go out for a beer together. They picked a well-stocked pub and went in. The guy from Corona goes up to the bar and says, "Hey, señor, I would like the world's best beer, a Corona." The landlord takes a bottle from the shelf and hands it to him. The bloke from Budweiser says, "Give me the King Of Beers, a Budweiser." The landlord passes him one. The chap from Coors says, "I'd like the only beer made with Rocky Mountain spring water; give me a Coors." He gets it. The bloke from Guinness sits down and says, "Oh, give me a Coke." The landlord is a little surprised, but gives him what he ordered. The other presidents look over at him and ask, "What's up, why aren't you drinking Guinness?" The Guinness guy shrugs and replies, "Well, I decided if you lot weren't going to drink beer, neither would I."

Down the Local

****

A middle-aged woman and her husband visit a disco, just to remember what it used to be like. After a few dances they sit down at the side to recuperate. A few minutes later a bloke comes over and asks the woman to dance. She is flattered and, with an approving glance from her husband, accepts the invitation. Well, after a few minutes bopping, the bloke leans over to her and says, "You know, I think you're really good-looking. Could I kiss you, please?" The woman is a bit bowled over but replies, "Certainly not - I'm a married woman and my husband is over there." The dancing continues, and after another few minutes the man leans over again and says, "I really do think that you're the most attractive woman I've seen for ages. Could I fondle your tits, please?" This time the woman is shocked, and she replies, "No! What sort of person do you think I am?" The bloke apologises, makes the peace and they continue dancing. After a little while more the bloke leans over for a third time and says, "I think you're so lovely that I'd like to turn you upside down, fill you with beer and drink it out of you." The woman is horrified, slaps the bloke in the face and goes back to her husband. "Do you know what that man wanted to do to me?" she asks him. "He wanted to kiss me." "What?" exclaims her husband. "That's not all either; he wanted to feel my tits too," she continues. Her husband gets up and asks "Where is he? I'll show him. I'll knock his block off!" "There's more," said his wife. "He wanted to turn me upside down, fill me with beer and drink it out of me." Her husband immediately sat down again. "What are you sitting down for?" she asked, "I thought you were going to go and sort him out?" "You must be joking," her husband replied. "I'm not messing with anyone who can drink 16 pints in one go!"

Down the Local

****

A small bloke is standing by the bar when he looks up and notices a really huge guy standing next to him. The huge guy glances down, sees the small bloke looking up at him and booms out "Turner Brown, seven feet tall, 350 pounds, with a 20-inch dick, a three-pound left testicle and a three-pound right testicle." The small bloke faints dead away. Concerned, the big guy picks the little one up, shakes him gently and brings him back to consciousness. "What's wrong with you?" he asks. The small bloke says faintly, "Look, what did you say?" The big guy shrugs and repeats, "Turner Brown, seven feet tall, 350 pounds, with a 20-inch dick, a three-pound left testicle and a three-pound right testicle." The small bloke says, "Thank God! I thought you said 'Turn around'."

****

A herd of buffalo can only move as fast as the slowest buffalo, so it follows that the brain can only operate as fast as the slowest brain cells. The slowest buffalo are the sick and weak ones so they die off first, making it possible for the herd to move at a faster pace. Like the buffalo, the weak, slow brain cells are the ones that are killed off first by excessive drinking and partying. This makes your brain operate faster...

An Irishman's been at a pub all night, drinking. The landlord finally says that the bar is closed, so he stands up to leave and falls flat on his face. He decides to crawl outside and get some fresh air, in the hope that it will sober him up. Once outside, he tries to stand up again and falls flat on his face again. So the Irishman crawls home. At the door he tries to stand up yet again, only to fall flat on his face once more, so he crawls through the door and up the stairs. When he reaches his bedroom, he tries one final time to stand up. This time he collapses right on to the bed and, exhausted, falls fast asleep. When he wakes up the next morning, his wife is standing over him yelling, "You've been out drinking again!" "How did you know?" he asks. "The pub called, you stupid eejit. You left your wheelchair there again."

A bloke walks into a pub and orders ten shots of vodka, no ice. As the landlord hands them over he crashes them down, one after the other. "Are you alright?" asks the landlord, "Why are you drinking so fast?" The bloke replies, "You'd understand if you knew what I had in my pocket." Thoroughly perplexed, the landlord asks "So what do you have in your pocket?" The bloke grimaces and says, "A grand total of 25p."

This bloke walks into a bar at the top of a very tall building. He sits down, orders a huge beer, knocks it back, walks over to the window and jumps out. Five minutes later, he walks into the bar again, orders another huge beer, necks it, walks over to the window and jumps out again. Another five minutes pass, he reappears and repeats the whole thing, and so it continues. About half an hour later, another guy at the bar stops the first bloke and says, "Hey, how the hell are you doing that?" The first bloke replies, "Oh, it's really simple physics. When you knock back the beer quickly it makes you all warm inside, and since warm air rises, if you just hold your breath you become lighter than air and float down to the sidewalk." "Wow!" exclaims the second man, "I've got to give that a go!" So he orders a huge beer, downs it, goes to the window, jumps out and plummets to land with a splat on the pavement below. The landlord looks over at the first bloke and says, "Superman, you're an asshole when you're drunk."

****

A Mexican, an Irishman, an African, a kilted Scotsman, a priest, two lesbians, a rabbi and a nun walk into a bar. The landlord looks up and says, "What the hell is this? Some kind of joke?"

****

An Indian scout was checking the area on behalf of some buffalo hunters, searching for the herds. He put his ear to the ground. "Ugg", he said, "Deer come!" The hunters looked at him with awe. "How the heck can you tell that?" asked one. The scout answered, "Simple. Ear sticky."

****

A bloke walks into a pub with a yellow, long-nosed, short-legged dog under his arm. "That's one ugly dog," says another patron, petting his Doberman. "Heh," says the bloke, "that he is, but he's a mean little bastard." "Is that so?" asks the other patron, "I'll bet you £50 my dog will kick his arse in less than two minutes." The bloke agrees, so they put their dogs face to face and each gives the command to attack. In the twinkling of an eye, the little yellow dog has bitten the Doberman clean in half. "Fuck!" shouts the Doberman's devastated owner, "He killed Fang! What kind of damn dog is this?" "Well," says the bloke, "before I cut off his tail and painted him yellow he was a crocodile."

****

A guy is having a drink in a very dark bar. He leans over to a large woman next to him and says, "Do you wanna hear a funny blonde joke?" The big woman replies, "Well, before you tell that joke, you should know something. I'm blonde, six feet tall, 210 lb., and I'm a professional triathlete and bodybuilder. The blonde woman sitting next to me is 6' 2", weighs 220 lb., and she's an ex-professional wrestler. Next to her is a blonde who's 6' 5", weighs 250 lb., and she's a current professional kick boxer. Now, do you still want to tell that blonde joke?" The guy thinks about it a second and says, "No, not if I'm going to have to explain it three times."

Down the Local

****

Two blokes decided to open a real ale brewery in the foothills. After several months of careful work, they produced a product with a golden straw-like colour and a good strong flavour of hops. They sent it to the chemical lab at the MAFF for testing, and after waiting impatiently for three weeks, the lab analysis came back. It read, "Dear Sirs, Our analysis of the sample sent to us indicates that your horse has diabetes."

****

A Jew and a Chinese guy were sitting at a bar drinking. All of a sudden the Jew turned and punched the Chinese guy in the face, knocking him off his stool. Stunned, the Chinese guy got up and said, "What the hell was that for?" The Jew replied, "That was for Pearl Harbour." The Chinese guy said, "That was the Japanese. I'm Chinese." The Jew says, "Well, you have black hair, slitty eyes and buck teeth. It's all the same to me." The Chinese guy says "Okay," sits on his stool and continues drinking. About a minute later the Chinese guy turns round and punches the Jew in the face, knocking him off his stool. The Jew gets up and says, "That had better not be for me hitting you before." The Chinese guy says, "No, that was for the Titanic." The Jew replies, "The Titanic? That was an iceberg." The Chinese guy looks coolly at the Jew and says, "Iceberg, Goldberg, it's all the same to me..."

****

A woman walked into a bar carrying a duck under her arm. "Get that dog out of here!" yelled the landlord. "That's not a dog, stupid!" she replied, "That's a duck!" "I wasn't talking to you!" said the landlord.

****

Two drunkards were sitting at the bar. One was crying. The other asked him what was wrong. "I've puked all over myself again, and my wife is going to leave me this time; she warned me about it." The other drunk said "Do what I do, pal. Explain to your wife that some other guy puked on you. Put a tenner in your shirt pocket, and tell her that he was sorry and gave you the cash to get your clothes cleaned." "Sounds like a great idea," said the first drunk. When he got home, his wife was furious and started shouting at him about his clothes, how disgusting he was and that she'd had enough; she was off. The drunk started telling his lie, saying: "Look for yourself; there's the money in my shirt pocket." His wife looked in the pocket and found twenty quid. "Hang on a minute," she said suspiciously, "I thought you said the bloke gave you ten pounds for puking on you, not 20." The drunk nods, "Yeah, he did, but he crapped in my pants too."

****

A bloke bounced into the pub grinning and said to the landlord, "The beers are on me! My wife just ran away with my best friend." The landlord smiled and said, "Well, that's a shame. How come you aren't sad?" "Sad?" replied the bloke, "They've saved me a fortune! They were both pregnant!"

****

This bloke walked into a pub with a large toad on his head. "Where the hell did you get that?" asked the barman. "Well," the toad replied, "You won't believe it, but it started out as a little wart on my arse!"

****

A bloke is in the toilet of his local pub taking a slash. He looks around, and notices this black guy also using the urinals, and he's got a huge cock. "Damn!" says the bloke, in awe, "I wish I had a cock like that." The black guy looks over at him, "Well, it's simple. All you have to do is whack your dick on the side of your bath tub every morning." "Really?" asks the bloke. "Really," answers the black guy. The following week the black guy sees the bloke in the pub again, so he walks over and says to him, "So, have you been following my advice?" The bloke nods. "Well," says the black guy, "I can't help you with the size, but at least you've got the colour right!"

****

A fish staggers into a bar. "What can I get you?" asks the landlord. The fish croaks "Water..."

****

A man walks into a butcher shop and asks the butcher "Are you a gambling man?" "I am" replies the butcher. "OK" says the man, "I bet you can't reach up and touch that meat hanging from those hooks." "I'm not doing that" replies the butcher. "I thought you said you were a gambling man?" "I am – but the steaks are too high."

****

Down the Local

The Lone Ranger rides into town during the hottest part of summer. He stops outside a saloon and tells Tonto to run in circles around Silver, waving his poncho to keep a nice breeze on the horse while he goes in for a drink. A couple of minutes later, a man dressed in black swaggers into the bar and says, "You the Lone Ranger?" "Yes, I am," the Lone Ranger replies. "Well," says the man in black, "Did ya know ya left your injun runnin'?"

****

A dark-haired woman was sitting in a pub, wearing a tube top. She never shaved her armpits so, as a result, she had a thick black bush under each arm. Every 20 minutes, she raised her arm to signal the landlord to pour her another drink. This went on all evening. Towards the end of the night, a drunk at the end of the bar pointed at her and said to the landlord, "Hey, I'd like to buy the ballerina a drink. What's she drinking?" The landlord replied, "She's no ballerina." The drunk said, "Come off it. Any girl that can lift her leg that high has to be a ballerina!"

****

A bloke stumbles home completely plastered. He spends an hour trying to get the key into the lock, with no success, when a policeman happens to pass by. "Is everything alright, sir?" asks the policeman. "I can't get the damn key in the lock, officer," slurs the man. The policeman helps him out with the key and starts to go on his way. "Wait, wait," shouts the drunk, "I really appreciate it. Let me show you my house!" "No, thank you, sir, I'll just be on my way," says the policeman. "I insist," presses the drunk, "It'll only take a second, and I really want to show you!" So the policeman agrees, to keep the peace, and they go inside. They enter the living room.

"There's my TV, my stereo, and all that," says the man. "That's nice," the policeman replies. They go through to the kitchen. "There's my microwave, the new refrigerator...pretty nice, eh?" says the man. "Lovely," replies the policeman. Into the kids' bedroom: "Those are my two baby boys." "Yes, they look cute." Finally they get through to the man's bedroom. "And that's my wife, and that's me next to her."

****

This American redneck walks into a bar and says, "Gimme a Coke." The landlord says "Nah, you want a beer, mate. Every night you come in, have three beers and leave." The redneck says "Yeah, but last night I had three beers here, then I went to the bar down the street and had ten more beers. Then I went home and blew chunks." The landlord says, "Well, don't worry, it happens to the best of us." The redneck says, "You don't understand. Chunks is my pit-bull!"

****

Down the Local

Three blokes are sitting with their dogs in a pub by a nice log fire, and they get talking about them. The first one says "My dog is called Woodworker...Go, Woodworker! At 'im, boy." The dog immediately grabs a log from the fire with his teeth and uses his claws to fashion a beautiful wooden figurine. The next one says, "My dog is called Stoneworker...Go, Stoneworker! Come by, lad!" The dog drags a stone from the fireplace, goes at it and a beautiful carving emerges. The third one looks at the other two and says, "Well, my dog is called Ironworker." He puts the tongs into the fire and leaves them until they get red-hot. "Now," he says, picking up the hot tongs, "I'll just slap him on the bollocks with these, and you watch him make a bolt for the door."

****

A Scots chap in England is walking home pissed from the pub, as usual, and decides to take a quick nap on a nearby bench, to provide stamina for the rest of the journey. While he's dozing, a couple of girls stroll by. One says to the other, "Hey, is it true that they don't wear anything beneath those kilts?" The other giggles and says, "Let's take a look". So, after finding that the chap is indeed naked under his kilt, the first one says, "We should leave something to let him know we were here." So saying, she removes a blue ribbon from her hair and carefully ties it around his bell-end. When he comes round a couple of hours later, the Scot nips behind a bush to relieve himself. He finds the ribbon, and in tones of awe murmurs, "I don't know where you've been, laddie, but I see you took first prize..."

****

Two vampires walked into a bar and called for the landlord. "I'll have a glass of blood," said one. "I'll have a glass of plasma," said the other. "Okay," replied the landlord, "that'll be one blood and one blood lite."

****

This bloke walks into a pub and orders a beer. The barman looks at the bloke and says, "Have you seen Eileen?" The bloke is rather confused and asks, "Eileen who?" The landlord replies, "How about I lean over and you kiss my hairy arse?" The man is fairly offended by this, and walks out of the door and into the bar across the street, where he sits down and orders a beer. While he is drinking his beer, he tells the landlord what the other barman said to him. The landlord says, "You know, what you should do is go back over there and ask him if he has seen Ben, and when he says 'Ben who?' you say 'How about I bend over and you kiss my hairy arse?'" So the bloke goes back across the street, and asks the barman if he has seen Ben. The barman immediately replies, "Yep, he just went out the door with Eileen." The bloke looks puzzled for a moment, then asks "Eileen who...?"

Down the Local

****

A bloke goes into a pub and orders five doubles. The landlord asks him, "Jesus, are you okay?" The bloke answers, "I just found out my brother is gay." The landlord nods sympathetically and pours the drinks; the guy downs them, pays up and leaves. The same bloke returns a week later, and this time he orders ten doubles. The landlord again asks him, "Are you okay?" The bloke shakes his head. "I just found out my other brother is gay, too." Well, the landlord pours, and the bloke drinks up. The next week, he goes back into the bar and orders 15 doubles. "Shit! Doesn't anyone at all in your family like girls apart from you?" the landlord asks. "Yes," replies the bloke dolefully, "my kid sister."

****

The Devil walks into a crowded bar. When the people see who it is, they all run out screaming except this one old man. So the Devil saunters up to him and asks, "Do you know who I am?" The old man sips his beer, looks at the Devil, and answers, "Yup, happen I do." The Devil says, "Well, aren't you afraid of me?" The old man looks him up and down and says, "I've been married to your sister for 47 years. Why the hell should I be scared of you?"

****

So, this dyslexic walks into a bra...

This bloke is really desperate for a shit, so he nips into a nearby crowded pub. He looks around and sees that the toilets are upstairs, so he pops up there. When he gets up to the first floor, though, he can't find the damn things anywhere. Eventually, after several minutes of hunting around, he finds a hole in the floor and decides it's better than dumping on the floor, so he craps into it. When he's finished up, he goes back downstairs thinking he'll have a quick beer. To his amazement, the place is deserted; just the landlord standing behind the bar. "Where is everyone?" he asks. The landlord looks at him in amazement. "Where the hell were you when the shit hit the fan?"

****

Down the Local

Our Beer, which art in barrels, hallowed be thy foam. Thy hopdom come, thou will be drunk, at home as it is down the pub. Give us this day our daily beverage, and forgive us our spillages, as we forgive those who spill over us, and lead us not into naughtiness, but deliver us from kebabs, for thine is the taste, the clarity and the head, forever and ever. Amen. That concludes today's service, gentlemen.

Pun Away! Pun Away!

15

Shaggy Dog Stories

Pun Away! Pun Away!

There was a bloke who was famous across the world for the quality of the tulips that he grew. People used to come from all around to admire them, and to try and get the secret of how he grew them out of him. He was very cagey, and would only say, "I just put the bulbs in, and they come up perfectly." No one believed him, of course, but no one could discover what it was that he used to turn ordinary bulbs into the most beautiful tulip blooms that had ever been grown. There were whole fields of them, ranks and ranks, all identical and all perfect. Eventually, a friend of his of long standing decided to get the secret out of the tulip-grower and, if it was a simple enough trick, to maybe turn a few quid on the side. He invited his horticultural friend over one evening; they settled down to watch the football and have a few tins of beer, and once the grower started to relax, they moved on to Scotch; eventually, the friend started to gently steer the conversation towards tulips. Well, by now the grower was drunk, and his guard was down. They chatted for a while about tulips, with the friend congratulating the grower on his skill, and eventually, when the friend asked, "So, how do you get them so good, anyway?" he tapped the side of his nose and announced, "Hamsters!" Well, the friend was taken aback, and peered at the grower suspiciously to see if he was taking the piss, but he looked sincere. "Don't be daft," said the friend, "how can hamsters make ordinary tulip bulbs produce flowers the quality of yours?" "Well," said the grower, "On my other plot of land, I breed hamsters. Not just one or two, mind you, but thousands of the little buggers. God! They don't half stink out a place, I can tell you. It's appalling. Anyway, when they become adults I wait until the evening, when they're asleep, then run over them all with a huge turbo-charged steamroller that I got especially for the purpose. It's a beauty — 12,000cc of growling monster, thundering around at 40mph. When they're all accounted for, I bulldoze the mush into a machine which cans them into barrels, which I store in a big warehouse. At the start of the growing season, I go out at night with the old fertilising machine, filled up from the tins of course, and spread the mess all over the fields. Then I then get the tractor out, and plough and plough until it's all thoroughly worked into the ground. The next day I plant the bulbs, and you've seen the results for yourself." The friend paused for a moment and thought it over, then said, "Well I suppose it must work, but I really can't see how!" The tulip-grower grinned at him. "Obvious, isn't it? I copied the idea from the Dutch flower-growers, 'cos they're the real experts when you get down to it. I grow tulips from hamster jam!"

Pun Away! Pun Away!

June 3, 1861. Out here, at the frontier, it's very easy to wonder if maybe those old missionaries weren't right all those centuries ago, and I have actually come to the edge of the world. There's no other white man — or woman, damn it — for 100 miles in any direction. I devote my time to reading my copy of the Bible and tending my patch of cucumbers. This outpost was supposed to hold back the Indians, but that's a joke, and it seems to be unnecessary, anyway.

June 11, 1861. I was excited this morning by an interesting, if silent, visitor. One of the Indians from the tribe that lives nearby stood at the top of the hill and watched me perform my chores for over an hour, and then left without a word. Contact with the local natives is a thrilling prospect, and I have resolved to do nothing to scare them away.

June 19, 1861. Breakthrough! I have finally managed to convince the Indians to make proper contact. I taught them the word for "fort", which seemed like a simple enough place to begin. They in turn taught me the Indian word "toitonka", which refers to a mysterious device, a tiny horseless carriage made of metal. I envy these people their simplicity.

Pun Away! Pun Away!

June 22, 1861. Today I was greatly flattered to be taken to the Indians' village. It is built on one of the many flat-topped plateaux, or mesas, in the area. As the buffalo herds decline, this noble tribe too will face a decline of its own. They need a fighting chance, so I will try to teach them agriculture. Their name for themselves is "Waatch," which, as far as I can make out, means "The people known as the Waatch" in their language. I am known to them — it seems that they've been observing me closely — as "Stinchapocla" which means "he who has bodily odour."

July 8, 1861. Today I received a rude awakening; I have been foolish. The Indians are in fact fully aware of agriculture, and have nothing to do with the buffalo. That makes sense, I suppose — no nomads would build a village on a mesa. Unfortunately, they are suffering from a drought, as they have no rivers on top of the mesa, and the rainfall has been poor recently. I can help at last! I have told them to dig a ditch from near the stream that runs past my fort, up the cliff, to their mesa-top fields. They seem doubtful, but they are desperate, and their shaman, Bahnee, has told them to go ahead. In the meantime, I am pickling my youngest cucumbers.

Pun Away! Pun Away!

July 20, 1861. The drought is getting critical, but the ditch is complete and my pickles are now ready. I have lined the ditch with pickles. The Waatch are nervous, but I have promised them results in the morning.

July 21, 1861. Success! The stream has been diverted, and is flowing up the cliff-face to the Waatch fields. I have gained much status by what they see as a feat of magic. The shaman asked about my powerful medicine, but I came clean and told him that I was simply making use of a common fact in my world. After all, everyone knows that Dill Waters run Steep.

Pun Away! Pun Away!

When I was young, I got separated from my parents in a crowd. Well, I was crying and crying, and eventually I found a found a policeman who said he would help. I asked him, "Do you think we'll ever be able to find them?" He replied "I'm not sure, lad. There are so many places to hide..."

It's a well-known fact that if you want an improvement in your working conditions, you should always tackle your boss about your issues one at a time. After all, you should never put all your begs in one ask-it.

Pun Away! Pun Away!

Charlie, a big green frog, hopped into a bank one morning, with a briefcase neatly tucked under his right foreleg. He waited in the queue for a bit, then hopped up to the cashier and leaped onto the counter, sitting down in front of the cashier, Miss Jane Grey. "I need a loan," Charlie announced. Miss Grey, not wanting to seem flustered by meeting a talking frog, paused a moment, then replied, "I'm sorry, sir, but the Northlands Savings Bank doesn't normally issue loans to amphibians." Rapidly flicking open the briefcase, Charlie got out a sheaf of planning permits, schedules, estimates and blueprints. He passed them over to Miss Grey, and said, "Look, I need a loan. I have a sure-fire construction project in mind. Down in the marsh, we're very short of affordable housing. All my relatives need places. I have the permits. Paul, an architect friend of mine — a newt, as it happens — has drawn up the plans. Everything is approved and in order. There's a lot of local interest. All I need now is the financing." For poor Miss Grey, the situation was getting stranger and stranger. It wasn't enough that there was a talking frog sitting just a few inches in front of her, but he was now talking about his architect newt, plans, permits and amphibian interests. On the verge of freaking out completely, she blurted, "I'm terribly sorry, sir, I can't help you. You'll have to see our loan officer, Miss Black. Wait here for a moment please, and I'll get her." Miss Grey was gone for a while. After several minutes of spirited conversation at the other side of the bank, she returned with the loan officer. "Hello, sir," she said, "I'm Patricia Black, the loan officer here. How can I help you?" Charlie repeated his speech

Pun Away! Pun Away!

again, telling her about his idea, the plans and permits, the housing situation and his friend Paul, the newt architect. Miss Black decided to put an end to the whole nonsense swiftly, so she said, "What do you have to use as collateral for this loan? You must have something of value that you can mortgage to obtain a loan like this." Charlie wasn't the least bit thrown; he dug into his briefcase again. "I have this," he said, and brought out a crystal trinket on a silver chain, "It's extremely valuable". "I can't give you a loan based on that thing!" said Miss Black. "I don't even know what it is!" Well, Charlie begged for a while. He pleaded. Finally, he demanded to see the bank manager. Miss Grey, the cashier, went to go and fetch him when Miss Black reluctantly agreed, and another lively conversation took place at the far side of the bank. The manager eventually came over and asked, "What appears to be the problem, Miss Black?" She looked at him doubtfully, then explained that Charlie wanted to take out a loan, to construct housing in the marsh for his friends and relatives, that he has plans and permits, but all he had for collateral was the trinket. The manager, perplexed by this whole situation, took the trinket from Charlie and had a long, close look at it. Finally, he handed it back to Charlie and nodded thoughtfully, then turned to the loan officer and said, "It's a knick-knack, Patty Black. Give the frog a loan."

Pun Away! Pun Away!

A little baby bunny rabbit was orphaned. Fortunately for him, a nearby family of squirrels took him in and raised him as if he were one of their own. As you might expect, a squirrelly upbringing produced some peculiar behavioural patterns on the part of the rabbit, including a tendency for him to forget about jumping but rather to run around like his step-brothers and step-sisters. When the rabbit hit puberty, he found himself faced with an identity crisis. What was he? He went to his foster parents to discuss the problem. They talked about how he felt different from his step-brothers and step-sisters, how he was unsure of his place in the universe, and how he was generally forlorn. His squirrel dad's wise response was, "Don't scurry, be hoppy."

****

There was an organic farmer who didn't want to use a tractor on his small fields, so instead he had a pair of shire-horses to pull his plough and his wagons. Unfortunately a group of small birds had made nests inside the horses' manes, weaving the hairs together, which prevented him from hitching the reins properly. He tried everything he could think of to get rid of the birds, but no matter what he did they just came back again. He tried lotions, potions, shields and notions. He kept the stable colder and he kept the stable warmer. He went to horse doctors, he went to bird specialists, he went to his local MP, he went to the vet, and he even called the MAFF. He trimmed the manes down as much as he could. He tried loud bangs, cats and little horsehair scarecrows. Nothing would make the birds leave his horses alone. Finally he took advice from a bloke down the pub and went to see a supposed wise woman at the end of the village. The wise woman listened to his story, nodded, and gave him some vile-smelling yeast extract to rub into the manes. To his delight and amazement, it worked. Within two days, all the birds had gone and the horses could get back to work. The farmer was extremely pleased, but puzzled. He went back to the wise woman, and asked her: "Well, you're obviously very wise, but how come your yeast extract was able to solve a problem that nothing, not even vets and bureaucrats hadn't been able to?" She smiled and said, "Ah, it's simple. Yeast is yeast, and nest is nest, and never the mane shall tweet."

Does fuzzy logic tickle your brain?

Pun Away! Pun Away!

****

In days of yore, a doughty knight was on a vital quest. The life of the King hung in the balance, for unless he was able to rush a special potion back to the palace that very day the King would surely die. He was still about a hundred miles from the palace when his horse, exhausted from the rate at which the knight was pushing it, became lame. Well, through the woods he could see a small inn, so he ran and ran up to the inn as fast as he could. He headed straight for the stables, found the inn's stable-keeper, and shouted, "I must have a horse! The life of the King hangs in the balance, for he will surely die unless I can get a special potion back to him this very day." The stable-keeper shook his old, grizzled head regretfully, and said, "Ahh, I'm dreadful sorry, Sir Knight. We haven't got any horses in the stable today. Patrons are a bit light on the ground at this point in the season, what with the crops and all." The knight was distraught. "This is disastrous! Oh, evil chance! You must have some steed, good man — a pony, a donkey, even a mule? Please?" The stable-keeper shook his head again, lank grey hair flying everywhere. "No, Sir Knight, we've not got anything at all. Well...no. No, nothing." The knight's eyes lit up. "You had an idea! What? Whatever it is, I'll take it

Pun Away! Pun Away!

and pay well." The stable-keeper sighed and said, "Well, it's not pretty, but we do have a specially-trained shaggy war-mastiff." "A war-mastiff?" asked the knight, "A dog? Show me!" So the stable-keeper escorted the knight into one of the stables. Inside was a dog like none the knight had ever seen. It was a giant, as tall at the knight himself. It also stank. It was the dirtiest, hairiest, mangiest, sorriest-looking dog that the knight had clapped eyes on in his entire life. He was revolted, but duty called..."It'll do," said the knight with resignation, "Saddle it up, stout stable-keeper." The stable-keeper nodded and headed over to the wall, where a saddle was hanging. As he reached for it, however, he started coughing so hard he convulsed. He fell on to the floor and lay there for 30 seconds, gasping, while the knight looked on impatiently. He recovered, got to his feet again, and reached for the saddle. Again, he was seized by coughing and convulsions, and he fell over. Finally, he struggled to his feet, looked and the knight regretfully, and said "I'm most dreadful sorry, sir knight, but I can't do it." "What?" asked the knight, thunderstruck, "Why not?" The stable-keeper shook his head. "I can't do it. I can't send a knight out on a dog like this."

Pun Away! Pun Away!

The Russians had been purchasing huge quantities of grain from the NATO countries. This placed Russia in a weak, dependent position so they instigated a research program and invested heavily. After a year or so Russian scientists discovered a new type of grain, called Krilk, that was good to eat, yielded twice as much as normal wheat and ripened in just half the time. The only catch was that it required special treatment during milling in order to provide usable flour. Well, that was OK, and huge prairies of Krilk sprung up all over Russia, along with super-secret milling stations, highly protected black buildings that took Krilk in one side and churned bags of flour out the other. The CIA teamed up with MI6 to discover the secrets of Krilk, either to appropriate it for the West or to find a way to stop production, because Russia was no longer dependent on the NATO countries. Either way, the key was the milling process. Teams of highly-trained infiltrators tried to get into the Krilk mills, but they all failed. Gorgeous femmes fatales attempted to seduce Krilk millers, but got nowhere; the pretty-boy gigolos did no better. Spy satellites could see the outside of the buildings, but not the milling process. Nothing worked. Someone even suggested offering to purchase the information through normal channels, but that suggestion was quickly squashed. One morning the Russian representative at the United Nations sent an offensive little note to the American and British representatives about the matter, which read, "Stop wasting your money and our time. The new super-grain will remain Russian secret. There is no use spying over milled Krilk."

Pun Away! Pun Away!

Cole's Law — Thinly-sliced cabbage.

****

Deep in the jungles of Africa lived two tribes, and they hated each other. One tribe lived at the foot of a gigantic mountain. They panned for gold in the river and mined for gold in the mountain. There was lots of gold in the area, and they were extremely rich. The other tribe lived in a swampland area and lived on crocodiles and fish, and they had nothing. They were extremely poor. The tribes never visited each other except to raid each others' grass huts and plunder them. There wasn't much gain for the rich tribe in raiding the poor tribe, but they did it out of a sense of vengeance for the poor tribe's raids, and to try to get their stuff back. One day the Chief of the rich tribe got wind of a raid planned for the following day. The poor tribe were going to sneak in and steal his golden throne. The Chief was furious. Determined not to let them get away with it, he called his wise man over to advise him. The wise man told him, "Chief, you will have to make your throne disappear. Get some men to stick long wooden poles into the grass roof. Then, using ropes, your strongest men can hide the throne up in the roof of your grass palace. The raiders will never think to look up there." The Chief thought this was a great idea, and immediately ordered it to be done. The next day, as expected, the poor tribe attacked and swept through the village, searching everywhere. They didn't find a thing. The rich tribe were hiding in the mines in the mountains, and all the valuables were safely hidden away on top of the throne. When the raiders had gone the tribe came out and went back down to their village, and had a great celebration. The Chief stood in the centre of his palace, looked up at the roof, and gloated, "We fooled those idiots! Right over their heads, and they missed it!" Suddenly there were several tremendous bangs. The wooden poles supporting the gold throne snapped. Two tons of gold came crashing down on top of the Chief, and killed him stone dead — which just goes to show you that people who live in grass houses shouldn't stow thrones.

****

There was once a wise, sensitive guy (no, really!) who loved a beautiful girl. She lived in the middle of nowhere, in a marsh where his car always got stuck. To make matters worse, her father had a gun and disliked the guy. Although the girl was fond of him, he could only get to see her by fooling her father into thinking he was someone else. However, he had a rival — a more energetic suitor. This second guy wasn't as wise or sensitive, but he was more persistent, so he bought a set of amphibious tyres for his car and, one night when her father was asleep, drove up and sneaked away with her. The moral of this is, of course, that treads rush in where wise men fear to fool.

****

How many existentialists does it take to change a light bulb? Two. One to screw it in, and one to observe how the light bulb itself symbolises a single incandescent beacon of subjective reality in a netherworld of endless absurdity, reaching towards the ultimate horror of a maudlin cosmos of bleak, hostile nothingness.

****

A crushingly poor farmer was down to his last meal. The only thing he had in the world, apart from his mud hut and the rags he wore, was his talking mule. This particular talking mule had a snappy line in comedy, and a great stand-up routine with a dry, understated type of humour, so the farmer was reluctant to sell up, but there was no choice. With much regret, he set off to the city to sell the mule. Relying on the mule's natural talents, he stopped at a street corner and let the mule go for it. Well, the mule was so funny that within five minutes he had a whole crowd around, rolling in the street with laughter. One guy near the front said, "Look, I'm a talent agent, and I've got to have that mule." "What will you offer?" asked the farmer. "I don't have any cash," said the man, "but I'll tell you what. Here is my key-ring, my Porsche, my flat in town, my house in the country — they're all yours. These people here can bear witness to the deal." "Alright," said the farmer, and they made the exchange. The agent walked off with the mule, and most of the people followed, while the farmer adjusted to the idea of being a wealthy property-owner. "That didn't take long," he mused. "Ahh," replied a guy who hadn't left the area, "A mule that is funny is soon bartered..."

Pun Away! Pun Away!

****

A team of scientists were nominated for the Nobel Prize. They had used dental equipment to discover and measure the smallest particles yet known to man. They became known as "The Graders of the Flossed Quark..."

****

An old farmer had spent his life collecting tractors. Whenever one finally broke down or became hopelessly out of date, he refused to sell it, instead keeping it in a large barn. He even bought tractors that were no longer any use from other farmers. He tidied up the bodywork and polished them, treating them like museum exhibits. Eventually, when it was time for him to retire, he decided to sell off his massive collection so that he could live comfortably with his wife in a nice country cottage. So he put advertisements in local and national papers, inviting offers. He didn't have long to wait. A few days later, he received a letter from a businessman whose company had built some of the tractors mentioned in the advert many years before, and who had an interest in old vehicles himself. The two men arranged to meet in the farmer's local pub on the

Pun Away! Pun Away!

following Sunday. The day came and the businessman arrived. Despite the heavy clouds of pipe smoke, the two passed an hour in most pleasant conversation, and turned out to have much in common. "Well," sighed the farmer eventually, "I haven't had such a good natter for a long time, but I suppose it's about time we got down to business, eh?" "Yes, I suppose so," replied the other, "but maybe we could go somewhere else? I'm finding it hard to think in such a smoky atmosphere." The farmer grinned, and said "Ah, there's no need for that. Watch this!" He then proceeded to take an amazingly long, deep breath, and sucked in every last wisp of smoke in the room. He then turned to the window behind him and blew all the smoke out of the pub. "Wow! How the hell did you manage that?" asked the businessman, astonished. "Oh, it was nothing," replied the farmer, "After all, I am an ex-tractor fan."

Would a pun about a Mexican long-haired chihuahua puppy qualify as a short shaggy dog story?

****

Pun Away! Pun Away!

A group of whales were fed up with ships. The things criss-crossed their feeding grounds, migration paths and breeding areas all the time. Occasionally, they turned out to be actively hunting them. So, they held a strategic meeting in the middle of the ocean, and decided to hammer out a plan of action. "We'll split into two groups, one behind the other," said the chief whale. "The first group can swim under each ship, and everyone will blow together. This will create a huge bubble of air, which will capsize the ship, dropping the sailors into the water. The second group of whales, which will have to be you killer whales over there, can then eat them all up. Soon word will spread, and we'll be left alone." After the cheering died down, one whale towards the outside of the group raised a flipper to get some attention. The chief said, "Yes, Moby? You have something to add?" "Well," replied Moby, "I can go along with the blow-job, but I refuse to swallow any seamen."

A truck carrying copies of Roget's Thesaurus overturned on the highway. The local newspaper reported that onlookers were "stunned, overwhelmed, astonished, bewildered and dumbfounded."

Pun Away! Pun Away!

A rich bloke decided to have himself cloned. After a long and expensive developmental process a clone was created and specially matured. Unsurprisingly, it turned out to be an exact physical duplicate of the man. Mentally, however, something went wrong, and all the clone could do was spew forth the most vile language and filthy profanities. After a couple of weeks of putting up with this torrent and trying to find out if the clone could respond or be somehow healed or repaired, the bloke decided to cut his losses. He took the clone up into the mountains, went to the edge of a steep cliff and pushed the clone over the edge. A policeman popped out from behind a tree and said, "I'm afraid you're under arrest, sir. I'm going to have to ask you to come with me." The bloke sighed, "Look, officer, it isn't what it looks like. I didn't murder anyone; that wasn't a real person." The officer shook his head. "I didn't say anything about murder, sir. I'm arresting you under suspicion of making an obscene clone fall."

A young guy had a job bagging groceries at the supermarket. One day, the shop got a flashy new machine for squeezing the juice out of fresh fruit. Because of the potential danger, someone from the shop would have to work the machine. Intrigued, the guy asked if he could switch jobs, but his request was denied. The store manager shook his head sadly, and said, "Sorry lad, but baggers can't be juicers."

Pun Away! Pun Away!

One day a snail got fed up with his reputation for being slow. He decided that he should get himself a fast car to compensate. After checking out the markets, he decided to go for the new Japanese Nissda 950-Z, which was clearly the best buy on the market, doing 0-60 in just 4.3 seconds. He went down to a car showroom, and asked about availability. The dealer was only to happy to help, after seeing the snail's platinum credit card, and assured him that he could have the car ready the following day. "Okay," said the snail, "it's a deal. But can you rebadge it for me as a 950-S? Change the paint-work to include an S, and modify the badge at the back." "Well, I guess so," said the salesman, "but it'll cost extra. Why do you want it done?" The snail smiled, "I don't mind about the price. 'S' stands for 'snail'. It's really important to me that everybody who sees me roaring past knows who's driving." The salesman thought "Fair enough", and the deal was concluded. The snail picked his car up the next day, and could be found blasting down roads and motorways happily for the rest of his life. Whenever he shot past, the people saw him zoom by and said, "Wow! Look at that S-car go!"

****

So this bloke walks up to a Buddhist hot dog vendor and says, "Make me one with everything..."

****

A good fairy was flying along over the Great Plains in Africa one afternoon when she heard a soft crying below her. She landed to investigate and saw a little yellow frog sobbing his eyes out. Feeling sorry for him, the fairy asked why he was crying. "None of the other frogs will let me join in all their frog games, because I'm not green," he cried. "Don't be sad," replied the fairy, and with a wave of her magic wand, turned the frog green. Delighted, the frog admired himself and was surprised to find that his penis was still yellow. He asked the fairy about it and, embarrassed, she said, "I'm sorry, but there are some things that a fairy just can't do. If you find the wizard, he can fix things up for you." The little green frog croaked his happy thanks and hopped off to see the wizard. Feeling like a good Samaritan, the fairy took to the skies again and hadn't gone much further when she heard more crying, although this time it was booming and loud. Down she flew again, only to discover a pink rhino. Although she had a fairly shrewd idea of the answer, the fairy asked him why he was crying. "None of the other rhinos will let me join in all their rhino games, because I'm not grey." So, again she waved her magic wand, and turned the rhino all grey. Happy again, the rhino was examining himself when he noticed that his penis was still pink. He asked the fairy about it and, embarrassed, she said: "I'm sorry, but there are some things that a fairy just can't do. If you find the wizard, he can fix things up for you." The rhino, however, heard this news and burst into tears again. "I don't know how to find him!" he lamented. "Oh," said the fairy pointing back across the plain a short distance, "that's simple. If you're off to see the wizard, you want to follow the yellow-pricked toad."

Pun Away! Pun Away!

This reporter was interviewing a wizened, decrepit, wrinkly old man about longevity. "Do you recommend any special diet for a long life?" she asked him. "Absolutely," said the man, "I drink six pints of beer and a bottle of whisky every day, and I smoke at least 60 cigarettes. My favourite food, which I eat at least four times a week, is chips cooked in lard, served with liver gravy, with a deep-fried, battered king-size chocolate bar for pudding." The reporter was astonished "Amazing!" she gushed. "How old did you say you were?" The old man nodded sagely, and said "28."

What do you call 20 floppy-eared mammals hopping backwards in a row? A receding hare line...

Lads' Night Out

16

Jokes about Women

How do you describe the perfect blonde? She'd be three feet tall, with no teeth and a flat head to rest your pint on.

****

How can you tell if an office has a blonde worker? There's a bed in the stockroom and big grins on all the bosses' faces.

****

What's the similarity between an blonde girl and a dog's turd? The older they get, the easier they are to pick up!

****

How many blonde girls does it take to make a chocolate chip cookie? Five. One to stir the mixture and four to peel the smarties.

****

What do you call a blonde mother-in-law? An air bag.

****

Did you hear about the blonde who thought an innuendo was an Italian suppository?

****

How does a blonde get pregnant? Christ, I thought blondes were dumb!

****

What nickname do blondes use to boost their popularity? "B.J."

****

What do blonde virgins eat? They're still on baby food, obviously.

****

You have to bury blondes in a Y-shaped coffin, because as soon as they're on their backs, their legs open.

****

Why do blondes wear green lipstick? Well, red means stop...

Why do blondes drive BMWs? Because they can spell the name.

****

How did the blonde burn her face? Bobbing for chips.

****

What is the worst thing about having sex with a blonde? Those bucket seats are damned uncomfortable.

****

How do you plant dope? You can start by burying a blonde.

****

How can you tell if a blonde owns a vibrator? By the chipped teeth.

****

How can you tell if a blonde has been in your refrigerator? Lipstick on your cucumbers.

****

How do you get a blonde to get up off her knees? Cum in her mouth.

****

Why do blondes have little holes all over their faces? They're from eating with forks.

****

How do you brainwash a blonde? Give her a douche and shake her upside down.

****

What two things up in the air will get a blonde pregnant? Her legs.

****

What happens when a blonde gets Alzheimer's disease? Her IQ increases.

****

What's the difference between a blonde and an ironing board? It's a real bitch trying to get the legs open on an ironing board.

****

Why do blondes drive cars with sunroofs? They've got more leg room.

****

What's the difference between a blonde and a limousine? There are people who haven't been inside a limo.

****

How many blondes does it take to play hide-and-seek? Oh, just one.

****

What's the difference between a blonde and a broom closet? You can only get two guys into a broom closet at the same time.

****

Why couldn't the blonde write the number 11? She didn't know which '1' came first.

****

How can you tell if a blonde writes mysteries? She has a chequebook.

****

Why did the blonde climb up onto the pub roof? She heard that the drinks were on the house.

****

How does a blonde turn on the light after sex? She opens the car door.

****

How do you know a blonde likes you? She fucks you two nights in a row.

****

Why do blondes insist on their partners wearing condoms? So she's got a doggie bag for later.

****

Why do blondes take the pill? So they know what day of the week it is.

****

How do you measure a blonde's intelligence? Stick a pressure gauge in her ear.

****

How do you tell if a blonde created your garden? The bushes are darker than the rest...

****

Why did the blonde die while drinking milk? The cow fell on her.

****

What is the difference between a blonde and the Grand Old Duke of York? The Grand Old Duke of York only had 10,000 men.

****

Why don't blondes double-up recipes at dinner parties? The oven doesn't go to 700 degrees.

****

Why do blondes have more fun? They're easier to amuse.

****

Why don't blondes work as lift attendants? They can't remember the route.

****

Why do blondes like lightning? They just love having their picture taken.

****

Have you heard that NASA recently hired a whole bunch of blondes? They're doing research on black holes.

****

Why do blondes wear earmuffs? To cut down the draught.

****

How many blondes does it take to make a circuit? Just two - one to stand in the bath tub, and one to pass her the hair dryer.

****

What does a blonde say after multiple orgasms? "Way to go, team!"

****

What's the difference between a blonde and a brick? After you've laid a brick, it doesn't follow you around whining for two weeks.

****

Why do brunettes take the pill? Wishful thinking.

****

How do you keep a blonde busy? Write "Please turn over" on both sides of a piece of paper.

****

Why is a blonde like a postage stamp? You just lick them, stick them, then send them off.

****

What's the difference between a blonde and a trampoline? You take off your shoes before using a trampoline.

****

What did the blonde say when she knocked over the priceless Ming vase? "It's OK, Daddy, I'm not hurt."

****

What do you call a woman who knows where her husband is all the time? A widow.

****

What do you get when you cross a blonde and a lawyer? I don't know. There are some things even a blonde won't do.

****

How does a blonde part her hair? By doing the splits.

****

A big-boobed waitress came up to a blonde in the café and asked her for an order. The blonde read her nametag, then said, "'Debbie.' Oh, that's sweet. What do you call the other one?"

****

A bloke received a telegram telling him that his mother-in-law had died and enquiring whether she should be buried or cremated. He replied immediately, saying, "Don't take any chances. Burn the body, then bury the ashes."

****

A blonde was standing on a street corner when a man stopped and said, "Excuse me, but do you know that you have a tampon hanging out of your mouth?" She went pale, and said, "Oh, my God! What did I do with my cigarette?"

****

A mother-in-law paid a visit to her daughter's husband. He opened the door and said, "Good afternoon, dear! I'm so glad to see you! It's been ages. Come in, please! How long are you staying?" The mother-in-law smiled and said, "Oh, until you get tired of me." The bloke looked at her and said, "Won't you at least have a cuppa?"

****

This woman was so jealous that when her husband came home one night and she couldn't find any unfamiliar hair on his jacket, she screamed at him, "God! Only you would cheat on me with a bald woman!"

****

What do you say to a blonde that won't have sex with you? "Have another beer."

****

A pair of newlyweds were on their honeymoon. The first night the groom asked, "Honey, you can tell me. Am I the first man?" She looked up at him and said, "Why does everybody always ask me that?"

****

This bloke was down the pub, chatting to his mates. "I called the local insane asylum this morning," he said, "to check on whether any inmates have escaped recently." One friend asks, "Oh? Why, feeling nervous?"

"No," the bloke replied, "Somebody ran off with my wife last night!"

****

A bloke was travelling down a country road when he saw a large group of people outside a house. He stopped and asked a farmer why such a large crowd was gathered. The farmer replied, "Joe's mule kicked his mother-in-law and she died." "I'm impressed," replied the man, "she must have had a lot of friends." "Nope," said the farmer, "We're all here to bid for the mule."

****

A dentist told his female patient she needed a root canal operation. "I'd rather have a baby," replied the woman in disgust. The dentist said, "Well, you'd better make your mind up before I finish adjusting this chair."

****

"My husband is an angel," a woman said to her friend. "You're lucky," replied the friend. "Mine is still alive."

****

What do you say to a blonde with no arms and no legs? "Nice tits, love."

****

.A wife was having coffee with a friend when she confided to her, "Our marriage has never been great, but this year has been an absolute nightmare. Bill shouts at me all the time, criticises me, puts me down, tells me I'm shit, never does anything at all around the house, and I know he's fucking that little tart of a secretary of his - I found her knickers in his briefcase. I can't eat, I can't sleep...in fact, I've lost eight pounds so far this month." "You should dump the bastard," her friend said, "then take him for everything he's got." The wife replied, "Oh, I'm going to, don't worry. First, though, I want to get down to eight stone."

****

A hippie with no job kept begging his girlfriend to marry him. She declined for months, saying he needed to get a job first. He always told her, "We can live on love, baby." Finally she relented, and they got married. The morning after their honeymoon, she got up, turned the cooker on to a low setting, and sat on the ring. "What are you doing, baby?" asked the hippie. "I'm heating your breakfast," she replied.

****

A woman asked her friend, "Would it kill you if your husband ran off with another woman?" The friend thought about it a bit, then said, "Well, it might. They say that sudden, intense delight can cause heart attacks."

****

What is the definition of gross ignorance? 144 blondes.

What's a 72? It's a 69 with three people watching.

What's five miles long and has an IQ of 40? A blonde parade.

****

It was this Essex bloke's first morning as a married man, and he'd had a wild night of mad sex with his new wife. Absent-mindedly forgetting where he was, he got up silently, dressed quickly, left fifty quid on the dresser and headed for the door. On the way out, he realised his mistake and sheepishly went back into the honeymoon suite. His new wife was there, tucking the cash into her bra...

****

What is the definition of the perfect woman? A gorgeous, deaf-and-dumb, blonde nymphomaniac whose father owns a pub.

What do you get by crossing a prostitute with an elephant? A whore who'll fuck you for peanuts and won't forget you afterwards.

What do you call a good-looking man with a brunette? A hostage.

Do you know what it means to come home to a man who'll give you a little love, a little affection and a little tenderness? It means you're in the wrong house.

What do you call a blonde sandwiched between two brunettes? A mental block.

What do you call a brunette with large breasts? A mutant.

What do you call a fly buzzing inside a blonde's head? A Space Invader.

****

What's the difference between a woman and a volcano? A volcano doesn't fake eruptions.

****

What do you call a basement full of women? A whine cellar.

****

What is the difference between a ten-year-old marriage and a ten-year-old job? After ten years, the job still sucks.

****

What was the blonde psychic's greatest trick? An in-the-body experience!

****

What do you call a brunette with a blonde on either side? An interpreter.

****

Bill and Kathy have gone to see their local vicar for some marriage counselling. After talking to them for a while, the vicar gets up and hugs Kathy, then sits down. He then gets up again and hugs Kathy a second and third time, before turning to Bill and saying, "Did you see that, Bill? Kathy needs that every single day!" Bill replies, "Well, I guess that's all well and good father, but I can only bring her over on Tuesdays and Thursdays."

****

What do you call it when a blonde dyes her hair brunette? Artificial intelligence.

****

A little boy at a wedding turns to his father and says, "Daddy, why is the girl wearing white?" His father replies, "The bride is in white to show that this is the happiest day of her life, son." The boy thinks about it, and then says, nervously, "Well then, why is the boy wearing black...?" His father nods slowly, and says, "You're catching on, son."

****

What's the difference between a dog scratching at the door and a woman scratching at the door? When you let the dog in, he'll stop whining.

****

Why do blondes wash their hair in the sink? Where else do you wash vegetables?

****

Why is a blonde like a door knob? Everybody gets a turn.

****

A blonde finally finished a jigsaw puzzle after six months, and she was really excited. On the box, it said, "From 2-4 years".

****

Why was the blonde upset when she received her driving licence? Because he'd given her an 'F' in sex.

****

I used to take my wife all over the place, but I've stopped now. There just wasn't any point. She always found her way back.

****

Why do brunettes sleep all night on their stomachs? Because they can.

****

Why don't women fart as much as men? Because they can't shut their mouths long enough to build up the pressure.

****

Why was the first football pitch sketched out on a brunette's chest? They needed a level playing field.

****

How are blondes like cornflakes? Because they're simple, easy and they taste good.

****

What's the difference between the Loch Ness Monster and a good woman? The Loch Ness Monster has, on occasion, been seen.

****

What has 80 balls and likes to screw little old ladies? Bingo.

****

How do you change a blonde's mind? Blow in her ear.

****

A bloke turned to his wife and suggested, "Let's go out and have some fun tonight." "Okay," replied the wife enthusiastically, "but if you get home before I do, leave the hallway light on."

****

How does a woman hold her liquor? By the ears.

****

What do you call a woman who can suck an orange through a hose pipe? "Darling."

****

69 + 69 = Dinner for four.

****

A bloke was at the altar getting married. The priest asked him to take his vows, and then he said, "I do." Immediately, his wife-to-be snapped, "Oh, no, you don't! I do!"

****

My wife is really immature. It's pathetic. Every time I take a bath, she comes in and sinks all my little boats.

****

In which month do women talk the least? February, of course. It's the shortest.

****

Why did the blonde cross the road? Road? What was she doing out of the bedroom?

****

The groom lay in bed on the first night of their honeymoon, while his blonde wife stood at the bedroom window, gazing at the stars. "Come to bed, darling," he whispered seductively after some time had passed. "Not likely," replied the bride, "my mother told me that this would be the best night of my life, and I'm not going to miss a minute of it."

What do you call a blonde with half a brain? Gifted!

****

A husband asked his wife, "Has the postman come yet, dear?" "No," she replied, "but he's panting hard and sweating a lot."

****

Phil came home from work and found his wife crying. "Your mother really offended me today," she sobbed. "My mother?" he asked. "How? She's on holiday in Australia!" "I know," she wailed. "This morning a letter addressed to you arrived, and I opened it, because I was curious." "Hmm, OK, and?" "Well, it was from her. At the bottom, she'd written 'PS: Dear Catherine, when you've read this, don't forget to pass it on to Phil.'"

An old man of 70 married a young girl of 18. When they went to bed the night after the wedding, he held up three fingers. "Oh, baby," said the young woman, "Does that mean we're going to do it three times?" "Nope," replied her husband, "it means you can take your pick."

****

How can you spot a woman wearing tights? Her ankles swell when she farts.

****

If a blonde is going to New York on a plane, how can you steal her window seat? Tell her the seats that are going to New York are the ones in the middle row.

****

Brian was dying, and his family were standing around the bed. In a weak voice, he said to his wife, "Dear, when I'm dead, I want you to marry Pete White." His wife was shocked, and said, "What? No! I couldn't marry anyone after you, darling." "But I want you to," said Brian. "Why?" asked his wife. "Well," he wheezed, "I've hated that bastard for 30 years."

****

What do a brunette and a freezer have in common? They've both got ice on the inside.

****

"If I died," asked Mike, "would you remarry?" His wife thought about it. "Well, I suppose so." "And would you and he sleep in our bed?" His wife thought again, and said, "I guess so. It makes sense." Mike pressed on, "Would you make love to him?" "Of course," replied his wife, "as he would be my husband then." "How about my golf clubs?" asked Mike, "Would you give those to him?" His wife shook her head. "There wouldn't be any point - he's left-handed."

****

How can two brunettes become invisible in a crowd of three? When they're with a blonde.

****

What did the blonde mother say to her daughter on Saturday night? "If you're not in bed by 12, come home."

****

What's the difference between a blonde and a cockerel? In the morning, a cockerel says, "Cock-a-doodle-doo", while a blonde says, "Any-cock'll-do."

****

Where did Prince Charles spend his honeymoon? In-Diana.

****

There is no reason for any wife to have an inferiority complex. All she has to do is to spend a week sick in bed and leave her husband to manage the household and the kids.

****

What's the difference between a blonde and a telephone? It costs 10p to use a telephone.

****

Why do brunettes like their hair dark? Because it doesn't show the dirt.

****

Did you hear about the blonde who waited up all night to see where the sun went? It finally dawned on her.

****

Why are brunettes flat-chested? It makes it easier to read their T-shirts.

****

Why is a brunette so proud of her hair? It matches her moustache.

****

Did you hear about the new girlie mag that caters for the married market? It's just like Playboy or Penthouse, but it's all the same model, month after month after month...

****

What does a blonde say when you ask her whether her indicator is working or not? "Yes, it is. No, it isn't. Yes, it is. No. it isn't..."

****

What's the difference between a brunette and a jelly? A jelly wobbles when you eat it.

****

Ian and Polly had just got married and were driving to Blackpool for their honeymoon. Along the way Ian, who was at the wheel, reached over shyly and stroked Polly's knee. Polly smiled, and blushed, and said, "We're married now, love. You can go farther if you want." So they drove to Edinburgh instead.

****

An elderly woman hurried up the stairs to the church, late for the wedding. An usher politely asked to see her invitation. "I don't have one," she said. "Well then," he said, "are you a friend of the groom's?" "I should think not," snapped the woman. "I'm the bride's mother."

****

What's the difference between a Rottweiler and a brunette with PMS? Lipstick.

****

How can you tell when a brunette's been using a computer? There are lipsticks marks on the screen.

****

Which disease paralyses women from the waist down? Marriage.

****

Generally speaking, mothers-in-law are generally speaking.

****

What's the difference between northern girls and southern girls on a date? Southern girls say, "Alright, I'll go to bed with you." Northern girls say, "Alright, I'll go to bed with all of you."

****

What did the blonde's right leg say to her left leg? Nothing. They had never met.

****

What do performing cunnilingus and being in the Mafia have in common? One slip of the tongue and you're in shit.

****

What is most women's idea of a perfect man? A bloke who is two-and-a-half feet tall, has a ten-inch tongue, and can breathe through his ears.

****

Why did they stop producing brunette Barbie dolls? Parents were scared that the dandruff might be contagious.

****

What does marriage teach women? Patience.

****

A blonde ordered a pizza and the guy behind the counter asked if he should cut it into six or eight slices. "Oh, six, please," said the blonde, "I could never manage eight slices."

****

What do you call a blonde with two brain cells? Pregnant.

How do you drown a blonde? Glue a mirror at the bottom of a swimming pool.

For dinner, what does a blonde make best? Reservations.

What is it called when a brunette dyes her hair blonde? Self-improvement.

The following sign was seen in a small restaurant: "Thanks for visiting. If you liked the food, send your friends. If not, send your mother-in-law."

How can you tell if your wife is dead? The sex is the same, but the plates are stacked up in the sink.

****

How can you tell when a blonde has an orgasm? She drops her nail file.

****

How can you tell if a blonde is a good cook? She can get the pop-tarts out of the toaster in one piece.

****

A blonde heard that 90% of accidents occur around the home, so she moved.

****

The true sign of a tough woman is that she rolls her own tampons.

****

How do you make a blonde's eyes light up? Shine a torch into her ear.

****

Why do blondes have vaginas? So guys will talk to them at parties.

****

Why do female paratroopers wear jockstraps? So they don't whistle on the way down.

****

Why did God create brunettes? So ugly men would have someone too.

****

What do you call a brunette whose phone rings on Saturday night? Shocked.

****

What's the best way to describe a blonde surrounded by drooling idiots? Flattered.

****

How do you get a blonde to marry you? Tell her she's pregnant.

****

How do you make a blonde laugh on Monday morning? Tell her a joke on Friday night.

****

What do you call a brunette in a waterbed? The dead sea.

****

When you gaze into a blonde's eyes, what do you see? The back of her head.

****

The night before her wedding, a young woman had a talk with her mother. "Mum," she started, "I want you to teach me how to make my new husband happy." The mother took a deep breath, steeled herself, and began, "When two people admire, honour, and respect each other, love can be a very beautiful thing..." "I know how to fuck, mum," the young woman interrupted. "I want you to tell me how to make that wonderful lasagne you do."

****

What do women and rocks have in common? The flat ones get skipped.

****

What do brunettes miss most about a great party? The invitation.

****

The morning after throwing a party for his boss, Nigel was nursing a king-size hangover and, finding his memory a bit sketchy, asked his wife, "What the hell happened last night?" She shuddered. "As usual, you made a complete wanker of yourself in front of your boss," replied the wife. "Piss on him," answered Nigel husband. "You did," said his wife. "He fired you." Nigel grunted, "Well, fuck him then." "I did," she replied, "and he gave you your job back."

****

What part of Popeye never rusts? His prick. He regularly dips it in Olive Oyl.

****

On their wedding night, a devout young man entered the bridal suite and found his wife lying languorously on top of the covers, naked. "I expected to find you on your knees by the side of the bed," he said disapprovingly. "Well, if I must," she replied, "but sucking cock always gives me hiccups."

****

At the marriage guidance bureau, a woman was complaining, "What's-his-name here says I don't give him enough attention."

****

Why can't brunettes do the splits? Their legs are welded together from the knee up.

****

How can you tell when a fax has been sent by a blonde? There's a stamp on it.

Lads' Night Out

****

Why is sex with your wife like a late-night grocery? The goods are unattractively packaged, there's very little variety and there's a high price to pay, but there's just nothing else available at 2am.

****

How can you tell if a blonde's been using your computer? There's Tipp-Ex on the screen.

****

What do women and spaghetti have in common? They both wriggle when you eat them.

****

Down in Cornwall, they say that customs have changed very little over the centuries. Many a man still sleeps with a battle-axe by his side.

****

What do a blonde and a bottle of beer have in common? Both are empty from the neck up.

****

The good thing about dwarf brunettes is that they're only half as ugly.

****

Why do blondes have TGIF on their shirts? It stands for "Tits Go In Front."

****

A man answered a knock on his front door to find an Encyclopaedia Britannica salesman standing there. "Sorry," he said to the salesman, "We don't need it. My wife always assures me she knows all about everything going on."

****

What's the difference between vultures and mothers-in-law? Vultures don't pick on you until you're dead.

What's the first thing a blonde does in the morning? She walks home.

A couple were sitting in the living room watching TV. The phone rang, so the husband picked it up. He listened for a moment, and then said, in a sarcastic tone of voice, "I have no idea. Why don't you call the weather centre?" and hung up. "What was that all about?" asked his wife. "Oh, I don't know," replied the husband. "Some idiot wanted to know if the coast was clear."

How do you get a one-armed blonde out of a tree? Wave to her.

An old man had died. The funeral was in progress, and the vicar was talking at some length about the good life of the dearly departed, what an honest man he had been, what a loving husband and kind father, and how his poor family would miss him. Finally, unable to cope any longer, the widow whispered to her elder son, "Just pop on up there a moment and have a look in the coffin, will you? I want to be sure he's talking about your father."

What three little words does a wife most want to hear? "I'll mend it."

A doctor rushed out of his study. "Quick, grab my bag, darling!" he said to his lovely young wife. "Why?" she asked, alarmed. "What's the matter?" "Some bloke just called and said he can't live without me," he gasped, reaching for his hat. His wife sighed. "Um, wait up a moment, will you," she said, gently. "I think that call was for me."

You know that your divorce proceedings are getting bitter and malicious when your lawyer no longer seems like a bloodsucking leech.

****

If a blonde and a brunette are thrown down a cliff, who hits the bottom first? It's the brunette. The blonde has to stop to get directions.

****

In the box that said, "Enter your husband's average income," the blonde wrote, "Oh, about midnight."

****

An upstanding, moral young man married a respectable convent girl, a young woman who had been kept away from the depravity of modern society. After the reception, the happy couple were on the way to the airport to go off on honeymoon. As they passed through one of the less pleasant areas of the city, she asked, "Darling, what are those women doing milling around dressed like that?" Her husband shook his head. "They're whores. They sell their sexual favours to men, for fifty quid a time." The bride was shocked. "Fifty quid? Those bastard monks only used to give us a damned apple afterwards."

****

How do brunettes comb the tangles out their hair after a shower? With a rake.

What is the advantage of having a blonde passenger? You can park in the handicapped zone.

What's the difference between a blonde and a toothbrush? Well, you wouldn't let your best friend borrow your toothbrush.

How do you confuse a blonde? Oh, you don't. They're born that way.

How do you know when a blonde has been making chocolate chip cookies? You find Smartie coatings all over the kitchen floor.

****

What's the difference between a woman and a computer? You only have to punch information into a computer once.

****

Steve was down the pub, nursing a beer in the corner. "Steve, mate, what's wrong?" asked the landlord. Steve sighed bitterly. "I had a quarrel with my mother-in-law. She swore to me she wouldn't talk to me for a month." The landlord looked puzzled. "What's so bad about that?" "You don't understand," sighed Steve. "That was four weeks ago, and today is the last day."

****

Are brunettes sexually active? Nope, they just lie there.

****

A newly-married couple checked into a hotel, and while they were signing in told the attendant that they'd just got hitched. "Congratulations!" said the girl, looking at the bride. "You'll be wanting the Bridal, then." "Oh, no thanks," replied the wife. "I'll just hold his ears until he gets the hang of it."

****

"Before I married my wife," this bloke complained, "everything was wine, women, and song. Now that I'm her husband it's all coffee, mother, and nagging."

****

"It's for my mother-in-law," a mourner leading a long funeral procession explained to an interested bystander. Tightening his leash, he gestured down at his dog and said, "My Doberman here mauled her one night." "God," sympathised the chap, "That's terrible. But...um...is there any way you might lend me your dog for a day or two?" The mourner jerked his thumb over his shoulder at the procession and answered, "I'm afraid you'll have to join the queue."

****

The doctor looked at the worried wife and said, "I'm going to be frank. I'm afraid your husband is at death's door." The wife said, "Isn't there any way you can open it and push him through?"

****

Lads' Night Out

A man came home one afternoon and discovered his wife busily trying to cover up the obvious signs of wild sex. "Was it my friend Steve?" he yelled, furiously. "No," she said. "Well, was it my friend Rael?" he then asked. "Look," she shouted back, irritated, "don't you think I have any friends of my own?"

****

"Simon," his wife said, nose buried in the paper, "it says here that the government is going to trim down the navy. They're going to destroy six superannuated battleships." Simon looked up and said, "I'm sorry to hear that, dear. You'll miss your mother."

****

"You're claiming that several men proposed marriage to you," asked the incredulous husband. "Yes, several," his wife replied. "God! I wish you'd married the first idiot who proposed," he lamented. "I did," she sneered, "but the others proposed anyway."

****

"Alright," said the wife, "I'll admit that I like spending money, but it's the only extravagance that I have."

****

A really arrogant bloke was shagging a really arrogant bird. "God, aren't I tight, baby?" she moaned. "Nope," he grunted, "just stretched."

****

A woman went into a hardware shop to buy an axe. "It's for my husband," she told the assistant. "Did he tell you what poundage he was after?" asked the guy. "Are you joking?" she said. "He doesn't even know I'm going to kill him!"

****

According to a recent report, the most common marriage proposal in use today is: "You're WHAT?"

****

Why do brunettes have to pay extra for breast implants? Because the plastic surgeon has to start from scratch.

****

The best way to stop the noise in your car is to let her drive.

****

This Essex guy called his local tax office, and asked if he could write off the cost of his daughter's wedding against his tax bill as "a total loss".

****

You know that the honeymoon is over when the husband takes his wife off the pedestal and puts her on a budget.

****

Why do men pay a psychiatrist to ask a lot of expensive questions that their wives ask for nothing?

****

This day of the year always brings back a lot of sad memories. It was two years ago to the day that I lost my wife and children. I'll never forget that poker game.

****

Most husbands don't like to hear their wives struggling through the housework, so they turn up the volume.

****

Never try to guess your wife's size when buying her clothes. Just buy her anything marked "petite," and keep the receipt.

****

The law prohibits a man from marrying his mother-in-law - a classic example of useless legislation.

****

It is better to have loved and lost than to have had to live with that bitch for the rest of my life.

****

Lads' Night Out

My ex-wife is an excellent laxative...If the sight of her doesn't make you crap yourself, she'll irritate the shit out of you in a couple of hours.

One For The Ladies

Jokes about Men

Men say that women wear make up and perfume because they are ugly and smell bad. Why don't men wear make up and perfume, then? They're ugly and smell bad too, but they can't tell...

****

What do women do with their assholes in the morning? Pack them a lunch and send them off to work.

****

How do men sort their clothes? Into two piles - "filthy," and "filthy but wearable."

****

What is the thinnest book in the world? "What Men Know About Women."

****

A sleazy guy asked a pretty lift attendant, "Don't all these stops and starts get you pretty worn out?" She shook her head, and replied, "It isn't the stopping and starting that gets on my nerves. It's the jerks."

****

Two women had met for coffee. One noticed that her friend seemed troubled, and asked, "Is something wrong? You look stressed." Her friend sighed. "Well, my boyfriend just lost all his money and life savings in a nasty stock market crash. He's totally bankrupt," she explained. "Oh, that's dreadful," the other girl sympathised. "You must feel really worried about him." "Yeah, I am," replied her friend, "I don't know what he's going to do without me."

****

What is a bloke's idea of a good a seven-course meal? A hot dog and a six-pack.

****

Before you marry, a man will lie awake all night thinking about something you said. After you marry, he will fall asleep before you finish saying it.

****

What do you have when you've got two little balls in your hand? A bloke's undivided attention.

****

Where do you have to go to find a man who is truly committed? A mental hospital.

****

What do most blokes consider safe sex to be? A padded headboard.

****

What do you call six nude blokes standing on each others' shoulders? A scrotum pole.

****

What's easier to build, a snowman or a snow woman? A snow woman is easier, because once you've made a snowman you have to scoop all the snow out of his head and use it to make his testicles.

****

What do you call an intelligent man in England? A tourist.

****

What do you give to the man who has everything? A woman who can explain how to work it.

****

Why are men's brains larger than dogs'? So they don't screw women's legs at cocktail parties.

****

Men are like chocolates. They never last long enough.

****

What's the difference between a new husband and a new dog? A year later, the dog is still pleased to see you.

****

Colonel Sanders was a typical man. The only three things he cared about were legs, breasts, and thighs.

One for the Ladies

****

Sadly, all men are created equal.

****

What's the definition of a bachelor pad? A flat where all the house plants are dead but there's something growing in the fridge.

****

What do a clitoris, an anniversary and a toilet have in common? Men always miss them.

****

What is a man's idea of foreplay? Half an hour of begging.

****

Most men think Mutual Orgasm is an insurance company.

****

Where is a women's asshole while she is having an orgasm? He's at home, looking after the kids.

Women would be better off if men treated them like cars. They'd get lovingly rubbed all Sunday morning, filled to the brim twice a weekand a damn thorough servicing every six months or 50,000 miles, whichever comes first.

****

Why is a singles bar different from the circus? At the circus, the clowns don't talk to you.

****

What should you give a man who has everything? Penicillin.

Why did God create man? Because a vibrator won't mow the lawn.

One for the Ladies

Do you know why the tribes of Israel wandered in the desert for 40 years? Even then, men wouldn't stop to ask directions.

****

Why do only 10% of men make it to heaven? If they all went, it would be sheer hell!

****

Most men prefer looks to brains, but that's because most men see more clearly than they think.

****

Why do so many women fake orgasm? Because so many men fake foreplay.

****

Why don't men get haemorrhoids? Because they are all perfect assholes.

****

Men are so reluctant to become fathers because they're still too busy being children.

****

Why don't men show their true feelings very often? They simply don't have any.

****

Why do blokes give names to their penises? Well, they don't like the idea of having a stranger make 90% of their decisions.

****

Men can't get mad cow disease. They're all pigs.

****

A man is like a snowstorm. You don't know when he's coming, how many inches you'll get or how long it'll stay.

****

One for the Ladies

The only way to make a husband love you and nobody else is to become his secretary.

★★★★

Why do blonde women have bruises around their navels? Blonde men are stupid too.

★★★★

What is the difference between savings bonds and blokes? It takes a few years, but eventually bonds mature.

★★★★

I really didn't want to marry him for his money, but I couldn't find any other way to get at it.

★★★★

Boys will be boys, but men will be boys too, and they're better at it, because they've had more practice.

★★★★

You see plenty of clever blokes with thick women, but you hardly ever see a clever woman with a thick bloke...

How do men exercise on the beach? They suck in their stomachs every time they see a bikini.

Women find it so hard to track down sensitive, caring, good-looking men for the simple fact that they already have boyfriends.

****

If a man appears sexy, caring and clever, give him a day or two. He'll soon be back to his usual self.

What do you do when your boyfriend walks out? Close the door!

One for the Ladies

At 35, a woman thinks about having children. At 35, a man thinks about dating children...

****

What do you call a woman without an asshole? Divorced.

****

What is the difference between blokes and ET? ET phoned home.

****

Men are like toilets. They're all either vacant, engaged or full of crap.

****

What has eight arms and an IQ of 60? Four blokes watching a football match.

****

How many men does it take to change a light bulb? Four - one to screw it in and three friends to brag about how he screwed it.

****

"Adam," said God, "Adam, I have some good news and some bad news, my lad. The good news is that I gave you a penis and a brain. The bad news is that I could only fit in enough blood to work one of the two at any one time."

****

How can you tell the difference between a present your husband buys for the hell of it, and a present he buys because he's feeling guilty? The guilty present is nicer.

****

A bloke's idea of planning for the future is to buy two crates of beer rather than one.

****

You tell if a guy is playing around when he sends you love notes that have been photocopied, and begin with the phrase, "To whom it may concern..."

****

How can you tell when it's puppy love for a bloke? He slobbers all over you.

If a bloke is better than you at something, he will tell you how important it is. If you are better than he is, he will claim it's nothing useful.

What's the difference between pink and purple? The woman's grip.

How can you tell if a bloke is aroused? He's breathing.

How do you know if a man is lying? Easy - his lips are moving.

What's the most stupid part of a man's body? The penis. It has a head without a brain, it hangs around with a nutcase and it lives just around the corner from an asshole.

One for the Ladies

****

What do you instantly know about a well-dressed man? His wife is good at choosing clothes.

****

This guy left the pub early, hoping to get home early enough not to get into trouble with his wife. When he got home, he discovered that his wife was in bed with his boss. Back at the pub later, he was telling the landlord the story. "That's dreadful," sympathised the landlord. "What did you do?" "Well," said the guy, "I crept back out again and got back here as fast as I could. They were just getting started, so I reckon I've got time for a couple of extra beers."

****

If blokes are so clever, how come you always see signs reading "Danger! Men Working"?

****

What's the greatest mystery about men? How can they continue getting older yet still manage to remain so immature?

****

One for the Ladies

What did God say after creating man? "Hmm. I can do better than that."

****

A priest and nun were on their way back home from a seminary when their car broke down. The garage didn't open until the morning, so they had to spend the night in the village's only B&B. It only had one room available, though. The priest said, "Holy Sister, I don't think the Lord would object, under the circumstances, if we spent the night sharing this one room. I'll sleep on the sofa, and you can have the bed." "Yes, I think that would be fine," agreed the nun. They prepared for bed, said some prayers, and then each one took up their agreed place and settled down to sleep. Ten minutes passed, and the nun said, "Father, I'm terribly cold." "Okay," said the priest, "I'll get you a blanket from the cupboard." Another ten minutes passed, and the nun said again, "Father, I'm still terribly cold." The priest said, "Don't worry Sister, I'll get up and fetch you another blanket." Well, another ten minutes passed, and the nun spoke up again. "Father, I'm still terribly cold. I don't think the Lord would mind if we acted as man and wife just for this one night." "I think you're right," said the priest. "Get up and get your own damn blankets."

****

A sure sign that a man is planning to be unfaithful is when he has a penis.

****

What do ceramic tiles and blokes have in common? If you lay them properly the first time, you can walk on them for life.

****

How can you tell that soap operas are fictional? In real life, blokes are only affectionate in bed.

****

Men are like animals. They're messy, insensitive and potentially violent, but occasionally they make great pets.

****

Men call women 'birds'. It must be because of all the worms women pick up.

****

When a man puts his best foot forward, it usually ends up in his mouth.

****

Why do men like masturbation? It's sex with the only person they love.

One for the Ladies

****

Men like love at first sight, because it saves them such a lot of time.

****

The top ten rejections used by men, and what they really mean, are:
10. I see you as a sister. (You're ugly.)
9. There's too big a difference in our ages. (You're ugly.)
8. I don't think about you in 'that' way. (You're ugly.)
7. My life is too complicated right now. (You're ugly.)
6. I've already got a girlfriend. (You're ugly.)
5. I don't go out with women from work. (You're ugly.)
4. It's not you, it's me. (You're ugly.)
3. I'm concentrating on my career. (You're ugly.)
2. I'm celibate. (You're ugly.)
1. Let's be friends. (You're hideous.)

****

Why is it dangerous to let a bloke's mind wander? It's too little to be allowed out on its own.

****

The bloke said, "Since I first laid eyes on you, I've wanted to make love to you in the worst way." "Well," she replied, "you've succeeded."

****

"Can you beat my total of 71 men?" asked Suzie. "Perhaps," replied Jane, "provided you supply the whips."

****

Why is screwing a man like watching a TV drama? Just when things get interesting, it's finished until next time.

****

What's a man's idea of helping with the housework? Lifting his legs so you can vacuum under him.

****

Why do gentlemen prefer blondes? Men always like company on their own intellectual level.

****

What do you do if your best friend runs off with your husband? Well, you miss her dreadfully...

****

What's the difference between a pub and a clit? Blokes have no trouble finding a pub.

****

What do blokes and atheists have in common? Neither believe in a second coming.

****

Why do men love computers? No matter what mood they are in, they can always get a floppy in.

****

I only wanted to have a child, not marry one...

****

A bloke's idea of a serious commitment is, "Oh, alright, I'll stay the night."

One for the Ladies

****

What is the difference between a man and giving birth? One is terribly painful, sometimes almost unbearable, while the other is just having a baby.

****

What is the difference between a bloke and a catfish? One is a bottom-feeding scum-sucker, and the other is a type of fish.

****

How many times ever, in total, is a bachelor's bed made? One - when it was in the factory.

****

How many men does it take to wallpaper a house? Only four, but you have to slice them thinly.

****

Why do bachelors like clever women? Opposites attract.

****

Men would find that their marriages lasted longer if they paid less attention to prenuptial agreements and more to postnuptial affection and sex.

****

How do blokes define a romantic evening? Shagging.

****

What's the best way for a single woman to get rid of cockroaches? Ask them for a commitment.

****

There was this guy who left his wife. She gave birth to twins, and he wouldn't believe her when she said that there was no one else.

****

What do you call a man who expects to have sex on the second date? Slow.

****

Do you know why men have holes in the end of their penises? It is to allow oxygen into their brains.

****

How do you save a man from drowning? Take your foot off his head.

****

It would be wonderful if there was a potion that could give an average bloke the physique of Sylvester Stallone, the brains of Steven Hawking and the humour of Jo Brand. Of course, it could be horrendous. One little slip and you might end up with a bloke who had Jo Brand's body, Sylvester Stallone's brain, and the charm of Steven Hawking. Actually, thinking about it, who could tell?

****

My boyfriend said that his doctor needed a urine sample, some faeces and a semen specimen. I told him, "Just hand them your boxers."

****

One for the Ladies

Why are so many men uncircumcised? The doctors were afraid of giving the infant brain damage.

****

What makes a man chase women he has no intention of marrying? I don't know, but it's the same thing that makes dogs chase cars they have no intention of driving.

****

What is the difference between a sofa and a bloke watching telly? The sofa doesn't keep asking for beer.

****

Whenever a man tries to hide his baldness by combing hair across his head, the truth comes shining through.

****

What do men and women have in common? Neither trust men.

****

One for the Ladies

Why do men like sleeping with virgins? They can't stand criticism.

****

Did you hear that they are going to stop circumcising men? They discovered they were throwing away the best bit.

****

Why don't women blink during foreplay? They simply don't have time.

****

Boyfriends are like cockroaches. They hang around the kitchen and are very hard to get rid of.

****

Real women don't have hot flushes. They have power surges.

****

Bankers are excellent lovers, because they have an excellent knowledge of the penalties for early withdrawal.

One for the Ladies

****

Why do men like frozen microwave dinners so much? They love being able to satisfy urges in under five minutes.

****

Why don't men have mid-life crises? They're all stuck in childhood.

****

Why does it take one million sperms to fertilise one egg? They won't stop to ask for directions.

****

Husbands are like lawn mowers. They're hard to get started, emit foul smells and don't work half the time.

****

What is the one thing that all the men at a singles bar have in common? They're married.

One for the Ladies

****

What do electric train sets and breasts have in common? They're intended for children, but it's the husbands who end up playing with them.

****

A man was sitting beneath a tree, thinking about how good his wife had been to him and how fortunate he was to be married to her. He asked God, "Why did you make her so kind-hearted, Lord?" The Almighty responded, "So you could love her, my son." The man nodded. "Why did you make her so good-looking, Lord?" "So you could love her, my son," replied God. "Why did you make her such a good cook, Lord?" he persisted. "So you could love her, my son," came the answer. The man thought about it. Then he said, "I don't mean to seem ungrateful or anything Lord, but why did you have to make her so stupid?" God sighed. "So she could love you, my son."

****

Two men who hadn't seen each other in years met on the street. While they were talking and trying to catch up on all those intervening years, one asked the other if he had got married. "Nope," the other man replied. "I look like this because someone just tipped a cup of coffee over me."

****

One for the Ladies

Two old men are sitting on a park bench watching the young women go by. One turns to the other: "You know, Pete, I'm still sexually interested in women. In fact, I always get excited when I see pretty young things walking by in those skimpy little numbers that are so fashionable nowadays. The problem is at my age I'm just not seeing so well any more."

****

A couple in their sixties, both of whom have lost their partners to illness, decide to get married and move to Bournemouth. To make sure that everything runs as smoothly as possible, they decide to organise the various details in advance. "What are we going to do about our old houses?" June asks Harry. He thinks about it, and replies, "Well, we ought to both sell our homes, and then we can both pay half of the cost of our new home. How do you want to organise the grocery bills?" June shrugs, and says, "Neither of us eat much, so we might as well just split the bill on a monthly basis. It's probably worth doing the same with the electricity and gas bills, too." Harry cheerfully agrees, and then asks his fiancée what she wants to do about sex. June shrugs, and says, "Infrequently, I think." "Tell me," replies Harry, "Was that one word or two?"

****

An old man and his wife decided to divorce. At the hearing, the magistrate was perplexed. Looking from one to the other in confusion, she said, "Mrs Matthews, you're 93. Mr Matthews is 95. You've been married for 74 years. Now, at such a venerable age, you want to divorce. Why? I don't understand." The old man shook his head and said, "That woman and I have loathed each other for 65 years." No less confused, the magistrate asked, "Why didn't you divorce earlier, then?" "It was the children, you see," replied the old woman. "We didn't want to hurt them, so we decided to wait until the last one had died."

****

What do you do if your bank account stops working? Ditch him.

****

Did you hear about the stupid guy who put ice in his condom? He wanted to keep the swelling down.

****

Why do doctors slap babies' bums after they're born? To knock the dicks off the clever ones.

****

Why do spiders kill the males after mating? To stop the snoring before it starts.

****

One for the Ladies

What do you call a handcuffed man? Trustworthy.

How many men does it take to change a roll of toilet paper? God knows. It's never happened.

Women are indeed silly. They sleep with men who - if they were women - they wouldn't even have bothered to have lunch with.

Most women's idea of the perfect man is someone who is obedient, well-mannered, faithful, can empty the garbage and is great in bed. If only you could train dogs to screw in positions other than doggie-style, and bestiality was more socially accepted...

Before money was invented, what did women find attractive about men?

The only time a woman values a man's company is when he owns it.

Why is psychotherapy so much quicker for men than for women? When it's time to take a bloke back to his childhood, he's already there.

Three guys were out fishing when one caught a mermaid. She offers to grant each fisherman one wish, in exchange for her freedom. "Alright, double my IQ," said the first fisherman. "Done," said the mermaid, and the man - to his amazement - began to recite Shakespeare. The second fisherman was so staggered that he forgot all about making his dick larger, and said to the mermaid, "Triple my IQ!" "Done," said the mermaid, and he started deducing solutions to mathematical problems that he had never even realised existed. The third fisherman was beside himself. "Quintuple my IQ!" he screamed. The mermaid looked at him and said, "Normally I wouldn't try to change someone's minds about a wish, but I'd really like you to reconsider." The bloke shook his head stubbornly. "No, I want my IQ increased five times. If you don't do it, I won't set you free." "Please," said the mermaid, "it will alter your entire view of the universe." No matter what the mermaid said, the third fisherman insisted. So the mermaid sighed and said, "Done." With that, the third guy became a woman.

One for the Ladies

What is the most important thing about female astronauts? When the crew gets lost in space, at least the woman will ask for directions.

****

The only time that a man thinks about a candlelight dinner is when the power goes off.

****

Why do men snore? When they fall asleep, their balls flop over their assholes and form an airlock.

****

The only way to hurt a man with your words is to hit him in the face with your dictionary.

****

Single women claim that all the good men are married, but married women complain that their husbands are appalling. This proves, for once and for all, that there is no such thing as a good man.

****

How do you tell if a man is happy? Who cares?

****

While shopping, women get excited and happy when they buy that perfect item. Men experience the same feelings when they find a good parking space.

****

They say that men only think about sex. That's not true. They're also fixated on power, world domination, money, football and beer.

****

Men are like adverts. You can't believe a word they say.

****

Why are blokes like UFOs? You don't know where they come from, you don't know what their mission is and you don't know what time they're going to take off.

****

One for the Ladies

When he asks you if he's your first, say, "I'm not sure. You might be. You do look slightly familiar."

****

Men are like blenders. You have this feeling that you need one, but you're really not sure why.

****

Why is a bloke like a diploma? You spend lots of time getting one, but once you have it, you don't really know what use it is.

****

If he asks you if you're faking it, tell him, "No. I'm just practising."

****

If you think he's listening to you, you're wrong. He's trying to find the childish innuendoes in what you just said.

****

"I don't know why you wear a bra," said the husband, "You've got nothing to put in it." "You wear boxers, don't you?" replied the wife coolly.

****

What's the difference between men and pigs? Pigs don't turn into men when they get drunk.

****

How do men define a '50/50' relationship? Women cook and they eat; women clean and they make messes; women iron clothes and they wrinkle them.

****

When a man says, "I hate to go shopping," he means "...because I always end up outside the changing room, holding your purse."

****

When a man says, "Can I help with dinner?" he means, "Why isn't it on the table?"

"Did you see that guy?" a woman asked a friend. "He doesn't sweat!" The second woman replied, "Yes, I know. Snakes generally don't."

****

When a man says, "Football is a man's game," he means, "Women are too sensible to play it."

****

When a man says, "Ask your mother," he means, "I am unable to make any decision."

****

When a man says, "Good idea," he means, "It'll never work, and I can spend the rest of the day gloating about it."

****

When a man says, "Have you lost weight?" he means, "I've just blown our last £50 on a power drill."

One for the Ladies

****

When a man says, "I've read all the classics," he means, "I collect Playboy, and have done since 1972."

****

When a man says, "I've got my reasons," he means, "I'll think of something soon."

****

When a man says, "Darling, we don't need material objects to prove our love," he means, "Fuck! I forgot our anniversary again!"

****

When a man says, "I split up with her," he means, "She ditched me."

****

When a man says, "I brought you a present," he means, "I won a free paperweight as a booby prize in the pub's meat raffle."

One for the Ladies

****

When a man says, "She's one of those rabid feminists," he means, "She refused to make me a cup of tea."

****

When a man says, "That's women's work," he means, "It's difficult, dirty and thankless."

****

When a man says, "Will you marry me?" he means, "Both my flatmates have moved out, I can't find the washing machine and the bin is full of pizza boxes."

****

When a man says, "You look terrific," he means, "Oh, please don't try on any more outfits. I'm starving."

****

The only problem with women is men.

Women prefer the simple things in life...like blokes.

****

Boy will be boys, but one day all girls will be women.

****

Every man has it in his power to make one woman happy...by remaining unmarried.

****

The trouble with some women is that they get all excited about nothing, and then marry him.

****

The average man is proof that women can take a joke.

****

One for the Ladies

They put a man on the moon. Why can't they put them all there?

****

If you catch a man, throw him back!

****

If men got pregnant, abortions would be carried out in high-street stores and at drive-throughs.

****

Only a man would buy a £300 car and put a £2,000 stereo in it.

****

Diamonds are a girl's best friend, while dogs are a man's best friend. You tell me which sex is smarter...

****

Men would rather pledge loyalty to a flag than to a woman.

****

Don't trust a man who says he's single and then collects you in a Volvo estate with a child seat in the back.

****

So many men, so many reasons not to shag any of them.

****

There are only two four-letter words that are offensive to men - "stop" and "don't".

****

Short skirts remind blokes of their manners. Have you ever seen a bloke push on to a bus in front of a girl in a short skirt?

****

Scientists have just discovered something that can do the work of five blokes - one woman.

****

Marrying a man for money is a terrible mistake. You'll have to earn every penny.

****

A bachelor is a man who has missed his opportunity to make a woman miserable.

****

The best way to get a bloke to do something is to suggest that he is far too old for it.

****

Men who say they can see through women are missing a lot.

****

Man was made at the end of the week's work. God was tired.

****

An unmarried man is an example of the failure of the 'Care in the Community' scheme.

****

My ex-boyfriend and I weren't compatible. I'm a Libra and he's an asshole.

****

Men...give them an inch, and they add it to their own.

****

90% of men give the other 10% a bad name.

****

My ex-boyfriend was a poor communicator. It's hard to drink beer and talk at the same time.

****

Few women admit their age, but fewer men act theirs.

Men piss like cheap cameras - they just point and shoot.

****

Never hit a man with glasses - hit him with a baseball bat.

****

Pre-menstrual tension is something that makes women act once a month like blokes do every day.

****

The bloke who said that all men are created equal never went to a nudist colony.

****

Being a woman is quite difficult, because it mainly consists of dealing with men.

Professional Misconduct

18

Jokes about Medicine, Law and Other Professions

A doctor began his examination of an elderly man by asking him what brought him to the hospital. The old man looked surprised, and said, "Why, it was an ambulance."

A bloke went to a private urologist and said, "Doctor, I have a problem. My penis is garishly red." The urologist replied, "Well, okay, let's have a look at the old fellow then. Hmm...yes, no problem. We'll have you sorted out in no time." He told the bloke to lie down, then fiddled about a bit with the bloke's prick, did one or two things and said, "Right. All done; that'll be £50." Sure enough, the bloke's penis was back to normal. Impressed, he paid up. A couple of weeks later, he was chatting to a friend of his who looked a bit shifty and said, "You know, I've got the same problem, but it's greenish, not red. That specialist sounds cheap – I'll go and try him out." So the next day the friend went to the same doctor. He showed the urologist his penis, and the chap said, "Hmm...well, we can sort you out, but it's going to cost you £4,100, I'm afraid, and we'll have to operate." The bloke looked at the doctor in horror. "£4,100 and an operation? You sorted my mate out for fifty quid!" "That's very true," nodded the doctor, "but he had lipstick smudges on his old chap. You've got gangrene!"

****

This Australian guy living in London went to see his GP. He walked in, and said, "Doc, it's my prick," then unzipped his fly and unfurled a thick, 12-inch penis, lovingly tattooed with a dragon, on to the doctor's desk. The doctor peered at it and asked, "And what appears to be the problem?" "Aw, there's no problem, doc," replied the Aussie. "He's a beaut, though, ain't he?"

****

Two psychiatrists walked passed each other in the corridor. "Morning," said one, and nodded. "I wonder what he meant by that," worried the other.

****

This bloke has just finished his painless five-minute check-up at the dentist's. "It must be a real bugger spending all day with your hands in people's mouths," he said. The dentist grinned. "I think of it as spending all day with my hands in their wallets. That'll be £25, please."

****

A man telephoned the mental hospital and enquired as to who was in Room 23. "That room is empty," replied the nurse. "Great!" said the bloke, "That means I must have escaped!"

A proctologist pulled a thermometer out of his inside jacket pocket. He looked at it in horror and said, "Shit! Some arsehole has walked off with my pen!"

A bloke was the private patient of a doctor mate of his. He went to see his pal one afternoon, explained his problem, let the guy look him over and then took a prescription from him. "Ah, lovely. Thanks, Ed," he said. "Since we're such good friends, I'm not going to insult you by offering to pay, but I'd like you to know that I have made a provision for you in my will." The doctor nodded and, touched, said, "That's very kind. Uh, Paul, before you leave, could I just have that prescription a moment? There's one little thing I need to correct..."

Old dentists never die; they merely get a bit long in the tooth.

****

Professional Misconduct

At a medical convention, a respected specialist gave a speech detailing a miraculous new antibiotic he had discovered. "What will it cure?" asked someone in the audience. "Oh, nothing that seven or eight other antibiotics won't fix more quickly," he replied. "What's so miraculous about that?" asked the questioner, surprised. "It has a major side-effect of short-term memory loss," explained the specialist. "Several of my patients have paid their bill three, four, even five times..."

What is 18 inches long and can be found hanging in front of an arsehole? A stethoscope.

A vet was feeling ill, and went to see her GP. The doctor asked her all the usual questions, such as which symptoms she had, how long they had been occurring, and so on, when she sneered and said, "I'm not very impressed. As a vet, I've been trained to find out what is wrong with my patients by direct observation. Why do you need to ask so many questions? Don't you know what you're doing?" The doctor nodded, and said, "That's a fair point." He looked her up and down, then wrote out a prescription. As he handed it to her, he said, "There you are. Of course, if it doesn't help, we'll have to have you put down..."

****

A new nurse spotted a couple of surgeons grubbing around in the flowerbeds outside the front of the hospital. "Excuse me, doctors," she said, "Can I help at all? Have you lost anything?" "Oh, no, thank you, nurse," replied one. "We're prepping a heart transplant for a tax inspector, so we're just hunting for a suitable stone."

✹✹✹✹

The worst thing you can hear as the anaesthetic starts to hit is, "Lord of This World, Father of Lies, Prince of Darkness, accept this, our Sacrifice..."

✹✹✹✹

An elderly bloke goes to his doctor to get the results of some check-ups. He sits down, and notices that the doctor has a grave look on his face. "Some bad news, I'm afraid. The worst of it is that you have cancer, and only have six months to live." The elderly bloke is devastated. "Is there more, doctor?" "Yes, I'm afraid so," replies the doctor. "You have Alzheimer's." The elderly bloke's face lights up. "Thank God! I was sure I had cancer!"

✹✹✹✹

A young woman went to the doctor and told him, "Doctor, I've got a problem. I'll need to undress to show you." The doctor nodded for her to continue, so she stood up, unzipped her dress and stepped out of it. "It's these," she said, pointing to the inside of her thighs, where two bright green circles were clearly visible. The doctor came round for a closer look, rubbed the circles and nodded thoughtfully. "Tell me," he asked, "do you have a gypsy lover?" The woman blushed, and said, "Well, um, yes, actually I do." "There you go then," said the doctor. "You'll have to tell him that his ear-rings aren't actually made of gold!"

****

I had to kill my psychiatrist. He helped me a lot, but he just knew too much.

****

This bloke dropped out of medical school. It was tragic. He really wanted to be a doctor, but he just couldn't stand the sight of cash.

****

"Would you do me a huge favour and scream in agony a few times?" asked the dentist pleadingly. "I'd really appreciate it." His patient looked dubious. "Well, OK," she said, "but would you mind telling me why first?" "Oh," he said, "The football's on in an hour, and I've got too many patients waiting to stand a chance of making it!"

****

"How much will it cost to have the tooth extracted?" asked the patient. "£50," replied the dentist. "£50 for a few moments' work?!" asked the patient. The dentist smiled, and replied, "If you want better value for money, I can extract it very, very slowly..."

****

An inmate went to see the prison doctor, and was dismayed to be told that he needed to have one of his kidneys removed. "Look," said the prisoner, "You're already whipped out my tonsils, my adenoids, my spleen and my gall-bladder, and now you want my kidney? I only came to you in the first place to see if you could get me out of here!" The doctor was unruffled. "And that's exactly what I am doing," he replied, "bit by bit..."

****

Mrs Jones got last-minute nerves about her plastic surgery operation. "Is it going to hurt, doctor?" she asked. "No, madam," he replied, "not until you get my bill."

****

"Doctor, my hair keeps falling out. What can you give me to keep it in?"
"Will a shoebox do?"

A man walked into the psychiatrist's office with a bit of buttered toast on his head, fried eggs on each shoulder, a sausage in his left nostril and a strip of bacon tied to each eyebrow. The psychiatrist looked at him, then calmly asked, "What seems to be the problem, sir?" The man looked at him, and replied, "Well, I'm really worried about my brother."

If there's one thing worse than your doctor telling you that you have venereal disease, it's your dentist telling you...

Howie had been feeling guilty all day long. He kept trying to put it out of his mind, but he couldn't: the sense of betrayal was overwhelming him. Every so often his soothing inner voice would try to rally his defences, saying reassuringly, "Howie, don't worry. You aren't the first doctor to sleep with a patient, and certainly you won't be the last." Invariably, though, the sneering voice of guilt would interrupt, accusing, saying, "Howie Reed, how can you call yourself Basingstoke's top vet?"

****

If I have sex with my clone, will I go blind?

****

A doctor and his wife were having a big argument over breakfast. "Well, you're no bloody good in bed either!" he yelled, and stomped off to work. By midday, he had relented, and decided he'd better apologise. He called home, and after a great many rings, his wife picked up the phone. "What took you so long to answer?" he asked. "I was in bed," came the reply. "What were you doing in bed this late?" There was a moment's silence; then she said archly, "Getting a second opinion."

****

There was a young dentist called Sloan,
Who catered to women alone,
In a moment's depravity,
He filled the wrong cavity,
And said, "Look! My business has grown!"

****

A mute bloke was walking down the street when he passed a friend of his. He tapped him on the shoulder, and asked how things were, in sign language. "Oh, pretty good actually," replied his friend, vocally. "As you can hear, I can talk now." Excited, the bloke asked for details. "Well," said his friend, "I went to a specialist who found I had no physical damage, and he put me on a program of treatment that eventually gave me the power of speech. It's wonderful." At the bloke's insistence, the friend cheerfully gave him the doctor's phone number; then, realising his mistake, laughed and gave him the address. Well, the mute bloke went along that afternoon. As luck would have it, there was a spare appointment time, so the specialist examined him and found that he, too, could be treated. The mute indicated that cost was no object – he'd pay whatever it took – and said that he'd like to start as soon as possible. "Very well," replied the doctor, and told him to go into the treatment room, get undressed, and lean over the table that was there. While the mute bloke did so the doctor got a broom handle, a hammer and a jar of Vaseline. He thoroughly lubricated the broom handle, then crept into the other room, where the mute was waiting, arse in the air, positioned the handle by the bloke's arsehole, then whacked it deep up his bottom with a firm stroke of the hammer. "AAAAAAAAAAAAA AAAAAAAAAAAAA!" screamed the mute in agonised horror. "Excellent!" congratulated the doctor. "Come back on Wednesday, and we'll get to work on 'B'..."

****

A doctor thoroughly examined his patient, and said, "Look, I really can't find any reason for this mysterious affliction. It's probably due to drinking." The patient sighed, and snapped, "In that case, I'll come back when you're damn well sober!"

****

You can always tell when a death certificate has been completed by a Russian doctor. He signs in the 'Cause of death' box...

****

A handsome doctor was so vain that whenever he took a woman's pulse he adjusted the results downwards by 10 over 2 to compensate for the fact that he had touched her.

****

Did you hear about the mystic who refused anaesthetic for his tooth extraction? He wanted to transcend dental medication.

****

"Tell me nurse, how is that boy doing; the one who ate all those 5p pieces?" "Still no change, doctor."

****

Professional Misconduct

A man goes to the doctor and says, "Doctor, I've got this problem you see, only you've got to promise not to laugh." The doctor replies, "Of course I won't laugh, that would be thoroughly unprofessional. In over twenty years of being a doctor, I've never laughed at a patient." "OK then," says the man, and he drops his trousers. The doctor is greeted by the sight of the tiniest penis he has ever seen in his life. Unable to control himself, he falls about laughing on the floor. Ten minutes later he is able to struggle to his feet and wipe the tears from his eyes. "I'm so sorry," he says to the patient, "I don't know what came over me, I won't let it happen again. Now what seems to be the problem?" The man looks up at the doctor sadly and says, "It's swollen."

"Doctor, Doctor, I've got five penises," said the worried patient. "How do your trousers fit?" asked the doctor curiously. "No problem," the guy replied. "They fit like a glove."

American doctors have the letters "MD" after their names to warn you that they are Mentally Deficient!

"Did you take the patient's temperature, nurse?" "No, doctor. Is it missing?"

****

What is the difference between a genealogist and a gynaecologist? One looks up the family tree and the other looks up the family bush.

****

The doctor looked at his patient. "Tell me, does it hurt when you do this?" The patient winced, and said, "Yes, doctor." The doctor nodded sagely. "Don't do it, then."

****

When a car skidded on a wet road and struck a telegraph pole, several bystanders ran over to help the driver. A woman was the first to get to the victim, but a bloke rushed in and shouldered her out of the way. "Step aside, love," he said, "I've got a certificate in first aid." The woman observed for a minute or so, then tapped the bloke on the shoulder. "I just thought you should know that when you get to the part about calling for a doctor, I'm right here."

Did you hear about the nurse who swallowed a scalpel by mistake? She gave herself a tonsillectomy, an appendectomy and a hysterectomy, and circumcised three of the doctors.

****

A famous artist started to lose her eyesight at the height of her career. Understandably concerned, she went to the best eye surgeon in the world, and after two months of painstaking treatment and delicate, intricate surgery, her eyes were repaired. She was extremely grateful, so in addition to paying his bill, she painted him a gigantic water-colour of a vivid eye, and had it hung in his office one weekend. The press were fascinated, so she and the doctor held an unveiling of the new masterpiece, followed by a press conference. "Tell me, Doctor Schwartz," said one journalist, "what were your first thoughts on seeing this exquisite new work of art?" The doctor shrugged, and replied, "I thought 'Thank Christ I'm not a gynaecologist!'"

****

"Doctor, should I file my nails?" "No, madam; throw them away like everybody else."

****

Professional Misconduct

A man takes his dog to the vet, because the dog has been feeling poorly of late. In the surgery the vet examines the dog, taking temperature, feeling the dogs abdomen and smelling his breath. The vet steps back and shakes his head ruefully. "I'm sorry" he says, "Your dog has kidney failure. He has two days left to live." The man is appalled at this terrible diagnosis, and demands a second opinion. "Well, okay" says the vet, and picks up the phone. He mutters into the receiver for a few seconds and then puts the phone down. A minute later a cat comes into the surgery. The cat looks the dog over for a short while, and then turns to the vet and says "Kidney failure?" "That's what I thought" says the vet. "Yep. I'd say he has two days, maybe three," and the cat walks out. The man reacts angrily to this. "What the hell was that? I'm not taking a cat's opinion. Get someone else." The vet replies "Okay" and picks up the telephone again. After a short conversation, and a little wait, a Labrador walks into the surgery. The Labrador examines the other dog briefly and then announces, "Kidney failure, by the look of it. Not much more than two days left in the old boy." "I concur" says the vet and the Labrador leaves the room. The man has had enough and decides to go, "Right. I'm leaving." "That will be £450" says the vet. "What! That's a fortune! What the hell do you think you're playing at!" "Well, if it had just been me" says the vet "it wouldn't be that much, but after the cat scan and the lab report..."

A woman went to the doctor with bad knee pain. After the scans had been run without any obvious causes turning up, the doctor asked, "Can you think of anything you might be doing that could be causing this irritation to your knees?" The woman looked a bit sheepish, and said, "Well, Sid and I screw doggy-style on the floor every night." The doctor looked severe, and said, "That would do it, all right. You'll have to change that. There are plenty of other positions you could have sex in, you realise." "Not so that you can both see the telly," she shot back.

****

There was a bloke whose tongue was so long that when he stuck it out for the doctor, it was the nurse who said, "Ohhhhhhh!"

****

How can you tell the head nurse? She's the one with scuffed knees.

****

"Doctor, what fish did you say I had?" "You don't have a fish, you idiot! You've got cancer!"

****

A depressed bloke turned to his friend in the pub and said, "I woke up this morning and felt so bad that I tried to kill myself by taking 50 aspirin." "Oh, man, that's really bad," said his friend, "What happened?" The first man sighed, and said, "After the first two, I felt better."

****

"Doctor, what should I do if my temperature goes up by more than a point?" "Sell! Sell!"

****

This bloke went to the doctor and said, "My tongue tingles when I touch it to a hard-boiled egg wrapped in baking foil taken from the bottom of the toaster. What's wrong with me?" The doctor looked at him. "You have far too much spare time."

****

My father always thought laughter was the best medicine. That's probably why half of us died from tuberculosis.

****

Four nurses decided to play jokes on the doctor they worked for, because he was an arrogant tosser. That evening, they all got together on a break and discussed what they had done. The first nurse said, "I filled his stethoscope with cotton wool so he won't be able to hear anything." The second nurse said, "That's nothing! I drained the mercury out of his thermometers and painted them so that they all read 106 degrees." The third nurse said, "Well, I did worse than that. I stabbed tiny holes in all his condoms; you know, the ones he keeps in his desk drawer." The fourth nurse just fainted.

****

If you cloned Henry IV, would he be Henry V, or Henry IV Part II?

****

Alzheimer's Disease has lots of advantages. You get to hide your own Easter eggs and buy yourself surprise presents. You are always meeting new people. Best of all, you never have to watch repeats on television!

Professional Misconduct

****

A patient with a sore throat goes to see his doctor. After examining him, the doctor says, "I'm afraid your tonsils will have to be removed." "I want a second opinion," says the man, unhappily. "OK," replies the doctor, "You're damn ugly, too."

****

An obese bloke visited his doctor, suffering from headaches. "Please get undressed," said the doctor, so the bloke did, puzzled. "Ah, excellent," said the doctor. "Now, please go and stand in the window, facing out, and thrust your penis towards the glass." Even more confused, the bloke obeyed. While he was standing there waving his flabby bollocks out of the window, he asked, "Look, doctor, I don't mean to criticise, but what has this got to do with my headaches?" The doctor was silent for a moment, then replied, "Nothing, actually. My ex-wife works in the office opposite my window."

****

"What kind of job do you do?" a woman asked the bloke next to her on the train. "Actually, I'm a naval surgeon," he replied. "Goodness!" said the woman, "You doctors do specialise in some arcane fields!"

****

A woman went to see her psychiatrist. "I'm really concerned," she said. "Yesterday, I found my daughter and the little boy next door together, naked, examining each other's bodies and giggling." The psychiatrist smiled. "There's nothing to worry about," she said, "It's not unusual." "Well, I don't know," said the woman, "It bothers me. It bothers my daughter's husband, too."

****

A woman visited her doctor for some advice. "Doctor," she asked nervously, "can anal sex make you pregnant?" "Of course," replied the doctor. "Where did you think we got lawyers from?"

****

A mother took her 17-year-old daughter to the gynaecologist and asked him to examine her. "She's been having some strange symptoms, and I'm worried," said the mother. The doctor carefully examined her daughter and then announced, "I'm afraid she's pregnant, madam." The mother gasped, and went pale. "What? That's impossible! My little darling has nothing to do with all those horrible men! Tell him, dear." "Yeth," lisped the girl fussily, "Thath abtholutely right. I've never even kithed a man!" The doctor looked at the mother, then at the daughter, then he got up and went over to the window and stared out. He stayed there for several minutes, until the mother finally asked, "Doctor, is there something wrong?" The doctor shook his head. "No, madam. It is simply that the last time anything like this happened, the father lit a star up out in the east, and I was just checking if another one had appeared."

A doctor lost his practitioner's license when he was caught having sex with one of his patients. It was a particular shame, as he had been the best mortician in town.

Scientists say that 92% of all ten-pound notes carry germs. That's not true. Not even a germ could live on a tenner.

What did the accordion player get on his IQ test? Spittle.

****

How can you tell when the stage is level? The drummer drools out of both sides of his mouth.

****

Why do some people have an instant hatred of jazz players? It saves time in the long run.

****

How can you tell the difference between heavy metal songs? By their names.

****

What is the definition of perfect pitch? Throwing a violin down a toilet without hitting the seat.

****

Professional Misconduct

What's the difference between a banjo and a chainsaw? A chainsaw has a dynamic range.

****

How can you tell if there's a banjo player at your front door? He can't find the key, the knocking speeds up, and he doesn't know when to come in.

****

I recently had surgery on my hand. I asked the doctor if, after surgery, I would be able to play the accordion. He looked at me and replied, "I'm operating on your hand, not giving you a lobotomy."

****

Professional Misconduct

A bloke decided to take a holiday and travel somewhere exotic, so he booked a trip to a small, relatively unspoiled Pacific island where the native culture was still intact. He flew into Thailand and set sail from Jakarta on a specially chartered boat to the island paradise. As the boat was approaching the island, he noticed the sound of drums. "How quaint," he thought, "the natives are performing an ancient drum ritual." He arrived at the island, and got something to eat in a charming local bar. He finished his meal, but the drums were still throbbing away. After a few hours, he began to wonder when they were going to stop. Curious, he asked a native why the drums were going on so long. Rather than reply though, the native ran away screaming with a terrified look on his face. Thinking he had probably broken some taboo by asking an intrusive question, the bloke decided to just forget about the drums and enjoy his holiday. After two days of continuous drumming, broken sleep, mild headaches and so on though, the drums were really starting to get to him. On the beach, he crossed over to a local, a man with his wife and kids, and asked, "When are the drums going to stop?" The native looked at him in horror. All of a sudden, the whole family was backing away, then they turned and fled. The bloke decided to leave it another night, ears stuffed with cotton wool. The next morning though, they were still pounding away in the hills. He went outside, found an old native man, then pounced on him and grabbed him in a vicious headlock. "Listen to me, old man," said the bloke, "You will tell me when the drums stop, or I'll snap your damn neck." The old man looked up at him, shuddering, and said, "I would rather die than be the one who stops the drums." The bloke, perplexed, asked him why. Slowly, reluctantly, the old man said, "You are a foolish young man. When the drums are over, the harmonica solo starts!"

Professional Misconduct

****

A Russian pianist, a Cuban guitarist, a Scottish piper and an English drummer were sharing a compartment on a train. The Russian, in an attempt to impress the other passengers, said, "In Russia we have so much vodka that we can afford to throw it away." He then pulled out a bottle of fine Russian vodka and, to the dismay of the Scot, threw it out the window. In a spirit of one-upmanship, the Cuban replied, "In Cuba, we have so many cigars that we can simply throw them away," and proceeded to dump a box of the finest Cuban cigars onto the track. Everyone looked at the Scot, who glowered back. He said, "Well, in Britain..." and then grabbed the English drummer and threw him out of the window.

****

What do you call a jazz musician without a girlfriend? Homeless.

****

What's the difference between a coffin and a cello? With the coffin, the corpse is on the inside.

****

What do you call someone who hangs around a bunch of musicians? A drummer.

****

A famous blues musician died. His tombstone bore the inscription "Didn't wake up this morning..."

****

A businessman was interviewing a nervous young woman for a position in his company. He wanted to find out something about her personality, so he asked, "If you could have a conversation with someone living or dead who would it be?" The girl thought about the question: "The living one," she replied.

****

Manager to interviewee: "For this job we need someone who is responsible." Interviewee to manager: "I'm your man then – in my last job, whenever anything went wrong I was responsible."

****

A businessman turned to a colleague during the course of a long lunch and asked, "So, how many do you have working at your office?" His friend shrugged and replied, "Oh, about a third."

****

How long have I been working at that office? As a matter of fact, I've been working there ever since they threatened to sack me.

****

How many company directors does it take to screw in a light bulb? Just one. He holds the bulb and the world revolves around him.

****

Mike was walking through the office when he came across a secretary sitting at her desk, sobbing her eyes out. "Are you alright?" he asked sympathetically. "What's wrong?" She sniffed, and replied, "My boss said that I'm not cute enough to make so many typing errors!"

****

The boss was in a good mood. He walked into the office and cracked a joke he'd heard that morning. The staff all creased up apart from one girl in the corner who just glared at him. "What's up," grumbled the boss, "no sense of humour?" The girl shrugged. "I don't need to laugh. I finish on Thursday."

****

My boss said that I would get a raise when I'd earned it. He's mad if he thinks I'm going to wait that long.

****

Government studies show that a 7% unemployment level is acceptable to 93% of the population.

****

A motivational speaker was making a speech, but kept getting interrupted. Finally, sick of it, he grabbed the microphone and said loudly, "We seem to have a great many fools here tonight. Would it be possible to hear just one at a time?" Someone at the back of the room laughed nastily, and said, "Yes, good idea. Get on with your speech."

****

A businessman was having a hard time lugging his lumpy, oversized travel bag onto the plane. With the aid of a flight attendant, he finally managed to cram it into the overhead cupboard. "Do you always carry such heavy luggage?" she sighed. "Never again," the man replied. "Next time, I'm going in the bag."

****

They say that a fool and his money are soon parted. What I'd like to know is how the fool and his money got together in the first place...

****

A bloke was sitting in his garden one afternoon when a lorry pulled up in front of his house. The driver got out of the lorry, walked to the grassy area by to the road, dug a hole, then got back into the truck. A few minutes later, a different chap got out of the passenger seat, walked to the hole, proceeded to fill it back in, and then returned to the lorry. The driver then moved the lorry 50 feet up the road, and the process repeated itself. This went on all up the road. The bloke, who was already a bit upset about the poor quality of the road, couldn't believe his eyes. He stormed down to the lorry, pounded on the window, and demanded to know what was going on. The driver replied, "We're part of a road improvement project. The bloke who plants the trees called in sick."

****

A young woman is getting ready for a shower. She's standing there naked, just about to go in, when there is a knock at the door. "Who is it?" calls the woman. A voice answers, "I'm a blind salesman." The woman thinks it would be quite a thrill to have a blind man in the room while she's naked, so she lets him in. The man walks in, looks up at her, and his jaw drops, then, as a broad grin spreads over his face, he says, "Well, I was going to try to sell you a blind...."

****

A door-to-door vacuum cleaner salesman manages to fast-talk his way into a woman's home in the Scottish highlands. "This machine really is the best ever," he gushes, and tips a bag of dust, dirt and rubbish over the lounge floor. "What the hell are you doing?" shrieks the woman. "Don't worry madam," replies the salesman, "this machine is wonderful. If it doesn't remove all the muck from your carpet, I'll lick it up myself." The woman looks at him, then shrugs and says, "Will you need some ketchup? The electricity won't be back on until Thursday, you see."

****

If the car had followed the same technological curve as the computer, a Rolls-Royce today would cost £50, do a million miles to the litre, and explode once a week, killing everyone nearby.

****

A doctor, an engineer and a computer scientist were sitting around late one evening, discussing which was the oldest profession. The doctor pointed out that according to the Bible, God created Eve from Adam's rib. This obviously required surgery to obtain the rib, so his was the oldest profession in the world. The engineer countered with an earlier passage in the Bible that stated that God created order from the chaos. That was most certainly the biggest and best engineering project ever, so her profession was the oldest profession. The computer scientist leaned back in her chair, smiled, and responded, "Yes, but who do you think created the chaos?"

****

Two Irish builders were working on a house. One was on a ladder, nailing planks. He repeatedly reached into his nail pouch, pulled out a nail, looked at it, and either tossed it over his shoulder or proceeded to nail it into the wood. The other one looked up at him, perplexed, and called out, "Why are you throwing some of the nails away?" The first bloke explained, "When I pull the nail out of my bag, it's either pointed towards me or pointed towards the house. I can only use the ones that are pointed towards the house. You can't hammer a nail in flat end first. Do you think I'm stupid?" His mate shook his head, and called back, "Sure and y'are stupid! You shouldn't throw away those nails that are pointed towards you! They're for the other side of the house!"

****

University: A fountain of knowledge where everyone goes to drink.

****

Two Media Studies graduates decided to have a reunion, and they arranged to meet at one's house, in Manchester. The visitor inevitably got lost, so he phoned his friend and said, "Hi, look, I'm on my way over, but I'm lost and I've got no idea where I am." His friend replied, "It's okay, just look at the nearest road junction. There will be a sign. Read it to me." The lost one looked around, and then said, "Oh, okay, I see it. It says 'No Parking'." "Oh good," replied his friend, "you're right down the street. I'll drop by to pick you up."

****

Ice is no longer available in drinks in the Student Union bar at the Agricultural college. The girl who knew the recipe has graduated.

****

A professor was known for being a generous marker. The grades he gave for one of his courses were based solely on two exams, and the stuff on the exams was covered entirely in the textbook. As word of the course spread, each term there was a larger group of students who turned up infrequently, or not at all, just showing up for the exams. Finally, it got so bad that one term, about half of the students never turned up at all until the exams. On the day of the first exam, the students sat down and a graduate assistant handed out the papers, explaining, "The professor is ill, so I'll be taking the exams." When they opened the booklet, the students discovered just one question. It listed twenty grainy staff photos, and the instructions read, "Circle the picture of the professor who teaches this course."

****

University is like a gorgeous woman. You try really hard to get in, then, nine months later, you wish you had never come.

****

Why is a degree like a condom? It's rolled up when you get it, it represents a lot of effort, and it's worthless the next day.

****

A professor is someone who talks in someone else's sleep.

****

When lecturers want your opinion, they'll give it to you.

****

Education boosts your earning capacity. Ask any professor.

****

You should never let your schooling interfere with your education.

****

Did you hear about the couple with three children in University? They're getting poorer by degrees.

Professional Misconduct

****

A student who changes the course of history is probably taking an exam.

****

If you took all the students that fell asleep in lectures and laid them end to end, they'd be a lot more comfortable.

****

While visiting a small primary school, an inspector interviewing the headmistress became irritated at the noise the children were making in the next room. Angrily, he opened the door and grabbed one of the taller girls who seemed to be doing most of the talking. He dragged her into the head's office, ordered her to be absolutely silent, and stood her in the corner. A few minutes later, a small boy stuck his head into the room and begged, "Please, sir, may we have our teacher back?"

****

A science graduate asks, "Why does it work?" An engineering graduate asks, "How does it work?" A business studies graduate asks, "How much will it cost?" A media studies graduate asks, "Do you want fries with that?"

****

One day, a very attractive undergraduate girl visited her professor's office. She pulled the chair closer to the professor, smiled at him shyly, bumped his knee "accidentally", leaned over towards him to fiddle in her bag for a moment, exposing her cleavage, and said, "Professor, I really need to pass your course. It is extremely important to me. It is so important that I'll do anything you suggest." The professor, somewhat taken aback, replied, "Anything?" The undergraduate nodded, and huskily murmured, "Yes, anything you say." After a moment's thought, the professor asked, "What are you doing tomorrow afternoon at 3:30?" The student smiled sexily, and said, "Oh, nothing at all, sir." The professor nodded, then smiled and said, "Excellent! Come to room 15. I'm holding a detailed revision lecture, so bring a notebook."

****

In a huge psychology lecture class, a professor took great pains each lecture to read a chapter of his weighty textbook, written by his good self, to the class. One student made a point of sitting in the front row, right in front of the podium, and knitted while the professor read the text. It irritated the professor no end, so after about five weeks of this, the professor paused mid-lecture, looked at the young lady, and said, "Miss, are you aware that Freud considered knitting to be a form of masturbation?" The student looked up and retorted, "You do it your way Professor – I'll do it mine."

****

An economics lecturer had a strict policy that the fortnightly examinations were to be completed in exactly one hour and anyone who kept writing on their paper after the bell would get a zero. Well, one session a student kept writing on his exam paper for a moment or two after the bell and then confidently strode up to turn it in. The professor looked at him and said, "Don't bother to hand that paper in... you get a zero for continuing after the bell." The bloke looked at him and said, "Professor, do you know who I am?" The professor replied, "No, and I don't care if your father is Tony Blair... you get a zero on this exam." The bloke, with a enraged look on his face, shouted, "You mean you have no idea who I am?" The professor responded, "No, I've no idea, and I couldn't care less." The bloke grinned, then said, "Good!" quickly whipped his exam into the middle of the stack, and sprinted out.

****

In a courtroom, a mugger was on trial. The victim, asked if she recognised the defendant, said, "Yes, that's him. I saw him clear as day. I'd remember his face anywhere." Unable to contain himself, the defendant burst out with, "She's lying! I was wearing a mask!"

****

A man on trial had pleaded "not guilty". When the jury, eight women and four men, had been seated, and the trial was under way, the defendant switched his plea to "guilty". "Why the change?" asked the judge, "Were you pressured to plead guilty?" "No Your Honour," the man replied, "When I pleaded 'not guilty', I didn't know women would be on the jury. I can't fool even one, so I'll never fool eight of them."

****

When you go to court, just remember that you are trusting your fate to twelve people who weren't clever enough to get out of jury duty!

****

This bloke happened upon a little antique shop, so he went in and took a look around. Way up on a high shelf he saw a little brass mouse figurine, and he really liked it. He asked the owner how much it was, and she replied, "It's £50 for the mouse, and £100 for the story that goes with it." The bloke thought about it, then handed over fifty quid and said, "I'll just take the statue, thanks." He walked out with the mouse. As he was walking home, he noticed the figurine was hollow, with two little holes. Holding it up to his mouth, it made a melodious whistle. No sooner had he started than he was being followed by three little mice. When he stopped, they stopped. When he turned left, they turned left. "That's strange," thought the bloke. As he continued walking, the mice were joined by more mice, until the bloke looked like the Pied Piper, leading a huge procession of mice. Spooked out, he ran over to the side of a nearby canal and flung the statue into the water. The mice leaped over the edge and down into the water, following the statue, and drowned. In a bit of a daze, the bloke went back to the antique shop. When he walked through the door, the owner gave him a smug smile and said, "So, you've come back to hear the story?" The bloke shook his head. "No. As a matter of fact, I was wondering if you had any little brass lawyers."

****

Professional Misconduct

A witness was called to the stand to testify about a head-on car crash. "Whose fault was this accident?" one lawyer asked. "As near as I could tell," replied the witness, "they hit each other at about the same time."

****

In the courtroom, the prosecutor thundered at the defendant, "Did you kill the victim?" The defendant shook his head, and replied, "No, I did not." "Do you know what the penalties are for perjury?" asked the lawyer. "Yes, I do," replied the defendant. "They're a hell of a lot better than the penalty for murder."

****

A policeman broke up a scuffle outside a pub. "He started it!" said one man, infuriated. "It's not my fault!" replied the other. "Perhaps you could tell me what happened, Gents," said the policeman. "He kicked me in the bollocks!" accused the first man. "I didn't mean to," replied the second. "How was I supposed to know you were about to turn round?"

****

A zombie popped down to his local brains shop to get some brain for supper. The sign boasted about the quality of the professional brain sold there, so he asked the butcher, "How much is it for Doctor's brain?" "That's £3 an ounce." The zombie nodded, and asked, "How about Engineer's brain?" "£4 an ounce, sir." "What about lawyer's brain?" "Ah," replied the butcher, "that's £100 an ounce." The zombie was aghast.

"Why is lawyer's brain so much more?" The butcher looked at him. "Do you have any idea how many lawyers you need to kill to get one ounce of brain?"

****

A primary school teacher was asking students what their parents did for a living. "John, you first," she said. "What does your mother do all day?" John stood up and said, "She's a doctor." "That's wonderful," said the teacher. "How about you, Amy?" Amy shyly stood up, scuffed her feet and said, "My father is a mailman." The teacher smiled, and said, "That's lovely. Thank you, Amy. What about your father, Billy?" Billy proudly stood up and announced, "My dad is a pimp at the local brothel." The teacher was horrified, and promptly changed the subject. Later that day, at lunchtime, she went round to Billy's house and rang the bell. His father answered the door. The teacher explained what his son had said and demanded an explanation. The man sighed, and said, "Actually, I'm a libel lawyer, but how do you explain a thing like that to a seven-year-old?"

****

A lawyer died and went to heaven. When he arrived before the pearly gates, a chorus of angels began to sing in his honour and St. Peter himself came out to shake his hand. "Mr Wilson," said St. Peter, "it is a great honour to have you here at last. At 1028 years, you've broken Methuselah's record." "What are you talking about?" asked the lawyer, puzzled. "I'm 56. Well, I was 56 anyway." St. Peter was surprised. "56? But aren't you John Wilson?" "Yes." "A lawyer?" "Yes." "From 23, Acacia Gardens, Wimbledon?" "Yes." "Let me check the records," said St

Professional Misconduct

Peter, and his eyes unfocussed. Suddenly, he slapped his hand against his forehead. "I see! Someone totalled your billing hours!"

A lawyer died in poverty and many barristers of the city subscribed to a fund for his funeral. The Lord Chief Justice was asked to donate a pound. "Only a pound?" said the Justice, "Only a pound to bury a lawyer? Here's twenty quid; go and bury a few more of them."

****

A kind woman died. At her funeral were her doctor, her accountant and her lawyer. Each had promised her that they would put £100 into her coffin before she was cremated. The doctor went up, said farewell, and placed his money in the coffin. The accountant then went up, said farewell and placed his money into the coffin. Finally, the lawyer went up, took the £200 out of the coffin, and dropped a cheque for £300 in its place.

****

A bloke was charged with stealing a car. After a long trial, he was acquitted by the jury. Later that day, the bloke came back to the judge who had presided at the hearing. "Your honour," he said, "I want that damn lawyer of mine arrested." "Why?" asked the judge, surprised. "He got you off. What do you want to have him arrested for?" "Well, your honour," replied the bloke, "I didn't have any money to pay his fee, so he went and took the car I stole."

****

"You seem to be displaying an unusual level of intelligence for a man of your background," sneered a lawyer at the witness. "If I wasn't sworn under oath," replied the witness, "I'd return the compliment."

****

A lawyer is a man who helps you get what's coming to him.

****

Little Katy turned to her mother as they were walking through a graveyard and asked, "Mummy, do they ever bury two people in the same grave?" "Of course not, dear," replied her mother, "Why would you think that?" "That tombstone back there said 'Here lies a lawyer and an honest man.'"

****

The defendant who pleads his own case has a fool for a client, but at least he knows that his lawyer won't be ripping him off.

****

God decided to take the devil to court and settle their differences once and for all. When Lucifer heard the news, he laughed and said, "Where does the old fool think he's going to find a lawyer?"

****

It has been discovered that lawyers are the larval stage of politicians.

****

There is no better way to exercise your imagination and creativity than to study the law.

****

A small town that cannot support one lawyer can always support two.

****

There are two kinds of lawyers – those who know the law, and those who know the judge.

****

At a convention of biologists, one researcher remarked to another, "Did you know that in our lab we have switched from rats to lawyers for our experiments?" "Really?" the other replied, "Why did you switch?" "Well, there were five reasons. First, we found that lawyers are far more plentiful. Second, the lab assistants don't get so attached to them. Third, lawyers multiply faster. Fourth, animal rights groups do not object to their torture. Finally, fifth, there are some things even a rat won't do. There is one big drawback, however – it can be very hard to project the test results to relate to human beings."

****

A lawyer's dog, running about unattended, heads straight for a butcher shop and runs off with a big joint of meat. The butcher, recognising the dog, goes to lawyer's office and asks, "If a dog running unleashed steals a piece of meat from my shop, do I have a right to demand payment for the meat from the dog's owner?" The lawyer nods, and replies, "Absolutely." The butcher smiles, and says "Then you owe me £14.23. Your dog got loose, and stole a joint from me earlier." The lawyer nods, and writes the butcher a cheque for £14.23. The next morning, the butcher opened his post and found a letter from the lawyer. Inside was an invoice – £100 for consultation without appointment.

****

Professional Misconduct

When a lawyer tells a client that he has a sliding fee schedule, what he means is that after he invoices you, it's hard to get back on your financial feet.

****

It was so cold last winter that I saw a lawyer with his hands in his own pockets.

****

An old lady paid a solicitor for an appointment to sort out her will with a £50 note. As she was leaving, the solicitor realised that there was a second £50 note stuck to the back. He suddenly found himself wrestling with an urgent ethical problem. "Do I tell my accountant?"

****

Professional Misconduct

At the turn of the century, a respectable western lawyer was filing some insurance papers when he came to a question which asked, "If your father is dead, state the cause." Unwilling to reveal that his father had been hanged for cattle rustling, the lawyer evaded the problem by answering, "He died taking part in a public ceremony; he was killed when the platform gave way."

After successfully passing the necessary exams, a man opened his own law firm. He was sitting at his desk when his secretary came in to inform him that a Mr. Jones had arrived to see him. "Show him in," the lawyer replied. As Mr. Jones was being ushered in, the lawyer picked up the phone and declared into it, "And you can tell them that we won't accept less then fifty thousand pounds. Don't even call me until you can agree to that amount!" Slamming the phone down, he stood up and greeted Mr. Jones. "Good Morning, Mr. Jones. What can I do for you?" Mr. Jones smiled, and said, "I work for BT. I'm here to connect your phones."

****

Professional Misconduct

Experts are people who know a lot about very little, and who go along learning more and more about less and less until they know everything about nothing. Lawyers, on the other hand, are people who know very little about many things, and keep learning less and less about more and more until they know practically nothing about everything. Judges are people who start out knowing everything about everything, but end up knowing nothing about anything, because of their constant association with experts and lawyers.

✳✳✳✳

An airliner was having engine trouble and the pilot instructed the cabin crew to have the passengers take their seats and prepare for an emergency landing. A few minutes later, the pilot asked the air hostess if everyone was buckled in and ready. "All ready back here, Captain," came the reply, "except for one lawyer, who is still passing out business cards."

✳✳✳✳

A gang of robbers broke into a lawyer's club by mistake. The old legal lions gave them a fight for their lives, and the gang was lucky to escape. "It ain't so bad," one crook noted when the gang got back to their den. "We got out with £50." "I warned you to stay clear of lawyers!" the boss screamed. "We had over £270 when we broke in!"

✳✳✳✳

Professional Misconduct

A man went into a police station in a small town, obviously desperate. He asked the bloke at the desk, "Is there a criminal lawyer in town?" The policeman nodded, and replied, "Yes, but we can't prove it yet."

****

Talk is cheap – until lawyers get involved.

****

Did you hear about the terrorist that hijacked an aeroplane full of lawyers? He threatened to release one every hour if his demands weren't met.

****

There was a doctor who refused to pay the rent on his outdoor toilet. He didn't like the lawyer living downstairs.

****

What do a lawyer and a sperm have in common? Both have something like a one in 3 million chance of becoming a human being.

The best place to find a good lawyer is in the graveyard.

The difference between a lawyer and a whore is that a whore only screws one person at a time.

****

Sporting Triumphs

19

Jokes about Sport

Two blokes were out playing golf. "Did you hear about William Rogers?" asked one. "No," said the other curiously, "what about him?" "Well," said the first one, "he went mad last Saturday and beat his wife to death with a golf club." The other one shuddered. "God, that's awful." They paused for a moment's reflection, and then the other asked, "How many strokes?"

Two blokes are out at the sixth, teeing off. The first makes a reasonable drive but the second gives it a tremendous wallop. Ahead, on the fairway, a groundsman wanders out and into the path of the ball. It hits him square on the temple, and he collapses. The two golfers rush up, but find the guy dead, with the ball lodged in the side of his skull. There's blood everywhere. "Oh, Christ, no!" yells the second guy, "what am I going to do?" The first guy looks at him. "Come on, it's not that bad. A pitching wedge has the loft to get that free."

****

An accountant has been working for a billionaire client for 25 years. To celebrate the event, the billionaire says he'd like to get the accountant a present, so the accountant asks for a set of golf clubs. "How many are in a set?" asks the billionaire. "Basically 14," replies the accountant. "Should be able to do that," says the rich man. A month passes, and the accountant is starting to wonder if perhaps he should have been more modest and asked for a watch, when the billionaire calls again. "I've got you some golf clubs," says the billionaire. "Thank you!" says the accountant, "It's really very generous and..." "Hell," says the billionaire, cutting him off, "it's nothing. I wasn't even able to get you a full set, just the ten. It's worse than that, too. Only six of them have hotels within the grounds."

****

A policeman called a bloke in to question him about his wife's death. "Could you tell me what happened?" he asked. "Well," said the bloke, "I didn't realise my wife was at the red tee getting ready to swing. I drove off, and the ball struck her in the head." The policeman nodded, and said, "That agrees with the coroner's report, but I have another question. Why did she also have a golf ball up her arse?" The bloke shrugged. "Oh, that was my mulligan."

****

Two golfers were playing near the edge of the course. One of them looked over the fence in amazement and said, "Look! Those idiots over there are out skating on the pond in this blizzard!"

****

The real reason men like to go fishing is that it's the only time anyone will ever say to them, "Oh my God, that's a big one!"

****

What's the difference between Middlesborough FC and a triangle? A triangle's got three points.

****

Do you know why they called it golf? Well, all the other four-letter words were taken...

****

A keen golfer was sometimes accompanied by his wife. On one particular afternoon he was having a disastrous time. Teeing off on the 14th he pulled his shot so badly it spun off towards a groundsman's hut. Unfortunately, the hut was obstructing the line. However, his wife, who was along that day, noticed that the hut had two doors, and it was possible that if both doors were opened he would be able to play through. Of course, he asked his wife to go round the back and open the far door. When she did, sure enough, there was a clear path through to the green, although the ball needed to keep flat. He pulled out a wood, lined up and took the shot. As the ball cracked off his wife, curious, looked round the doorway. Tragically, the ball hit her in the centre of the forehead, killing her stone dead. Well, a few weeks later the widower was playing the same course with a friend. Again, he pulled his shot at the 14th, and ended up in front of the hut. "Hey, you might be able to play through if we opened both doors," observed the friend. The bloke shuddered and went pale. "No way. Very bad memories. Last time I did that, I ended up with a seven."

****

Three blokes assembled for a round of golf on Mothering Sunday. All were quite surprised at having been able to escape from the family for the day, and so they compared notes on how they managed it. The first bloke said, "I bought my wife a dozen red roses, and she was so surprised and touched that she let me go." The second guy said, "Yeah. I bought my wife a diamond ring, and she was so thrilled that she let me go." The third guy shook his head, and said, "I woke up this morning, farted thunderously, scratched my arse, then turned to my wife, belched and said, 'Golf course or intercourse?' She blinked and replied, 'I'll put your clubs in the car.'"

****

Why doesn't Mexico have an Olympic team? Because everybody who can run, jump and swim is already in the U.S.

****

Boxing is a lot like ballet. Except, of course, that there's no music, no choreography, and the dancers punch each other. All-in wrestling, however, is exactly like ballet...

****

A golfer was practising at the driving range after work one evening. He got a large bucket of balls from the kiosk and worked his way through them, but couldn't correct the slice he was trying to iron out. He didn't have the cash for a second bucket of balls, and as he was alone at the range he decided to go and scavenge some, so he walked up the edge of the range collecting balls from bushes and weeds, trying to be inconspicuous. To be able to carry more, he loaded the big, deep pockets of his baggy trousers. Walking back to the tee, he noticed a pretty young woman who had started practising. When he got closer, he saw that she was staring at the strange-shaped bulges in his groin. A bit embarrassed, he explained to her: "Um...they're just golf balls." She looked at him with a mix of sympathy and awe, and said, "That's like tennis elbow, yeah?"

****

Three blokes arrived late at the ski resort, and when they got to the hotel found that they'd have to share a room until the morning, because nothing else was available. When they got up there they found it just had one large bed. "It's just for one night," they thought, and went to bed. The next morning, the one on the far right said, "I had a really odd dream last night. I kept dreaming that I was wanking like a furious donkey, but I couldn't feel my hands." "That's really strange," said the bloke on the far right, "because that's what I dreamt, too. Exactly the same. Eerie." "You lads!" laughed the guy in the middle. "I just dreamt I was skiing..."

****

A man was walking down a street in Brazil when he heard a woman screaming and noticed a smell of burning. He ran round the corner to find a huge crowd of people watching a building burn and wringing their hands. On the eighth floor, a woman was leaning out of a window screaming for someone to save her baby. The man stepped forward and called, "Throw down your baby. I'll catch her." The woman yelled back, "No! You'll drop her, and she'll die!" "No, I won't," shouted back the man. "I'm the goalkeeper for the Brazilian national team. I've played every international for ten years. I've never missed a match, and I've never let in a goal. I'm not going to drop your baby." The woman was incredulous. "You've never let in even one goal?" "No, never," he calls back. "I am the greatest goalkeeper the world has ever seen. Throw down your baby." And with that he went into a crouch, legs bent, body angling forward, arms ready. The woman looked at the flames licking up the building, realised she had no choice, shouted, "Okay, here she comes!" and with a shriek threw her baby down. Unfortunately, as she did so, she knocked her elbow against the window frame, jerking it, and the baby went flying, tumbling wildly off-course. The crowd gasped, the woman screamed, but the man never took his eye off the baby. He stayed dead still as the child fell, watching it tumble and spin, until it was just feet from the pavement. Suddenly, like a panther, he leapt across the street, a jump of 25 feet, snatched the child from the air, rolled and came up with the baby clutched to his chest. He looked around at the crowd, acknowledged their admiration, and lifted an arm to the woman in a salute. Then he turned and, in one swift motion, drop-kicked the baby through a plate-glass window and into the back of a hardware shop.

A very rich bloke wanted to give his sons presents, so he called them to him and asked them what they wanted. The oldest son asked for a train set, so his father purchased London Underground for him. The second asked for a CD player, so his father bought him Virgin Radio. The final son wanted a cowboy outfit, so his father gave him Everton.

****

A poor golfer was having a bad round. He was 30 over par after four holes, had lost 14 balls in the same piece of water and had practically ploughed the rough trying to get a ball out. Then, on the green of the fifth, his caddy coughed just as he took a ten-inch putt, and he sliced it. The golfer went wild. "By God! You've got to be the worst damn caddy in the whole wide world!" The caddy looked at him sourly, and replied, "I doubt it. That would be too much of a coincidence."

****

A keen golfer was granted an audience with the Pope on a visit to the Vatican. When he got to see the pontiff, he kissed the hem of his robe and said, "Holiness, I have a question that only you can answer. Is there a golf course in heaven?" The Pope blessed the man, and replied, "My son, I do not know the answer to your question, as I do not play golf. But I will ask God for you, and pass on his answer." The next morning the man was awoken, feeling a bit groggy, at seven in the morning, by a hotel porter bringing him a note. It was from the Pope himself, and read: "My son, Heaven has the most fantastic golf course. It is eternally in perfect condition, the weather is ideal and the greens play like a dream. I'm afraid you're booked in to tee off at 11 o'clock this morning, however."

****

A guy out on the golf course takes a high speed ball right in the crotch. Writhing in agony, he falls to the ground. As soon as he could manage, he took himself to the doctor. He said, "How bad is it doc? I'm going on my honeymoon next week and my fiancée is still a virgin in every way." The doctor told him, "I'll have to put your penis in a splint to let it heal and keep it straight. It should be okay next week." So he took four tongue depressors and formed a neat little 4-sided bandage, and wired it all together; an impressive work of art. The guy mentions none of this to his girl, marries and goes on their honeymoon. That night in the motel room she rips open her blouse to reveal a gorgeous set of breasts. This was the first time he saw them. She said, "You're the first, no one has ever touched these breasts." He drops his pants and says, "Look at this, it's still in the CRATE!"

This bloke was a passionate fisherman, and spent all weekend at the waterside regardless of the weather. One Sunday he headed off to the riverside as usual. However, it was freezing cold and pouring with rain and, uncharacteristically, he decided to go home. When he got back, he noticed that his wife was still in bed, so he made a cup of coffee for the two of them, went up to the bedroom and said, "Hello, darling. I've made some coffee. It's really dreadful out there, freezing cold and lashing with rain." "Yeah," she said sleepily, "and that stupid bloody husband of mine went fishing anyway!"

****

The Irish parachutist realised that he had problems when his snorkel wouldn't open.

****

"I have a confession, love," a bloke said to his new wife. "I'm a golf-player. Much as I love you, you're not going to see me at weekends during the golfing season, I'm afraid." "That's OK," she replied, "I have a confession too. I'm a hooker." "No problem," replied the bloke. "Just keep your head down and straighten your left arm."

****

Two Scotsmen, Jim and Freddie, were out playing golf, and they decided to put some competition into the game by putting money on the round - 50p. Well, with such a sum at stake both men were concentrating fiercely, and they were perfectly matched for the first nine holes. On the tenth, though, Jim drove into the rough and couldn't find his ball. He called Freddie over to help and the pair searched around. Finally, desperate to avoid the four-stroke penalty for a lost ball, Jim popped a new ball out of his pocket when Freddie wasn't looking. "Freddie lad, I've found the ball," said Jim. "You filthy, cheating swine!" exploded Freddie. "I never thought that any friend of mine would stoop so low as to cheat in a game that had money on it!" "I'm not cheating!" protested Jim, "I've found my ball, and I'll play it where it lies." "That's not your ball," sneered Freddie. "I've been standing on your ball for the last five minutes!"

****

Two Irish blokes were out hunting ducks. Despite a whole day of vigorous hunting, though, they completely failed to harm even one duck. Finally, one turned to the other and said, "Maybe we'd do better if we threw that dog a bit higher."

****

A bloke was walking his three-legged greyhound through a park when he spotted something in the undergrowth. Going for a closer look he found that it was a lamp, so he gave it a quick buffing on the off-chance and out popped a genie. "Oh, hello," said the genie. "I suppose you want a wish?" The bloke nodded, too surprised to speak. "Well, you can have the one." "Alright," said the bloke. "Um...can you fix it so my dog will win all six races one evening at the dog races? They'll put ludicrous odds on it, because he's three-legged, and I can put my life savings on and be a rich man." The genie looked doubtful and said, "Well, I dunno. I mean, a three-legged dog winning six races is a pretty obvious sign of supernatural intervention, and things are supposed to be more subtle than that, according to the Codes and Regulations For Supernatural Semi-Divinities Act 1941. Can't you think of anything else?" "Well, I suppose so," said the bloke. "I'm a Southampton fan, so could you fix it so we win the Premiership this year?" The genie sighed. "About that dog of yours..."

****

Two blokes were on an African safari when they came across some lion tracks. Suddenly nervous, one said to the other, "You follow these forward and find out where the lion's got to. I'll follow them backward, and find out where it's been..."

Sporting Triumphs

A poor golfer spent the day at an expensive country golf club courtesy of a rich friend, playing badly and enjoying the luxury of a caddy. By the time he got to the 18th he was 88 over par. Seeing a pond over past the green, he said to the caddy, "I've played so badly today that I'm tempted to go and drown myself in that lake." The caddy looked back at him and said, "To be frank, I find it difficult to believe that Sir could keep his head down long enough."

If at first you don't succeed, BASE jumping is not your sport.

****

Sporting Triumphs

Why did God invent golf? So men had an excuse to dress like pimps.

****

In Africa, some of the tribes have a peculiar custom of beating the ground with clubs and uttering unearthly cries. Anthropologists have described this as a form of demonic exorcism. In Europe, we call it golf.

****

Have you ever thought about which game came first? Tennis has often been suggested, because the Old Testament states, "Joseph served in Pharaoh's Court." Others prefer the cricket hypothesis, because Genesis itself starts with "In the big Inning." There's no doubt about the last game that will ever be played, though. It's bridge. At the end of the world, we are told, "Gabriel will play the last trump..."

****

In the mornings, directors talk about golf in their offices. In the afternoons, they talk about work on the golf course...

****

Two alien scientists visited Earth to examine local customs. When they met to pool their knowledge the first alien told of a peculiar religious ceremony it had seen, of impressive magical power. "I went to a large green arena shaped like a meteorite crater. Several thousand worshippers were gathered around the outside. Two priests walked to the centre of the field, where a rectangular area was marked, and hammered six spears into the ground, three at each end, then linked the spears in each set of three with small tubes. Then 11 more priests came out, clad in white robes. Finally, two high priests wielding clubs walked to the centre area. One of the white-robed priests produced a red orb and hurled it at the ones with the clubs." "Wow," replied the other alien, "what happened next?" The first alien said, "Every time they performed the ceremony, at this point it began to rain!"

****

Three friends were getting ready to play golf when a bloke walked down the path to the first hole and asked if he could join them. They agreed, and began golfing. The new guy played left-handed, and shot a wonderful round. After they finished, the fourth golfer was invited back the following week. "I'd love to, thanks," he said, "But I might be a little late." The next week, he turned up on time and again shot a great round, but to everyone else's surprise, he was playing right-handed. Again he was invited back, and again he said. "I'd love to, thanks, but I might be a little late." The following week he again turned up on time and played left-handed. He played another good round, and when he was asked back another time, replied, "I'd love to, thanks, but I might be a little late." Well, he was on time again, played left-handed again, and got another good round in. When he was invited back to his now-regular slot, he again warned the others that he might be a little late. Unable to bear it any longer, one of the three friends asked him: "We've seen you play superbly both left- and right-handed, which I think is fantastic, and you always tell us you might be late. Why is that?" The golfer responded, "Well, like many players, I'm superstitious. When I wake up to go golfing, I look at my wife. If she's sleeping on her left side, I golf left-handed. If she's sleeping on her right side, I golf right-handed. If she's on her back; well, I'm going to be a little late..."

****

"When you go diving," warned the Caribbean instructor, "always take a friend with you. If you run out of air, your friend can help you. If you forget which way the surface is - I know it sounds silly, but it's easy - your friend can help you. If you have equipment problems, your friend can help you. Most important of all, though, is that if a shark turns up, your chance of survival is 50%, not 0!"

****

The manager of Reading Football Club was woken up by a call from his local police station. "I'm afraid the club has been broken into, sir." Horrified, the manager asked, "Did they get the cups?" "No, sir," replied the policeman, "they didn't go into the kitchen."

****

A parachutist who always carried his parachute as hand luggage had checked in for a commercial flight to the States and was entering the departure lounge. At the X-ray machine, the inspector did not recognise the 'chute, and insisted that the bloke unpack it to prove he wasn't hiding anything in there. They argued over it for a while, and eventually the supervisor came over, calmed the bloke and the inspector down and let the bloke go on his way. Later, on the plane, he found that he was sitting next to an old couple who had seen him at the X-ray machine. The old boy turned to his wife and said, "Ellie dear, that young man has a parachute in his backpack," and pointed to where the bloke had placed his 'chute under the seat. The old woman looked doubtful, turned to the parachutist and asked, "Is that really a parachute?" Still irritated by the inspector, the bloke turned to her and said, "Yes, of course. Did you not get yours?"

****

Why do mountain climbers rope themselves together? It's to stop anyone who accidentally comes to his or her senses from going home.

****

A Scot and a Yank were talking about golf. "In most parts of the United States we can't play in winter. We have to wait until the spring," said the American. "Och, ye big softies," replied the Scot. "Surely ye can play if ye put a will to it? We dinnae let the snow and cold fess us." The Yank looked doubtful. "Well, what do you do, paint your balls black?" he asked. "No," replied the surprised Scot. "We'll just put on a thick pair of thermal troosers."

****

Two blokes were out fishing. One of them was making a cast when a stunningly beautiful young woman ran past, stark naked, laughing. Well, it put him off his cast, but he let the matter slip. As he was about to cast again two men in white coats pounded past, neck and neck, grinning. They were less of a distraction, and he was almost ready to cast again when a third bloke ran past, panting desperately, carrying a heavy bucket of sand in each hand. Unable to bear it any longer, the fisherman called to the bloke in the next bay: "Sorry, mate, but do you have any idea what was going on there?" The guy nodded. "There's a nut-house just through those woods. Once a week, regular as clockwork, that woman escapes, rips off all her clothes and runs around the lake. Those three blokes in the white coats are care nurses. They have a race to see which of them can catch her first. The winner intercepts her, and carries her back to the mental home. Occasionally, she insists on having wild sex with her captor before she'll go back." "What about the buckets of sand?" asked the first bloke. "Well," replied his informant, "that's the one who caught her last week. The buckets of sand are his handicap."

****

Do you know that sport in the Olympics where you track through deep snow, stop to shoot your gun, and then continue? Most of the world calls it the biathlon. In America though, they refer to it as 'winter'...

****

Sleeping with a woman never harmed any professional footballer. It's staying up all night hunting for a woman to sleep with that does the damage...

****

Fishermen are proud of their rods.

Sporting Triumphs

****

BASE jumping is an excellent way to relax. It really takes your mind off your problems...

****

You know that you've been watching too much all-in wrestling when the top of your wardrobe has footprints on it from where you've been jumping off the ropes.

****

A rugby player was jailed for six months for biting an opponent's ear off. The judge ruled that this action was "not within the normal give-and-take that the sport allows"!

After Dinner

Jokes about Restaurants and Food

After Dinner

A Polish restaurant was in the habit of putting buckets of shit around the edges of the dining-room to draw the flies away from the diners. The air was so polluted anyway that the smell didn't really make an impact. They had to stop, though. They found that their customers kept getting drunk and eating everything in sight...

****

I ate in a Chinese restaurant a few days ago. It was appalling. I called the waiter over and yelled at him, "This bloody chicken is rubbery!" He smiled at me, and yelled back: "Thank you berry much!"

****

What is the most common speech impediment? Chewing gum.

****

There are four classes of food: Instant, Fast, Frozen and Snack. Within those four classes, the food is broken up into the five different types of nutritional value: Fat, Salt, Caffeine, Sugar and Chocolate.

****

This bloke was having chicken noodle soup in a restaurant. The food arrived, he started tucking in, and then hit a hair. Well, he choked for a while, then called the waitress over and said, "Take this away. There's a hair in it. It's disgusting; I'm not paying for it." Well, the waitress wasn't very happy about this, and the two of them got into an argument over it. Eventually, the bloke stormed out, leaving the soup unpaid-for and an expensive steak going cold in the hatch. Opening the door to yell after him, the waitress saw him going into a brothel down the road, so ten minutes later she nipped out and followed the guy into the brothel. She dashed in while the madam's back was turned, went upstairs and burst into the room where the bloke was. As she had hoped, he was up to his ears in the whore's muff. "You arsehole!" the waitress yelled at him, "you wouldn't eat our damn soup because of a hair, and now look at you!" Unperturbed, the guy turned to the waitress and said, "Yes, and if I find a noodle in here I won't be paying this lady, either."

****

This mushroom girl was gushing to one of her pals about a new boyfriend. "Oh, Lucy," she said, "He's such a fun guy..."

After Dinner

****

As Sid sat down to a big plate of chips and gravy down the local pub a mate of his came over and said, "Here, Sid, me old pal, I thought you were trying to get into shape? And here you are with a high-fat meal and a pint of stout!" Sid looked up and replied, "I am getting into shape. The shape I've chosen is a sphere."

****

"Waiter, I distinctly remembering asking for bread with my meal." "Yes, sir. It's in the sausages, sir."

****

This bloke in a restaurant calls to the waiter, "Excuse me. I can't eat this meal you've just served me." The waiter, shocked, comes over and says, "I'm dreadfully sorry, sir. What's the matter?" The bloke looked at him. "You haven't given me a knife and fork yet!"

****

The other day, I dropped a piece of bread and it fell butter-side up. I was dreadfully shocked, until I realised what had happened - like an idiot, I'd buttered the wrong side.

****

In a particularly callous and heartless move, the owners of a large mail order diet pill business with tens of thousands of clients sold their mailing list to the boss of a quality chocolate company which was preparing a mailing. The chocolate company's sales rose immediately by 400%; a few weeks later, so did the diet pill company's sales.

****

The most exciting part of a bulimic's birthday party is the bit when the cake leaps out of the girl!

****

This bloke had a nasty accident in a fish-and-chip shop, and tipped some vinegar into his earhole. He now has a bad case of pickled hearing!

After Dinner

****

A bloke was in a restaurant, trying to plough his way through a revolting meal. After a little while he called the waiter over and said: "Waiter, bring the chef out here. I want to complain about the quality of this disgusting muck you've served me." The waiter looked apologetic. "I'm afraid you'll have to wait for half an hour, sir. He's just popped out to get something to eat."

****

This woman was ordering a meal. "I'd like the lamb chops, please - and make them lean, would you?" "Certainly, madam," replied the waiter. "In which direction?"

****

After Dinner

A man and a woman were eating in a swanky restaurant. Their waitress, taking another order at a table a few feet away, noticed the man slowly sliding down his chair and under the table. The woman dining across from him appeared calm and unruffled, apparently unaware that her companion had disappeared. Wanting to make sure that no monkey business was going on the waitress finished taking her order, crossed over to the table and said to the woman, "Pardon me, madam, but I believe your husband just slid under the table." The woman calmly looked up, shook her head and replied, "No, he didn't. As a matter of fact he just walked in, and is heading in this direction..."

****

A Polish couple went into a restaurant and ordered their food. When it was served a few minutes later, the husband started tucking in ravenously while his wife just watched, not touching her food. After a little while the waitress came over and asked, "Is something wrong?" "I'm waiting for my husband to finish," said the woman. The waitress looked at her and said: "But your dinner's getting cold. You don't need to wait." The woman nodded vigorously. "Yes, I must. It's his turn to go first with our false teeth."

After Dinner

****

"Waiter, there's a flea in my soup!" "Don't worry sir, I'll tell him to hop it."

****

A Scotsman and a Jew were arguing over who could make 20p go further. They decided to give it a try and meet up later to compare notes. When they got back together again, the Jew said, "Well, I used my 20p to buy two cigarettes off a tramp. The first day I smoked one and saved the ashes. The second day I smoked the other and saved the ashes. On the third day I ate the cigarette-butts and used the ashes I'd saved to fertilise my plants." "Ah, you were robbed," replied the Scot smugly. "I used my 20p to buy a black pudding from the butcher. The first day I slit open the casing, scooped out half of the pudding and ate it. The second day I scooped out the other half and ate that. The third day I crapped into the empty black pudding skin. I then took it back to the butcher and said, 'This black pudding smells like shit!' He agreed, and gave me my 20p back!"

After Dinner

This bloke was in a curry house, flicking through the menu and idly munching on poppadoms. After a few minutes he called the waiter over. "Waiter, could you possibly explain something on the menu to me?" "Oh, most certainly, sir," replied the waiter cheerfully. "I know Indian food pretty well," said the bloke, "but I've never heard of this dish here, Lamb Tarka. Surely you mean Lamb Tikka?" The waiter shook his head and said, "No sir, we mean Lamb Tarka. It is very similar indeed to Lamb Tikka, you are most correct, but it's just a little 'otter."

We reserve the right to serve refuse to anyone.

An Indian chef was sacked for being divisive after a week in his new job. He keep favouring curry.

After Dinner

****

A couple of lads had a go at using pickles for a ping-pong game. They found themselves in The Volley of the Dills...

****

Eat a prune! Start a movement!

****

An Irish bloke walked into a café and ordered a big mug of tea. When it arrived he carefully spooned ten teaspoons of sugar slowly into the tea and then started sipping it gently, leaving all the sugar on the bottom. Puzzled, the waitress asked him, "I know it's none of my business, sir, but why didn't you stir your tea?" The bloke looked at her, smiled, and replied, "Well now my lass, I don't like sweet tea."

****

There was a bloke who was absolutely devoted to baked beans. He ate them at every chance he got. He adored them. He even found himself dreaming about them. Unfortunately, they were not as fond of him as he was of them, and they always had a vicious reaction, making him fart like an elephant. One day he met a girl, and they fell in love. As their relationship deepened, he came to understand that they would be married, and he thought to himself, "She's a sweet and gentle girl. She'd never

After Dinner

understand me farting all the time like a platoon of troopers," and realising how much it would embarrass and humiliate her he decided to do the only thing he could - he gave up the baked beans. Shortly afterwards they were married. Some months later his car broke down, and, working in a village not that far from his home, he decided to walk home, there not being any taxis. He called his wife and explained that he'd be an hour or two later for dinner because of the breakdown. As he left his office, he thought, "I'll just pop in and grab a quick snack at the café round the corner, to fortify myself for the journey." But when he got inside, the scent of baked beans overwhelmed him. He thought about it, and decided that he'd be able to walk the effects off on the way home, and he'd been so good for so long, and so he'd treat himself, just this once. Next thing he knew, he'd eaten four platefuls of beans. Even as he was leaving the café he could feel the effects; he barely made it out of the door before letting off a fart that rattled the window-panes. He farted constantly all the way home. Two hours later, he was feeling fairly confident that he'd farted his last. He knocked on the door and his wife rushed out, hugged him impulsively and said, "Oh, I'm so glad to see you, darling. I have the most wonderful surprise for you for dinner tonight." He smiled, kissed her, and then she blindfolded him, led him by the hand to the table and sat him down. She was about to remove the blindfold when the phone rang. "I'll just be a moment, love," she told him. "Now wait there, and don't you dare touch that blindfold!" She dashed into the hall and closed the door. As she did so, a terrible spasm rippled through his intestines - the beans' final message to his bottom. Thanking God that his wife was in the hall, he eased his weight onto one buttock and farted. It was a legendary thing; a fart from the pages of history itself. It started off slow and squeaky, then rapidly grew in volume as it dropped in pitch, becoming so thunderous that the table rattled. It went on and on and on, for over 30 seconds. It stank like the very Pit itself, too; thick and sulphurous, with the sickly-sweet odour of rotting fruit. It was enough to make him gag silently, and he'd been used to his own wind for a long time. Grinning in amazement, he grabbed his napkin from the table, and started fanning the air to disperse this astonishing last stand before his wife got back. The last vestiges of the stench were just fading five minutes later when she came back from the hall, and apologised for taking so long. "Did you peek, darling?" she asked him. He smiled, and assured her that he had not moved a muscle. She went round behind him, hugged him and whipped off the blindfold. "You're going to be a father," she gushed, "and everyone's come round to celebrate." His parents, his wife's parents, the vicar and his wife, the local GP, her husband and his boss and her husband all stared back at him, reproachfully.

****

"Waiter, there's a dead beetle in my soup." "Yes, sir, they're dreadful swimmers."

****

This bloke was in a café. He took a big swig out of his mug of coffee and spat it out. "Waiter!" he called, "This is disgusting. This coffee tastes like soap." The waiter rushed over. "I'm dreadfully sorry, sir! I've given you a mug of tea by mistake! I'll bring you a coffee at once. It tastes like glue."

****

Did you hear about the man who drowned in a bowl of muesli? He was dragged under by a strong currant.

****

Most Japanese do not know that the English have their own word for sushi. We call it 'bait'.

****

If a vegetarian eats vegetables, what does a humanitarian eat?

****

This bloke was in a restaurant and the waiter brought him his meal in a nosebag. "What's the meaning of this?" asked the man indignantly. "Oh, sorry, sir," said the waiter, "I must have misunderstood. The chef told me that you come in every Tuesday and eat like a horse."

After Dinner

Despite what many people think, eating oysters will actually improve your sex life. When you eat an oyster, members of the opposite sex feel safe in the knowledge that you'll eat anything.

"Waiter, you're not fit to serve a pig!" "I'm doing my best, sir."

This bloke walked into a fast-food restaurant, went up to the counter and said to the girl taking the order: "Yeah, I'll have fries and a Chicken Special burger with no lettuce." The attendant gazed at him. "Would you like fries with that, sir?"

After Dinner

A bloke in a café late one evening called the waitress over and said, "You're really cute. I'd love to shag you." The waitress looked at him and said, "Look, I've been stood on my feet all day. I'm exhausted." The bloke shrugged, and said, "Great, let's go and lie down..."

****

This bloke picked up a tin of sweetcorn in a supermarket and looked at the label. "Contains no artificial additives or preservatives," it read. Then, a few inches below, was another message saying, "Contains reclaimed aluminium." The bloke showed the label to his wife and said, "Frankly, I'd rather have the additives..."

****

There was a restaurant that had a sign in the window which read, "Eat now - pay waiter."

After Dinner

****

A bloke went into a pizza parlour with a friend. Naturally they could not decide what type of pizza to get, so to save hours of pointless wrangling they decided to go half and half. "I'd like a large ham and mushroom pizza, please, but with extra pepperoni on one half." The dumb-looking guy behind the counter looked at him and asked, seriously, "Which half do you want the pepperoni put on?" Quick as a flash the bloke said, "Put it on the left-hand half." The guy at the desk duly wrote down, "Ham and mushroom, pepperoni on the left," and handed the order to the chef, who grinned and got on with making the pizza. About half an hour later, the guy at the desk called the bloke over to give him his pizza. When he got there, he noticed that the pepperoni half was facing him so, unable to resist, he said, "Hey, I wanted that pepperoni on the left, not on the bottom!" The desk guy looked upset, grabbed the pizza and with one swift motion threw it into the rubbish bin. "I'm really sorry, sir," he apologised. "I'll get the chef to make you another one..."

****

After Dinner

An elderly couple died in a car accident and found themselves being given a guided tour of heaven by Saint Peter himself. He took them to the area they would be living in, saying, "Over there is your beachside villa - the tennis courts and swimming pools are round the back; the community centre is down the road a bit, there's a pair of golf courses just past that hill, and if you feel hungry or thirsty, just drop by one of the pubs or restaurants. Everything is free, of course, and you'll find that you have plenty of energy if you do want to exercise. I know you'll be happy; everybody is." Then he smiled and flew off. The bloke turned to his wife and muttered, "Honestly, Alice. If you hadn't insisted on all that damn bran and low-fat milk, we could have been here 15 years ago!"

****

A Scotsman was in a restaurant. "How much do you charge for one single drop of whisky?" he asked the waitress. "That would be free, sir," she smiled. "Excellent," said the Scots bloke, "drip me a mugful."

****

Did you hear about the restaurant that had a sign in the window reading "Now Serving Food"? You really have to wonder what they used to serve...

After Dinner

****

There's a small snack-bar next to the atomic accelerator at CERN. It's called "The Fission Chips Café"!

****

A bloke was eating in a Polish restaurant when to his horror he found a dead cockroach at the bottom of his soup. He screamed for the waitress, "There's a cockroach in my soup!" She smiled, and said: "Eat. We have more. I bring you fork."

****

This guy was in a greasy spoon, drinking a cuppa, when he found a dead dormouse in the bottom of the cup, nestled among the tea-leaves. "Hey!" he yelled to the woman behind the counter, "What the hell is the meaning of this?" She looked at him and shouted back, "I ain't got no idea, love. I'm a London gal, not a gypsy!"

****

This Polish guy walked into a restaurant. "What would you like?" asked the waitress. "You know what I like," replied the man, "but first, we eat, yes?"

****

A bloke reading the menu in a small café called the waiter over. "Are you ready to order, sir?" asked the waiter. "I have a question," said the bloke. "Why do two hard-boiled eggs cost twice as much as a three-egg omelette?" "Ah," said the waiter, "Well, you can't count the eggs in an omelette..."

****

Being overweight is something that just sort of snacks up on you...

After Dinner

****

Dieting is the triumph of mind over platter. You just need to keep your willpower dominant over your won't power.

****

It was a brave man who ate the very first oyster...

****

There was a sign in the baker's window that read, "Cakes 66p. Upside-down cakes 99p"!

****

Scientists have discovered that we actually live on only about a third of what we eat. Health farms, gymnasiums and diet pill manufacturers live on the other two-thirds.

****

A new experimental car was designed that ran on used chip fat. It did 400 miles to the gallon and let off very few fumes, but you had to stop every twenty miles to change the vinegar.

After Dinner

****

There are many things on offer on restaurant menus around the world that perhaps aren't exactly what the kitchen staff had in mind. Even worse, some are...

Beef rashers beaten up in the country people's fashion	Poland
Buttered saucepans and fried hormones	Japan
Cock in wine	Cairo
Cold shredded children and sea blubber in spicy sauce	China
Dreaded veal cutlet with potatoes in cream	China
Fillet streak, popotoes, chocolate mouse	Hong Kong
French creeps	America
French fried ships	Cairo
Fried fishermen	Japan
Fried friendship	Nepal
Goose barnacles	Spain
Indonesian Nazi Goreng	Hong Kong
Lioness cutlet	Cairo
Lobster Thermos	Cairo
Muscles Of Marines	Cairo
Pork with fresh garbage	Vietnam
Prawn cock and tail	Cairo
Roasted duck let loose	Poland
Sole Bonne Femme (i.e. "Landlady Style")	France
Strawberry crap	Japan
Sweat from the trolley	Italy
Teppan Yaki, Before Your Cooked Right Eyes	Japan
Toes with butter and jam	Bali

Similarly, some products have a certain image problem:

Ass Glue   Chinese glue

After Dinner

Ban Cock	Indian cockroach repellent
Cat Wetty	Japanese moistened hand towels
Colon Plus	Spanish detergent
Creap Creamy Powder	Japanese coffee creamer
Crundy	Japanese gourmet candy
Homo Sausage	East Asian fish sausage
Hornyphon	Austrian video recorder
I'm Dripper	Japanese instant coffee
Last Climax	Japanese tissues
Libido	Chinese soda
My Fanny	Japanese toilet paper
Pipi	Yugoslavian orange drink
Pocari Sweat	Japanese sport drink
Polio	Czechoslovakian laundry detergent
Shitto	Ghanean pepper sauce
Superglans	Netherlands car wax
Swine	Chinese chocolates

What did OJ Simpson say to Ronald Goldman when he found the bloke with his ex-wife? "Hey, buddy; mind if I cut in?"

The Day Today

21

Topical Jokes Past and Present

The Day Today

What did OJ Simpson say to Ronald Goldman when he found the bloke with his ex-wife? "Hey, buddy; mind if I cut in?"

****

What do you call three days of filthy weather followed by bright sunshine? A bank holiday.

****

Chandran, a classical Indian dancer of some standing, has complained about an upcoming Spice Girls concert scheduled to be held near certain ancient Indian sculptures. Her protest is that the Spice Girls are "inappropriate for the locale." Rumour suggests she would think it far more suitable to have the Spice Girls dropped into a pit and then stoned to death.

****

Two men sentenced to die in the electric chair on the same day were led to the room in which they would meet their Maker. The priest had given them the last rites, a formal speech had been made by the warden and the final prayers had been said. The warden turned to the first bloke and with a grave expression on his face asked, "Well, son, do you have any last requests?" "Yes, sir, I do," replied the condemned man. "I love dance music. I really want to listen to the Spice Girls for one last time before I die. Can that be organised?" "Of course," replied the warden. He then crossed to the second bloke, and asked, "How about you, son? Do you have a final request?" "God, yes," pleaded the prisoner, "Have mercy. Kill me first!"

As the new Welsh assembly gets ready to take over administrative affairs, a new white paper has been tabled suggesting that housing benefit could be extended to same-sex couples. Farmers are likely to be disappointed at the paper, which requires that the couples still have to be the same species.

Steven Spielberg was discussing his new project – an action document drama about famous composers starring top movie stars. Sylvester Stallone, Steven Segal, Bruce Willis, and Arnold Schwarzenegger were all present. Spielberg strongly desired the box office 'oomph' of these superstars, so he was prepared to let them choose whichever composer they would want to portray, as long as they were very famous. "Well," started Stallone, "I've always admired Mozart. I would love to play him." "Chopin has always been my favourite, and my image would improve if people saw me playing the piano" said Willis. "I'll play him." "I've always been partial to Strauss and his waltzes," said Segal. "I'd like to play him." Spielberg was very pleased with these choices. "Sounds splendid." Then, looking at Schwarzenegger, he asked, "Who do you want to be, Arnold?" So Arnold says, "I'll be Bach."

John Wayne Bobbitt has turned to the church for solace, and been ordained as a minister in Las Vegas. Rumour has it, however, that his chapel has no organ...

Reports from military intelligence sources say that Iraqi president Saddam Hussein has placed his wife under house arrest, and forbidden her to leave the palace. The presidential compound contains over 100 rooms, a bowling alley, indoor and outdoor pools and three satellite dishes. Civil liberties groups in the UK have condemned Hussein for subjecting his own wife to a regime even worse that than suffered by British convicts.

****

Many commentators were astonished that Pan-Am could actually lose one of the engines from an aeroplane. It later transpired that the engine had a luggage sticker on it, and it was found, sad and lonely, on the baggage carousel at Karachi International.

****

A recent campaign calling for car safety awareness was launched with a national Child Car Safety Week. A spokesman said, "Over the course of this week we hope to make everyone think about the safety of children in cars. All children should wear a seatbelt. Then, next week, everyone can go back to slinging their kids through windscreens as normal."

****

Early reports suggest that at least six men have already died after using the new anti-impotence drug Viagra. Ironically, sales of the drug have been increased. One customer said that the fact it could keep men stiff indefinitely was a huge plus.

****

Rumour has it that Tony Blair and Paddy Ashdown are left-handed...That's peculiar for politicians because they are all, without exception, under-handed.

****

Notoriously stupid American politician Dan Quayle has announced that he will be standing for president, but he has yet to decide when. One colleague close to Mr. Quayle has said campaign officials are praying that it happens to be a year when there's an election on.

****

The stock market may be bad, but I slept like a baby all through the Black Friday crash and its aftermath. Every hour, on the hour, I woke up crying.

****

How does Michael Jackson pick his nose? By catalogue...

****

Florida was recently submerged under a huge blanket of smog, causing officials to issue the first ever state-wide health alert. Residents have been advised against all strenuous outdoors activity, including gardening, jogging, beach-ball and slaughtering British tourists.

****

What do you get when you cross a lesbian with a draft dodger? Chelsea Clinton.

****

George Tenet, Director of the CIA, has been called before the American Congress to explain why US intelligence forces were unaware that India and Pakistan were both about to start detonating nuclear weapons. Reports suggest that Tenet blamed the lapse on the workload involved in finding and killing all of Bill Clinton's former business associates, adding, "We've got most of them now, though, so soon it'll be business as usual."

****

The Hindenburg was in fact very similar to Waco in Texas. When push came to shove, both proved to contain flammable compounds.

****

David Koresh had a lot of wives, it's true, but they were all excellent matches.

****

The former president of the Swiss National Bank, Markus Lusser, died recently at the age of 67. His family have announced their plans to bury him in a secret grave somewhere in Zurich, marked only by a long string of coded numbers.

****

In the wake of the Challenger shuttle disaster, NASA are said to have banned a particular brand of canned drink from their bases - 7 Up.

****

The Colombian navy recently discovered a ship transporting more than a ton of cocaine out of the country in direct violation of Colombian law. Under current directives, no vessel is allowed to leave Colombia carrying less than three tons of coke.

The Day Today

****

What's the difference between OJ Simpson and Christopher Reeve? OJ hit the ground running and then walked away, while Christopher Reeve got the electric chair.

****

Singer George Michael was recently arrested and charged with performing a lewd act in a Beverley Hills public toilet. Music critics have hailed the event as a breakthrough for George Michael, saying that it's the first time ever that he has been more humiliated than former Wham partner Andrew Ridgely. Meanwhile, in the States, the pop star has been busily turning the event into a PR coup for himself. Like Hugh Grant before him, it appears that the Americans will forgive any pervert, so long as they've got a British accent.

****

Right-wing politicians have recently defended tobacco advertising, saying that kids don't start smoking because of posters, but because of stars like Leonardo DiCaprio smoking in high-impact films such as Titanic. There is of course no proof of this, but since the release of the film there has been a marked increase in the numbers of gay American teenagers shagging fat English girls as part of an attempt to prove that they're heterosexual.

****

In a vital boost for the Internet recently, several countries have agreed not to tax it, in order to help increase the prominence of electronic commerce and to foster the growth of a truly worldwide communications network. Consumer groups have hailed the move as a great breakthrough, saying, "An Internet tax could have been disastrous. Most 11-year-olds are already strapped for cash, and would have real difficulty coping with any further rises in their weekly hardcore pornography bills."

****

Elton John was recently knighted by the Queen. Interviewed after the event, Sir Elton said that it felt odd to get down on his knees only to end up not swallowing the sword.

****

A worrying new study has linked women's alcohol consumption with breast cancer, suggesting that women who get drunk regularly are more likely to suffer from the disease. The effects of this may be counterbalanced, however, by the fact that drunk women are likely to get their tits felt by a wide variety of blokes, and some of them could be doctors.

****

Bob Hope, the 95-year-old legend of comedy, has been knighted by the Queen. Hope, who was born in Britain, has been suffering from ill-health for some time. When told to kneel before the Queen, Hope was heard to mutter in confusion: "Bing? Is that you? I heard you were dead."

****

In 1969 the Apollo 11 mission went to the moon and sent back live images of Neil Armstrong and Buzz Aldrin bouncing around on the surface. More recently, in 1997, a special probe to Mars passed back images of the red planet's surface live as scientists sent the little buggy around the place. Why the fuck then can Channel Five not get a signal from the transmitter down the road to my house?

****

Sources indicate that Madonna, the bad girl of rock and roll, has started studying the Qaballah, an ancient form of Jewish mystical occultism. One commentator expressed no surprise, saying, "After you hit 40, have a kid and lose your interest in sex, becoming Jewish is the next logical step."

****

The Day Today

An evil-tempered old farmer died and went down to Hell. A couple of weeks later the Devil checked up on him and noticed that he didn't seem to be suffering like the rest of the damned souls. He checked the gauges and observed that the room was set to 80% humidity and a temperature of 28 degrees, so went in and said to the farmer, "What are you so cheerful about?" The farmer grinned and said, "I like it here. It's just like ploughing my fields in June." Well, that pissed the Devil off, so he went back to the controls and turned it to 90% humidity and a temperature of 32 degrees. He then went back to check the farmer again, who was standing around happy as a sandboy. "Oh, honestly," thought the Devil. "What are you so damn cheerful about now, then?" he asked the farmer. "This is even better," replied the farmer. "It's like tugging weeds out of the fields in July, except that my back's not breaking." Well, the Devil was even more pissed off, so he went to the controls and reset them yet again - 99% humidity and 40 degrees. When he looked in, the farmer was still grinning broadly. With a sinking feeling, the Devil asked him what this reminded him of. "Oh, it's just like spending the day in the grain silo in the middle of August," replied the farmer. Suddenly the Devil had a brainwave, thought, "I'm going to sort out this smug little wanker," and went to the controls, where he turned the temperature to minus ten degrees. Well, sure enough, at that humidity it started snowing. "We'll see what happy summers this reminds the fucker of now!" thought the Devil. He went back, only to find the farmer leaping up and down and shouting for joy. "Yes! Away the Gunners! Arsenal have finally won the Premiership!"

Pol Pot, the evil Cambodian dictator, is finally dead. The leader of the Khmer Rouge, his reign saw the murder of more than a million intellectuals and urbanites in an attempt to turn Cambodia into a nation of farmers. He eventually realised his mistake and repented after being forced to listen to 12 hours of The Archers non-stop.

****

Mikhail Gorbachev, the former leader of the USSR responsible for the dismantling of the communist system, has reportedly received $1 million as payment for acting in a Pizza Hut advert. Pizza Hut officials commented that Mr Gorbachev was the perfect choice, as he already had a splodge of tomato sauce on his forehead.

****

Recent discoveries of ancient primate remains suggest that humans evolved in several different places at the same time. That fits predictive models based on the British political system - a close look at Whitehall, the Houses of Parliament, Downing Street and Buckingham Palace clearly shows that there is all sorts of monkey business going on all over the place.

****

Elizabeth Taylor, the legendary 66-year-old actress, was recently hospitalised following a fall in which she injured her hip. Doctors said that Miss Taylor was extremely fortunate, and that her injuries would have been much worse if her fall had not been cushioned by her revoltingly saggy tits.

****

Word has it that Michael Jackson, the world's first trans-racial, is about to release a new book. The working title (allegedly) is, "The Ins and Outs of Child Rearing."

****

In these up-and-down market periods there is one sure-fire way to secure the attention of your broker. Snap your fingers in the air and call, "Waiter! Waiter!"

****

This bloke was in Devon, walking along a country path, when he noticed a young lad over to one side busy making something. He took a closer look, and was horrified to see that the boy was playing with cow manure. A bit taken aback, he went over and said, "What on earth are you doing, lad?" The boy looked up and said, "I'm making John Prescott." Amazed, and unable to think of anything sensible to say, he asked "Prescott? Why are you making John Prescott? Why not Tony Blair?" The boy looked at him seriously and said, "Oh no, I could never make Tony Blair." "Really? Why's that?" asked the man. The lad shrugged, and replied, "Come off it. There's not enough bullshit in all of Devon to make Tony Blair."

****

What's the difference between a pigeon and a stockbroker the day after Black Friday? Well, the pigeon can still put a deposit on a new Merc.

****

Unemployed French citizens occupied government buildings recently as part of a protest movement demanding greater social security benefits. The disturbance was quickly settled however, when the French government appealed to the Germans to send the tanks back in.

****

Lorena Bobbitt visited Equador, where the President treated her like his very own long-lost sister. To be fair though, can you imagine any bloke not wanting to be careful around her?

****

"Get my broker, Miss White." "Certainly, sir. Stock or Pawn?"

****

Did you hear about the "OJ Simpson Special Deal" from Hertz? When you rent a white Bronco, you get a free police chase, TV helicopters and a 'Get Away With Murder For A Small Fortune' card.

****

"Ol' Blue Eyes" is dead. Frank Sinatra, who thrilled millions worldwide with his voice, will now be known as "Ol' Shut Eyes." President Clinton saluted Sinatra, saying that the famous entertainer "really did do it his way." Clinton vowed that he too would try to follow Sinatra's sterling example, adding that he would be endeavouring to keep his Mafia links secret and saying, "I'm sure going to smack that bitch Hillary around next time she starts getting lippy, too."

****

The Inland Revenue have been trying to cheer people up regarding their self-assessment taxation by using snappy slogans and jolly catch-phrases. They're currently considering, "We've got what it takes to take what you've got!"

****

New tests have revealed that survivors of the bubonic plague that swept through England and the rest of Europe in the Middle Ages may have passed on a genetic resistance to the HIV virus to their modern ancestors. The researchers have however warned people at risk from AIDS not to test for the immunity by stuffing live rodents into their rectal cavities.

There's no doubt - the two worst things about Tony Blair is his face.

The Branch Davidian Church has split into two sects - Revisionist and Extra Crispy.

****